THE FLETCHER JONES FOUNDATION

HUMANITIES IMPRINT

The Fletcher Jones Foundation has endowed this imprint to foster innovative and enduring scholarship in the humanities.

The publisher and the University of California Press Foundation gratefully acknowledge the generous support of the Fletcher Jones Foundation Imprint in Humanities.

Hungry for Revolution

Hungry for Revolution

THE POLITICS OF FOOD AND THE MAKING OF MODERN CHILE

Joshua Frens-String

UNIVERSITY OF CALIFORNIA PRESS

University of California Press
Oakland, California

© 2021 by Joshua Frens-String

Library of Congress Cataloging-in-Publication Data

Names: Frens-String, Joshua, 1985– author.
Title: Hungry for revolution : the politics of food and the making of modern
    Chile / Joshua Frens-String.
Description: Oakland, California : University of California Press, [2021] |
    Includes bibliographical references and index.
Identifiers: LCCN 2021003557 (print) | LCCN 2021003558 (ebook) |
    ISBN 9780520343368 (cloth) | ISBN 9780520343375 (paperback) |
    ISBN 9780520974753 (epub)
Subjects: LCSH: Food security—Political aspects—Chile. | Chile—
    History—20th century.
Classification: LCC HD9014.C52 F74 2021 (print) | LCC HD9014.C52 (ebook) |
    DDC 338.1/983—dc23
LC record available at https://lccn.loc.gov/2021003557
LC ebook record available at https://lccn.loc.gov/2021003558

30 29 28 27 26 25 24 23 22 21
10 9 8 7 6 5 4 3 2 1

For Frankie and Abby

CONTENTS

ILLUSTRATIONS

FIGURES

TABLES

ACKNOWLEDGMENTS

The research that has gone into reconstructing the various histories in this book has extended over many years in many different locations. Most importantly, it has involved the assistance and support of countless friends, teachers, colleagues, and collaborators.

When I was an undergraduate student, the School for International Training's program in the Southern Cone, then directed by Brenda Pererya, first introduced me to the critical work of grassroots social movements as they not only confronted the physical violence of Latin America's Cold War but envisioned alternative economic futures as well. At the University of Michigan, my interest in the history of social movements and the Latin American left grew through classes and conversations with mentors like Gustavo Verdesio and the late Fernando Coronil. After I finished my undergraduate studies, my intellectual attraction to Latin America during the Cold War period became more defined while working and living in Washington, D.C., and Montevideo, Uruguay. I'm especially grateful for the time I spent learning from and working with the late Marcus Raskin at the Institute for Policy Studies, Peter Kornbluh at the National Security Archive, and members of the Open Society Institute's Latin America Program. I'm also indebted to the Fulbright program, which provided me an opportunity to study at Montevideo's Universidad de la República and Centro Latinoamericano de Economía Humana (CLAEH) while researching Uruguay's New Left of the 1960s.

I drafted a skeleton of what became this book when I was a graduate student in the History Department at New York University. Greg Grandin served as a scholarly example, adviser, and constant advocate of my own research and writing. The dissertation I completed in 2015 would have been impossible without the collaborative counsel of the broader NYU faculty.

I'm especially grateful for the mentorship of NYU's eminent group of Latin American historians, particularly Barbara Weinstein, Sinclair Thomson, Ada Ferrer, and Alejandro Velasco. Special thanks is due to Alejandro. I'll forever be proud of our work resurrecting the still vital NACLA *Report on the Americas*.

The graduate school experience is only as rich as the camaraderie one shares with his/her fellow graduate students. For that I feel truly fortunate. Sincerest thanks to friends and intellectual interlocutors during my time at NYU, especially Christy Thornton, Stuart Schrader, Claire Payton, Ernesto Semán, Carmen Soliz, Michelle Chase, Jennifer Adair, Aldo Marchesi, Daniel Rodríguez, Natan Zeichner, Federico Sor, Tony Wood, Sara Kozameh, Rachel Nolan, David Klassen, Marcio Siwi, Anasa Hicks, Gabriel Rocha, Alex Manevitz, Katy Walker, Julia Leiken, Geoff Traugh, Samantha Seeley, and Tej Nagaraja.

With many of the aforementioned friends, political experiences and accomplishments overlapped with academic ones. Thank you to the tenacity of union comrades like Daniel Aldana Cohen, A. J. Bauer, and other founding members of NYU Academic Workers for a Democratic Union. I will always hold special admiration for AWDU bargaining committee members Ella Wind, Ayesha Omer, Natasha Raheja, David Klassen, and Shelly Ronen (WORKR), who modeled moral clarity to the graduate workers of GSOC-UAW Local 2110 during a long contract fight in 2014–15.

Conversations that occurred at various stages of this project, particularly with fellow scholars of Chile, also helped this book take shape. For insights on that long road, I thank Marian Schlotterbeck, Tanya Harmer, Rodrigo Henríquez, Soledad Zárate, Fernando Purcell, Tomás Ariztía, Martín Arboleda, Marianne González le Saux, Alfonso Salgado, Andra Chastain, Michael Lemon, Peter Krupa, Ona Flores, Steven Bodzin, Juan Andrés Abarca Castro, Reed Kurtz, and Macarena Guerrero. As I have completed both the dissertation and book, I've also had the unwavering support of Peter Winn, whose inimitable *Weavers of Revolution* inspired me (and many others) to pursue a career as a historian.

In Chile, the Marambio/Castro family opened their home in La Reina to me on various Santiago research visits. Thank you also to the many archivists and librarians in Chile and elsewhere who helped locate key documents. Without such hospitality and assistance, the at times alienating work of "doing history" would have been far less productive and enjoyable.

The process of revising my original dissertation into a book manuscript occurred largely at the University of Texas at Austin. Thank you to my generous colleagues in the Latin American history program and at UT's Teresa Lozano Long Institute of Latin American Studies (LLILAS), especially Ann Twinam, Matthew Butler, Seth Garfield, Ginny Garrard, Jonathan Brown, Lina del Castillo, Jorge Cañizares-Esguerra, and Susan Deans-Smith. The support and feedback of colleagues Julie Hardwick, Megan Raby, Abena Dove Osseo-Asare, Ashley Farmer, Al Martínez, Michael Stoff, and Daina Ramey Berry were also appreciated as I finished the book. Ahmed Deidan de la Torre aided with crucial translations. Nathan Stone graciously tracked down final documents and offered suggestions on the draft manuscript. UT's College of Liberal Arts generously supported this book through its Humanities Research Award Program. On multiple occasions, Jackie Jones, as chair of the History Department, provided the time and resources that I needed to complete research and writing. Miriam Bodian, as director of UT's Institute for Historical Studies, offered forums for that research to be shared with a broader audience. Special thanks to the UT History Department's tremendous administrative staff, especially Art Flores, Jackie Llado, Courtney Meador, Martha Gonzalez, and Michael Johnson, for the regular assistance they provided.

Heidi Tinsman and Natalia Milanesio joined Ann Twinam, Matthew Butler, Seth Garfield, and Julie Hardwick in offering insightful comments on a draft of the manuscript as I embarked on revisions. I am forever grateful for Audra Wolfe's sharp editing eyes and encouragement. Her close reading of each chapter undoubtedly made the final product far better than it otherwise would have been. Also, for their suggestions on conference papers and early draft chapters that, in one form or another, have made their way into this book, I thank Brodwyn Fischer, Nara Milanich, Gabrielle Kuenzli, Augustine Sedgewick, Steve Volk, and Rachel Laudan. Participants in Columbia University's Latin American History Workshop provided helpful feedback on the book's final chapter while I was a visiting scholar at Columbia's Institute for Latin American Studies—a stay that was facilitated by the generosity of John Coatsworth.

It has been a pleasure working with the editorial team at the University of California Press. Kate Marshall saw promise in my work early on. She and Enrique Ochoa-Kaup have made the process of delivering this book into the world an especially smooth one. Given the press's strengths in food studies and Latin American history, I can think of no better place for *Hungry for Revolution* to appear. I am appreciative of the critiques raised by Heidi Tinsman, Camilo Trumper, Ed Murphy, and one anonymous reader, all of whom commented on the manuscript for the press. The final monograph was greatly improved as a result of these brilliant scholars' suggestions. Of course, all shortcomings and errors lie with me, the author.

Finally, deepest gratitude goes to my friends and family. My parents, Richard and Mary, provided me with the security and freedom to explore the world and pursue my own path starting at a young age. Though my brother and I approach the world in very different ways, I've looked up to him since we were kids. He and his wife, Sandra, are a source of support in good times and bad. As I finished polishing the manuscript, the laughter, conversation, and friendship of Ben Katz, Tara Starin-Basi, Lizzy Smith, Bryan Smith, and Jackie Alexander pushed me over the finish line. My in-laws, Michael and Maggie, provided constant support—and during the final leg of the journey, a refuge from a city in the throes of a pandemic. No other person has had to endure this project longer—witnessing the many highs and lows that accompany the book-writing process—than Abby Weitzman. When fatigue sets in, she is the sounding board that keeps me on track. Most importantly, she continually pushes me to grow not just as a teacher and writer but as a person. With our daughter, Frankie, she provides a constant reminder of what's most important in life.

Introduction

BUILDING A REVOLUTIONARY APPETITE

AROUND NOON on January 26, 1972, Dr. Salvador Allende arrived at Pier D in the bustling Chilean port of San Antonio. As the Popular Unity (UP) revolution (1970–73) entered its second year, Chile's socialist president had come to the coastal city to officially welcome a fleet of Soviet fishing ships into Chilean waters. The ships owed their presence off the Pacific coast to an accord Allende's government had signed with the Soviet Union just a few months earlier. The goal of that pact was to increase the supply of *merluza*, or hake, available to Chilean consumers.[1]

At a time when popular cuts of red meat had largely disappeared from butcher counters around the country, UP officials hoped that the domestically caught fish would satisfy consumers' growing appetite for inexpensive protein. In Chile, the revolution would be "flavored with empanadas and red wine," UP leaders were fond of saying, and while merluza was neither of these two traditional gastronomic goods, the goal of producing a plentiful supply of the cold-water fish reflected Allende's promise that material sacrifice would be minimized on the country's revolutionary march. As government officials were well aware, forging a peaceful, democratic road to socialism in many ways depended on the state's ability to successfully link nutritional abundance with the construction of a more just and sovereign national economy.[2]

The Soviet-Chilean fishing agreement ultimately fell short of UP supporters' expectations. Domestic fish production surged in 1972, but alone, the initiative could not make up for shortfalls in other subsectors of the food economy, many of which grew more acute during the last eighteen months of the revolution. As the cost of food imports rose steadily and as agricultural production in the Chilean countryside struggled to rebound amid the feverish pace of land seizures, food security became a topic of impassioned debate—and eventually of sustained protest. In this context, state-backed efforts to promote domestic alternatives to more customary, but frequently imported, foodstuffs did little to keep the government's opponents at bay. Fish was supposed to sate consumers' appetites, but the displeasing texture of a piece of once-frozen merluza instead became a symbol of state overreach and everyday economic uncertainty. In short, the Soviet-Chilean accord only inflamed the desire of Allende's opponents to remove the UP from office by any means necessary.[3]

Yet a deeper analysis of Allende's visit to the port of San Antonio reveals a long-standing, far more complicated portrait of the relationship between nutrition, food security, and revolutionary politics in twentieth-century Chile. Rather than being an isolated episode, the UP's attempt to boost fish production and alter traditional consumption habits shines a light on the recurring spates of urban mobilization that food matters generated, the growing prominence of food science in Chile's midcentury state-building process, and the emergence of ever-more-defined economic proposals about how best to ensure that food was produced, distributed, and eventually consumed in an equitable fashion. When observed through the lens of food, the Allende years appear as the culmination of, rather than a break with, decades of struggle to reimagine Chile's social and economic future by transforming the bonds that tied together production, distribution, exchange, and consumption.

Since at least the 1930s, a period when many UP leaders, including Salvador Allende, first cut their teeth in national politics, urban workers, feminist activists, and Chile's organized political left had vocally asserted that it was the modern state's duty to guarantee popular access to affordable and healthy foods by exercising a more active role in national economic affairs. To better understand the social, cultural, and economic milieu out of which such demands emerged, officials embraced new methods of survey research and the latest findings and theories of international public health experts. Using the ideas of midcentury nutrition science as one important guide, prominent figures in the medical field argued that popular discontent about food prices was a sign of both economic anxiety and physical despair. Scientists' and doctors' efforts in the late 1930s and early 1940s to make protein, calcium, vitamins, and other essential nutrients accessible to all, irrespective of income, represented, in the words of a young Dr. Salvador Allende, a "noble experiment aimed at conserving and strengthening the prodigious raw material that is mankind."[4] Allende's position posited a deep association between physical health and diet and between working-class wellness and national economic productivity, and it manifested itself clearly in the work of a generation of researchers who toiled fastidiously to improve the poor nutritional practices that exacerbated Chile's already high rates of tuberculosis and infant mortality.

By mapping and confronting the inequities of the food system, scientific experts and medical practitioners constructed the artifice of Chile's emergent social welfare state. Upon assuming positions of elected power, some designed experimental nutrition programs to first contain the social and political fallout of a long-existent popular food crisis and then consolidate a new social compact from which to move their country forward. Embracing Keynesian-style policies of state economic intervention and regulation, other midcentury state builders backed higher worker wages, the creation of one of twentieth-century Latin America's most expansive systems of consumer price controls, and the establishment of state-subsidized food stores and restaurants. Health experts and social workers also led the charge to establish special consumer health initiatives that brought basic nutrition habits—the consumption of fruits and vegetables as well as milk and meat—more closely in line with what Chilean farmers actually produced. At times such programs were articulated as a brand of socially inflected economic nationalism or "creole" socialism.[5] In other moments, efforts to improve national nutritional outcomes were decidedly transnational endeavors, involving collaboration with foreign advisers and consultants who encouraged Chile to adopt new agricultural techniques and household cooking practices to meet the country's social reality.

The post–Second World War era was a particularly active period when it came to building a developmental state that could turn nutritional scarcity into nutritional security. As one of Latin America's most ambitious agrarian reform projects went into effect in the 1960s, agricultural officials pursued national food sovereignty by promoting trade, investment, and production policies that would lessen the country's outsized dependence on imported wheat and beef. As two of the most significant items in a bloated national food import budget, these commodities were a financial drain on other urban development initiatives. Therefore, a generation of reformers trained in a range of scientific and social scientific disciplines, including genetics, agronomy, and agricultural economics, dispersed across the Chilean countryside to plant new crop varieties, manage food-processing industries, oversee experimental hog and chicken farms, devise alternative land tenure arrangements, and organize infrastructure improvements that would more efficiently connect sites of rural production with urbanizing consumer centers. Consumer education campaigns, many of which had been piloted in urban areas a few decades earlier, complemented these production efforts by teaching rural consumers—and particularly women—how to prepare food in ways that mimicked their urban counterparts during times of economic plenty but to embrace values of household thrift and resourcefulness when economic times got tough.

When it came to food, Allende's democratic revolution represented a continuation of this earlier period. By first instituting a series of wage increases and price controls and then later consolidating a more formalized system of state-led economic planning and community-led food distribution, the UP worked tirelessly to ensure that the anticipated bounty generated by agrarian reform settlements would be earmarked for the urban poor and working classes. Additionally, the leftist coalition guaranteed fair profits and wages to the often undervalued laborers who worked Chile's foodways. When it came to determining the content and conditions of food production, the revolution promised to give a voice to those who harvested the land and cultivated the sea. A report on Allende's visit to San Antonio noted that the Chilean government's investments on the coast would ensure that an "avalanche" of protein-rich merluza would "inundate" grocery stores, open-air markets, and butcher shops throughout Chile.[6] Seemingly mundane food-engineering initiatives, like the state-supported production of salted fish and fish croquettes, represented the UP's attempt to make good on its promise of nutritional equity.[7]

Throughout late 1971 and into 1972, the UP coalition also established more than two thousand consumer committees in poor neighborhoods around Santiago and other urban areas. Known as *juntas de abastecimiento y precios* (supply and price control boards), or JAPs, this network of neighborhood consumer watchdog and distribution committees soon became an important channel through which basic foods, including beef, chicken, and fish, entered the peripheral neighborhoods of Santiago and other metropolitan areas. The individuals who staffed the JAPs, many of them women UP militants, were trained by the state's consumer protection agency and acted as local economic advisers and price inspectors. Through this process, ordinary citizens transmitted new ideas about family nutrition and in-home food preparation to their fellow community members. Harvesting, buying, preparing, and consuming domestically produced foods all became unlikely acts of loyalty to Chile's socialist revolution.[8]

The daily experience of revolutionary food politics was eloquently captured by pro-UP women like Eloisa Díaz. A leader in a women's organization in a working-class community near Santiago, Díaz told a Chilean newspaper in March 1972 that the group she helped run in her home community had financed the purchase of some five hundred kilos of frozen fish. Her hope for the second year of the revolution was that familial consumption of merluza would increase as more and more women participated in classes on how best to prepare the fish. "We are helping the Government in its task of teaching the people that fish, one of our most important riches, is the best substitute for beef," Díaz said. "Eating fish is ten times cheaper than beef, and by increasing familiarity with fish, we'll be helping the country save foreign exchange."⁹ Determining what type of food was produced, deciding to whom it was distributed, and finally directing how it was consumed were, in Díaz's view, all measures of a community's adherence to the nation and the construction of democratic socialism.

MAKING FOOD POLITICAL

From the making of Chile's Popular Front in the 1930s to the Popular Unity revolution of the early 1970s, *Hungry for Revolution* reconstructs how decades of struggle over food fueled the rise of one of Latin America's most expansive social welfare states. In the process, the book stitches together two of the most significant processes in twentieth-century Chile: a growing urban population's political fight to gain reliable access to basic foodstuffs and the state's herculean efforts to undo the inequitable power structures that had, by the 1960s, conditioned life in both cities and the countryside. By following a broad cast of historical actors—from trade unionists to communists, women activists to Catholic reformers—the book's narrative arc follows two generations of Chileans as they sought, sometimes in collaboration and sometimes in conflict with one another, to make basic consumption a fundamental social and economic right and the foundation of a more socially inclusive economic democracy. The book shows how Chile's food system was a reflection of the inequalities embedded in Chilean social and economic life. It also illuminates the critical role that the politics, science, and economics of food played in shaping the trajectory of the Chilean state and the evolving visions of citizenship and development that such a state promoted for nearly a half century.

By chronicling how popular conceptualizations of an alternative socialist future in Chile grew out of the simple belief that urban workers and their families were entitled to nutritional equality, *Hungry for Revolution* challenges a tendency in the scholarly literature to associate the politics of consumption in Latin America primarily with the era of economic deregulation and liberalization that emerged in the late 1970s and early 1980s. During those years, right-wing governments suppressed socialist movements across the continent. According to an argument that is particularly notable in the scholarship on Chile, politicians' attention to consumer desires marked the retreat of the interventionist state and the rise of the marketplace as a substitute for the contestation that had accompanied mass politics. In his widely read 1987 book, the conservative Chilean intellectual and politician Joaquín Lavín articulated such a position most clearly when he claimed that the emergence of a supposedly self-regulating, market-based consumer society was the centerpiece of the "silent revolution" that took hold under the iron fist of dictator Augusto Pinochet. In Lavín's vision of the modern capitalist economy, the state had a minimal role to play when it came to protecting consumer welfare; rather, market forces would dictate the standard of living for Chileans of different social classes.[10]

In countering Lavín, *Hungry for Revolution* reveals how, for much of the mid-twentieth century, consumption in Chile was understood as a social relationship that both generated and reflected larger concerns about the nature of citizenship, the responsibilities of the state, and the fundamental purpose of economic development. As historian Heidi Tinsman has argued, the problem of consumption is deeply embedded in the political fibers of twentieth-century Chile, and as such, it should not be seen as an act that is always or necessarily "reactionary" in nature—even if it often became so during the darkest days of Chile's Cold War.[11] Indeed, a growing body of historical scholarship has demonstrated the unlikely ways that citizens' embrace of consumer regulations and institutions expanded, not restricted, the state's administrative purview throughout the twentieth century, thus politicizing, rather than having a dampening effect on, society more broadly. In her analysis of the US New Deal, for instance, Meg Jacobs convincingly showed more than two decades ago how mid-twentieth-century state consumer institutions and consumer laws radicalized popular understandings of democracy, provided new space for citizens to organize themselves politically, and widened the expected boundaries of state regulation. This "dialectical relationship between state and society" is one that Jacobs calls "state building from the bottom-up."[12]

Modern Latin America presents numerous corroborating examples of the processes that scholars such as Tinsman and Jacobs describe. In their respective studies, historians Eduardo Elena, Rebekah Pite, Natalia Milanesio, and Jennifer Adair have traced the cultural and political history of food and consumption in twentieth-century Argentina to illuminate how the food and consumer economies were not only highly political spheres, but also arenas in which citizens and the state concretized ideas about social justice, social and economic rights, and gender.[13] In the Mexican context, historians Jeffrey Pilcher, Enrique Ochoa, and Sandra Aguilar-Rodríguez have similarly shown how both cultural and physical concerns about food and nutrition became integral components of Mexico's revolutionary institutions and the state's construction of respectable citizenship.[14] In midcentury Brazil, broad-based cost-of-living struggles, as the historian Brodwyn Fischer has demonstrated, became a mode of organization for that country's political left, particularly the Brazilian Communist Party, which went beyond the workplace to mobilize shantytown residents in urbanizing Rio de Janeiro.[15] In Venezuela, recent scholarship by historians like Alejandro Velasco has revealed how urban popular sectors' demands for improved urban provisioning of basic collective services and goods—from trash collection to drinking water—grounded radical democratic practices of accountability in the period after the Second World War.[16]

Hungry for Revolution thus fits squarely within a growing body of historical literature on the centrality of consumption matters to the practice of popular politics across the Americas. By distinguishing "consumerism"—that is, a narrow and individual concern with the subjective allure of conspicuous forms of consumption—from a moral and deeply classed notion of "consumption politics," this work elucidates how poor and working-class citizens became politicized by a perceived absence of everyday household products and services. In turn, this book and others with which it dialogues demonstrate why urban residents, in particular, mobilized as consumers to make economic demands on an incipient regulatory state.[17] It is abundantly clear that as a Cold War dictatorship dismantled the institutions of an interventionist state in Chile, consumption became a key characteristic of neoliberal citizenship during the late 1970s and 1980s. However, in an earlier time period and different political context, the politics of consumption in Chile and around

Latin America was also integral to progressive visions of economic and social democracy. Thus, this book is an attempt to recover the historical relationship between the experience of hunger, citizens' desire for food security, and the emergence of mass politics in twentieth-century Latin America.

In pushing beyond an exclusive focus on food consumption, *Hungry for Revolution* also explains how persistent concerns about basic food availability in Chile fostered expansive visions of a just and democratic national economy. Scholarship in the field of food studies offers important ways for making sense of these broader economic consequences of food's ubiquity in modern Chilean history. With their focus on food production, historians of agriculture and food industrialization have underscored how social problems like hunger or malnutrition set the stage for farmers to embrace new agricultural methods, crop types, and processing techniques.[18] Social historians of food have uncovered how food distribution and price-monitoring activities provided openings for political participation, however unequal, to social groups that were historically marginalized in formal politics, like women and the urban poor.[19] Cultural historians of food, meanwhile, have illuminated how states have at times pushed the consumption of certain foods to forge national communities, particularly during moments of political upheaval.[20] To interrogate the food system is thus to disentangle the political, cultural, social, and economic "webs of life" that sustain the nation-state and global capitalism, as well as visions of a life beyond such modes of political and economic organization.[21]

In Allende's Chile, we see all of these facets of food politics and more. Drawing upon decades of plans drafted by past governments, the UP revolution sought to turn the popular consumption of nationally produced goods into a key component of a new and revolutionary economic culture. A decade of agrarian reform in Chile blended together a pursuit of mechanized agriculture with the introduction of higher-yield crops and animal species to beat back food inflation and urban hunger. At the same time, the creation of alternative channels for food distribution became an important way for women and shantytown dwellers to shape the direction of Chile's food revolution at various moments in the mid-twentieth century. Each of the social and economic linkages that connected rural farmland to the marketplace and the marketplace to the household kitchen table became spaces in which organized citizens and the state could reimagine the boundaries of democracy, the economy, and citizenship. This book, then, is an attempt to probe the material inequities that became associated with the Chilean nation-state and show how food offered a way to envision a political economy that was more just.

PRODUCING AND CONSUMING INEQUALITIES

Following the insights of the eminent food scholar Sidney Mintz, to study food politics is to observe a great contradiction between two competing, and often irreconcilable, citizen demands: a social group's public desire to have a governing institution regulate what and how food is produced in order to ensure the affordability and quality of essential products, on the one hand, and a rival private wish that an individual's freedom to choose what and how food is actually consumed never be restricted, on the other hand.[22] In many ways, midcentury Chile offers a canvas on which to see how this "conundrum," to use Mintz's words, has historically resolved itself. During its three years in power, the UP devoted great energy to reconciling the tension between a cultural nostalgia for foodways past and the promise of a more egalitarian "culinary modernism."[23] But as the state increasingly intervened in the production and distribution of basic foods during the 1960s and early 1970s, a chorus of oppositional figures—rural landowners, urban merchants, female consumers—lined up together, united around the claim that their individual preferences for both producing and consuming certain foods should never be constrained, even if the ultimate goal was to generate more equitable nutritional outcomes for the population at-large. Over time the polarization that emerged at sites of food production, distribution, and consumption spawned very distinct visions of economic democracy, citizenship, and the role of the state in economic life. If the food economy could fuel a socialist revolution, Chile in the early 1970s showed that it could also become a foundation of far-right counterrevolution.

A consumer counterrevolution was in many ways enabled by the fact that state food policy often exacerbated insidious inequities and exclusions. By creating mechanisms of food provisioning that were bound up with an individual's employment status, as many early nutrition-related policies were, the state created a social welfare system that relegated many of the country's most socially and economically marginal communities to second-class status (if they were included at all). By embracing a quantitative and overly schematic vision of what constituted "proper" food consumption, nutrition experts and agricultural engineers tended to view food as a collection of minerals and nutrients, whose taste, social meaning, or cultural significance were secondary to its life-sustaining properties. In casting women as the principal source of the country's poor nutritional habits, agents who staffed new state offices that dealt with food matters reproduced a highly gendered and often racialized characterization of modern masculinity and femininity: while proper masculinity was associated with one's participation in the traditional workplace and a willingness to abstain from nonvirtuous forms of consumer activity, such as alcohol consumption, to be a respectable woman was to adhere to traditional ideas of domesticity and perform acts of maternal care. Finally, by overemphasizing technical solutions to the country's crisis—in essence, turning a question about power and politics into a matter of science that was beyond reproach—medical and agricultural experts unwittingly laid the groundwork for those who, in the context of a global Cold War, would later attempt to banish "political" activity and associations from Chilean society.

Chile's agrarian reform project of the 1960s and early 1970s, which Chilean state officials approached as a regional project that affected not only the spatial organization of the city but also the rural hinterlands, showcased some of the aforementioned contradictions.[24] When urban-based agrarian reformers conflated the objectives of rural land redistribution with the desires of a growing urban consumer class, rather than the living standards of rural laborers, they reinscribed the primacy of urban desires over rural needs. When social reformers fashioned the rural home as one of the only spaces where women could assert themselves politically, they reproduced normative understandings of gender and respectability. Finally, when those involved in building the Chilean state articulated a notion of the "national economy" that was, in contrast to the old export-oriented model, rooted in the ideal of mass consumption, they found it impossible to successfully enact a program of economic development that did not depend on access to foreign markets—especially food imports.

During the final months of the UP revolution, the persistence of contradictions that were embedded in the food economy opened space for certain members of Chile's counterrevolutionary right to present their own vision of a consumer society. As the state relied upon food imports to make up for domestic shortfalls, large, and increasingly, medium-sized landholders argued against the prevailing view that smaller landholdings would necessarily improve agricultural productivity. Amid growing citizen concerns about food scarcity, food distributors, small merchants, and housewives attacked the Chilean state's long-standing argument that more active state participation in consumer distribution and exchange would make it easier for consumers to fulfill their essential nutritional needs. And as the value of Chile's national currency went into a free fall, free-market economists, known as the Chicago Boys, laid the groundwork for a decades-long project of recategorizing access to food and other essential goods not as a social and economic right of citizenship but instead as commodities whose allocation would be dictated by the market. Such a hyperindividualized understanding of consumption would define political and economic life under the dictatorship of Augusto Pinochet, and its legacies remain widely visible in contemporary Chile.

The history of food that I tell in this book is both a story of how understandings of welfare and economic justice were made and lived in twentieth-century Chile and an account of the limitations of a politics, state, and economy too fixated on consumption. In sum, it is a meditation on one of the most fundamental matters in Chile, both past and present: the question of whom national development efforts have historically been set up to benefit, and at whose expense.

ORGANIZATION AND ROAD MAP

The abovementioned themes and arguments are developed over the course of seven chapters. Taken together, these largely chronological chapters weave together a social history of popular mobilization around consumer issues; a cultural and intellectual history of Chile's midcentury middle-class reform movement and its evolving approach to human ecology, agriculture, and the economy; and a new political history of Chilean state formation that is centered around the many underexplored state institutions that were created to improve urban food security and guarantee Chilean citizens a social and economic right to basic consumption.

The book's first chapter explores the social and economic context out of which food-focused political movements first emerged in the twentieth century, identifying the mining camps of northern Chile and the urbanizing streets of Santiago as two key arenas. As a series of global economic crises shook Chile's position within the international economy, the price and scarcity of food became a rallying cry of early workers' organizations in these two distinct but increasingly intertwined economic environments. At the center of this story is the organizing of early Chilean labor leaders, like socialist activist Luis Emilio Recabarren. As Chile's production of nitrate fertilizers made it increasingly integral to the global food economy, Recabarren and his allies contended that the state's unwillingness to address the basic consumer needs of those who produced that abundance was a defining feature of inequality and social exclusion in the country. The early Chilean labor movement argued that hunger was one of the most concrete and immediate manifestations of working-class exploitation and identified persistent problems of inflation, basic cost-of-living increases, and episodic food scarcity as signal indicators of an economic system that was rotten at its core.

Chapter 2 follows the grassroots mobilization of consumers from the end of the First World War through the beginning of the Cold War, focusing on how the emergent political left mobilized around food distribution and the regulation of the urban marketplace during this era. In the period immediately after the First World War, the Asamblea Obrera de Alimentación Nacional (Workers' Assembly for National Nutrition, AOAN), a labor-based consumer organization, rallied tens of thousands in the capital's streets to demand, among other things, popular access to protein-rich beef and grain. Amid the creation of the Chilean Popular Front (FP) in the mid-1930s, leftist organizers again placed food and other basic consumer needs at the center of their nascent economic programs. In the 1938 election, the PF successfully appealed to voters by promising "bread, shelter, and a warm overcoat" to all Chileans. In the years that followed, the Chilean Communist Party (PCCh) took up consumers' cause. Using the new channels of state economic intervention, the PCCh made the case that citizen-consumers would blaze the trail toward economic justice in the postwar world. To that end, the PCCh organized major protests around the scarcity of two symbols of culinary modernity—white bread and cooking oil—on the eve of the Cold War. Taken together, these three moments demonstrate when and how food distribution and consumption became integral to midcentury mass politics.

The next two chapters track the Chilean state's response to the organized left's politicization of food and nutrition. As chapter 3 shows, in the 1930s and 1940s a generation of middle-class reformers trained in various health-related fields staffed new social welfare institutions, like the Consejo Nacional de Alimentación (National Nutrition Council, CNA), which had been established to battle urban hunger and malnutrition. For medical doctors, poor nutrition and antisocial consumer habits, such as excessive alcohol ingestion and inadequate dairy consumption, represented a threat to the vitality of the country's working class, upon whose shoulders industrial prosperity depended. A cultural reading of the relationship between state nutrition policies and the expanding scope of state price controls reveals how the state's embrace of modern scientific claims about popular health and state intervention in the economy reproduced gendered ideas about work and domesticity.

Chapter 4 builds upon the previous chapter by mapping a second wave of state responses to popular food protests in the post–Second World War era. Specifically, it explores how a national consensus about the urgency of agrarian reform grew out of lingering concerns over urban consumer insecurity in 1960s Chile. While most histories of Chilean agrarian reform depict the initiative as an attempt to improve the living and working conditions of rural workers, *Hungry for Revolution* suggests that the state's promotion of rural reform emerged largely from two urban concerns: the inability of the Chilean countryside to efficiently feed Chile's urban centers and the desire of urban manufacturers to build a larger consumer market for their own goods and services. By centering state-led attempts to boost domestic food production and alter the practices of food producers (as well as rural food consumers), the chapter examines the work of a generation of Chilean agronomists, engineers, and state policy makers, for whom resolving the nutritional consequences of agrarian stagnation became their life's work.

The book's fifth chapter reconstructs the importance of consumption to the UP government's pursuit of socialist modernity in the early 1970s. The chapter maintains that Chile's "road to socialism" was the culmination of some five decades of political and economic organizing around food. First, it illuminates just how integral consumption was to the UP's vision of economic democracy during Salvador Allende's first year in office. Second, it highlights the UP's belief that it could provide for the basic needs of urban consumers while simultaneously deepening the agrarian reform efforts of Allende's predecessors. The UP coalition would initially be quite successful in accomplishing the first task. However, it would stumble when faced with the second. In the final months of the revolution's first year, a series of economic challenges emerged. As food demand outpaced supply, the government resorted to importing record amounts of foodstuffs. As scarcity of certain traditional staples grew more severe, the revolution pushed unconventional consumer substitutes—as well as restraint—on consumers, generating popular frustration and anxiety.

Chapter 6 examines the vision of a more participatory and egalitarian economy that was enacted in many of the urban communities that supported Chile's revolutionary process. It begins by examining the UP's promotion of an ad hoc network of local food distribution sites and neighborhood grocery stores, the JAPs. Theses neighborhood consumer committees became a key institutional channel through which grassroots actors confronted the top-down nature of the revolution, offering an alternative vision of a revolution driven by "popular power." Over time, these informal networks of food distribution produced tensions between the government, which sought to maintain firm control of the revolutionary process, and elements of its grassroots base, which aimed to expand the scope and speed of Chile's transition to socialism. For those who identified with the Communist left, consumer organizing became a way of demonstrating unity and discipline. For the radical, Cuba-inspired left, direct participation in the food economy increasingly became a site of revolutionary praxis. The chapter considers some of the critiques of the UP's political economy that emerged on the coalition's left flank as the country's consumer revolution stagnated.

The book's last chapter interrogates the demise of Chile's socialist revolution, demonstrating how the state's inability to maintain the consumer abundance it had promised was central to its collapse. The chapter details how landowners, conservative women, and a broad middle class formed an anti-Allende oppositional bloc as food shortages and inflation increased in severity. It also explains how, in the wake of such opposition, a new conservative intelligentsia appropriated consumer concerns as its own. While landowners took steps to halt land redistribution and sabotage agricultural production, middle-class women took to the streets. Together, these disparate groups argued that the state's presence in the basic economy, not its absence, was the driving force behind food shortages and rising inflation. This new generation of conservative consumer activists attacked the JAPs and other forms of neighborhood-based food distribution. In the final months of the UP revolution, a small cohort of economists, most of them educated in the monetarist theories of the so-called Chicago school, began to voice an intellectual challenge to the long-standing role of the state in the economy as well as the era's prevailing assumptions about the origins of consumer inflation. Shortly after a military coup toppled the Allende government in September 1973, this coalition of political actors transformed consumption into the centerpiece of a radical free-market project. As several years of sustained protest in the South American country demonstrate, many Chileans today remain committed to challenging the exclusions that Chile's free-market counterrevolution deepened.

PART ONE

A Hungry Nation

ONE

Worlds of Abundance,
Worlds of Scarcity

AFTER SEVERAL MONTHS working the mineral-rich nitrate plains, Juan Chacón arrived back in Santiago as the First World War wound down, discovering a city brimming with both social discontent and political possibility. Speaking to his biographer some four decades later, the longtime Chilean Communist Party (PCCh) activist remembered how in those years global demands for equality and democracy reverberated throughout the city's working-class districts. "The Russian Revolution brought the most heated debates and discussions," Chacón recalled. "We devoured the press which reported every day on how the revolution was advancing, how it was stalling, how it was moving backward, and then how it advanced again."[1]

What proved especially intriguing to Chacón, however, was the way the organizers of those demonstrations—mostly students and workers—tied their support for the Soviet revolution to local campaigns against high rents and unjust evictions and for better salaries, what the leftist called "our own struggle against the rising cost of living." In this respect, a gathering organized by the AOAN, a labor-based organization committed to capping food prices, left a particularly lasting impression. Chacón recollected how, as one public meeting to discuss inflation and food scarcity concluded, attendees broke out into a spirited rendition of "The Internationale."[2]

The early decades of the twentieth century represented a significant conjuncture for poor and working-class Chileans like Chacón. As livelihoods and work opportunities became ever more tied to global circuits of trade and foreign investment, Chile experienced some of its most sustained years of economic prosperity to date at the turn of the century. And yet as the early lives of Chacón and his political contemporaries demonstrated, the beginning of a new century was also plagued with deepening social inequities. With each passing year, workers and their political allies saw ever more clearly how the economic growth of the era was being built upon the backs of the excluded.

Centered around the early years of the twentieth century, this chapter maps the rise of these two contrasting phenomena in Chile: economic prosperity on the one hand, and economic marginalization on the other. Following the movement of money, people, and political ideas between the country's urbanizing capital city, Santiago, and the export-oriented mining regions of the Chilean North, the chapter examines how food came to shape Chile's place within the global economy while simultaneously becoming a defining feature of the exploitation and exclusion that urban workers and their families faced on a daily basis. By exploring when and why inequitable access to basic consumer essentials became commensurate with what reformers of the era dubbed the "social question," the chapter also illustrates how popular organizing around food insecurity set the stage for the emergence of mass politics in Chile and a vision of what a more just national economy might look like.

LIVING IN A LAND OF PLENTY

An observer arriving in Santiago around the turn of the twentieth century would have undoubtedly been struck by a city replete with markers of modernity. Telephones, electric streetlights, paved streets, and electric trams all appeared in the capital's city center in those years. At the same time, larger infrastructure projects were quickly reshaping the city's physical landscape, turning Santiago into a model of urban progress in South America. The historian-turned-politician Benjamín Vicuña Mackenna jump-started a first wave of modernization in the late 1870s and early 1880s. As governor of Santiago province, Vicuña Mackenna channeled state revenue gained from commodity export duties toward the re-creation of the capital's urban geography. Vicuña Mackenna was credited, for example, with turning Cerro Santa Lucía, site of the city's 1540 founding, into one of the continent's most attractive public parks. He also promoted the construction of the tree-lined Alameda as the city's main east-west artery and poured unprecedented amounts of public capital into large-scale building projects.[3]

By the late nineteenth century, state and municipal officials had built upon Vicuña Mackenna's initiatives by completing the construction of a new central market, municipal theater, and congress building. The expansion of the small Mapocho River into a canal that, according to some, resembled Italy's Tiber or

Central Europe's Elbe, followed, as did the establishment of a narrow, mean-dering greenbelt, known as the Parque Forestal, along the Mapocho's southern banks.[4] In 1897, the city's central train station, designed by French architects, was rebuilt, streamlining the movement of goods and people between Santiago, the country's rural countryside, and its chief port cities. As further evidence of Chile's urban development, by 1903 some 275 streetcars crisscrossed the capital city, linking together new neighborhoods to the north, south, and west of Santiago's city center.[5] Santiago may not have had the sophisticated architecture or culture of the Argentine capital, Buenos Aires, one eyewitness noted at the turn of the century, but it had certainly distinguished itself from the capital cities of its other Latin American neighbors.[6]

A high-powered coterie of bankers, large landowners, foreign merchants, and industrialists were among those who took up residence in metropolitan Santiago during this period, their evolving consumption habits becoming a symbol of Chile's newfound prosperity.[7] Between 1875 and 1903, annual wine consumption in the country more than tripled, from 81 million liters to 275 million liters, a result of bountiful supplies of European imports.[8] Similarly, increases in beef consumption suggested a country in the throes of transformation. By the end of the 1880s, per capita beef consumption in Santiago reached almost 150 kilograms of beef per year, a figure that was roughly double the average amount of red meat consumed by residents of New York or Paris at the time and nearly three times the national average in England.[9]

Amid these changes, the demographic character of Chile also evolved. According to historian Arnold J. Bauer, by the late nineteenth century, "every landowner who could afford it" had built a second home in the Chilean capital and was spending more and more time away from his country estate.[10] New job opportunities for rural people of modest means, particularly poor women who flocked to the city to work as domestics, cooks, and laundresses for the country's political and economic elite, accompanied the process of spatial centralization. As a result, the population of the department of Santiago, a geographic unit that included two dozen parishes of different sizes and at various stages of urbanization, more than tripled in the four and a half decades between 1885 and 1930. Whereas the population of the department was scarcely 11 percent of Chile's total population in 1885, forty-five years later Santiago constituted nearly a fifth of the country.[11]

As was the case throughout turn-of-the-century Latin America, the driving economic force behind the urbanization and geographic centralization of Chile did not lie in the dynamism of the country's capital. Rather, urban

TABLE I Urban Growth in Late Nineteenth-
and Early Twentieth-Century Chile

Year	Total National Population	Population of Santiago Department[a]	Population of Santiago Department as Percentage of Total National Population[b]
1885	2,507,380	272,524	10.9%
1895	2,695,911	351,425	13.0%
1907	3,231,496	444,614	13.8%
1920	3,731,573	604,598	16.2%
1930	4,287,445	836,928	19.5%
1940	5,023,539	1,100,725	22.0%

SOURCE: Robert McCaa, ed., *Chile: XI Censo de Poblacíon (1940): Recopilación de cifras publicadas por la Dirección de Estadísticas y Censos* (Santiago: Centro Latinoamericano de Demografía, 1972), 450–451.

a. Santiago department includes the following *comunas* (parishes): Santiago, Conchalí, Providencia, Ñuñoa, San Miguel, Maipú, Quinta Normal, Renca, Quilicura, Tiltil, Colina, Lampa, Barrancas, La Cisterna, La Granja, Puente Alto, San José de Maipó, Peñaflor, Talagante, Isla de Maipo, Curacaví, Las Condes, La Florida, and Pirque

b. Numbers in column 4 are rounded to the nearest one decimal place.

development was fundamentally shaped by—and frequently dependent upon—Santiago's intimate and inescapable relationship to the political economy of raw material extraction.[12] As midcentury demand for Chile's agricultural imports subsided, mineral exports became the primary fuel of national economic growth. In this respect, no part of Chile's national territory was more critical to the growth of cities like Santiago than Tarapacá and Antofagasta, the country's two most northern provinces, which together represented the unsuspecting wellspring of the global agricultural economy.

Known simply as the Norte Grande, the mining regions of Tarapacá and Antofagasta were home to the world's largest deposits of saltpeter, a sodium-nitrate compound that, when processed down into a soluble, crystalline fertilizing agent, restored agrarian vitality to fruit, vegetable, and grain fields in Europe, the United States, and beyond. In the late 1870s and early 1880s, the Chilean military had waged an aggressive war to annex the resource-rich Atacama Desert from its neighbors to the north and east, Peru and Bolivia. With the Norte Grande under Chile's full sovereign control beginning in 1884, extraction of nitrates from its arid plains, or *pampa*, proceeded apace, soon succeeding Peruvian guano as the fertilizer of choice for agriculturalists around much of the world.[13] Estimates suggest that annual global exports of

Chilean nitrates surpassed one million tons around 1890. During the first decade of the twentieth century, that figure surged over the two-million-ton mark. By 1913, just one year before the First World War began, Chilean nitrate sales abroad hit a record 2.75 million tons per year, thus constituting 80 percent of the country's total exports and approximately 50 percent of all ordinary public revenue in Chile.[14]

Nevertheless, throughout the nitrate era—a period that most see as beginning with the War of the Pacific (1879–83) and ending with the global economic crisis of the early 1930s—Chile's control over its most important economic sector remained circumscribed. For the first three decades of the twentieth century, foreign investors and engineers followed the demands of foreign agricultural consumers in developing the industry. By extension, foreign interests directed Chile's national economic trajectory as well. At the end of the 1880s, Great Britain was the dominant player in the Chilean nitrate trade as British capitalists secured effective control of production at a plurality of the nitrate *oficinas* (processing centers) that dotted the Chilean desert highlands.[15]

Nitrate baron John Thomas North was the most recognizable face of British economic influence on the pampa. A shrewd and demanding businessman, North is credited by scholars with successfully reducing the cost and increasing the scale and intensity of nitrate production in late nineteenth-century Chile. However, the economic power of the "Nitrate King," as North became known, also provoked resentment. By the late nineteenth century, North claimed a controlling stake in almost every facet of the region's development, operating shipping lines and railway networks as well as enterprises that provided potable water, electricity, and basic foodstuffs to the region.[16]

The work of international marketing agents bolstered the intensity of extraction by foreign investors like North. In fact, even more than European and later North American capitalists, those who served as foreign distribution agents for Chilean-made nitrate fertilizers were responsible for turning the South American country into an axis around which an ever-more-globalized food economy turned. Or at least that was how many sought to portray themselves. In preparation for the 1893 Chicago World's Fair, the London-based Permanent Nitrate Committee, a marketing company run by a conglomeration of prominent nitrate producers, printed and distributed half a million pamphlets detailing the indispensability of nitrate fertilizers to the international agricultural economy.[17] A few years later, in 1899, a group of US-based nitrate agents embarked on a roughly twelve-thousand-mile, sixteen-state tour of the United States and western Canada to promote Chile's "all-natural" fertilizer to North American farmers, the editors of popular agricultural publications, and fertilizer retailers.[18] "A portion of our earth, namely Chile, has by accident or by design been set aside as a storehouse for nitrogen in its most available plant food form," William S. Myers, the longtime head of Chile's nitrate marketing operations for the New York–based Chilean Nitrate of Soda Educational Bureau, declared in a speech presented to a group of US businessmen in the early 1900s. As he touted the future prospects of Chile's most important industry, Myers, a chemist by training, added that nitrates— an "All-America product," in his words—provided US farmers with "first aid and continued nourishment" against the sort of soil depletion that was decimating Chilean agriculture.[19]

Marketing agents played a particularly decisive role in demonstrating to US farmers that a deep ecological interdependence bound North American agriculture to Chilean mineral extraction. In one 1910 memo, the New York office of the Educational Bureau wrote proudly that there was no doubt that an "enormous increase" in nitrate use in the United States was due to the "missionary work" of nitrate advertising specialists. There was "hardly an issue of any farm paper today which does not have some reference somewhere in its pages" to the agricultural importance of Chilean nitrate of soda fertilizer, the memo maintained.[20]

Nearly a decade and a half later, and shortly after US president Calvin Coolidge warned that the United States should prepare itself to become a food-importing nation, nitrate industry officials in New York underscored the then president's "repeated references" to US overreliance on fertilizers to meet its domestic food needs.[21] "Foremost among all of the American farmer's plant food resources," the Educational Bureau wrote, "stands Chilean nitrate of soda"—a commodity whose proper use had the potential of "postponing" US "dependence on foreign supplies of agricultural products" for at least a generation.[22] During the early years of the twentieth century, the United States had already become the second largest consumer of Chilean nitrates, surpassing all other European markets save Germany.[23]

FIELDS OF HUNGER

Beyond the façade of affluence that Chile's position in the global food economy exuded, the social conditions that most Chileans experienced at the turn of the century presented a far less sanguine portrait of economic progress than the one sketched by nitrate capitalists and propagandists. Struggles to feed Chile's working class figured prominently in the country's social reality, and everyday life on the pampa was revealing in this regard. For one thing, the sort of extensive mining operations that consumed the pampa demanded a consistent and reliable supply of cheap labor—no easy task in a region where the nutritional necessities that nitrates helped produce were scarce, to say the least. Thus, turn-of-the-century nitrate producers constructed a far-reaching system of labor recruitment known as the *enganche*—literally the "hook"—to relocate large numbers of strong, able-bodied workers to the pampa at the lowest possible cost.[24]

First utilized in the middle of the nineteenth century to complete construction of the railways that would connect isolated mining enclaves in the interior of the Atacama to port cities along the then Peruvian and Bolivian coastline, the enganche was repurposed by nitrate manufacturers in the late nineteenth century to meet the labor needs of the global fertilizer economy. Itinerant labor recruiters, known as *enganchadores*, acted as the anchors of this system of labor conscription. Working at the behest of the country's powerful Nitrate Producers' Association, these headhunters were sent to rural towns and cities around the Central Valley, where they peddled handbills promising high wages and plentiful work opportunities to young, job-seeking men.[25]

For "hooked" *enganchados*, the journey to the Norte Grande began in a public plaza, a tavern, or around a town's central train station. There, recruiters loaded the enlisted onto railcars headed for ports like Valparaíso and Coquimbo. At the docks, the voyagers then went below deck on steamships destined for the northern coastal towns of Antofagasta, Taltal, Tocopilla, Iquique, and Pisagua: the five gateways to the Chilean nitrate market. Recruiters typically covered a new conscript's travel fare while also distributing coupons to purchase food and basic supplies at a network of canteens that dotted the path to the pampa. Nevertheless, access to food and clean water on nitrate clippers was often precarious. Members of one enganche that originated in the agricultural town of Chillán in the mid-1920s faced such horrific conditions on board the steamship transporting them north that Chile's national police force produced an incident report for the country's national labor office. The report documented that dozens of women and children had been crowded into the ship's forward hold with nothing to eat or drink for the duration of the trip.[26]

Upon the ships' arrival in the Norte Grande, representatives from the privately run nitrate companies organized the inspection and hiring of new workers. A company health official was among the first to greet the arrivals, checking recruits for maladies and testing their general physical fitness. By the time ships arrived in the north, it was common for diseases like smallpox to have run their course in the dank steerage. Men whom labor inspectors deemed capable of tolerating the extreme climactic conditions of the pampa were then shuttled ashore for a shower and midday meal; the "unfit" were often left to fend for themselves on the docks of port towns. Finally, with basic employment paperwork completed, recruiters directed contracted laborers to railcars to complete the final three- to six-hour leg of the journey to the high plains of Tarapacá and Antofagasta. Whereas just over sixty-four hundred people worked in the nitrate industry during the first decade after the War of the Pacific, by the 1910s the industry employed around fifty thousand people in any given year.[27]

New nitrate miners found working and living conditions on the pampa to be physically demanding and socially isolating. "The typical nitrate oficina was a noisy, smoky, smelly industrial company town set incongruously in the quiet grandeur of the Atacama Desert," the historian Charles Bergquist once wrote in a vivid account of working-class life in northern Chile.[28] This description aptly reveals the inescapable challenges that new laborers faced in most nitrate mining communities: constant exposure to dust, mud, and fumes, which often resulted in respiratory infections; an always-present concern that sections of the earth's crust could buckle at any moment because of misplaced explosives; and the threat of physical mutilation—from severed limbs to horrible burns—which was a consequence of nonexistent workplace safety measures.[29] To make matters worse, the Norte Grande was almost completely devoid of proper medical services. As late as 1912, just a single hospital existed on the entire nitrate pampa.[30]

This was part of the reality that Juan Chacón confronted in 1916 when, after being laid off from his factory position at Santiago's main glass manufacturer, he joined some three hundred other enganchados on an Iquique-bound ship that departed from Valparaíso. Just twenty years old at the time, Chacón had only lived in Santiago for six or seven years when he departed, having originally left his rural home village, some thirty kilometers northwest of the capital, to find work in the growing metropolis. Now settled in the small nitrate town of Oficina Paposo in the distant province of Tarapacá, Chacón must have felt that he had arrived in another world.[31]

As demand from the First World War drove production of nitrates for use in both explosives and fertilizers, Chacón spent much of 1916 and early 1917 readying the craggy surface of the Atacama to be dynamited so that the desert rocks, known as *caliche*, could be extracted with a pickax and shovel, transported to a nearby processing factory, boiled down, and dried under the heat of the desert sun. In the final stages of the nitrate production process, workers bagged the refined product—*salitre*, as it was called in Chilean Spanish—into large burlap sacks for transportation, first to the Chilean coast and then on to points north and west.[32] The work was strenuous and not for the faint of heart. "The bags were of various sizes," Chacón recalled. "They weighed between 100 and 140 kilograms. You had to have a strong back to haul them off."[33]

But for Chacón, as for many other nitrate workers, the contradictions between the challenging living conditions he experienced on the pampa and the prosperity that his labor sustained in faraway lands generated some of the most vivid memories of exploitation. Struggles over food, in particular, conditioned how class was lived and how political struggle would be waged in the Norte Grande; indeed, company officials' failure to meet dietary expectations was very often the spark that ignited regionwide instances of social mobilization. Chacón reconstructed one such moment in a discussion with his biographer decades after he had returned to Santiago. He recalled a day sometime in late 1916 or 1917 when Oficina Paposo's company store, or *pulpería*, inexplicably refused to sell daily food rations to the women of the community who operated the local cantina that miners frequented for their midday meal. As a response to the store's action, the workers organized an impromptu political rally. Chacón said around two hundred individuals turned out for the demonstration, raising their collective voice to demand that the nitrate company immediately recommence the sale of affordable foodstuffs. As the workers congregated in the local plaza, members of the Chilean national police met them, and in a matter of minutes began to detain those they deemed political agitators. When some protestors resisted arrest, a peaceful demonstration turned violent. Chacón remembered one police officer firing on the crowd indiscriminately, killing at least one of his fellow workers. "[T]here it happened," he said, "right in front of the administration building, some 20 steps from the company store."[34]

Chacón's memories of consumer struggle on the pampa were typical. The prolific chronicler of the nitrate region, historian Sergio González Miranda, has argued that nitrate workers' discontent frequently originated from their disillusionment with the monopolistic practices of the company store and the contradictions they embodied in workers' daily lives.[35] Such grievances included workers' discovery that, upon being resettled in the Norte Grande, producers extracted large deductions from their initial compensation so that the debts workers owed to labor recruiters could be reimbursed.[36] For much of the late nineteenth and early twentieth centuries, new arrivals on the nitrate plains scarcely saw anything resembling a full wage, paid out in Chile's national currency. Instead, private employers preferred to compensate workers in company-backed tokens, known as *fichas*, an alternative form of remuneration used by mining companies and on large agricultural estates throughout the nineteenth century but one whose exchange value did not extend beyond the gates of privately owned properties.[37] As a consequence of debt and the ficha system, laborers were often trapped on the desolate pampa with no savings and restricted economic mobility when global commodity prices dipped and employment opportunities dried up.[38]

The inequities produced by the nitrate economy's labor system, together with the problems of quality and affordability in the consumer marketplace, marked working-class encounters with export-dependent capitalist development, an observation that is captured in the many reports and dispatches that worker advocates filed to document the plight of nitrate workers.[39] When investigators from Chile's recently formed Labor Office traveled to the Norte Grande in 1904 to assess social conditions in the region, they called it a "well-established fact" that the nitrate pampa had "brought many millions of pesos into Chile." And yet in a region that "had relied for twenty years on the strength of the Chilean worker," both the state and private companies had failed to "find the minimal resources" needed to provide for the basic nutritional needs of their workers.[40]

In what reads like an allusion to the agricultural abundance that workers' own sweat and blood had created in the distant lands of North America and Europe, one group of petitioners, whose grievances were documented in the same 1904 report, argued that had the most minimal wealth obtained from the export of nitrates been reinvested in the provinces of Tarapacá and Antofagasta, Chile could have transformed "the sandy plains into fertile and productive valleys."[41] This commentary echoed the words of one European visitor to Chile's nitrate zone a few decades earlier. If the Chilean state ensured an adequate "supply of water and of labour," the observer wrote, the pampa "could be made to teem with vegetation."[42]

Few summarized the contradictions of the nitrate economy more clearly and succinctly than a North American traveler and diplomat named William

Reid. During a brief stopover in the province of Tarapacá in the early 1900s, Reid described how "foodstuffs for man and beast" had to be imported into the nitrate region." Reid added that this curious process, in which food for human consumption entered a country on such a large scale only so that "food-growing materials" could "be sent out of the country," represented one of the greatest "ironies" of global commerce.[43] In assessing those observations, as well as the particular impact that Chilean nitrate fertilizers had on the westward expansion of the United States, the environmental historian Edward Melillo has written that, thanks to the plentiful supply of Chilean nitrates, "far more food than [California's] residents could ever consume" was produced at the turn of the century.[44] Few facts, notes Melillo, provided a finer description of the "global nature of the metabolic rift in modern agriculture" at the turn of the century.[45]

Reid's words laid bare a problem that haunted Chilean state builders for much of the early and mid-twentieth century: the challenge of simultaneously satisfying basic needs and sustaining economic growth. As the feminist activist Enriqueta de Carpio would perceptively ask in the 1930s, how was it possible that a country like Chile, so "blessed by Nature" that it contributed to the feeding of thirty million people around the world, remained incapable of "guaranteeing the subsistence" of its own population of just four and a half million?[46]

STREETS OF HUNGER

Hardship and want defined life for the nitrate workers who fueled the engine of Chile's economy in the early twentieth century. But conditions for many workers in Santiago, the city that supposedly reaped the material benefits of the nitrate economy, appeared scarcely more just. As a generation of prominent national writers and social critics observed, squalid living conditions in the working-class neighborhoods of the capital rivaled those in the most impoverished parts of the continent during the early years of the century.[47] A common observation throughout this period was just how close the city was to a full-fledged public health crisis. Persistent outbreaks of cholera, smallpox, yellow fever, tuberculosis, measles, influenza, and typhus, to name but a few of the illnesses that most worried public officials, choked working-class districts of the city. Such diseases spread rapidly through the poorly ventilated, cramped quarters of multifamily, tenement-style residences, known as *conventillos*, killing untold numbers in any given year. Young children were particularly vulnerable.[48]

One European traveler who visited the country in the first decade of the twentieth century underscored the severity of such conditions when he declared that Santiago was not worth the journey required to arrive. Chile's capital was filled with over 200,000 slum-dwelling *rotos*—the pejorative term used for Chile's lower classes—he opined, adding that it was a bastion of crime, disease, squalor, and air that was among the most foul smelling he had ever encountered.[49] "[M]unicipal officials have contented themselves with putting up adornments in the downtown areas of the city, the place where the most well-to-do live and where they take comfort in well-ventilated, light-filled salons," a group of protestors wrote of Santiago in a 1918 petition that identified the emergence of two distinct Santiagos, segregated from one another. "It's not like this in the slums where the poor live in filthy pigsties . . . inferior in quality to what hog producers offer to their own pigs."[50]

Santiago's problems of disease, an inadequate and substandard housing stock, and poor sanitation were exacerbated by Chile's dependence on commodity exports because temporary dips in global commodity prices often displaced thousands of workers into the capital, thus intensifying overcrowding. For some, Chile's major cities were temporary stopping-off points, places where the jobless might spend a few days or weeks in a makeshift flophouse before moving on to seasonal agricultural work farther south or quickly returning north to catch the rising tides of a new commodity cycle. For most, however, Santiago and other urban centers, like Valparaíso, gradually became permanent homes where the unemployed looked for work in construction, in manufacturing, or as informal street vendors.[51]

As a result, the modern, centrally planned downtown area of Santiago was gradually encircled by a ring of more precarious working-class neighborhoods. According to Chilean government estimates, in 1911, 120,000 people, roughly 40 percent of the population of the *comuna* (parish) of Santiago, lived in multifamily tenement complexes that grew in and around the city center.[52] Three years later, after the international price of nitrates collapsed, an editorial published in the leading newspaper of Chile's second city, Valparaíso, compared the social situation that had resulted from the arrival of thousands of ex-nitrate miners to a natural disaster. "We should remember how life was in Valparaíso in the days following the 1906 earthquake, when whole families, prudent families, lived for months in nothing more than a small shack. They had nothing to spend on clothing; they only ate the barest of essentials," the paper wrote.[53]

In this environment, the growing nutritional divide between rich and poor became a metaphor for urban inequality, just as it had become synonymous with exploitation on the nitrate pampa. As historian Daniel Palma has written, "nutritional scarcity" defined daily existence for the majority of Chile's city dwellers in the late 1800s and early 1900s, as consumer options were limited to a few inexpensive dishes produced with just a handful of local ingredients that could be purchased at city markets.[54] Upon waking for breakfast most urban residents fought off hunger pangs with a piece of plain bread and a cup of yerba maté, toasted wheat or barley that was brewed as a cheap coffee substitute, or tea, which British importers began to popularize in Chile in the late nineteenth century. Among the most common midday meals were simple dishes produced with a limited selection of rural staples: a bowl of *porotos* (beans); a bone-broth noodle soup with onions, known as *pantrucas*; a potato-heavy casserole mixed with onions, peppers, and scraps of beef or horsemeat, called *charquicán*; or *pequenes*, a hand pie filled with onions that served as the poor man's stand-in for the more delectable *empanada de pino* (meat hand pie). For most urban residents, the typical day would conclude with more tea and bread.[55]

In stark contrast, the dining table of the Chilean elite was consistently a feast of culinary delights, many of them imported from abroad and prepared according to European-inspired recipes. If recipes in popular cookbooks of the early twentieth century are any indication, expensive cuts of beef, veal, and lamb were relatively common in the homes of Santiago elites, as were popular French and Spanish dishes such as Parisian- and Andalusian-style calamari, Provençal-style trout and cod, and *caracoles a marsellesa*—Marseillaise snail.[56] In their study of elite consumer habits in turn-of-the-twentieth century Chile, Arnold Bauer and Benjamin Orlove write that despite high tariffs in the late nineteenth century, French wine, rather than cheaper, domestically produced wines and spirits, remained the drink of choice at important banquets and state functions, even during some of the country's deepest recessions.[57] According to the memoirs of one notable member of Chile's upper crust, it was typical for mealtime in the homes of Chile's landed aristocracy to consist of "four or five different plates, of all different styles and all of the highest quality."[58] Suffice it to say, urban workers themselves rarely shared such experiences. As historian Raymond Craib has observed, translations of Belgian playwright Maurice Maeterlinck's 1908 play *The Blue Bird*, a work that begins with the

FIGURE 1. Commercial activity at Santiago's principal market, the Vega Central, circa 1900. Colección Museo Histórico Nacional, Santiago de Chile.

poor looking down with confusion at a group of wealthy neighbors who sit at a table with untouched plates filled with food, was a widely read best seller in the early decades of the century, particularly within Chilean radical circles.[59]

THE HUNGRY REVOLT

It did not take long for hunger to become more than the stuff of social criticism. In this regard, the year 1905 marked a turning point—one of the first moments in twentieth-century Chile when food sparked a political awakening.[60] In early September of that year, a group of Santiago market vendors joined with city labor leaders and members of the country's left-leaning Democratic Party (PD) to plan actions against a much-despised national tariff on imported beef. In an attempt to insulate the country's inefficient and uncompetitive agrarian sector from imports of cheaper red meat, Chile's largest landowners' association, the Sociedad Nacional de Agricultura (National Agricultural Society, SNA), had first promoted the tax as a response to the opening of a trans-Andean railroad between Chile and its larger beef-producing neighbor, Argentina. This development, Chile's landowners argued, would flood Chilean markets with cheap Argentine beef, thus suffocating the country's fledgling cattle industry.[61]

Controversy surrounding the tariff issue persisted for nearly a decade before Congress officially adopted the new tax in 1897. Unsurprisingly, the tariff's approval became an immediate source of resentment. Chilean consumers, laborers, and small butchers contended that the policy would increase the price of beef, which it quickly did. The most curious complaints came from the poorest members of Santiago society, who at best enjoyed a chunk of beef every few weeks. The concern for this broad cross section of the urban consuming public was that the new law would incentivize agriculturalists to convert rich croplands into more profitable free-range pastures, thus raising the price and decreasing the supply of beans and wheat, which predominated in their daily diets.[62]

The aforementioned September 1905 meeting that was called by the Santiago consumer-merchant coalition to strategize against the cattle import tax resulted in the creation of an organizing committee dedicated to fighting the rising price of basic foodstuffs. The Central Committee to Abolish the Cattle Tax, as the ad hoc association of butchers, working-class consumers, and representatives of various Santiago labor organizations called itself, argued that the time had come for the city's residents to put aside sectarian disputes and vocally reject the all-too-common xenophobic claim that foreign-born workers and merchants were to blame for the country's economic troubles. Instead, the anti-tax committee turned its frustrations against a singular enemy: Chile's landed agrarian elite.[63]

On October 22, 1905, a Sunday, the committee's organizing work culminated in a citywide march in which thousands of *santiaguinos* took to the streets of their city to demand the immediate repeal of the state's tariff on imported beef. Crowds—totaling somewhere between twelve and fifty thousand people, according to various reports—poured onto the Alameda in the early afternoon of that day and from there marched on the presidential palace, determined to win an audience with Chilean president Germán Riesco Errázuriz. A petition written by the demonstration's lead organizers cited the basic dietary importance of red meat to the building of a strong nation. Calling meat prices a "problem on which the vitality and greatness of this nation depends," the marchers vociferously denounced the revolving door through which large landowners circulated between positions of economic and political power.[64]

The October demonstration was intended to have ended there. However, with the speechmaking concluded and the country's president nowhere to be found, a single orderly march—what was by all accounts a festive event—divided in two. One group of protestors continued on to demonstrate in front of the president's personal residence, while the other split away from the planned demonstration, subsequently splintering into a series of more raucous marches that directly confronted the symbols of inequity in the capital. Demonstrators in these latter groups smashed storefront windows of the commercial establishments that lined the Alameda as they rushed through Santiago's downtown streets. They tore down recently installed streetlamps. Some attempted—albeit unsuccessfully—to knock down the doors of the city's foreign-owned banking houses and the National Treasury building. Others directed their fury toward the city's pawnshops and grocery stores, twin symbols of the inequities facing urban consumers. In at least one instance, a group of demonstrators took out their economic frustrations on the landlord of a Santiago tenement, threatening to destroy his property if that month's rent was not immediately canceled for the building's residents. In another publicized encounter, protestors reportedly disarmed a group of national guardsmen who had been deployed to put down the protests, seizing the security agents' weapons and throwing them into nearby sewer drains.[65]

State officials shuddered at the prospect of their modern capital city going up in flames—a concern that intensified when city officials realized that much of the country's armed forces were away from Santiago, conducting training exercises, when the protests broke out. To fill their place, Chile's Ministry of War authorized the distribution of hundreds of rifles to bands of paramilitary militias composed largely of young men from the same landholding families that the demonstrators had denounced in their protests.[66] After three days of simmering street battles between bands of urban rebels and state-backed militia groups, one Santiago newspaper reported that "nearly every bank" on the Alameda had been destroyed; only the "ancient stones with which they had been built" remained. The destruction, the paper went on to report, had transformed Santiago into a smoldering "battlefield."[67] So traumatic was the experience that one North American writer who visited Chile a decade later described the 1905 uprising as South America's reenactment of France's 1652 Battle of the Fauborg Saint Antoine.[68]

Though no official figures on casualties were released, various estimates suggested that anywhere between seventy and three hundred protestors were killed in the October conflagration.[69] Whatever the exact figures, the episode constituted one of the most notable examples of state-supported repression in twentieth-century Santiago, at least until the military coup of 1973.[70] So bloody was the week that political commentators would dub the events *semana roja*—"red week"—a moniker that referenced the bloodshed that the demonstrations had provoked, the tax on red meat that was under siege, and the leftist ideology of those who were believed to have organized the demonstrations.

The protests of 1905 did not immediately usher in the repeal of the controversial 1897 cattle tax. For two years the SNA succeeded in blocking such action, and although enforcement of the tax was paused in 1907, its suspension proved only temporary. It was not until the late 1920s that the cattle tax was repealed once and for all, replaced by a sliding duty scale that was pegged to wholesale cattle prices.[71] Nevertheless, in the wake of the 1905 uprising, the Chilean government did take several concrete steps to address other matters of social concern, if only to contain the possibility of future unrest. In 1906, for example, the government approved passage of a special worker housing law. Considered by many to be Chile's first piece of explicitly "social" legislation, the new law granted the Chilean state power to take a more active role in regulating the national housing market. The law also allowed the public sector to promote the construction of new housing complexes for the country's urban working and middle classes.[72]

Additionally, in 1907 a presidential decree established the national Office of Labor Statistics, an agency that would eventually grow into the national Labor Office, a first-of-its-kind body with the power to investigate workplace conditions on the state's behalf.[73] That same year, Chile's Congress also approved a new law mandating Sundays, Christmas Day, New Year's Day, and Chilean Independence Day as official holidays on which no Chilean workers could be forced to work. Over the next decade, other pieces of social legislation would extend special protections to child laborers, employees of commercial establishments, and women workers. These measures ultimately paved the way for the ratification of one of Latin America's most progressive constitutions in 1925 and an inclusive national labor code in the early 1930s.[74]

Just as events in 1905 had revealed the contradictions of capitalist growth in Santiago, in 1907 the inequities of economic liberalism were put on display in the Norte Grande. In December 1907, sites of consumer exchange across the nitrate plains were transformed into arenas of popular unrest as thousands of nitrate miners walked off the job in dozens of nitrate communities to protest, among other matters, the nitrate industry's policies on consumption.

Filling Iquique's wood-clad streets just a few days before the Christmas holiday, an estimated twelve thousand *pampinos* demanded that the state end the pulpería's monopoly on commercial exchange in nitrate communities, abolish the ficha payment system, guarantee wage stability, and more strictly monitor the scales used by merchants to weigh consumer goods sold in company towns.[75]

When leaders of the strike movement camped in the inner courtyard of Iquique's Escuela de Santa María, demanding they be allowed to continue their demonstrations, regional authorities reluctantly granted them their wish. Just days later, however, the province's governor declared a state of siege across the province of Tarapacá. After workers refused to pack up their belongings and return home, the governor ordered troops to evict the occupiers by force on December 21, 1907. During the action, members of the Chilean military were given orders to fire on the demonstrators, and an estimated two thousand pampinos, among them dozens of women and children, were killed in a barrage of gunfire that became known as the Santa María School massacre.[76]

In the wake of the massacre, consumer grievances became an ever-more-present topic of labor petitions. In a report issued by a Chilean Labor Office inspector in the early 1920s, it was estimated that as a consequence of malnutrition, perhaps 60 percent of all nitrate workers suffered from tuberculosis and that nearly all were stricken with internal organ ailments of one form or another.[77] Despite the approval of far-reaching social legislation during that same decade, including a ban on the use of fichas as a form of worker compensation, poor living conditions persisted, as observed by the Chilean journalist Atilano Oróstegui, who wrote to the governor of Antofagasta in 1934 about conditions on the pampa during the Great Depression. The product of a year of on-the-ground observation, Oróstegui's thirty-one-page report highlighted the social neglect many northern nitrate communities continued to endure and made the case that a defining experience of life on the pampa was hunger in nitrate camps. "The people fear hunger . . . which knocks at the door insistently day in and day out," he wrote. "Every working-class woman carries the concern that her husband will have to go to work without eating first, that there will not be sufficient money to buy the most urgent and necessary products at the pulpería, or that she'll be unable to find milk for her small children." Calling the problem of nutrition on the pampa an issue that "deserves its own chapter," Oróstegui described the quality of consumer goods in nitrate communities as "detestable." "The system of rationing, through cards, which has been implemented in the majority of pampa oficinas, is the most odious thing you can imagine," he wrote, underscoring the fact that in some places basics like rice, flour, and sugar were unavailable for weeks on end.[78]

Decades later, the trauma of consumer struggle would also color the memories of those who reflected back on working-class life on the pampa. "The issue of food and nutrition left much to be desired," Julián Cobo wrote of his childhood in the Norte Grande. "Worm-ridden potatoes, rotten eggs, maggot-infested cans of fat, old legumes filled with dirt and pebbles, throwaway fruits and vegetables, and the arrival of beef cows that suffered from tuberculosis and were often nothing more than bones" were the items that defined everyday life, he recalled.[79] Another woman who grew up on the pampa in the middle of the twentieth century described her childhood to historian Lessie Jo Frazier, relaying that during periods of bread scarcity, her mother would locate some old, discarded bread, scrape off the mold, knead the remaining bread in water, and rebake it so her hungry family would have something to eat.[80]

Few did more to elevate consumer inequities as a class-based grievance than the political organizer, typesetter, newspaper publisher, and eventual founder of the PCCh, Luis Emilio Recabarren. The stomach and the wallet, Recabarren argued, represented inequity in its most immediate and physical form. The socialist leader contended that if working-class emancipation was to occur at all, it needed to happen not only at the workplace but in the consumer marketplace as well. During a 1910 speech, Recabarren maintained that Chilean workers had witnessed their standard of living steadily decline since the late nineteenth century. Chile's infant mortality epidemic was a symptom of this popular economic anxiety, he argued, as he provided a systematic accounting of the eroding value of workers' wages by approximating wage values to the declining number of basic consumer products that could be purchased with them.[81] While the typical Chilean blue-collar worker (peón) earned just 1.50 pesos per day in 1890, Recabarren's figures illuminated that some twenty years later that wage, even when adjusted for inflation, had not even come close to keeping up with the soaring cost of living. In 1910, for example, the cost of living—calculated in terms of a basket of basic goods that included sugar, milk, shoes, housing, bread, meat, potatoes, and paraffin—was approximately four times greater than it had been twenty-five years prior. A box of sugar, which sold for 7 or 8 pesos in the late 1880s, could not be bought for less than 15 or 16 pesos at the time of his writing. One liter of milk, then 5 or 10 pesos, cost between 20 and 40 pesos just a few decades later. The price of bread had doubled. The same was true for beef, potatoes, and paraffin, the main source of heating fuel in working-class homes.[82] Recabarren went on: "All of the most basic and necessary consumer goods have increased in price by more than one hundred percent in the last quarter century. . . . I'll repeat this one more time, the cost of living has increased by more than one hundred percent in the last twenty-five years, while wages . . . have not even gone up by forty percent over that same period. Life then is today more agonizing than before. Given these facts, is it really possible to say that the proletariat is emancipated, or that it is free or independent?"[83]

In a series of articles that were published a short time later, Recabarren turned his economic findings into a call to action. In the working-class newspaper *El Grito Popular*, he urged workers to join consumer cooperatives. Local, community-controlled commerce would provide them the capacity to meet their everyday needs through mutual aid, he said, rather than deepening dependence on private food purveyors and distributors.[84] The socialist leader even argued that cooperatives represented an institutional innovation on a par with more traditional forms of worker organization, like workplace trade unions and class-based political parties.[85]

Speaking to a meeting of the Gran Unión Marítima (Grand Maritime Union), one of Iquique's largest workers' associations, in 1911, Recabarren took this proposal further, declaring that the socialist cause should be expanded to the marketplace, where "intermediaries," who were guilty of "making more expensive the means of subsistence," needed to be confronted.[86] Just a few months later, Recabarren and his political allies put their ideas into action by founding the city's first cooperative organization, the Sociedad Cooperativa de Pan (Cooperative Bread Society). Within just four months of its creation, the endeavor included 250 members and was supplying the city with nearly eighty-eight hundred pounds of bread per day.[87]

Through the work of journalist-muckrakers and political agitators, the marketplace problems of malnutrition, speculation, and hoarding gradually came to define what working-class Chileans—whether on the streets of Santiago or in the desert fields of the pampa—meant when they talked about exploitation. For many, food politics wove together a common story about what the abuse of Chile's working class looked and felt like. Following what historian James Vernon has written about the politics of hunger in the British context, hunger also helped establish "where the boundaries would be drawn between the market and the state, the subject and the citizen, the individual and the collective, the nation and the empire."[88] In short, food protests helped working-class Chileans and the urban poor understand what the "social question" was and identify who was to blame for the inequities they so viscerally experienced. Struggles over food also helped these same groups begin to imagine what actions the state could take to resolve such problems.

But just as quickly as labor leaders like Recabarren focused their energies on the problem of working-class food provisioning in the north, the political center of the labor movement and working-class politics began to move south, this time for good. The global catastrophe that was the First World War marked the beginning of the end for Chile's nitrate economy.[89] The closure of shipping lanes across the Atlantic temporarily halted the export of nitrates to consumer markets in Europe and beyond. Meanwhile, as global production turned toward immediate wartime needs, nitrate producers found it increasingly challenging—and expensive—to find the inputs and credit they had come to rely on for the production of nitrate-rich fertilizers. Between July 1914 and February 1915, monthly production of nitrates in Chile fell from 262,863 tons to just 80,654 tons, while the total number of nitrate processing plants operating on the pampa declined from 134 to just 43.[90] The long-term prospects of the industry would be thrown into even greater doubt when a group of German chemists produced the world's first synthetic fertilizers.[91]

As a result, tens of thousands of nitrate miners picked up their lives and their scarce belongings and returned south in search of some better future— the first in a series of migratory waves that intensified the urbanization of Chile's Central Valley. Once in cities like Santiago and Valparaíso, however, many former nitrate workers quickly discovered that hunger had followed them. In 1914, a Santiago newspaper reported on the living conditions at a state-run urban shelter in the port of Valparaíso, where 350 jobless men and 80 women and children were living together after escaping unemployment on the nitrate pampa. When a journalist from the paper visited the site, he was told that on two days that week the residents had scraped together enough potatoes and *cochayuyo*, a nutrient-rich kelp that is abundant on the Chilean coastline, to prepare one meal for the day. On another day that week, the residents ate just beans. On the day of the reporter's actual visit he witnessed nearly two dozen open flames tended by the female residents of the shelter as they prepared a soup consisting of old fish carcasses donated by a group of local fishermen.[92]

Juan Chacón joined one of the many southbound caravans of displaced nitrate miners when the First World War ended. Arriving back in Santiago penniless and fearful that he might be conscripted into military service, sometime in 1918 or early 1919 Chacón was fortunate enough to be rehired in the same glass factory at which he had been previously employed. There he joined his fellow workers not only on the factory floor but also at political meetings. He recalled attending numerous anarchist gatherings after his return and also participating in the recently formed national labor federation, the Federación Obrera de Chile (Workers' Federation of Chile, FOCH). Enamored of the ideals and early successes of the Russian Revolution, Chacón ultimately turned to Recabarren's Socialist Workers' Party (POS). It did not take long for him to join—and eventually become a leader within—the POS's successor organization, the PCCh.[93]

Offering a glimpse into his own political worldview at the time, Chacón told his biographer that what inspired him most in those years were the writings of anarcho-syndicalist thinker Pëtr Kropotkin, in particular *The Conquest of the Bread*, published in 1892. "I liked the way it focused on concrete social issues," he said. "As a political work, it was very well-done."[94] In the decades that followed Chacón's homecoming, the problem of food security would become an ever-more-integral part of popular political life and organizing. The topic also shaped popular visions of a more equitable national economy and more interventionist social welfare state. Rather than being bound to the dictates of economic liberalism, the organized left in which Chacón became a committed militant argued that economic development in Chile needed to be tailored to working-class needs, popular consumption foremost among them.

TWO

———

Red Consumers

LIKE THE STORY of Juan Chacón, the political biography of Carlos Alberto Martínez captures well the contours of social struggle that defined the march of Chile's organized left in the mid-twentieth century. Born in 1885 to a working-class Santiago family, Martínez began helping his family scrape by economically at a remarkably young age. He entered the workplace when he was just twelve, first as an apprentice to a Santiago woodworker and then as a full-time employee at a local printing company. For the first three decades of the twentieth century Martínez dedicated himself to the latter trade, eventually opening his own print shop, which remained in operation until at least the early 1940s.

Trade union politics consumed most of Martínez's life in those early years. In the 1910s and then again in the 1930s, the political responsibilities that Martínez assumed within Chile's printers' union funneled him into positions of authority within an incipient national labor movement. His regular correspondence with Luis Emilio Recabarren during the second decade of the century points to the two men's complementary organizing work, as well as a close friendship. While Recabarren mobilized nitrate workers in Tarapacá and Antofagasta, Martínez relayed messages north about union activists' successes uniting Santiago's growing working- and middle-class populations. For a time, Martínez even joined Racabarren's Socialist Workers' Party, though he appears to have left the party for the more nationalist Chilean Socialist Party (PSCh) as the former's relationship with Moscow grew closer.

During the 1930s and 1940s, Martínez migrated from the union hall to the halls of congress. As an elected legislator, he became a vocal advocate of land reform; if Chile hoped to sustain the social and economic well-being of its people, he argued, underutilized agrarian properties needed to be handed over to those who actually worked the fields. At three different moments in the mid-twentieth century Chilean leaders called on Martínez's expertise on food and agricultural matters, requesting that he serve as the country's minister of land and colonization. Three times he agreed. When agrarian reform finally began in the early 1960s, Martínez, then an adviser to Chile's state development corporation, pushed those efforts forward by advancing credit and subsidies to better link urban consumption patterns with new lines of food production. For a time he also directed Chile's state-controlled fertilizer company as it sought to transform a commodity that during the early twentieth century had been primarily exported into a motor of nutritional self-sufficiency.[1]

In a long life committed to economic justice, it's difficult to select just one moment that captures Carlos Alberto Martínez's emergence as a leader on the Chilean left. However, the final months of 1918 seem as formative a period as any. Starting around midday on the fourth Friday of November of that year, factories throughout Santiago halted production and local businesses closed their doors, the result of Martínez's and his comrades' tireless efforts to turn out tens of thousands of urban workers and middle-class professionals to denounce the rising cost of basic foodstuffs. Within hours, nearly all traffic and economic activity had come to a standstill as protestors amassed on the city's downtown streets.[2]

Around five o'clock on November 22, 1918, Martínez and his fellow protest organizers addressed the crowd on Santiago's main east-west thoroughfare. The "consciousness and popular energy" of Chile had been roused at last, the orators observed, staring out over a "human sea" of somewhere between 50,000 and 100,000 demonstrators in a city whose total population was only around half a million at the time. In early evening the march, with Martínez at its head, wove its way through Santiago's city center and toward the presidential palace. The demonstrators' objective was to deliver to then Chilean president Juan Manuel Sanfuentes more than a dozen economic proposals to halt inflation and end food insecurity once and for all.[3]

This chapter explores the mobilization of Chile's midcentury organized left by reconstructing the struggles over food that Martínez led, which became a defining feature of political life in the country's growing cities. From the formation of the AOAN in 1918 through the growth of the Chilean Communist Party (PCCh) and the rise of a progressive women's movement in the decades that followed, working-class Chileans combined a commitment to popular-front-style coalition building and direct action to combat urban food scarcity.

FIGURE 2. AOAN protestors flood downtown Santiago in late November 1918. International Institute of Social History, Marcelo Segall Rosenmann Collection, Amsterdam.

By politicizing their identities as consumers, activists engaged in a wide range of grassroots actions to pressure multiple reform-minded administrations to protect the rights of working-class families not just on the shop floor but at the marketplace as well. However, later on, as the Second World War ended and scarcity and inflation intensified once again, the state's concern about the PCCh's influence over urban consumers—together with deepening fissures between different elements of Chile's diverse Popular Front (FP) coalition—precipitated one of the most severe government crackdowns on the political left anywhere in Latin America.

HUNGER ON THE MARCH

The hunger marches that the AOAN organized in 1918 and 1919 made manifest the dire social conditions that a spike in consumer prices had created for urban families at the end of the First World War.[4] Indeed, the mobilizations, in which demonstrators carried precious grains of rice or crumbling pieces of bread, still rank among the most sizable and ecumenical political convergences in all of twentieth-century Chilean history. Led by Martínez during its active first year in existence, the AOAN invited "all worker organizations, without ideological discrimination" to take part in its activities, the student leader and future Radical Party activist Santiago Labarca recalled shortly after the AOAN disbanded.[5] In Labarca's view, this made the movement one of the first truly cross-class political organizations in Chile's twentieth century. As one of the movement's early public statements maintained, the AOAN sought to create a "bridge" uniting producers and consumers.[6]

By emphasizing the problem of food when making claims on the Chilean state, the AOAN was arguably the first of many Chilean social and political movements to articulate a vision of economic democracy that was grounded in the construction of a more just system of economic exchange. In its first call to action, authored by Martínez and his political collaborator Manuel Galaz in October 1918, the eclectic movement of labor activists and reformers castigated Chile's political and economic leaders for arguing that "free trade" was a sacred and unassailable principle and defending the behavior of merchants who profited from speculation in basic food staples.[7] Days later, in one of its first public declarations, the AOAN called on the Chilean "pueblo"— a category that excluded only politicians, high-ranking state officials, large landowners, bankers, and businessmen—to "reclaim its sovereignty."[8] Whereas earlier labor protests had originated in the distant Norte Grande, the AOAN's marches represented a moment in which residents of the city took the organizing lead, doing so with a clear and compelling message and disciplined organization.[9]

The AOAN's first public manifesto presented a list of fifteen food-related problems that limited the ability of city dwellers to live their lives with dignity. National policies regulating the importation of sugar and beef needed to be amended, the movement argued, so that these two essential goods— the former a cheap source of energy that could be added to one's morning and evening tea and the latter a symbol of masculine strength and national economic vitality—would be as readily available to workers as they were to elites.[10] In requesting restrictions on the export of nationally produced grains, especially wheat, the AOAN similarly focused its attention on the inequitable distribution of that most humble icon of Chile's culinary heritage: bread. Finally, by demanding that the state offer incentives for agriculturalists to increase vegetable cultivation and promote small-scale fishing operations, the AOAN anticipated midcentury food science's concern with cultivating alternative sources of vitamins and other essential nutrients to guard against so-called diseases of poverty, like scurvy and rickets.[11] Together with calls for land reform; more concerted state regulation of local food sellers and distributors; and the promotion of alternative mechanisms for food distribution, such as urban farmers' markets, the AOAN maintained that food policy, health policy, and economic policy were intimately bound up with one another.[12]

The specific demands that the AOAN made on the Chilean government—and the moral claims and assumptions that infused those demands—would shape the political and institutional development of Chile for decades. As the AOAN demonstrated, organizing around *alimentación*—a term that, depending upon its use, could mean either nutrition or sustenance, in a more general sense—was not just an attempt to suppress the rising numbers that appeared on price tags in local retail establishments. Rather, decisions about how the most essential staples of everyday life would be produced, distributed, and consumed determined how a modern state and national economy—and by extension the notion of citizenship itself—should be organized. In short, to rethink how the food system functioned was to imagine a new social and economic future. In a public statement released by the AOAN in 1919, movement leaders thus pushed Chileans of all social classes to rethink the obligations that the state owed its citizenry. It was outlandish, AOAN activists maintained, for critics to call the movement and its supporters "demanding" for arguing that the state should guarantee all of its citizens a "right to live" or for complaining that the country's elected leaders did "nothing for the general well-being of the common people."[13]

While turn-of-the-century labor leaders and left-wing militants tended to equate the exploitation carried out by the state with that of capital, the AOAN envisioned the state as a set of fungible institutions that could be adapted as popular needs evolved—and that, most importantly, were capable of supporting a politics of social and economic emancipation. As the movement's leadership wrote when mobilizations against rising food prices began to peak in late 1918, "The life of a people [pueblo] is not defended simply by creating armies and purchasing ships; it is also defended . . . by providing affordable foodstuffs, advancing industrial progress, and providing real freedom in the workplace."[14] For the AOAN, the promotion of fairness at the workplace and in the marketplace was a state obligation on a par with more traditional functions like national defense.[15]

What's more, leaders of the AOAN suggested that matters of popular well-being and public health were the metrics by which the success—or failure—of the national economy should be measured. The "health of the people," Carlos

Alberto Martínez declared in a speech in December 1918, represented the "supreme Law" of the land.[16] National deputy Malaquías Concha, a defender of consumer rights going back to the early twentieth century, articulated a brand of socially inflected popular liberalism that was similar to that of the AOAN. "The products of the soil belong, first and foremost, to the citizens of the country," Concha maintained in early 1919. "They are a social resource, produced by capital, land, and labor in concert. . . . The right of property," he insisted, should be limited by "the social interest."[17]

To be sure, the Chilean state's repressive functions tested the durability and staying power of the AOAN as a movement. Starting in the final weeks of 1918, the government disseminated rumors that some involved in the AOAN's protests were in fact provocateurs, working on behalf of the Peruvian government to take back parts of northern Chile for Peru. When vandals targeted multiple Chilean consulates in Peru that same year, the Chilean state used the attacks as a pretext to crack down on the AOAN. Chilean lawmakers' passage of a new "residency law" constituted the first significant act taken by the state to restrain the movement's activities. Approved in late 1918, the measure prohibited those whom the state deemed politically undesirable from entering the country. The law also granted local officials the power to register foreigners living in their communities and fast-tracked deportation proceedings for accused political agitators. In mid-December 1918, the first expulsion order was issued using the law. Its target was the Spanish anarchist, AOAN militant, and fourteen-year Chilean resident Casimiro Barrios.[18]

The crackdown on the AOAN reverberated throughout Chile. At times it even inspired those on the political right to take violent action against movement sympathizers. In mid-January 1919, right-wing vigilantes ransacked the Iquique offices of the left-wing newspaper that Recabarren had founded, *El Despertar de los Trabajadores*, destroying the paper's printing presses. A few days later, as socialist militants in the city of Antofagasta planned a meeting to form their own local branch of the AOAN, the national police arrested Recabarren himself, along with three other socialist activists. The state sent all four men to an isolated prison in the south of Chile. Chilean security forces swept up an estimated ninety workers in the city of Antofagasta alone during a two-month state of siege. The threat of a general strike in February 1919 made government officials and economic elites particularly nervous about the political threat that sustained protests posed as the price of food imports soared.

TABLE 2 Food Prices and Cost of Living in Chile, 1913–1925

Year	Domestic Food Price Index	Imported Food Price Index	General Cost of Living Index
1913	100	100	100
1914	116	112	108
1915	128	136	120
1916	109	144	117
1917	112	141	118
1918	110	151	121
1919	132	238	143
1920	165	256	168
1921	151	230	169
1922	146	227	173
1923	152	236	176
1924	164	240	186
1925	200	217	202

SOURCE: Dirección General de Estadística, *Sinópsis estadístico, año 1925*, 118. Cited and originally reproduced in Thomas C. Wright, *Landowners and Reform in Chile: The Sociedad Nacional de Agricultura, 1919–1940* (Urbana: University of Illinois Press, 1982), 106.

The question of how to react to such measures provoked divisions within the AOAN. On the one hand, some movement activists, particularly those associated with Chile's anarchist tendencies, demanded more intense mobilizations against the state in response to repression. On the other hand, a more moderate wing of the AOAN, which included progressive Catholics and middle-class reformers, believed it best to postpone the AOAN's scheduled demonstrations until social peace was restored. In the winter of 1919, the movement briefly regrouped, carrying out a successful day of protest in late August, followed by a multiday work stoppage. Nevertheless, the AOAN's rebirth proved short-lived. The organization's leadership ultimately collapsed weeks later after the state refused to address any of the AOAN's proposals.[19]

Throughout the 1920s, the workers' movements and political parties that had channeled their supporters into the AOAN continued to serve as spaces of discussion for a broad-front Chilean left. In his 1920 presidential bid, Arturo Alessandri proved the most immediate beneficiary of such organizing. Orienting his victorious campaign around the demands of Chile's increasingly unified and visible urban working-class constituency, Alessandri promised the construction of an interventionist state capable of providing Chilean workers the "necessary elements to defend themselves physically, morally, and intellectually."[20] Despite the fact that Chile's small socialist left ran Recabarren as its own candidate against Alessandri, many who had been involved with the AOAN were drawn to Alessandri's populist economic message and his trenchant critique of economic liberalism. "Yes, I too was an Alessandrista in 1920, just like the majority of the working-class," the eventual Communist activist Juan Chacón admitted in an interview with his biographer. "We went out each day to march [for Alessandri]. We swore that we would strike to back Alessandri if the oligarchy did not recognize his [1920] victory. . . . We felt like we were socialists, we were with [POS presidential candidate] Reca in every union struggle, and we admired him for his toughness but . . . you had to vote for Alessandri."[21]

In 1925, after a military coup temporarily unseated Alessandri, the spirit of the AOAN was briefly rekindled by a broad-based citizens' organization that sought to rewrite Chile's constitution with direct popular participation.[22] One year later, ex-AOAN activists, including Martínez and the recently formed PCCh, also advocated for a broad-front political strategy when they aligned themselves with the presidential campaign of medical doctor and social reformer José Santos Salas.[23] Though Santos Salas was defeated, the persistence of social movement leaders ensured that the state addressed many of the AOAN's original proposals. In the late 1920s, Chile's national Congress approved a full repeal of the country's 1897 tariff on Argentine beef. During those same years, the state also allocated large sums of money to purchase and sell basic foodstuffs to poor and working-class consumers in state-administered grocery stores.[24] Finally, in 1925 the ratification of a new national constitution codified the principle, articulated by Concha and others, that property possessed a "social function"; as such, the state held the power to limit the rights of private property holders when said rights impeded the fulfillment of more pressing social needs. As had occurred with the passage of Mexico's 1917 Constitution, Chile's 1925 Constitution laid the legal groundwork for new forms of state economic intervention in subsequent decades, including land redistribution, state-led industrialization, and consumer protection.[25]

CONSUMERS BUILD A POPULAR FRONT

During the first three years of the 1930s, when the crash of international financial markets precipitated a subsequent collapse of global commodity prices, the value of Chilean exports, measured in real terms, tumbled by some 80 percent.

In Chile, the crisis was defined by a cascading list of problems. When foreign credits and the country's reserves of gold dried up, Chile's access to foreign imports was restricted.[26] National rates of unemployment skyrocketed. In 1931 alone, estimates suggested that some 100,000 jobs were lost. The country's total GDP fell by over half that same year. A report issued by Chile's Central Bank in early 1932 predicted that the previous year was likely to be remembered as "one of the most severe crises" in the country's history.[27] An oft-cited League of Nations study concurred, assessing the crisis in global terms and stressing the devastating result for the country: "Chile was hit harder by the effects of the depression than any other nation in the world."[28]

Running on his reputation as a reliable reformer, Arturo Alessandri was reelected to a second, nonconsecutive term as president amid the economic collapse of the early 1930s. Although both the breadth and depth of the crisis were daunting, Alessandri's economic measures, which included a combination of tax hikes and subsidies to balance the national budget and jump-start an economic recovery, restored public confidence in Chile's political and economic institutions. Bolstered by renewed international demand for Chilean copper and nitrates, the new government had largely staunched rising unemployment and pulled the country out of depression by the mid-1930s.[29]

However, for Santiago consumers the economic outlook remained bleak. As inflation crept upward again, price increases for basic consumer goods outpaced scheduled wage increases, and shortages of numerous foodstuffs disrupted everyday life.[30] Over the course of just a few weeks in the spring of 1936, the price of key ingredients in a filling culinary staple like charquicán, potatoes and beef, registered such considerable price hikes that even middle-class consumers could scarcely afford them. "If these people can barely eat, what conditions must the working-class family, who sweats day in and day out, confront to put bread on the table?" an article published in the PCCh newspaper *Frente Popular* in September asked its readers after a journalist had visited a Santiago market.[31] The long-term ramifications of the unresolved consumer problem were dire, according to the paper: "The nation is being consumed by hunger and nothing is being done to prevent it."[32]

As Chilean citizens grappled with the uneven nature of the economic crisis and the recovery from it, critics of the Alessandri government fixed their attention on the state's continued failure to protect the everyday economy. Some underscored the state's hesitation to use the powers embodied in new state agencies and social laws established in the late 1920s and early 1930s.[33] Others attacked the outsized influence that large agricultural producers continued to exert by successfully lobbying for price floors for key agricultural commodities.[34] Whatever the individual criticisms, nearly all observers agreed on one thing: the national government's muddled response to the world economic crisis had created a vacuum, and urban activists—many of them partisans of a growing collection of left-leaning parties and the country's labor movement—actively sought to fill this void.

The emergence of informal price-monitoring brigades was illustrative of the popular response to Chile's crisis of the mid-1930s. Staking its claim as the heir to the AOAN, the Popular Nutrition Assembly, a citizen-led watchdog group that Santiago consumers formed sometime in 1936, started to monitor the prices and availability of staple goods in local markets in the spring of that same year.[35] Activists affiliated with Chile's recently created FP coalition quickly followed suit. Within weeks of the first reports on the Popular Nutrition Assembly's activities, the FP's provincial council in Santiago drafted a list of proposals to beat back the surging inflationary tide and guarantee the nutritional well-being of urban consumers.[36] A short time later, FP supporters convened a hunger march through the streets of downtown Santiago to publicize their concerns to the Alessandri government.[37] For several hours each evening, FP militants collected citizens' complaints about consumer issues at an office just a few blocks from Chile's presidential palace. Subsequently, they filed said petitions in a general registry administered by the Provincial Committee of the FP so they could be presented to the proper authorities. Most dramatically, the coalition's leadership also authorized its members to requisition food items that they determined to be ineffectively distributed in an attempt to pressure the state into action.[38]

Women were a driving force behind many of these early consumer actions. As such, they assumed a position of leadership within Chile's emergent food justice movement while also becoming the public face of hunger and consumer despair.[39] When *Frente Popular* interviewed a female shopper in Santiago's Vega Central market during a period of rising food costs and shortages, the woman told a reporter from the daily that a cup of tea and a piece of bread were all her family, and hundreds of others like hers, were able to afford. "Sir, we're simply unable to eat anymore," the woman remarked. "Life has gotten to be so expensive that my husband has found it impossible to make ends meet." In response to the interview, the paper editorialized that the marketplace had become synonymous with economic insecurity. "People can dress themselves poorly and walk about without a jacket, but it's simply not possible to stop eating."[40]

This deeply gendered depiction of who constituted the consumer public conferred on women a notable amount of influence. Illustrative of what historian Temma Kaplan calls "female consciousness"—that is, women's embrace of their normative feminine identities to exert collective political power—the pages of *La Mujer Nueva*, the monthly bulletin of the Movimiento Pro-Emancipación de la Mujer Chilena (Movement for the Emancipation of the Chilean Woman, MEMCh), provided women a public space to denounce food-producing monopolies and identify those they believed were guilty of price gouging.[41] In presenting consumer claims before the state, female activists also reproduced the message that a just food economy was the foundation of both household and national economic well-being. At a time when the questions of how to improve the fitness of a predominantly masculine workforce—and thus increase national economic productivity—were much-discussed topics across Latin America, an article in *La Mujer Nueva* in 1936 demanded the state find a way to guarantee access to protein-rich foods, like meat, in order to bolster industrial progress. "[O]ur children need food not only so they do not die but so they are also able to grow strong and be useful to their country (*patria*)," a writer at the magazine argued.[42]

Contrasting working-class families' actual consumption of bread and tea with nutrition experts' recommendations about calcium and vitamin D intake, especially for children and nursing mothers, women consumers also drew upon their maternal identities to press for state intervention around products like milk. In 1937 MEMCh activists scored an important victory in this regard. In the winter of that year, the Chilean state accepted a petition from a MEMCh delegation that laid out why fresh milk substitutes for infants should be added to the list of goods to which state price controls applied.[43]

The small-scale but highly effective grassroots efforts of consumer campaigners likely contributed to the election of the FP's first candidate to national office in late 1936. During the country's 1938 presidential election, the leadership of the FP continued to mobilize voters around issues of nutritional anxiety by incorporating the problem of rising prices into its national platform. "Facing the steep rise in the price of staple goods produced by the twisted political economy of the Government," the coalition's National Committee declared that the state had an "obligation to requisition primary necessity goods" and then resell said goods to the public at fixed prices. In an attempt to reshuffle the traditional priorities of an economy that was dependent on foreign trade and investment, FP leaders even suggested that if money was needed to fund such activities, it could be found by delaying payments of Chile's foreign debt obligations.[44] The landowning reformer and former interior minister Pedro Aguirre Cerda won a narrow victory in that year's presidential contest by articulating that very message. His defeat of former Alessandri finance minister Gustavo Ross—a man the FP denounced as Chile's "minister of hunger"—made the country the first in the Americas to elect a coalition that included both the Communist and socialist left. What's more, Aguirre Cerda's campaign slogan *pan, techo, y abrigo* (bread, shelter, and a warm overcoat) made clear that the essential concerns of Chile's popular classes would guide coalition leaders as they reformed the institutions of Chilean democracy.[45]

Consumer activists made the operationalization of a little-used decree from the early 1930s one its chief priorities when the FP took office.[46] A variation of the AOAN's original demand for a system of enforceable price controls, Decree-Law (DL) 520 had in 1932 established one of the first permanent consumer protection agencies anywhere in the Americas. Known as the Comisariato General de Subsistencias y Precios (General Commissariat of Staple Goods and Prices), or simply the Comisariato, the agency's economic powers were truly unprecedented. Arguably no other institution associated with the early Chilean social welfare state had a broader legal charge than the Comisariato's directive to "guarantee the most decent conditions of life" for all Chileans.[47]

Concretely, the work of Comisariato officials pertained most directly to matters of consumer protection. This included setting and enforcing national price ceilings, controlling housing rents, and conducting unannounced state inspections of retail shops and distribution warehouses. DL-520 also granted the Comisariato the power to seize distribution and transportation networks that it deemed inefficient, requisition consumer goods and agricultural commodities when markets were in short supply, and establish new businesses that catered exclusively to poor and working-class consumers. The latter included dozens of *almacenes reguladores*, or yardstick stores, which offered staples at below-market prices to provide relief to consumers and pressure private retailers to adjust their own pricing.[48] To fund its operations, the office assumed the power to fine those found guilty of economic speculation or hoarding.

The vastness of the Comisariato's mandate derived from a mundane source. In coordination with Chile's executive branch, the Comisariato's chief, the colorfully named "general commissar," would formulate and continuously

FIGURE 3. A Comisariato inspector closes a local retailer in the 1940s. Colección Museo Histórico Nacional, Santiago de Chile.

update multiple registries of products that he deemed to be of either "basic necessity" or "habitual use or consumption."[49] In response to the demands of the AOAN, the state had experimented with its first list of such staples in the 1920s, suggesting, but rarely enforcing, price caps on essentials like medicines, farming fertilizers, and construction materials.[50] After the Comisariato's creation in 1932, the list of items that fell under the purview of state price controls began to grow, such that by 1945 the state had the power to set maximum prices on well over two hundred products. Central, though not exclusive, to this growing list were foodstuffs—everything from peas, rice, and sugar to eggs, cooking fats, fish, flour, and potatoes. The agency even set prices for certain manufactured durables that made food storage and preparation possible, such as refrigeration.[51]

A review of some of the types of goods added to such lists early on provides a glimpse into the state's evolving definition of what constituted "subsistence" or "staple" goods. For example, coffee, fresh vegetables, and dried fish were a few of the first items to be declared "articles of basic necessity" or "habitual consumption."[52] Although the goods hardly reflected the actual consumption habits of most Chileans, particularly those of the least well-off, their presence underscored the state's willingness to use its regulatory power to expand what it saw as a dignified and decent *subsistencia*, or existence.[53]

The Comisariato's functions of categorization enshrined the concept of basic need as the key metric by which state intervention in the national economy was to be judged and executed. However, to make good on enforcing its capacious understanding of human welfare, the FP needed to first staff job vacancies at the Comisariato, many of which had gone unfilled since the agency's creation.[54] Fresh out of law school, Volodia Teitelboim, who would later become one of Chile's most famous twentieth-century writers and a PCCh leader, was one of those who began work at the price control office under the FP. For much of the 1940s, Teitelboim worked in the Comisariato's Judicial Assistance Bureau, where he dealt with citizen rent and eviction complaints against landlords. "My job consisted of preventing the police from throwing the poor out onto the sidewalk," he would later write, adding that his post within the growing welfare state of the 1940s is what gave him his status as a member of Chile's "petit bourgeoisie."[55]

Other Comisariato officials sought to enact economic fairness in more bureaucratic ways. In late March 1943, for example, the Comisariato approved petitions from butchers in the cities of Viña del Mar and Santiago, each of whom hoped to open a new retail establishment in parts of their respective cities where other meat sellers already operated. In the case of the former, the butcher convinced the Comisariato that the services he would provide to consumers of the area were distinct by noting that his focus would be the sale of domestically produced lamb, not beef. In the case of the Santiago butcher, proof that a reasonable geographic distance existed between the door of his shop and that of his nearest competitor—227 meters and 80 centimeters, to be exact—contributed to the Comisariato's eventual approval of his request.[56]

At the same time that the FP increased staffing at the Comisariato, it also elevated the political profile of women. The case of Graciela Contreras de Schnake was emblematic in this regard. The wife of PSCh leader Oscar Schnake, Contreras de Schnake was a longtime supporter of MEMCh and other women's causes when President Pedro Aguirre Cerda appointed her to be the head of Santiago's city government in early 1939. Throughout her tenure as mayor she made assisting female consumers a top priority.[57] Less than two weeks after taking office, for example, Contreras de Schnake outlined her most notable public policy initiative: the creation of a system of locally regulated *ferias libres* (community farmers' markets) to directly link small fruit and vegetable farmers to popular consumers.

Through this initiative, Santiago's municipal government initially permitted six such markets to operate two or three days each week in various neighborhoods around the capital. At each location, consumers could purchase fresh produce directly from small farmers, rather than assuming the costs associated with the various intermediaries that transported fruits and vegetables from farms to the country's primary wholesale market in Santiago, the Vega Central. In this way, consumers of modest means would avoid paying high prices for vitamin-rich foods that kept childhood illnesses at bay.[58] When the *New York Times* interviewed former Santiago mayor Contreras de Schnake during a visit to the United States in 1943, the paper praised her "free fare" exchange system, noting that her urban farmers' market idea had "spread all over Chile."[59]

Chile's new open-air markets were not the object of unanimous praise, however. Indeed, the fact that Contreras de Schnake's tenure as mayor abruptly ended just over a year after she was appointed—at least in part because she had challenged the interests of established retailers—was evidence of the distinct visions on economic exchange within the broad FP coalition. On one side, public sanitation officials voiced criticisms of Contreras de Schanke's street market system, arguing that such installations dirtied neighborhood streets. On the other, food distribution agencies and *regatones*—small retailers who engaged in the common practice of purchasing vital consumer goods to then resell at marked-up prices—said that ad hoc neighborhood markets were an unfair source of competition to their own more established businesses.[60] At one meeting of the city council, members of these latter two opposition groups reportedly packed the balcony of the council's gallery at Santiago's city hall to heckle a socialist councilman who championed the free fare idea. So intense had deliberations over the issue become that when the group of protestors refused to leave the councilman's office, the elected official allegedly pulled out a gun and fired multiple shots in the air, forcing his opponents to scatter.[61] In many ways, the political encounters between consumers, their political advocates, and those whose livelihoods depended upon the production, distribution, and sale of foodstuffs offered a preview of the political infighting that would tear the FP apart in the wake of the Second World War.

Food politics in midcentury Chile was frequently infused with a deeply partisan flavor. Socialists of various tendencies were among those most insistent about the need for rigorous enforcement of national price controls. Many of the MEMCh organizers who protested the rising cost of living in urban areas and northern mining regions were also militants of progressive parties and FP auxiliary groups. As discussed in a subsequent chapter, Catholic activists, many of them affiliated with Chile's Conservative Party, would play a leading role in devising and implementing national nutrition standards and policies.[62] However, the influence of one political party, the PCCh, within the country's consumer movement proved to be a step too far for both opponents of the FP and many of the coalition's original supporters.

A series of consumer actions in and around Santiago in late 1946 put the distinct political cosmologies of the midcentury PCCh and Chile's more traditional political establishment in clear relief. In September of that year, a group of women and PCCh activists assembled a few blocks south of downtown Santiago to protest failed state efforts to normalize the distribution and sale of two items: tea and cooking oil. According to consumers, the two staples had become almost impossible to find at neighborhood food markets in the weeks preceding the gathering. In the face of the Comisariato's ineptitude, local consumers decided it was time to "take justice into their own hands," in the words of the PCCh's daily.[63]

Marching together, the small citizens' brigade proceeded to the small grocery store of Don Diego Crespo, where suspicions of hoarding were allegedly confirmed. Discovered inside Crespo's shop were two barrels of cooking oil being held off the shelf. The shopkeeper was pushed aside as the demonstrators hauled the hoarded oil to the curb. But instead of ransacking Crespo's inventory, as opponents of the action believed would occur, the women and PCCh militants, in a very organized and orderly fashion, began to sell the product to neighborhood consumers at a cost of 16 pesos per liter—some 30 pesos less than the store's marked sale price for oil. Similar events followed at a store operated by another small merchant, where packages of tea were allegedly found hidden away from consumers' view.[64]

An editorial in *El Siglo* described the events as acts of "justice-seeking ire" and a "warning to speculators and the government, which either does not know how to attend to the most basic demands of the people or is simply unwilling to do so. The men of government," the paper concluded, "now know the '*vox populi.*'"[65] In the days that followed, PCCh members sought to institutionalize a new system of distribution for select staples. Special ration cards were distributed to PCCh members and fellow travelers, and within weeks of the first seizure, the party was reportedly running more than seventy distribution sites around Santiago. By late 1946, the party estimated that some eighty thousand liters of cooking oil had been sold through its improvised system of grassroots exchange.[66]

The aforementioned events call to mind historian E. P. Thompson's notion of "moral economy." Thompson described how in eighteenth-century England food riots and other similar demonstrations were often "triggered off by soaring prices, by malpractices among dealers, or by hunger." However, such consumer "grievances," as Thompson called them, were almost always grounded in shared assumptions about the social and economic duties of various actors in a given community, including the state and merchants.[67] According to a Thompsonian reading, the joint actions of the women and PCCh activists during the Chilean spring of 1946 reflected a shared community belief that the state's duty to enforce fairness in the consumer marketplace was not being met, and that in its absence, consumers had a responsibility to act.

But the fact that many, including some who had been longtime supporters of robust state consumer protections, disagreed with the PCCh's actions suggests that the moral economy of urban Santiago was not accepted by all. In fact, among those who protested the PCCh's cooking oil schema were individuals like Juan Bautista Rossetti, a former minister of labor and the official most responsible for the Comisariato's creation a decade and a half earlier. Having become a prominent anti-Communist voice within independent socialist circles, Bautista Rossetti used the newspaper that he directed, *La Opinión*, to wage an aggressive media campaign against the PCCh in the mid-1940s. In particular, he attacked Communist partisans' efforts to resell cooking oil in party strongholds, arguing that the alternative distribution initiative was marred by inefficiencies and rooted in political discrimination against non-Communist families.[68] As a counter to Communist calls for direct action, *La Opinión* amplified the voice of Chile's small merchant community, which recommended that the sale of cooking oil in the country be exclusively administered by the country's retailers' guild—a proposal that echoed shopkeepers' earlier attacks against former Santiago mayor Contreras de Schanke and her ferias libres idea.[69]

This clash between Communists and their political opponents over the proper relationship between consumers and the state was more than a decade in the making. On the streets of Santiago and in isolated mining communities, party members had led disciplined marches against speculation, unjust prices, and suspicions of hoarding starting in the mid-1930s.[70] For just as long, party activists had used the pages of the PCCh's daily newspapers to demand distribution firms that committed "economic crimes"—for instance, violating state-mandated price controls or holding necessary consumer goods off the shelf in hopes of larger future profits—be charged and even jailed under the country's penal code, just as common criminals were.[71] Following Pedro Aguirre Cerda's victory, an editorial in one Communist newspaper even defined the party's mission as including two very distinct key fronts: the global fight against fascism and the everyday struggle against the *vida cara*, or expensive cost of living.[72]

Consumer scarcity during the Second World War created fertile organizing soil for the PCCh to recruit new members. Comprised of blue-collar laborers, community leaders, and housewives, community-organized "cost of living committees" that emerged in cities like Santiago became hubs for planning local street demonstrations and petitioning the state for collective economic redress in the face of wartime food shortages.[73] In other Communist strongholds, citizen-activists were emboldened by the FP's willingness to finally use the enforcement mechanisms of the Comisariato to directly challenge merchants and private food distributors. For example, a 1941 report on working and living conditions in Lota, Chile's most important coal mining town, criticized coal companies for allowing private concessionaires to buy up what had formerly been company-controlled stores and restaurants, subsequently jacking up prices well above the limits set by Chile's price control agency.[74] As the Second World War drew to a close, the Confederación de Trabajadores de Chile (Chilean Confederation of Workers, CTCh) expressed its displeasure with the government's failure to take "effective measures" against the "rise in the price of articles of daily consumption." In 1945 it issued a statement that identified the subject of its fight for better wages and workplace protections as the "consumer public"—a notable shift from the more traditional nomenclature that emphasized the worker as such. The CTCh also instructed its member unions to organize coordinated campaigns against price increases and rent hikes.[75]

Indeed, while the Chilean labor movement restrained its militancy on the shop floor to meet the wartime production needs of those fighting fascism in Europe, consumer defense became an alternative outlet for worker militancy during and immediately after the war.[76] Alongside dockworkers who refused to load Chilean nitrates and copper onto ships headed for fascist Spain and Nazi Germany, workers at a cold-storage food distribution warehouse for fruits and vegetables in one Chilean port city set up their own workplace vigilance committees in 1943 to monitor the actions of the company's owner, the importer Gianoli Mustakis. One of the first worker-led inspections carried out by several PCCh members discovered that the company was holding back several tons of food from the market, in anticipation of higher prices. After workers reported the crime to their local union, price control officials visited the warehouse to seize the goods in question—an astounding 590 tons of wheat, beans, garbanzos, and lentils—and resell them at their official price. The incident led unions to advocate for the formation of similar watchdog committees in the country's factories, as well as a national economic council that would focus its attention on promoting the production of domestic foodstuffs.[77] In each of these instances, the popular organization of Communists as food producers and consumers became an important means through which economic democracy was demanded from below. Rather than waiting for the state to summon them, the mobilization of workers around food allowed citizens to call on the state to make good on its promise of economic justice.

It was not until the PCCh's 13th National Congress, held in early 1946, that food matters—what party members referred to as a social and economic "right to basic existence"—became an enumerated objective of the PCCh. The Central Nacional de Defensa de los Consumidores (National Organizing Committee for Consumer Defense, CENADECO), an urban consumer organization in which PCCh members would play an active and outsized role, became one of the party's primary outlets for mobilizing working-class families in the postwar world. Through CENADECO, Communist activists coordinated public campaigns against the actions of food distribution monopolies run by international firms like W. R. Grace Company, Williamson Balfour, and Gildemeister, with party members often organizing their own teams of informal consumer inspectors to investigate claims of hoarding and other illicit economic activity.[78] In one such instance, local residents in the working-class community of San Felipe discovered that food distributors were shipping red meat to more well-heeled municipalities where consumers could pay higher prices for their product. The group turned over their evidence to a local inspector of the Comisariato and then proceeded to organize what one Communist activist described as a "combative demonstration" in the town's central plaza, demanding that such speculative activity not go unpunished. When the Comisariato failed to act, the residents organized a second mobilization, which finally drew the attention of the national office of the Comisariato. Shortly thereafter, the agency issued a new price ceiling for beef.[79]

During this period, women again played a notable role in pushing a more confrontational agenda when it came to matters of food. As mining companies scaled back employment at a number of oficinas in the province of Tarapacá, MEMCh activists, many of whom exercised a double militancy in the PCCh, highlighted women's ability to shut down the economy by shutting down the kitchen. Kitchen strikes, in which female cantina employees and wives simply refused to cook for their male customers and partners as a way of protesting against food shortages, became a popular means of grassroots resistance in those communities most affected by the third major economic crisis in a generation. Such demonstrations often triggered work stoppages across entire nitrate oficinas.[80] At La Santiago nitrate camp, more than six hundred workers went on a twenty-four-hour strike in late January 1946, citing the inability to obtain basic foodstuffs, like potatoes, at the company-owned pulpería as the reason for their action. Lacking a nourishing meal before they left for their shifts on the pampa, men put down their tools as well. The strike paralyzed La Santiago completely. Two months later housewives and *cantineras* repeated their protest, shutting down their kitchens once again.[81]

Ultimately, grassroots mobilization around food, stretching from urban Santiago to the mining centers in the country's north and south, contributed to two important, albeit divergent, political results. First, the electoral power and mobilizational capacity of the PCCh surged in the years immediately following the Second World War. In fact, at the same moment that many leaders of the Socialist Party and Radical Party began to sour on the FP idea, the PCCh sought to return the FP to its more radical roots. Those efforts proved even more popular than most PCCh leaders could have imagined. While the PCCh had won just 6.4 percent of all votes cast in municipal elections held in 1944, just three years later, in the country's 1947 local elections, the PCCh received nearly triple the total number of votes it had in the previous election, obtaining some ninety thousand votes, equivalent to 16.5 percent of all votes cast. The increase in votes solidified the PCCh as the third most powerful party in the country and arguably the most formidable in the country's capital.[82]

Second, the power that the PCCh wielded made it a key political constituency in Gabriel González Videla's 1946 electoral coalition. As a reward for its support of his campaign, newly elected González Videla gave the PCCh several important social and economic posts in his administration. These included three cabinet-level positions, as well as key jobs in several state agencies, including the Comisariato and a parallel state agency that set price floors for agricultural commodities. In large part because of these consumer organizing efforts, Chile's Communists had assumed unprecedented, formal political power within Chile's executive branch by the end of 1946.[83]

The growing influence of the PCCh was not well received in all quarters of Chilean political society. Just as the global alliance between the Soviet Union and the United States frayed, anti-Communist fervor was also tearing the Chilean FP apart by the mid-1940s, and the country's consumer movement became one of many sites of political tension. As the end of the Second World War came into sight, women activists associated with Chile's centrist Radical Party established their own consumer advocacy group to reduce the power that the PCCh exerted over such matters. Rather than pressuring the Comisariato from outside the government, as the PCCh had advocated, this decidedly noncommunist consumer movement gradually subsumed its activism to the needs of the state and its consumer watchdog agency. Their objective was to dilute the power of more confrontational forms of consumer organizing. As they turned their focus toward the behavioral aspects of consumer activity—promoting consumer education over state consumer regulation, for example—anti-communist consumer activists sidelined the more radical elements of the movement, including the demand that merchants who did not abide by price ceilings be sanctioned or even imprisoned. Within a year and a half of its formation, this countervailing movement had led nearly six hundred classes on issues of nutrition and proper consumption habits and counted some thirty-four hundred women among its membership—a demonstration of how food politics could serve to restrict imaginings of a more just economy as much as they could nurture them.[84]

When González Videla took office in late 1946, he initially charted a middle path between these two competing tendencies. In a nod to more moderate consumer activists, the new president tried to channel extra-institutional forms of consumer action, like popular requisitions of supposedly hoarded foodstuffs, back into the institutional channels of the state. At the same time, González Videla sought to appease members of the PCCh, aware of how important the party had been to his electoral victory. González Videla set in motion various measures, among them the organization of state-supported vigilance committees across the country, and for a brief period citizen price inspectors joined formal inspectors from Chile's national price control system in monitoring retail stores and distribution sites, particularly around Santiago. The decision was as much pragmatic as it was political; by providing the government volunteer staff to fight what González Videla called a "war on speculation," the measure offered much-needed relief to Chile's cash-strapped price control agency. The new Chilean president also named one CENADECO organizer to a top post in the Comisariato and authorized Chile's police to monitor and arrest those found guilty of market-place infractions. But by mid-1947, González Videla was siding with those in his own Radical Party who sought to counter Communist influence within the country's consumer movement.

Juan Chacón recalled in great detail the process by which he personally was transformed from an ally of the new government into a target of an intense government witch hunt in early 1947. Having risen through the ranks of the PCCh in the 1930s, Chacón had established himself as a leading voice on food and agriculture issues by the mid-1940s. So respected had he become that González Videla tapped the former glassworker and nitrate miner to be his adviser on agrarian issues during the 1946 campaign. When González Videla assumed office, Chacón was named the executive vice president of the state agency in charge of setting price floors for key agricultural commodities.

Almost immediately, however, Chacón became a symbol of leftist over-reach for Chile's anti-communist crusaders. During his four-month tenure in the González Videla government, conservative figures with close ties to the country's landowning elite boycotted the agency Chacón ran, citing his membership in the PCCh. What's more, Chacón's political adversaries disregarded directives and policies that bore Chacón's signature. Some of his anti-communist opponents dubbed him a "demagogue" and "dictator" for requiring employees of the agency to show up to work promptly at eight o'clock in the morning and work a full eight-hour workday. Others attacked him for supposed acts of patronage. Some criticisms bordered on the absurd. In one instance that Chacón recalled, his detractors attacked him for "sullying" the reputation of the state by sitting next to his state-assigned personal chauffer in the front seat of the car, rather than sitting in the back, as was customary for state officials.[85]

Chacón's decision to take on the economic interests of Chile's wheat farmers provoked the greatest backlash. When Chacón's agency refused to raise wholesale prices for Chilean wheat, major Chilean planters refused to bring their harvest to market. The distribution boycott sent immediate ripples through the consumer economy. As flour became scarce, so too did the availability of affordable bread. In response, Chacón authorized the use of state vehicles belonging to his agency, as well as the national price control agency, the Comisariato, to seize wheat from farms around the country and deliver it to local markets. "The sabotage of our policies was strong," Chacón recalled. "The Right carried it out with all of their affiliates as well as officials in the government itself."[86] González Videla soon relieved Chacón of his appointed position.

It was in this highly charged political environment that the government's otherwise routine reclassification of bread prices, an issue Chacón would have dealt with had he still been in his government post, set in motion a national crisis on an unprecedented scale. In August 1947, a presidential decree increased the price of both flour and bread in Chile. Originally intended as just one part of a larger fight against speculative activities, González Videla's rollout of the price hike proved disastrous. In particular, workers interpreted the president's decision to eliminate the sale of two different loaves of bread in local bakeries—one "special" and the other more "basic"—at the same time that prices were raised as an affront to the needs of popular consumers.[87]

In Lota, the center of the country's coal production and a town already racked with concerns about the declining demand for raw materials in the postwar period, such protests became especially heated. When the town's Communist mayor declared that it would be "impossible" for workers to accept the price hike given the uncertain nature of their wage rates and employment opportunities, coal miners in Lota started an indefinite strike, highlighting, among other matters, the need to rescind González Videla's decree regarding bread. The strike action quickly spread, with bakers, mill workers, and dockworkers all joining in as well.[88]

González Videla used the work stoppage as a pretext to vacate all appointment-based offices that PCCh members held throughout the country. "With the stroke of a pen," the historian Jody Pavilack writes, González Videla "threw out of work tens of thousands of civil servants at all levels of government," among them many of the country's most experienced and committed labor officials. In the weeks that followed, political tensions grew as labor unrest spread through the Chilean economy, from transportation to the mining sector.[89] Exemplary of the cruel measures the state would adopt in response, the Chilean military proceeded to cut off food provisions to striking workers in Lota, the epicenter of the strike wave. State officials loyal to González Videla publicized the action with the slogan "those who don't work, don't eat." When it was discovered that some workers were surreptitiously fishing in the waters below the town, the military even prohibited fishing in the area. The military also banned marches in which women's groups banged empty pots and pans to protest the hunger, which they blamed on González Videla.[90]

In the final months of 1947 and into 1948, the Chilean state forced between seven and ten thousand people from the coal region into either internal exile or state-run internment camps. In Lota, nearly one in every twelve inhabitants was forcibly removed from their residences. Nationally, an estimated fifteen thousand workers and PCCh members were detained or relocated by force.[91] In September 1948, these actions were codified when González Videla approved the Law for the Permanent Defense of Democracy, more commonly known by its colloquial name, the Ley Maldita, or Damned Law. The decree, one of the most draconian attempts to vanquish the left from institutional political life anywhere in the Americas during the Cold War, immediately reconfigured the political landscape of Chile. Overnight the Chilean government purged tens of thousands of PCCh voters from the country's electoral registry. Through the law, González Videla also proscribed the PCCh itself from participating in public political life for nearly a decade. Among the few legislators who cast a vote against the anti-Communist measure was former AOAN leader Carlos Alberto Martínez.[92]

The stress created by the state's repression reverberated throughout the most intimate spaces of family life in the late 1940s, scarring those who had participated in the food and consumer campaigns of the postwar period. "I followed the call made to housewives by the National Government to combat speculation, and in my role as a housewife, I have made various complaints to the authorities and have helped to close various businesses on orders from the Comisariato," one woman wrote to First Lady Rosa Markmann in late 1947 as she pled with the First Lady to help free her son, a PCCh member, from state detention. "I beg you, distinguished *Señora*, as only mothers know what it is to love their children and how much pain it gives a mother to be incapable of providing our children with sustenance."[93] From the archival material available, it is unclear if the mother's plea was ever heard.

As a gesture toward the role that food insecurity had played in producing postwar unrest, González Videla did take small steps to lessen consumer anxiety, creating a new national consumer organization, the Asociación de Dueñas de Casa (Association of Housewives, ADC). However, the structure of the ADC assumed the same vertical organization and authoritarian political culture of the post-1947 González Videla government. The president appointed his wife, Rosa Markmann, as the organization's figurehead, while a Radical Party activist and anti-Communist consumer leader ran the ADC's day-to-day activities. Wives of prominent politicians and professionals were handpicked to serve in many of the organization's other positions of leadership. Moreover, when González Videla issued a long-awaited decree outlining the duties of new neighborhood vigilance committees that would regulate local commercial activity, only women associated with the ADC were granted positions on such boards, effectively erasing anyone who was believed to have been a PCCh sympathizer or enabler.[94] In the words of one historian, the efforts represented the state's "vigorous and successful attempt . . . to co-opt the consumer movement."[95]

Starting with the creation of the AOAN in 1918 and continuing through the FP years of the 1930s and early 1940s, working-class consumers in Santiago and other urban centers mounted campaigns against the rising cost of living—and particularly the rising cost of food. In the process, labor activists, women, and the organized left helped to build and activate new state institutions, like the Comisariato, to protect Chilean workers in their role as consumers. Working-class activists would have to wait another three decades, until the 1970 election of Salvador Allende, to reassert the same degree of political power they had exhibited during the FP era. However, initiatives that the Chilean state pursued in the decades surrounding the Second World War suggested that the new common sense about food, the state, and the economy that three decades of activism had helped to forge remained squarely on the minds of state officials as they navigated their relationship with the social groups that had found their political voice through midcentury mass politics. At the center of this new common sense was the notion that the functioning of the national economy was dependent upon how the state managed the production, distribution, and consumption of food.

PART TWO

Containing Hunger

THREE

Controlling for Nutrition

HISTORIANS ARE FREQUENTLY ADVISED to engage sparingly with counterfactuals—those moments in which one identifies a turning point in the historical record, only to then reconsider how an alternative outcome might have resulted had said event occurred in a distinct manner or with a distinct set of actors. Yet it's hard not to wonder if and how the dawn of the global Cold War in Chile might have looked different had Dr. Eduardo Cruz-Coke, rather than Gabriel González Videla, ushered Chile into the postwar world. The Chilean writer, one-time Comisariato official, and long-time Chilean Communist Party (PCCh) leader Volodia Teitelboim indulged in precisely this sort of thought experiment when he commemorated the late physician more than three decades after his passing. "It's too late to repair the error," Teitelboim remarked about his own party's ill-fated decision to support González Videla over Cruz-Coke in Chile's 1946 presidential election. Nevertheless, a half century on, it was still worth remembering the alternative to repression and authoritarianism that the doctor's more humane approach to politics represented.[1]

In the years leading up to 1946, Cruz-Coke had steered state efforts to build a robust system of social protections for the most vulnerable in Chilean society. A 1937 law that granted special health-care assistance to new mothers and their newborn children, and the country's Preventive Medicine Law, which one year later codified a prophylactic approach to worker health, both bore his signature as Chile's minister of health.[2] Though he was a leader of Chile's Catholic Church–aligned Conservative Party, Cruz-Coke made common cause with the country's midcentury political left on a surprising number of occasions. His steadfast commitment to a robust system of economic regulation mimicked, for example, the left's own vision of the economy and made him a friend of influential Communists like Teitelboim and Pablo Neruda. For all three, economic and social development required an active state, capable of ensuring the economic rights of workers and their families and remedying the social injustices that Chile's position within the global capitalist economy helped produce.[3]

Given the fact that Cruz-Coke dedicated much of his professional career to the study of human nutrition, including the impact of high food prices on working-class living standards, it would violate the historical imagination to not also wonder if Cruz-Coke felt a special bond with the miners of Lota. A surge in the cost of nutrient-poor bread, after all, was what ignited the 1947 coal miners' strike and precipitated González Videla's crackdown on his erstwhile progressive allies.[4] Cruz-Coke's sensitivity to the issue might partially explain why, just one year later, he joined just seven other senators—a group that included the ex-AOAN leader Carlos Alberto Martínez, Cruz-Coke's fellow physician Salvador Allende, and a handful of PCCh officials—in voting against the Law for the Permanent Defense of Democracy.[5] In summarizing his position against the 1948 anti-communist decree, Cruz-Coke reiterated his commitment to an inclusive democracy. If containing political radicalism was the goal—and at times Cruz-Coke almost certainly believed it was—then "strengthening the cause of justice" would be far more effective than promulgating legislation rooted in "punitive" principles.[6]

This chapter examines the social, cultural, economic, and scientific concerns that contributed to the formation of Chile's robust, yet ultimately unfinished, midcentury welfare state. Centered around the period from the early 1930s to the late 1940s, it focuses specifically on a broad cast of physicians, social scientists, and physical scientists—people like Eduardo Cruz-Coke—who stood at the center of this state-building process. In an environment racked by economic insecurity and global conflict, members of Chile's incipient professional middle class became leading figures in a decades-long crusade to expand the institutional structures of the Chilean state, and in particular the country's public health system. To that end, the national agencies that they helped guide worked tirelessly to protect the physical and economic health of all Chileans. In so doing, these state builders sought to secure an objective shared by both the midcentury political left and those who promoted a socially conscious variant of Catholicism: the right to a decent standard of living.

Nutrition science played a critical role in this story. On the one hand, a scientific approach to the increasingly politicized topic of food access provided

FIGURE 4. Dr. Eduardo Cruz-Coke during his 1946 presidential campaign. Colección Museo Histórico Nacional, Santiago de Chile.

officials associated with Chile's young welfare state a new, seemingly objective language for addressing the nature and consequences of the urban crisis that workers, women, and social movements had brought to the arena of public debate in those same years. On the other hand, food surveys and new food policies offered the state an important tool to both assess and then begin to remedy said crisis. The development of everything from national nutrition guidelines to supplemental feeding programs became a means of enacting a more just social contract. At the same time, these same initiatives served to contain the influence that mass political movements exercised in an environment of persistent social and economic uncertainty.

NUTRITIONISM'S RISE

The sort of nutrition science that proved so alluring to Eduardo Cruz-Coke in the middle decades of the twentieth century was the product of decades of intellectual exchange that crisscrossed the North Atlantic before moving south. Working out of his London laboratory in the 1800s, British chemist Dr. William Prout made some of the earliest breakthroughs in the scientific study of food—or what in the nineteenth century was commonly referred to as "dietetics." It was Prout who in the 1820s identified what experts believed were the three building blocks of all comestibles. Protein, fat, and carbohydrates, he observed, were the vital elements that accelerated muscular and nerve development and provided the body with ample stores of energy.[7] A short while later, Prout's German contemporary, Justus von Liebig, built upon these findings, positing that, of the Englishman's triad of macronutrients, protein constituted the primary fuel for animal growth. What nitrogen provided to the plant world, protein supplied to the human species, he maintained.[8]

By the turn of the twentieth century, however, the field of nutrition science stood at something of a crossroads. Following the trail blazed by the North American chemist Wilbur O. Atwater, one group of researchers dove into nutritional research with utilitarian purpose. Atwater's research, which he famously conducted in his Middletown, Connecticut, laboratory in the mid-1890s, suggested that food's primary value lay in the quantifiable amount of energy that it transferred to its consumer.[9] This thermodynamic approach to nutrition science, which reduced food's importance to its caloric composition, offered social scientists and government officials, many of them steeped in variants of eugenicist thinking, a purportedly universal metric with which to rank and naturalize differences between cultures and races.[10]

Nutritionists' "discovery" of the calorie also provided economists and labor engineers a quantitative unit that could be deployed instrumentally as part of a larger attempt to improve worker productivity and rationalize the workplace. By affixing a minimum caloric value to the bodily needs of workers, especially those engaged in demanding physical labor, industrialists might set more efficient wage rates and work schedules.[11] Underscoring the goal of economic optimization that motivated much of his own interest in nutrition, Atwater also suggested that his findings provided public officials new tools for instructing workers how to economize their earnings and prioritize foodstuffs that maximized energy intake.[12] As the prominent British political economist J. A. Hobson observed at the turn of the century, food science was fast becoming a "tributary science" of sociology.[13]

Around these same years, a second cohort of intrepid researchers pivoted toward food with a slightly different emphasis. Rather than fixing their attention on the caloric composition of working-class dietary regimens, this latter group adopted a more holistic approach to nutrition, one that centered around the special healing properties that certain foods possessed in greater quantities than others.[14] Chemists called these special molecules "vital amines," or vitamins for short, and the ingestion of foods rich in such compounds were believed to transmit exceptional protective and restorative value. Public officials quickly latched onto such findings, seeking to improve the general public's access to a variety of fruits and vegetables as well as meats and dairy products, especially milk. What and how the urban poor and working classes ate took center stage in a broader discussion about the causes and consequences of poverty, the purpose of public health policy, and the meaning of social welfare.[15]

TUBERCULOSOS AND DYING CHILDREN

Both the thermodynamic approach to nutrition, with its focus on food's caloric value, and the biochemical approach, which emphasized vitamin deficiencies, appealed to physicians and health experts in turn-of-the-century Chile. Indeed, well into the middle decades of the century, the line between these two nutritional approaches remained blurry at best. In an early example of the state's desire to instrumentalize international breakthroughs in nutrition science, officials at Chile's recently established Ministry of Hygiene, Social Assistance, and Welfare began to develop in the 1920s plans to better integrate Prout's three building blocks of nutrition—fats, proteins, and carbohydrates—into working-class diets. Given the caloric energy produced by these macronutrients, ministry officials argued that the primary goal of any future national nutrition policy should be to increase their consumption. "The human organism is like a machine," the ministry maintained in reiterating the tenets of the thermodynamic theory. "As such, it needs fuel in order to function and that means foods that nourish cells and leave it ready to work."[16] A decade later, at a regional meeting of the International Labor Organization (ILO), held in Santiago in 1936, Chile's delegation to the conference echoed such views when it maintained that future economic productivity depended upon improving the diet of the country's laboring population.[17]

But other voices in the public health community argued that a lack of qualitative diversity in an individual's consumption habits left society as a whole susceptible to communicable illnesses.[18] This latter group began to take interest in the protective properties that certain foods contained, irrespective of their caloric value. The Catholic Church was a leading voice in this regard. Through the Patronato Nacional de la Infancia (National Foundation on Infancy)—a philanthropic institution that the church and other social reformers had jointly established in the early twentieth century to address issues of childhood poverty and abandonment—activists created some of the first channels through which poor mothers in and around Santiago could access free milk for their children. Eventually the initiative, known as the Gotas de Leche (Drops of Milk) program, provided some three thousand Chilean children with a supplemental source of essential vitamins and minerals each year. Concurrently, church leaders also began to organize educational courses about nutrition for women of modest economic means.[19]

In the decades that followed, the ideas of international nutrition experts bolstered the Catholic Church's focus on improving vitamin consumption. In a landmark nutrition report that it issued in the mid-1930s, the League of Nations began promoting what it referred to as the "new teachings" of nutrition science. New developments in the study of food emphasized the importance of what food experts referred to as "protective foods," the League noted. This category of food and drink, which included meat, milk, cheese, legumes, vegetables, and fruit, helped shield the human body from the most prevalent diseases of poverty, and as such, their consumption needed to form the basis of the population's daily caloric intake. In contrast, so-called energy-bearing foods, like grains, fats, and sugar, should be consumed on a supplementary basis, League health experts advised.[20]

Throughout the 1930s and 1940s, back-and-forth discussions between those who emphasized food as a source of energy for the laboring body and those who underscored food's protective and restorative capacities found their way into debates over national economic policy. An article published in the monthly bulletin of Chile's Sociedad de Fomento Fabril (National Manufacturers' Association, SOFOFA) argued, for example, that the country's labor force should be divided into six different categories based on the intensity of physical labor that each class of worker was engaged in. Industry officials could then work with nutrition specialists to determine the recommended daily caloric intake for each category of the workforce. Once those recommendations had been established, state health and labor officials would together craft a multitiered wage system that corresponded to consumer prices at a given moment. In this way, every worker would have the appropriate earnings to consume the recommended daily calories for his type of work. But SOFOFA affiliates added one important caveat to his plan: somewhere between a quarter and half of a worker's daily caloric intake needed to come from food with high protective value.[21]

Few public health concerns in Chile brought the issue of protective foods to public view more than the threat posed by tuberculosis (TB). By the late 1920s, the communicable bacterial infection, which attacked the respiratory function of its mostly poor, urban-dwelling victims, had become a metaphor for a society suffocated by poverty and an economy struggling to industrialize. Between 1925 and 1932, the total number of deaths in Chile attributed to TB rose by an estimated 20 percent as the country's densely populated urban centers, which suffered from overcrowding, poor sanitation, and inadequate access to essential foods, became the epicenter for community spread of the disease. In the mid-1930s, as Chile struggled to recover from the collapse of its national economy just a few years earlier, Santiago registered a death rate from TB of just over 314 for every 100,000 people—a figure that was nearly twice that of the country's smaller, less densely populated regional cities.[22] A piecemeal attempt to conservatively quantify the economic damage wrought by the disease posited that if on average, every Chilean worker's labor produced just two pesos of total value each day, and if the number of people sidelined from the workforce by TB numbered just 200,000 people—a figure that represented less than half the total number of such cases—Chile would have lost an estimated 120,000,000 Chilean pesos per year due to worker incapacitation. Such figures said nothing of the additional costs that the state assumed to nurse the ill back to health or to assist poor families who lacked a primary breadwinner because of the disease.[23]

A chorus of respected medical experts agreed that the underlying cause of Chile's TB epidemic was obvious: its urban poor and working-class population were "starving and naked."[24] An understudy of Eduardo Cruz-Coke, the doctor and nutritional expert Jorge Mardones Restat, laid the blame squarely on diet. The country's stunning rates of TB were, in Mardones Restat's words, clear evidence of the chasm that existed between the country's "typical nutritional regimen" as it existed in real life and the medical community's assessment of "an individual's basic nutritional needs"—that is, the nutritional ideal.[25] And so to fight the epidemic, physicians joined forces with industrial leaders and the state to improve Chileans' consumption habits.

In highlighting the recommended course of treatment for those who had already contracted TB, a public health bulletin produced by the Welfare Division of Chile's state railway company advised blue-collar laborers that a dietary regimen that included high amounts of protein and fat, as well as vitamins, would expedite the recuperation process after infection.[26] Other popular education materials focused on how high-risk communities could alter their traditional food preparation habits to avoid contact with the bacteria that caused the disease. Such advice included boiling milk, then storing it in a cool location before consuming it. Experts also advised consumers to sufficiently cook all meat that was prepared at home in order to kill contaminants.[27] One of the most common, yet controversial, pieces of public health advice was that workers decrease their consumption of alcohol, as high levels of alcohol were thought to weaken the body's immune system.[28]

For public health officials working in the 1930s, the problem of TB was rivaled only by Chile's startling rate of infant mortality. At the beginning of the twentieth century, public records suggested that more than 342 infant deaths occurred for every 1,000 live births in Chile. Although that rate had slowly begun to decline in the first two decades of the century—by 1920, for example, infant mortality had fallen by nearly a third, to 263 deaths per 1,000 births—Chile still stood in the unenviable position of having among the highest recorded infant death rates anywhere in Latin America, if not the world.[29]

A young, bespectacled medical doctor named Salvador Allende cast the problem of infant mortality in particularly dramatic relief. In his 1939 *La realidad médico-social chilena* (The Chilean medical-social reality), the newly minted physician compiled existing data to show that for every twenty children born alive in Chile, one child was born lifeless. The figure was just the first of a parade of disquieting statistics in a book that quickly became a public health manifesto for social reformers of various political stripes. For every ten children born alive, one would die in his or her first month of life, Allende reported. A quarter would die during their first year of life, while an astonishing 50 percent would not live to see their ninth birthday.[30] As challenging as those figures were to accept, Allende argued that understanding the social reality that such statistics revealed was an essential first step toward devising a way out of the crisis. "A succinct and objective examination of our medical-social reality is the best guarantee that exists for first diagnosing [the problem] and then identifying the appropriate remedies that can restore the vigor and health of our people," the socialist doctor concluded.[31]

As with TB, public health officials saw dietary consumption as both a cause of and solution to the crisis of preventable infant death. An editorial published in a 1939 issue of the Ministry of Health's monthly bulletin put it most concisely: "There is . . . a basic problem and that problem is nutrition." According to the health officials, the problem required intervention in the everyday consumption regimens of infants themselves as well as those of underresourced mothers. "Poor mothers, poorly nourished and skeleton-like, inevitably pass on to their ricket-stricken children" an inability to defend themselves against disease and sickness, Ministry officials pointed out, referencing the prevalence of bone deformities among children deficient in vitamin D. The bulletin concluded that such matters intensified in severity during the nursing period due to the fact that poor mothers were "incapable of properly nourishing" their children. In this way, inadequate access to nutrition perpetuated a cycle of childhood illness and increased the probability of early death.[32] In making the case for new policies to combat Chile's high infant mortality figures, Allende himself kept his eye on the larger socioeconomic picture. If the "first condition" of any nation's economic prosperity was the growth of a robust and healthy population, then the continued existence of high infant and childhood death rates would prevent such a future from ever coming into being.[33]

CALCULATING MALNUTRITION

In Europe, the study of food's restorative and protective capacities—what some later refer to as the "new nutritionism"—emerged in response to food scarcity during the First World War, Chilean historian María Soledad Zárate has observed. By contrast, in Chile, public health officials' growing concern with nutrient deficiencies was a response to the fact that the advent of industrialization was ravaging the physical health of Chile's working-class communities.[34] The threat of TB and the seriousness of infant mortality thus became bodily markers of Chile's nutritional inadequacies, as well as omnipresent reminders of the need for sweeping social and economic reforms to suppress the many injustices created by global capitalism.[35]

But as the Chilean state took concrete steps to remedy such problems, many social reformers discovered that they lacked essential data. In particular, health officials needed empirical information about the actual dietary habits of Chile's citizenry. Chile's national Labor Office had tried to initiate the gathering of such data in the early decades of the century. In response to the food riots and cost-of-living strikes that that had rocked the country in 1905 and then again in 1907, Labor Office researchers began entering homes and workplaces around the country in the 1910s, documenting the social conditions in which Chile's working-class population lived and labored. Among other things, the office's early surveys detailed the relationship between worker wages and the rising cost of essential family expenditures, like food. As such, they offered an early numerical description of working-class life. They also prepared the way for the later argument that the declining exchange value of workers' wages acted as the primary brake on family consumption.[36]

In the years that followed, scientists and medics, many of whom would eventually occupy positions within Chile's early public health institutions, blended findings about the economic constraints on food consumption habits with inquiries into more substantive concerns about the Chilean diet. Given the economic limitations on consumption and the inequities in distribution of basic foodstuffs in the country, what, in fact, constituted a "typical" Chilean consumption regimen? Physical and social scientists began to answer that question in an ever-more-systematic fashion as Chile pulled itself out of the doldrums of the Great Depression, by utilizing methods of survey research to assess the caloric and nutrient composition of household food intake.[37] At times, these studies presented conundrums. A thesis completed at the University of Chile in 1933 used publicly available agricultural data to show that when it came to average daily caloric consumption, general dietary intake had improved in the preceding decades.[38] That same year, a study conducted by another young medical doctor, this time on the consumption habits of four dozen working-class families located in the coastal city of Viña del Mar, also revealed relatively high caloric consumption. Among the researcher's forty-eight-family sample, average daily caloric consumption reached as high as 3,275 calories—just shy of most international recommendations.[39] If such findings were generalizable—and it was not yet clear if they were—why were so many Chileans dying an early death?

A series of investigations in the mid-1930s provided further answers. In nearly all such studies, the resounding conclusion was that the quality of the typical Chilean consumer's diet was poor. A 1935 study by a young medical doctor named Ramón González confirmed, for example, that most working-class Chilean families used just a handful of ingredients, many of them devoid of essential vitamins and minerals, to make a few key dishes. Basing his findings on larger and more diverse samples than prior work, González highlighted that two goods in particular, bread and potatoes, constituted nearly half of survey participants' total calories.[40] Contemporaneous nutrition studies filled out the nutritional picture, suggesting that approximately 60 percent of the calories consumed by both urban and rural consumers came from potatoes and wheat-based products, especially bread and noodles. Another 12 percent of total calories came from sugar. Just over 7 percent came from beef, while 5 percent was derived from wine.[41]

The defining account of nutritional deficits in Chile came not from within but from outside the country. In the winter of 1935, two European nutrition experts, Etienne Burnet and Carlo Dragoni, arrived to begin a monthslong study of Chile's national food economy under the auspices of the League of Nations' Health Committee. Collaborating with Chilean public health officials and social workers, the League consultants drafted, printed, and circulated thousands of questionnaires on the country's nutritional habits. They then quickly got to work collecting data in fifteen different localities across Chile over the course of two weeks in 1935. To carry out the survey, the League relied on community nurses and *visitadoras sociales*—social workers trained to do house calls in mostly poor communities—each of whom received training in survey methodologies before being sent into the field. An unprecedented undertaking in terms of its size and geographic scale, the survey captured information from nearly 600 different families: 3,383 participants in all.[42]

When the results of the research were analyzed by League experts, the findings both qualified and affirmed what earlier researchers had postulated. Although Chileans consumed 2,357 calories per day on average, the gap between rich and poor was stark. The poorest Chileans—those earning less than one peso per day—consumed just 979 calories, but the most well-off in the survey—those earning approximately five pesos per day—consumed more than 3,540 daily calories. According to the study, the line between "underconsumption" and proper consumption (set by Burnet and Dragoni at around 2,500 calories per day) fell somewhere between those who earned three and four pesos per day. Approximately 60 percent of families did not even reach 2,000 calories per day.[43] Such findings tempered the earlier claims that Chileans consumed a sufficient number of calories and that the larger problem was the fact that such calories were "empty"—that is, devoid of essential vitamins and minerals. Absolute caloric intake and the types of foods that constituted such consumption both seemed to be matters of concern, according to the rigorous study.

This discovery about caloric insufficiency notwithstanding, the League agreed that the greatest problem in Chile was the issue of dietary quality. Like González's study, Burnet and Dragoni's report painted a stark portrait of a nation getting by on wheat products, especially bread, and potatoes. Together, the two sets of comestibles overshadowed all other foods, and often by astounding margins. As a point of comparison, average daily per capita consumption of meat was around 107 grams per day, according to the Burnet and Dragoni survey, but consumption of potatoes and wheat each topped 300 grams each day. Indeed, just as González had demonstrated, the two nutrient-scarce, carbohydrate-rich staples together constituted nearly 50 percent of total consumption when measured by total weight.[44]

To provide some perspective on their survey findings, the study compared Chileans' consumption of five subcategories of protective foods rich in vitamins A and C as well as calcium—milk, butter, eggs, fruit, and fish—to available consumption data in the United States and a smattering of countries in Europe and Asia. Chileans consumed just one-tenth the milk of their Danish counterparts, Burnet and Dragoni discovered. When it came to daily cheese consumption, a German national, on average, ate 160 times more cheese than the average Chilean. Similar findings emerged for eggs, fish, and fruit. For the latter food group, Burnet and Dragoni underscored that citizens of the United States consumed an astounding 300 times more fruit each day than a typical Chilean.[45]

BEYOND A STATE OF HUNGER

The results of the Burnet and Dragoni study were first published in French in 1936 and then translated into Spanish roughly one year later. For Chilean social scientists, the report's methodology became a model in rigorous survey research. Even more important, though, was the empirical content of the League of Nations' study. On the one hand, the data collected by social scientists and public health experts painted a remarkably clear and consistent picture of everyday life in Chile—one in which the cost and availability of food staples conditioned how the household budgets of Chile's urban poor were allocated and what dietary practices then became customary. On the other hand, the quantifiable data that flowed forth from the research provided a certain logic to the cost-of-living protests and food riots that working-class Chileans had participated in during the previous decades. Through charts and statistics, social reformers gained a better understanding of the depth of social and economic anxiety that fueled so much disquiet. As one prominent Chilean physician wrote around the time that the main findings of the League-sponsored nutrition surveys were released in Spanish, few Chileans believed the "troubles" affecting Chile were "so profound" before the Burnet-Dragoni study.[46] The Burnet and Dragoni report proved to be as much a political document as a scientific one. Just as the AOAN's 1918 manifesto had mobilized the street, the League's findings generated a feeling of urgency in the chambers of government.

No single figure became more intimately involved in harnessing that sense of urgency than Dr. Eduardo Cruz-Coke. The child of a French mother and Chilean father, Cruz-Coke was born on the eve of the twentieth century in Chile's second city, Valparaíso. Rising through the ranks of an elite preparatory school in the port, the young Cruz-Coke departed for Santiago when he was a teenager to begin his medical training in a world being torn asunder by global war and depression. At the University of Chile, where he studied from 1915 until 1921, Cruz-Coke's final thesis offered a scientific appraisal of Chile's nascent TB crisis, an artifact of the intellectual age in which he would soon become a leading figure. In the ensuing years, he split his time between teaching and clinical work, all the while maintaining an active laboratory that became an incubator for new knowledge about the social determinants of health, and specifically nutrition.[47]

A trip Cruz-Coke took to Europe in the late 1920s had a profound impact on his medical trajectory. Visiting Germany, France, Britain, and Spain in 1926 and 1927, the young Chilean medic gained firsthand exposure to the laboratories of several scientific giants of his day, including German physiologist Otto Warburg, French physicists Jean Baptiste Perrin and Louis de Broglie, and the British biochemist Frederick Gowland Hopkins.[48] Upon his return to Chile, Cruz-Coke used what he had learned from those encounters to train a generation of medical students who would quantify the problem of malnutrition in Chile. His work surveying the nutritional habits of approximately fifty families in Santiago exemplified scientific rigor for many of the aforementioned researchers as they began collecting their own empirical data about working-class living conditions and consumption habits in the 1930s.[49]

Following the release of Burnet and Dragoni's damning findings about Chile's nutritional inadequacies, President Arturo Alessandri appointed Cruz-Coke to head Chile's Ministry of Health, the successor to the earlier Ministry of Hygiene. From that post, he became the architect of a series of unprecedented public health measures. Chile's Mother-Child Law improved and expanded access to health services for new and pregnant mothers and their children. A short while later, the country's landmark Preventive Medicine Law sought to ensure that all Chilean workers received an annual wellness exam. If a worker was found to be suffering from an ailment during such a checkup, the state would guarantee temporary employment leave, even if the illness had not yet impaired one's ability to work. Ultimately, the goal of the public health legislation was to diagnose debilitating infections, like TB, as early as possible. In this way, the state hoped to improve treatment success rates and limit the spread of the disease through crowded job sites and residential communities.[50]

It was a third achievement, however, that ultimately provided the institutional home from which a cadre of nutrition experts would effect the most long-lasting change. Situated within Chile's Ministry of Health, the Consejo Nacional de Alimentación (National Nutrition Council, CNA) was one of several state nutrition agencies set up around Latin America in the late 1930s.[51] To head the office's day-to-day operations, Cruz-Coke tapped his former student and trusted collaborator Jorge Mardones Restat. Under Mardones Restat's watch, the CNA pursued the singular mission of bettering nutritional outcomes for poor and working-class Chileans—what its founding decree identified as the "foundation" for improving national health.[52]

Almost overnight, the CNA became a vital institutional space in which medical researchers and public health officials grappled with the country's entrenched hunger pangs. First there was the research. As experts cycled through the new agency, the CNA promoted and publicized new findings in the area of public health and social medicine. A host of journals, some technical and others more public facing, became media for sharing new knowledge about domestic and international developments in the area of nutrition.[53] Food policy even entered the realm of more general publications that otherwise had little to do with nutrition science. For example, Chile's *Boletín Municipal de la República*, a monthly publication of the Ministry of Interior's Department of Municipalities, spent its first six issues in 1938 relating how and where Chile's new network of state-backed *restaurantes populares* (popular restaurants) would be run.[54] An editorial published in the bulletin in 1939 similarly called for all municipal governments to make consumer education a core task. In subsequent months, the municipal *Boletín* also released a series of nutrition "primers" and consumer guides intended for both social workers and the general consuming public.[55]

Medical journals committed to advancing intellectual discussion about the social and environmental aspects of public health also became a forum for discussing matters that could be best described as "applied science." As the cost and availability of protective foods spiked during the Second World War, Jorge Mardones Restat, writing in the *Revista de Medicina y Alimentación*, highlighted the great physiological and economic promise of enriching domestically produced foodstuffs with critical vitamins and minerals. This process, the nutrition expert wrote, represented a "new way to resolve the nutritional deficiencies present in the general population" at a time when the availability of many basic goods was limited and prices were on the rise.[56]

The Santiago-based Instituto Médico Técnico Sanitas took the lead in such efforts, creating a special protein- and vitamin-enriched consommé, called Sopal, and a starch supplement, known as Farinol. Both were intended for young children who did not receive adequate supplies of milk.[57] Other nutrition researchers experimented with how to naturally fortify basic foods, especially dairy products, often by simply improving the nutritional quality of the forage that animals in the countryside grazed upon.[58] Within a few years, a focus on enrichment expanded to the production of bread in Chile. Rather than redirecting popular consumption habits away from this most essential staple, as some early nutrition experts might have advocated, food engineers at Chile's Instituto Nacional de Comercio (National Institute of Trade, INACO) explored ways to enhance the nutritional content of bread by infusing it with life-supporting vitamins and minerals, like vitamin B, calcium, and iron.[59]

The publication in 1942 of the more than 275-page study *La Alimentación en Chile* (Nutrition in Chile), by Mardones Restat and Ricardo Cox, represented a watershed moment in Chilean food research. The product of copious data accumulation, the study represented a synthesis of Chilean nutrition experts' work over the previous decade. On the one hand, it offered a comprehensive diagnostic of Chile's food economy, assessing everything from the productivity, fertility, and usage of the country's agricultural lands to national patterns of consumption, trends in food prices, and improvements—both completed and pending—to the country's food distribution infrastructure. On the other hand, Mardones Restat and Cox explored the problem of nutrition in Chile from a physiological perspective, seeking to build a bridge between the actually existing and the ideal when it came to the nutritional habits of Chile's popular classes.[60] The study's concluding section built upon the findings of Burnet and Dragoni's League of Nations report by squarely emphasizing that the "fundamental defect" of Chile's popular diet was an absence of "protective foods." In the case of children, this largely meant a limited consumption of milk; for adults—and especially men who engaged in physical labor—the report emphasized a dearth of foods rich in vitamin B, including vegetables, meat, fish, and eggs.[61]

In some of the report's most urgent language, Mardones Restat and his coauthor maintained that no serious expert on the topic could deny a few elementary facts any longer. First, until the persistent instability of Chilean workers' purchasing power was stabilized, deep class divisions in the area of food consumption would continue to reproduce themselves. Second, to increase the popular consumption of nutrient-rich foods that improved the overall health and productivity of the Chilean nation, the state would have to take a more active role in promoting the domestic production and distribution of food. In essence, eating was intimately bound up with economic life.[62]

Policies that addressed these conclusions were already being developed when Mardones Restat and Cox's authoritative report was released in 1942. In the CNA's 1937 Plan de Gobierno, Cruz-Coke and his associates made the case that environment and society, including nutritional intake, conditioned an individual's physical health and well-being.[63] In the years that followed, the Ministry of Health partnered with state offices and economic institutions who shared its goal of resolving Chile's nutritional crisis.[64] Together with the Junta de Exportación Agrícola (Agricultural Export Board, JEA), the agency charged with setting agricultural commodity prices in the country, the CNA advocated for limits on the export of vital, nutrient-rich foods from Chile as part of an effort to prioritize domestic consumer needs.[65] In a similar vein, the CNA also collaborated with the country's main agricultural credit provider, the Caja de Crédito Agrario (Agricultural Credit Fund), and its land colonization office, the Caja de Colonización Agrícola (Agricultural Colonization Fund). The CNA urged the former to reorient its offerings of low-interest credit toward farmers who specialized in producing nutritionally rich foods, especially dairy products. The CNA also suggested that the Caja de Colonización Agrícola promote the subdivision of large agricultural land holdings that were not being "intensively exploited."[66]

Placing the problem of food within a broader developmentalist framework that emphasized the importance of an active and interventionist state, Cruz-Coke and his allies at the CNA contended that any effort to increase production of a particular food product that was "not accompanied by a similar initiative to stimulate that good's consumption" ultimately ignored the "basic needs of the country" and would thus be "ineffective."[67] The CNA's vision of economic complementarity constituted a reimagining of the foundations of the Chilean national economy and the role that the state should play in it. Put differently, Chilean state builders set popular nutrition—and by extension, public health—as key metrics by which state officials should measure the national economy's success.

The CNA's relationships to two agencies that came out of the social reforms of the mid-1920s and early 1930s—Chile's national consumer protection and price control office, the Comisariato, and its national worker's insurance fund, the Caja de Seguro Obligatorio (Obligatory Insurance Fund, CSO)—were especially notable examples of the CNA's growing social and economic reach.[68] State-run popular restaurants, which operated under the jurisdiction of the Comisariato, offered low-cost, nutrient-rich lunches, which were designed in partnership with the CNA and its affiliated nutrition experts. The facilities served a largely male, working-class clientele.[69] The offerings at one of the earliest such restaurants, located in the Santiago parish of Providencia, were typical. There, starting in the late 1930s, customers paid a fixed price for one of three savory menus—either charquicán, a large bowl of beans, or a chunk of beef, potato, and vegetables drowned in a rich broth, known as *cazuela*. Although each dish also included a piece of bread, a cup of tea, and an after-lunch dessert, the menus directed workers toward protein- and vitamin-rich options when it became difficult to return home for their midday meals.[70] At the same time, the CSO, whose wide range of responsibilities included administering a network of popular consumer goods stores, turned to the CNA for advice about which basic foodstuffs required state-imposed price controls and which did not—a decision that the CNA based on each product's "physiological value and the state of national production."[71]

FIGURE 5. Showcasing modern bottling technologies at a Central de Leche processing facility in the 1940s. Colección Museo Histórico Nacional, Santiago de Chile.

The state's growing role in the production of milk similarly underscored its role in fostering the production of protective foods. As part of the state's attempt to expand dairy production, the CSO, under the leadership of the former AOAN activist and Radical Party member Santiago Labarca, bought controlling shares first of Chile's principal pasteurization and bottling company, the Santiago-based Central de Leche, and eventually of a series of smaller, regional milk pasteurization plants as well. This not only moved a significant portion of domestic milk processing into the hands of the Chilean state; the incorporation of new bottling technologies and an emphasis on standardization at the Central de Leche also quickly boosted total production.[72] Between 1939 and the end of 1941, total milk production at the Central de Leche increased from just 28,000 liters of milk per day to some 250,000 liters per day.[73]

State efforts to more equitably distribute milk followed these changes in production. As previously discussed, many poor Chileans had come to rely upon the goodwill of philanthropic organizations and the Catholic Church, which together had administered a network of milk dispensaries for infants during the early decades of the century. But in promoting the idea that milk was a right of citizenship, not an object of charity, the Popular Front of the early 1940s secularized milk distribution by establishing approximately half a dozen *bares lácteos* (milk bars) in Santiago and a handful of regional cities. At these sites, the state sold an array of delectable, calcium-rich dairy products—everything from *arroz con leche* (rice pudding) and flan to chocolate milk and ice cream—all at fixed prices.[74] The first such bar, which operated at the corner of Alameda and Bandera Streets in downtown Santiago, was said to be serving at least five thousand customers daily by the end of 1941. A popular milk bar in the port city of Valparaíso was an even larger sensation; one report suggested that as many as eight thousand orders were being placed each day by the end of that same year.[75]

When Salvador Allende took over Cruz-Coke's position at the Ministry of Health in 1939, he expanded milk distribution efforts in Santiago. By the early 1940s, the Central de Leche was distributing between twelve and fifteen thousand liters of milk daily to working-class communities in Santiago. What's more, the state required distributors to sell all milk at cost—that is, with a profit margin of 0 percent.[76] As a result, from 1937 to 1946 per capita milk consumption in Chile was twice that of the previous decade.[77] Such efforts reflected a first step, however partial, toward the fulfillment of one of Cruz-Coke's dreams: that one day milk consumption in Chile would be on a par with that of the United States and Sweden, two countries whose health outcomes the Chilean medic greatly admired.[78]

FOR A WORLD FREE FROM WANT?

In a report that Salvador Allende presented in 1942, shortly after his tenure as minister of health, the rising socialist leader declared that the public health efforts of the Chilean FP offered a shining example to countries around the hemisphere, if not the world. Chile had become a "a vast laboratory for experimentation," the physician said, expressing great pride that his country had "mobilized . . . a fervent crusade against physical suffering . . . the most rational and technically accomplished" in all of Latin America. The benefits of such efforts would have "Hemisphere-wide usefulness," Allende promised, adding that they approximated US president Franklin Delano Roosevelt's vision of a world in which every person was allowed to "live his own life, free from fear and from want."[79]

Allende was hardly the only figure in midcentury Chile who saw Roosevelt and the US New Deal as pole stars for a more social democracy. Nor was Allende the only one to associate the Roosevelt administration's notion of a world "free from want" with Chile's own struggle to guarantee a right to essential consumption. "The best guarantee we have for the rights of sovereignty and independence for our country and for the development of its economy and the welfare of its people" lay with the "program of the Atlantic Charter," an editorial in Chile's leading PCCh newspaper had declared in March 1943.[80] In the introduction to his 1946 survey of consumption practices in Chile and around Latin America, the longtime Chilean labor advocate, legal expert, and sociologist Moisés Poblete Troncoso pointed toward former US vice president Henry Wallace's notion of a "century for the common man" as an idea worth fighting for around the region.[81] "Modern science . . . has made it technologically possible for peoples around the world to have enough to eat. The object of this war is to make sure that everybody in the world has the privilege of drinking a quart [*litro*] of milk a day," Poblete Troncoso wrote in the preface of his book, a direct gesture to Wallace's vision of social and economic democracy in the postwar world.[82]

But by the time that Poblete Troncoso's book was published, cracks were already beginning to appear in the Chilean state's expanding social welfare architecture. Hopes of a Pan-American New Deal were fast fading as well. Speaking before members of Chile's Socialist Party just a year and a half after declaring that Chile represented a model for the Americas, Allende, who had since resigned from his ministerial post, struck a decidedly disillusioned tone about the course the FP's leadership was charting. In that speech, given to his party's annual convention in 1943, the young medical doctor underscored the many "contradictions" of the broad front coalition. The union of Socialists, Communists, and middle-class reformers had succeeded in bridging sectarian differences on the reformist left. It had also raised the power and profile of Chile's national labor federation, arguably the single most important grassroots force behind the coalition's official establishment. But unable or unwilling to break with decades of liberal economic thought, Chile's progressive reformism, in Allende's assessment, was failing in its social mission.[83]

Of particular concern to Allende was the gap between the persistently low wages paid to most Chilean workers and the high prices Chilean consumers were forced to pay in the marketplace. Between 1941 and 1943, that problem grew more severe as the value of the average wage in Chile fell by some 12 percent.[84] This fact, Allende pointed out, meant Chilean workers had to toil longer and harder to feed themselves and their families. The average Chilean worker had to work for roughly thirty-eight minutes to earn enough to buy a single piece of bread—more than three times as long as a typical French worker and six times as long as an average worker in the United States. For other household items, like sugar and eggs, the figures were even more skewed; an entire hour of labor might get a worker one hundred grams of sugar, while six hours of work bought a dozen eggs. By contrast, in the United States, the corresponding numbers were just seven minutes for an equal amount of sugar and fifty-five minutes for a carton of twelve eggs.[85]

In concluding his speech, Allende condemned the FP's continued adherence to liberal orthodoxy. All across the globe, men and women were demanding their "right to live and to subsist," he concluded. "The people have realized that a lasting peace will not be maintained if there exist rich people and poor people" or if the "insecurity of the individual who lives on a simple wage or salary" is not alleviated.[86] Only if basic consumer needs, not market forces, dictated the output of national production, Allende argued, would Chile begin to break with the old, increasingly discredited assumptions of economic liberalism.[87]

The broader ideological shifts that Allende condemned in his 1943 speech—namely, the FP's reticence to imagine a world beyond liberal capitalism—foreshadowed the increasing reluctance of nutrition experts to engage in structural critiques of Chile's food economy. Whereas the CNA's early publications had readily attacked wage differentials and other economic forces for propagating malnourishment and childhood illness, by the mid-1940s the CNA's willingness to advocate for state intervention in the national economy slowly receded. In its place, a discourse that focused on the culture of poor and working-class consumers became ascendant. "[T]he possibilities that a Chilean has to nourish him or herself properly are influenced by economic matters . . . but it must be pointed out that ignorance also plays a role of evident magnitude in every social stratum," the prominent nutrition expert Julio Santa María wrote as he reflected anew upon the underlying causes of nutritional inequality in postwar Chile. "[T]he influence that 'habits' have on the nutritional situation of the country cannot be underestimated," he concluded.[88]

Illustrative of a behavioral turn in nutrition, state food officials looked inward by promoting, for example, group cooking demonstrations in the homes of poor and working-class women. One part educational outreach tool and one part research instrument, public cooking demonstrations were offered by public health officials, nutrition experts, and consumer inspectors to more than 1,150 women between October 1944 and December 1946. These events provided an arena to teach new methods of food preparation, but they also helped researchers to glean new knowledge about existing habits.[89]

In the wake of González Videla's 1946 electoral victory, the integrative approach to public health that Cruz-Coke had once advocated splintered further. Under the leadership of First Lady Rosa Markmann, the Asociación de Dueñas de Casa (Association of Housewives, ADC) popularized the stereotypical image of the "unfit" Chilean mother whose ignorance about basic household matters, like food preparation, was seen as detrimental to the physical health and well-being of her family and the nation as a whole.[90] For much of the late 1940s and early 1950s, one of the ADC's most notable activities involved publishing short consumer handbooks and primers, known as *cartillas del consumidor*, which social workers and well-to-do professionals affiliated with the organization distributed to poor and working-class women, all in an effort to educate them about how nutritional outcomes might be improved while embracing values of thrift and frugality. As one article in the group's memorably named magazine *Fiel* (Loyalty) argued, "the education of the consumer is today the most urgent necessity for those segments of the population with limited resources."[91] While nutrition had been at the center of Chile's vision of national economic development in the late 1930s and early 1940s, by the end of the decade, the CNA and consumer politics more generally had largely become focused on how best to alter the "improper" consumer habits that existed within the traditionally feminine domestic sphere.

Writing in 1950, the statistician Juan Crocco Ferrari reported the latest midcentury data regarding basic living conditions in Chile. As part of a larger effort by Chile's national development agency to chart Chile's "economic geography" following the Second World War, Crocco Ferrari's report considered how inflationary pressures had chipped away at the value of Chilean workers' salaries over the course of the 1940s. It then went on to quantify per capita consumer spending data. It also considered the availability of the most widely consumed food products in Chile over part of that same period, specifically the years 1944 to 1948. The numbers did not suggest as desperate a situation as some might have argued, but Chile certainly had little to brag about. Among the study's most alarming revelations was that Chileans were, on average, consuming the same amount, if not less than they were a half decade earlier, when it came to nearly every basic food product—this despite the noble efforts of scientists, doctors, and policy makers to put the problem of nutrition at the center of the state-building process.

The report's most incriminating conclusion came in the statistician's own analysis of the data he had collected. "The problem of nutrition appears to have grown more serious in Chile," Crocco Ferrari wrote. He went on: "There exists the impression, justified in part by statistical data, that until the year 1930, and probably going back to the start of the century, the availability of agricultural food products allowed the [Chilean] population to feed itself in a better way than it does at present, even if it did not meet the nutritional requirements associated with basic scientific norms. After that time, however, shortages for certain products, like beef, wheat, legumes, and potatoes, started to appear, which has translated into a decline in the quality of the [Chilean] diet, particularly with respect to proteins."[92]

Over the next two decades, popular consumers in Chile would only be squeezed further as inflation intensified, becoming, in President González Videla's own words, a "scourge" akin to an ecologically devastating drought.[93] The ADC would continue as the primary national organization that integrated women into national political life, and much of that work interpellated women as consumers. However, by the early 1950s the group's influence was in decline. In the association's place, the populist military general Carlos Ibáñez del Campo, who was elected to a second nonconsecutive presidential term in 1952, backed the creation of a new set of organizations to deal with consumer problems, but such organizing was most often channeled toward narrow electoral ends.[94]

To be sure, many of the legislative accomplishments of Cruz-Coke and his disciples endured. Already by 1946, Cruz-Coke's Preventive Medicine Law was responsible for more than 968,500 wellness health exams among the approximately 980,000 workers who were actively insured by the CSO. A few years later, in 1952, those accomplishments expanded when, under the watch of former CNA chief turned minister of health Jorge Mardones Restat, Chile established two new welfare and health agencies, the Servicio de Seguridad Social (Social Security Service) and Servicio Nacional de Salud (National Health Service). Together, the two initiatives superseded the old CSO system of worker-based health provisioning and allowed all Chileans—no matter their employment status, marital status, age, or class background—to receive comparable health-care services in the same medical facilities.[95] When it came to infant mortality, meanwhile, the number of Chilean infants who died for every 1,000 live births fell from 252 in 1936 to just 143 one decade later.[96] One factor that contributed to that drop was almost certainly a doubling in per capita consumption of milk during that same ten-year period.[97]

But for at least the first two decades of the post–Second World War era, the impulse to organize key elements of Chile's social welfare state around nutrition and food consumption matters appeared to be in retreat. As Chile's dependence on expensive food imports grew more stark, a new generation of scholars and activists began to shift their gaze from questions about demand to matters of supply, and thus from the immediate problems of the food-consuming city to those of the food-producing countryside.[98] If the earlier studies of urban workers and their families had demonstrated that unstable prices of food sucked household budgets dry, this new intellectual cohort—many of them trained as sociologists, agronomists, and economists—considered the food economy as a set of productive and distributional relationships that cut across regions within Chile and beyond. To emancipate Chile economically, it was not enough to fix prices and monitor the marketplace. Rather, the Chilean state would have to encourage its farmers and food processors to effectively produce more at the lowest possible cost and then adequately distribute that bounty to those who needed it most.

FOUR

Cultivating Consumption

IN THE MIDDLE OF 1958, as lawmakers prepared to repeal Chile's ten-year-old political ban on the Communist left, Jorge Ahumada celebrated the defining work of his academic career. In *En vez de la miseria* (Instead of misery), one of the leading thinkers in Chile's Christian Democratic Party (PDC) grappled with the growing consensus that despite the social and economic reforms that had begun in the 1940s, Chile was plunging ever deeper into an economic abyss. Three years earlier, a group of US financial consultants had proposed that Chile embrace austerity and liberalize its trade policies to halt rising inflation and attract new foreign investment. Ahumada, among others, watched as President Carlos Ibáñez del Campo's partial implementation of such recommendations provoked a wave of social unrest unlike any Chile had experienced since the end of the Second World War. Tensions exploded in April 1957 when thousands of urban protesters took to the streets to oppose the rising cost of living in a multiday uprising that became known as the "Battle of Santiago" or Santiagazo.[1]

Assessing the economic landscape after the dust had settled, Ahumada suggested that to understand the origins of Chile's travails and begin to chart a way forward, one needed to look beyond the immediate site of social protest: the city streets of Santiago. In short, the social scientist was part of group of intellectuals who said Chile's unwillingness to modernize its agrarian sector during the boom years of the nitrate era had sent the country down a path toward the crisis it was now living. The failure to address the rural-urban divide was akin to a family that receives all of its food from outside the home and therefore has never "put its own kitchen in working order," he wrote in *En vez de la miseria*. Like the Chilean nation itself, such a family believed instead that it was enough to maintain a "presentable dining room" for those who viewed the house from afar.[2]

Jorge Ahumada's metaphorical use of food to describe the condition of the Chilean economy in the late 1950s was hardly coincidental. Rather it was informed by several years studying the food-producing economies of Chile and its various neighbors around the hemisphere. Born in Santiago in 1917, Ahumada had pursued a degree in agricultural engineering in the 1930s, not long after his father's wholesale distribution business collapsed amid the economic depression of the era. Upon finishing his studies at the University of Chile, Ahumada joined Chile's Popular Front (FP) government, and as a midlevel functionary in the Ministry of Agriculture he watched as the Chilean state's regulatory powers expanded at breakneck speed. When Chile finally broke off formal diplomatic relations with the Axis powers, Ahumada's professional trajectory became closely linked to the new circuits of inter-American cooperation that defined the era. In 1943 he accepted a fellowship from the US Department of Agriculture's (USDA) Bureau of Agricultural Economics to complete graduate coursework in Washington, DC. At Harvard, Ahumada continued his training, studying with some of the intellectual giants of his day, like Keynesian theorist Alvin Hansen; John Black, a leading US scholar on agrarian matters; and the heterodox Austrian political economist Joseph Schumpeter.[3]

As a young social scientist, Ahumada intended to bring the skills gained from his formal work in economics back home, and for a brief period he returned to Chile's Ministry of Agriculture, where he helped draft one of the country's first plans for comprehensive reform of the rural sector. The failure of Chile's landowning elite to consider even the most modest agrarian reform measures disillusioned him, so Ahumada soon departed his home country again, this time circulating among international institutes and agencies. In Puerto Rico he observed efforts at planned agricultural development and industrialization, which became known as Operation Bootstrap. In Washington he worked at the International Monetary Fund (IMF) at a time when the new Bretton Woods system still advocated an interventionist approach to economic development. And in Guatemala, where he served as an adviser to that country's Institute for Development and Central Bank, Ahumada gained an up-close view of the Central American country's historic push for land reform under President Juan José Arévalo. It wasn't until the early 1950s that Ahumada returned to Santiago, recruited by the UN's Comisión Económica para América Latina (Economic Commission for Latin America,

CEPAL) to help lead an organization that argued Latin America's rising inflation was tied to stagnating domestic food production.[4]

Back home, Ahumada set out to write a major treatise that tackled the
relationship between rural underdevelopment, on the one hand, and urban
blight, on the other. *En vez de la miseria* became that work. In digestible
academic prose, Ahumada advanced a variant of the dominant *cepalino*
position, which said rural modernization, including the dissolution of large
agricultural estates, was a necessary first step toward securing Chile's domestic
food supply. Whereas many advocates of land reform in Chile focused their
attention on the needs, demands, and organization of the rural populations
who would become the immediate subjects of such an initiative, Ahumada
emphasized that agrarian reform and urban modernization efforts should be
linked processes.[5] As he argued in his 1958 opus, declining agrarian productivity, not excessive public spending, fueled persistently high rates of inflation.
If any future agrarian reform initiative was to be successful, it would need to
focus on two critical problems: how to produce a greater quantity of agrarian
goods more efficiently and how to raise the income of rural wage laborers so
they might one day constitute a domestic consumer market. Working with
Chile's insurgent PDC in the late 1950s and early 1960s, Ahumada prescribed
policies that sought to address both concerns.[6]

This chapter, like Ahumada's life, outlines the larger political, economic,
and intellectual world that made food and agricultural development—and
eventually the complete dismantling of the large estate system—the centerpiece of a national reform agenda in midcentury Chile. Building upon the
political demands of earlier social movements, like the AOAN, as well as
the policies enacted by physicians and scientists, like Eduardo Cruz-Coke,
the cohort of agronomists, economists, and agricultural engineers of which
Jorge Ahumada was a part forged deeper into understanding the nature of the
country's urban crisis. Like many leftist political organizers and labor activists
before them, they asked how it was possible for a country so well endowed
with agricultural resources to have become dependent on the agricultural
bounty of others to feed its own people.

While nutrition researchers had examined household consumer habits
to answer that question, Ahumada and his contemporaries eventually came
to the conclusion that Chile's urban crisis was the product of the rigid social
and economic structures that restricted agricultural production. The concentration of land in the Chilean countryside offered farmers few incentives
to change what, how, and how much food was produced. Semifeudal labor

conditions and a generalized lack of economic opportunity for rural laborers precipitated the unplanned migration of thousands of Chileans into urban spaces. As a result, invaluable amounts of foreign exchange were diverted away from broader development projects to fulfill the country's basic nutritional needs with expensive imports. Chileans were struggling to just keep their collective economic head above water, and as Ahumada saw it, the country needed to undo the uneven relationship between city and country if it hoped to create a sustainable model of growth.

MODERN FOODWAYS

Ahumada and his generation of postwar social scientists were hardly the first to draw connections between urban needs and Chile's untapped agrarian potential. In its 1918 manifesto, the trailblazing labor-consumer association, the AOAN, had led the way in demanding a new model of integral development that crossed the rural-urban divide. As it denounced the tariffs the Chilean government levied on food imports, the movement attacked the state's willingness to prioritize the profits and property rights of inefficient domestic food producers over the nutritional needs of working-class consumers.[7] While its base of support resided in expanding metropolitan areas like Santiago, the AOAN was also arguably the first national movement in Chile to call for the expansion of a moderate program of national land redistribution—what reformers of the era called "colonization"—to reduce the cost of basic foodstuffs.[8] In what today might be categorized as a variant of urban ecosocialism, one of the AOAN's lead organizers, Evaristo Ríos, even argued that socialism in the Chilean context meant ending, once and for all, a situation in which "death by hunger" threatened a large segment of society. In the movement militant's view, such a position extended the promise of the French Revolution, a world historical event that had "liberated humankind" but notably failed to "liberate the land."[9]

When a global economic crisis consumed Chile in the 1930s, scenes of urban bread lines and soup kitchens, as well as the familiar sight of worker itinerancy between the countryside, mining camps, and cities, provided a propitious entrée for the state and labor leaders to further assess the ties that both bound urban and rural spaces together and pulled them apart. As surging unemployment taxed the social and economic infrastructure of Santiago and Valparaíso, public officials and economic thinkers considered plans to resettle the jobless in underproducing rural parishes, imagining the countryside as an escape valve. The social stress of urban migration, state builders maintained, could be quelled if those who fled shuttered nitrate camps were encouraged to work the fertile lands of Chile's agricultural regions. In this way, the social and economic burdens of physical displacement would be redirected away from the formal wage economy of the city and toward forms of subsistence production in the rural sector.[10]

Such proposals were at times amplified by the demands of rural workers themselves. Brian Loveman has described how in the years surrounding the Great Depression many agricultural workers, lacking legally recognized unions, took up forms of resistance based on "pilferage, sabotage, strikes, work slowdowns, or individual acts of violence." These everyday acts of defiance sought to reestablish "customary prerogatives," like pasture rights and access to special land allotments for the purpose of subsistence agriculture.[11] To demonstrate how access to food constituted a means of social and physical control in the countryside, the Trotskyist labor activist Emilio Zapata even used his own savings to pay for chemical analyses of the often adulterated food rations that landowners provided to their peasant labor force.[12]

Speaking during this period of economic uncertainty, former AOAN leader Carlos Alberto Martínez called land the most "vital problem" facing the country: "We should never forget that, as a country with so much cultivatable land, capable of producing food for more than 20 million people, we have the shameful distinction of having among a population of just four and a half million people, many thousands of families that are unable to meet their most basic nutritional needs."[13] As Chile's minister of lands and colonization in the 1930s, Martínez took preliminary steps toward remedying these disparities by initiating pilot projects in land redistribution, including the establishment of small agricultural colonies that resettled more than one thousand Chilean families.[14]

Worries about food insecurity helped set the stage for Pedro Aguirre Cerda's 1938 electoral victory, and with the FP in power, progressive activists expected that an agrarian plan that addressed rural labor exploitation and concerns over land tenure and reformed antiquated methods of food production would be atop the new government's agenda for change. Martínez himself confidently proclaimed that the FP government would move quickly to carry out such reforms, thus providing "to all Chilean homes" the "sustenance they required."[15] Upon assuming office, however, the Aguirre Cerda government offered only qualified support for the multifaceted organizing work around food, labor, and land that left-wing political movements had spearheaded. A new system of labor courts theoretically recognized the rights of rural workers as equal to their urban counterparts, but in practice the government continued to back the interests of large landowners. Despite having campaigned on a platform that included support for rural unionization, the FP also upheld an earlier order from Chile's Labor Department that had indefinitely suspended state recognition of rural unions.[16] In the absence of a rural agenda that included trade union rights or land redistribution, the FP and the various governments that guided Chile into the post–Second World War period promoted agrarian development when it bolstered the broader push toward urban industrialization.

The perspective of Chilean lawyer and diplomat Hernán Santa Cruz was illustrative in this regard. A leading figure behind the creation of the Santiago-based, UN-run CEPAL, Santa Cruz became one of the foremost voices on agricultural matters across Latin America during the postwar period, first serving as the UN Food and Agriculture Organization's (FAO) senior representative for Latin America and later convening the UN's first conference on agrarian reform in 1966.[17] But throughout much of this period, Santa Cruz argued that malnutrition and hunger should be viewed through a productionist prism—that is, as social problems that could be remedied through new foreign trade arrangements and intensified industrialization. Food was first and foremost a "problem of production" rather than a matter of inequitable "distribution," the diplomat maintained in a speech in 1947 that celebrated the UN's formation of CEPAL. Industrialization and economic diversification, he went on to argue, were widely recognized by the most respected economic minds of the day as the best way to improve a given population's living standards.[18]

Early food policies tended to reflect the emphasis that diplomats like Santa Cruz placed on production. Consider, for example, the push to develop Chile's canning industry in the 1940s and 1950s—an initiative that was driven, at least in part, by the state's desire to meet the nutritional needs of urban workers and their families. As Chile entered the postwar era, industrialists contended that canned foods, or *conservas*, were an effective means of stretching Chile's existing agricultural bounty in order to ensure urban consumers' access to inexpensive, healthy, domestically produced food options year-round.[19] In the absence of readily available refrigerated railcars and storage sites, a variety of "home-grown" foodstuffs—everything from fish and seafood to fruits, vegetables, and meats—could be quickly preserved at one of the more than sixty canneries that operated in Chile by the late 1940s. By using tin produced at Chile's Huachipato steel factory, in the southern province of Concepción, canning also generated new industrial employment opportunities.[20]

To overcome popular skepticism about the taste of conservas, Chile's canning industry took it upon itself to teach Chilean consumers about the economic and gastronomic benefits of canned goods. One of the most notable such campaigns involved an advertising icon named Tía Paulina (Aunt Paulina). Conceived by the Chilean canners' association in the 1950s, the marketing initiative established special "test kitchens" at various canning facilities. At each kitchen, Tía Paulina—part chef, part home economics instructor—prepared two stews, or *guisos,* each day using a variety of canned products. When the meals were plated, a special radio broadcast shared the recipes and results of Tía's daily culinary creations. Every two months accompanying recipes were also printed in the bimonthly trade bulletin of the canners' association.[21]

Milk and bread were two other staples that showcased Chile's commitment to modernizing how food was produced after the Second World War. Adopting methods and technologies developed by international food and dairy giant Nestlé, the Compañía Chilena de Productos Alimenticios (Chilean Food Products Company, CHIPRODAL), expanded manufacturing of long-lasting processed milk products, particularly powdered and condensed milk. At three processing facilities, CHIPRODAL nearly tripled its annual production of condensed milk and more than quadrupled its annual production of powdered milk between 1937 and 1946.[22] A decade and a half later, Chile had the capacity to produce some sixty thousand liters of powdered milk daily at sixteen processing plants.[23] As with canned fruits, vegetables, seafood, and meat, a growing prevalence of stable, long-lasting, and easily transportable dairy products promised to increase nutritional options for those living in urban areas and the far-flung population centers of the Norte Grande, where fresh milk was often impossible to find or prohibitively expensive.[24] When it came to bread, meanwhile, the Instituto Nacional de Comercio, formed in 1953, used a special Santiago facility that it established with FAO assistance to showcase modern yeast fermentation chambers and large British-manufactured baking ovens. The new state economic agency also offered training classes so Chilean bakers could learn about more efficient baking technologies and production methods.[25]

While the Chilean state played a key role in subsidizing the industrialization of food, the modernization of the agrarian sector received public sector attention as well. During its first half decade of operation, Chile's national development agency, the Corporación de Fomento (CORFO), extended credit and other forms of financial assistance to beef and dairy farmers. It also supported the country's main milk processing and distribution company, the Central de Leche, and facilitated the importation of new, award-winning cattle pedigrees into Chile to create a more robust national beef and dairy stock.[26] CORFO agents had particular interest in the production of fertilizers for domestic use and the introduction of new farming implements. While the development agency helped import new farm machinery from abroad, it also provided seed capital to Chilean industrialists to begin domestically manufacturing said implements, particularly tractors. As a result of these combined efforts, the number of total tractors in Chile more than doubled, from 1,557 in 1936 to 3,337 in 1943.[27]

At the same time, CORFO experimented with new agricultural crops to reduce dependence on food imports. The cultivation of oil-producing plants like sunflowers, soybeans, sesame, peanuts, and turnip seeds was a principal focus in this regard. After discovering that many of these plants did not require especially fertile soil to thrive, agricultural engineers affiliated with CORFO's Committee for the Promotion of Oleaginous Plants brought acres of previously disregarded agricultural land into cultivation. Motivated by the cooking oil shortages that had struck Chile after the Second World War, development officials also extended special credit to industrialists who were willing to process the plants into cooking oils.[28] By 1960, thirty-one factories in Chile produced nearly thirty-two metric tons of edible oils annually, covering roughly two-thirds of Chile's domestic needs.[29]

CORFO's various experimental efforts in the agricultural sector were synthesized in Chile's 1954 Plan Agrario (Agrarian Plan). Drafted jointly by CORFO and Chile's Ministry of Agriculture, the document represented arguably the most comprehensive policy statement on Chile's agricultural modernization efforts to date, laying out objectives that included improving national consumers' access to key nutritional goods, reversing the country's trade imbalance by replacing food imports with domestic production, intensifying per hectare productivity, and creating new markets for nonagricultural goods in the countryside itself.[30] These plans assumed that if existing rural estates adopted new techniques and technologies, total agricultural production in Chile would increase by approximately 40 percent, with important urban staples, like wheat and comestible oils, leading the way.[31]

CORFO technicians approached the agriculturally rich Central Valley and Bío-Bío regions as sites of experimentation to begin translating their ideas into action. With the assistance of the US Point IV development program, the FAO, and the World Bank, the Chilean development agency transformed the rural provinces of Maule, Ñuble, and Concepción into "demonstration areas" for rural development in the early 1950s. Dubbed Plan Chillán, after the rural Chilean town that sat at the geographic center of the program, the pilot project first focused on the establishment of an agricultural college in Chile's Central Valley, where a combination of Chilean and US technicians, most of them hailing from the University of California system, would teach a new generation of agricultural engineers and agronomists to manage everything from public works projects, such as road building, irrigation, and railway construction, to new crop experiments. Hoping that a more well-integrated countryside would resolve Chile's agrarian woes, just as the Tennessee Valley Authority had in the US South, planners expected that the lessons learned from reforestation and soil rehabilitation initiatives would eventually be extended to other parts of the Chilean countryside.[32]

Though the origins of the development of Chile's national sugar beet industry fell slightly outside the specific parameters of Plan Chillán, few state-supported agricultural enterprises received more political attention and state support during this period. Chilean lawmakers and intellectuals touted the creation of the CORFO-backed Industria Azucarera Nacional (National Sugar Industry, IANSA) as a natural spark for a more economically harmonious mode of agricultural and industrial development. A robust national sugar industry would save Chile valuable foreign exchange by reducing dependence on imported sugar. The cultivation of sugar beets would also generate important by-products, such as animal feed, ethanol, and nutrient-replenished farm soil.[33] Sugar beet farming had the added benefits of bringing underused land into year-round production and, at least initially, employing a permanent rural labor force as well. As such, state officials believed the industry would slow out-migration from the countryside to the city. Of greatest long-term significance, at least to the country's urban observers, was the possibility that the industry might channel new industrial technology into other sectors of the national economy.[34]

Development experts hailed Chile's national sugar beet industry as one of the region's great success stories in state-led economic planning. Just one decade after IANSA opened its first processing plant, annual domestic production of sugar in Chile surged from 4,530 tons to nearly 110,000 tons.

IANSA's existence meant that, by the mid-1960s, Chile was producing half of all sugar its citizens consumed, and as government officials and sugar beet farmers pursued plans for continued expansion, domestic production was projected to reach 220,000 tons in 1970.[35]

The social impact of domestic sugar production was even greater. The industry provided steady employment, whether in IANSA plants or sugar beet fields, for some ten thousand rural workers and their families.[36] In the area around the provincial city of Llanquihue, data collected in 1969 showed that 58 percent of all income earned by small agriculturalists in the area came from sugar beet cultivation. When small farmers in the region were asked in the late 1960s if they were satisfied with the purchasing agreements signed with IANSA's four sugar processing plants in operation at the time, 84 percent responded yes.[37]

But despite such instances of fanfare and success, neither food industrialization efforts, nor agrarian development efforts like Plan Chillán, nor the creation of IANSA fully resolved the contradictions and inequities that marked the Chilean countryside and much of the bucolic Pacific coast. While major infrastructure projects expanded the amount of agricultural land under cultivation, the adoption of new, labor-saving technologies frequently led to fewer and less stable employment opportunities than rural residents anticipated. With the richest soil still primarily in the hands of large landowners, economic prospects for rural residents, particularly those of indigenous origin, scarcely improved as speculators grabbed the land on which they depended to meet subsistence needs. When national austerity led to a decline in rural investment and access to credit, production fell, sparking widespread rural unemployment.[38] Those infrastructure projects that did continue through the lean years of the 1950s and early 1960s proved largely incapable of halting seasonal migration and itinerancy across the countryside. While the population of Chile's countryside grew by approximately 2 percent in the 1950s, the population of Santiago grew by twice that figure. In sum, roughly 550,000 Chileans left the countryside for more urban areas during the 1950s, despite agricultural improvement efforts.[39]

Urban life presented its own set of challenges. In the 1920s and 1930s, migrants typically found shelter in the tenements of downtown Santiago. In contrast, the predominantly rural migrants who entered Santiago in the 1950s and 1960s were pushed to the capital's geographic periphery, where land and housing disputes pitted migrant squatters against absentee property owners. Facing prohibitive public transportation costs and irregular service, rural migrants found it difficult to obtain a stable, well-paying job. Increasingly, migrants found political allies in the country's middling sectors, whose own social mobility was constrained by the same economic concerns. But such alliances hardly prevented tensions from boiling over into public conflicts.[40]

Two of the most prominent such incidents occurred in 1957, when thousands of members of Chile's increasingly organized community of *pobladores* (urban poor) joined Chilean students to protest the rising cost of basic goods and services. As the once-subsidized price for urban transport soared, popular protests on the streets of Santiago peaked. During the first week of April, state security forces killed dozens of protestors in one of twentieth-century Chile's largest urban uprisings. Just a few months later, a smaller group of pobladores carried out the first massive urban land invasion, known as the *toma* (occupation) of La Victoria, in response to the state's failure to prioritize the construction of affordable housing for low-income residents.[41]

Writing in 1958, one year after the Santiagazo, Ahumada identified growing urban inequality as the most striking symptom of Chile's social crisis. The unplanned nature and rapid pace of urbanization was transforming Santiago into a "spectacle" where the "sordid poverty of the many" existed alongside the "boastful ostentatiousness of the few," Ahumada declared in *En vez de la miseria*. One would be hard pressed to find another city in all of Latin America composed of both "such luxurious homes and 'mushroom-like' shantytowns (*callampas*) that were so miserable," the social scientist contended.[42] A pamphlet promoting rural reform in the 1960s took Ahumada's observation one step further, arguing that the urban unrest Chile experienced in those years was rooted in the "backwardness" of the rural economy. The pamphlet's authors declared that because state officials had not "suitably dealt with the agrarian problem," "misery" was being "transported from the countryside to the marginalized squatter settlements in the city."[43]

CITY AND COUNTRY

Chile's PDC, the political party with whom Ahumada's political allegiance rested, began to break up and redistribute the country's largest agricultural estates after winning a decisive victory in the 1964 presidential election. During the subsequent decade, the Chilean state would expropriate nearly half of the country's agricultural lands, promote the unionization of thousands of rural workers, and channel an unprecedented amount of public money into nonurban communities. As a result, a semifeudal social structure based upon peonage and patronage was gradually replaced by a wage labor system that combined private, cooperative, and collective property arrangements. Through a web of new state-run agricultural agencies, rural peasants also received training in modern farming techniques and gained access to basic social services, like education and medical care. Until 1973, these accomplishments made the Chilean Agrarian Reform arguably the most far-reaching, peaceful such project carried out by a democratically elected government anywhere in Latin America and perhaps the world.[44]

By offering a path between socialist revolution, which members of Chile's organized left demanded, and the retrenchment of landholder interests, which the country's right-wing forces supported, perhaps the boldest promise of Chile's Christian Democrats was that they could fulfill the divergent pleas of the city and the country at the same time. After hearing Eduardo Frei discuss his ambitions for the Chilean countryside, one US agricultural official working in Chile in the 1960s saluted the new government. "In Chile . . . city people want a better diet, peasants their own land," the North American observer noted. "Chile hopes its agrarian reform will help satisfy both demands."[45]

The form and content of agrarian production promoted during Frei's tenure underscored the Christian Democrats' desire to fulfill the expectations of these two distinct constituencies. State efforts to develop the country's chicken and pork industry were illustrative in this regard. On the one hand, agricultural experts believed that the domestic production of these two relatively fast-replenishing sources of protein would satisfy the appetites of a growing urban class of consumers, particularly at a time when red meat remained scarce and expensive.[46] When it came to pork, agricultural officials not only sought to increase production by extending credits to new hog farming cooperatives for infrastructural improvements and animal purchases, but they also trained a new cohort of hog farmers in modern techniques of butchering, salting, curing, and eventually commercializing their products. Agricultural experts believed modern meat-processing methods would ensure that no part of a given pig went to waste. Farmers' use of proper preservation methods also extended the time in which their product needed to reach market and be consumed. Ultimately, a more holistic approach to meat production decreased the need for expensive refrigeration capacity and allowed the state to hold back from the consumer market a portion of the country's total pork stock during moments of excess supply.[47]

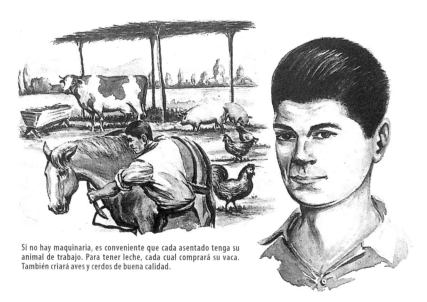

Si no hay maquinaria, es conveniente que cada asentado tenga su animal de trabajo. Para tener leche, cada cual comprará su vaca. También criará aves y cerdos de buena calidad.

FIGURE 6. The Chilean state encourages agrarian reform beneficiaries to produce new sources of protein, including chickens and pigs. "If machinery is unavailable, each asentado should have a work horse. To obtain milk, he will possess a cow. He will also raise quality chickens and pigs." Land Tenure Center Files, Steenbock Memorial Library, University of Wisconsin, Madison.

On the other hand, agricultural officials emphasized that chicken and hog production represented a unique economic opportunity for a new generation of small landholders—a long-term pathway toward the second goal of the Christian Democrats' agrarian reform efforts: raising the incomes of small-scale farmers.[48] "Raising chickens" will be "good business," the country's bimonthly bulletin optimistically declared in an article on the importance of chicken production to small farmers' livelihoods.[49] These sorts of proclamations were supported by projections about growing consumer demand: while domestic chicken consumption was estimated at fifty-four thousand tons in 1968, state consumption models projected that the country was on track to be eating nearly seventy-nine thousand tons of the bird just a few years later.[50] New chicken farmers would need to be patient, however. According to a 1967 profile of one new chicken enterprise in the province of O'Higgins, expenditures were calculated to be more than double the profits earned during the farm's first year of production. Experts estimated that it could take as long as three years for the cooperative to get out of the red and into the black.[51]

The state's focus on the cultivation of garden produce—things like tomatoes, carrots, potatoes, cabbage, and a variety of greens—was motivated by similar desires to both expand small farmers' opportunities to earn income and provide urban consumers with inexpensive, nutritious, and relatively abundant food options. From the state's perspective, very few economic resources were needed to, for example, teach small farmers how to produce cabbages and carrots year-round, properly store vegetable seeds, and warehouse harvested potatoes in cold-storage facilities to prevent spoilage and sprouting.[52] Though the investment was more substantial, state and international assistance for the construction of canning facilities in the heart of Chile's agricultural regions provided rural farmers with a new market of buyers. Starting in late 1966, a new cannery in the city of Los Andes was expected to churn out as many as five hundred units of canned fruit and legumes daily. Officials anticipated that a similar facility, opened in the southern province of Cautín that same year, would have the capacity to produce as many as fifteen hundred units of canned tomatoes, artichokes, various local fruits, meats, and fish each day.[53] Just as development experts had insisted a decade earlier, urban consumers would ultimately benefit from this new economic relationship as they gained the ability to eat fruits and vegetables throughout the year.

For many reformers, a model of the rural-urban economic harmony they sought to create was embodied in a cooperative garden system near the southern city of Concepción. Known as the gardens of San Pedro, the network of small vegetable patches produced a variety of produce, flowers, and fruit, especially apples, in addition to a small amount of poultry and pork. According to a leader of one of the cooperatives that comprised the network, the gardens' creation was motivated by a desire to "resolve food supply matters" in the nearby city of Concepción. But the benefits to rural producers were also readily apparent. Upon visiting San Pedro in early 1966, a writer from Chile's agrarian reform bulletin who was sent to visit the gardens reported that he was struck by two things. The first was that through the formation of a cooperative, small farmers were able to "achieve the most advantageous marketing of their products." The second was that the consumer public got the best prices possible for those same products. "Nobody abuses anybody else," he concluded.[54]

The case of San Pedro also illustrated the Frei administration's push to extend the principles of economic rationalization to one of Chile's long-standing logistical problems: how to move agricultural products across the

"Al término del Asentamiento, dentro de nuestra Cooperativa, seremos todos propietarios.

El título de propiedad se entregará a aquellos de nosotros que hayamos demostrado apti-

tud y capacidad para el trabajo agrícola. A los flojos les llegará al pihuelo".

FIGURE 7. A drawing in an agrarian reform pamphlet promotes vegetable growing and the establishment of cooperatives. "When the Asentamiento is complete, we'll all be property owners within our Cooperative. A land title will be given to those who have demonstrated aptitude and capacity for agricultural work. Those who are undisciplined will not be tolerated." Land Tenure Center Files, Steenbock Memorial Library, University of Wisconsin, Madison.

country's complicated national geography. A report produced by North American agricultural expert Frances Foland in 1968 provided a vivid account of how an outdated distribution system strangled Chilean consumers and producers alike. In what Foland described as a model of logistical inefficiency, fruits, vegetables, and numerous other foodstuffs were in the 1960s still being hauled from the country's agricultural heartland to a single market, the Vega Central, in Santiago. There the country's agricultural bounty was promptly unloaded and divvied up to concessionaires in a chaotic auction system. After auction, buyers then reloaded much of their acquired bounty back onto trucks, often for a return trip to its place of origin, only to be resold yet again, this time at a price that ensured profit to the various intermediaries through whose hands the foods had passed. "In a plexus emanating from this center, a 'negative flow' returns potatoes to Melipilla from whose soil they were dug, tomatoes to the truck garden area of Quillota, and apples to the orchard country north of Chillán," Foland astutely observed. Neither producer nor consumer benefited from such an arrangement.[55]

As an alternative to the perplexing system that Foland and others described, agrarian technicians and state planning officials envisioned a distribution system that was under partial state control. The Empresa de Comercio Agrícola (Agricultural Trading Company, ECA), a national agricultural agency that had been established under the government of Jorge Alessandri in 1960, was envisaged as the axis of this new system: an institutional mechanism to skirt the logistical inefficiencies of places like the Vega Central and its price-gouging distribution syndicates. Starting in the late 1960s, the Bío-Bío region would become a pilot case for the government's efforts in this area. Centered around the growing urban hub of Concepción but encompassing the provinces of Ñuble, Arauco, Malleco, and Bío-Bío itself, ECA sought to begin what it described as "a new stage of decentralization" when it came to food distribution.[56]

Indeed, a key objective of logistics planners at ECA was to reduce the distance between rural farms and urban tables. The advantages of this were twofold: regional consumer markets would not be depleted by the consumer demands of those living in Santiago, while those living in Santiago would gain a semblance of nutritional independence from the country's more distant agrarian hinterlands. With that in mind, the Frei administration devoted particular energy toward improving agrarian productivity in those areas closest to urban consumers. Some of the Frei administration's earliest attempts to promote a new model of regional development occurred in the Maule region—a three-province, 21,670-square-kilometer area located some 300 kilometers south of Santiago. Launched by Chile's Ministry of Agriculture in the winter of 1964, the Maule Project sought to construct a system of regional irrigation, promote intensive agriculture practices and hydroelectric power production, and build value-added food manufacturing plants on arguably Chile's most agriculturally rich lands.[57] In the early 1970s, the project became the basis for the Allende government's proposal to create a special agro-industrial development corporation for the region.[58]

Attempts to promote regional agricultural production and streamline consumer access to basic foodstuffs embodied economic experts' vision of nationally inclusive but regionally based agrarian economies. In 1969, the primary public bulletin of Chile's agrarian reform initiative, *Quiubo Compadre*, reported glowingly on the Frei administration's plan to divide the country into fifteen distinct agricultural development zones. In each, the state would work with local farmers to set production goals for nearly every agricultural crop imaginable: from wheat to corn, oats, barley, rice, and potatoes to beans, sunflower, rapeseed, sugar beets, peas, onions, melons, green beans, tomatoes, peaches, apples, oranges, grapes, beef, lamb, chicken, pork, milk, and eggs.[59] By 1970 the foundation for such a system was solidified through the creation of zonal agrarian development offices, which aimed to coordinate production matters with agrarian reform settlements in each region.[60] According to Jesús González, the Chilean agronomist and former UN economic official who helped to devise the plan, regional planning was a prerequisite for Chile to achieve "self-sufficiency" in the area of food production.[61]

In a book he published in 1964, Jacques Chonchol stretched ideas of regional agricultural development across a continental canvas. As a leading voice for agrarian reform within the Chilean PDC and the vice president of the state-run technical assistance agency, the Instituto de Desarrollo Agropecuario (Institute for Agrarian Development, INDAP) during much of the Frei era, Chonchol argued for the creation of multiple zones of agrarian development across Latin America. He maintained that Latin American agricultural experts needed to think about economic and agricultural development not in terms of "the national boundaries of each country" but rather as a project of "Latin American geographic unity." To that end, Chonchol proposed working with Chile's Latin American and Caribbean neighbors to establish more than a dozen agricultural zones in the region. The planned, cooperative coordination between neighbors would make not just Chile but the entire region more nutritionally self-sufficient. It would also deflate the threat posed by competing forms of economic nationalism.[62]

A GREEN REVOLUTION IN LIBERTY

The Frei government's attempt to balance urban and rural needs frequently included an emphasis on technology and technique. The professional scientist turned agrarian reformer Manuel Elgueta exemplified this fact, while also illuminating the diverse circuits of agricultural knowledge that Chile's Christian Democrats drew from to break the country's dependence on foreign food sources and simultaneously improve rural and urban living standards. A plant geneticist by training, Elgueta, like his contemporary Ahumada, had traversed the hemisphere during the middle decades of the twentieth century, studying and collaborating with leading midcentury agricultural scientists. In Elgueta's case, his Pan-American journey had included coursework at the University of California, Berkeley in the early 1930s as well as observational stints and collaborations with agronomists and plant scientists at leading US agricultural institutions like the University of Minnesota, Cornell University, and the University of California, Davis. After the conclusion of the Second World War, Elgueta became a widely respected scientific voice in the hemisphere, promoting agricultural cooperation from a post at the newly created, Costa Rica–based Inter-American Institute for Agricultural Cooperation (IICA), the brainchild of hybrid seed promoter and former US vice president Henry Wallace.[63]

When the new Frei government assumed office, Elgueta's expertise and professional connections around the Americas made him the ideal candidate to run the day-to-day operations of Chile's Instituto Nacional de Investigación Agrícola (National Institute for Agricultural Research, INIA). The successor to a smaller research unit that had been housed within the state's fisheries and agriculture agency, INIA became a laboratory for agricultural experimentation after its founding in 1964. At three primary research stations, opened between 1959 and 1964 in three distinct agricultural regions of Chile, plus another seven experimental substations, agronomists rigorously examined everything from the relationship between fertilizer usage and the density of crop yields to the susceptibility of various grain varieties to destructive insect infestations. INIA's research stations also became testing sites for assessing the impact of newly developed pesticides and herbicides and experimenting with new pasturing techniques.[64]

INIA's ultimate goal reflected some of the core objectives of what in the late 1960s became known as the "Green Revolution": to intensify production on agricultural lands through the development of higher-yield food crops and crossbreeding of animal species.[65] The fundamental staples of the Chilean working-class diet were the most notable subjects of INIA's early inquiries. In 1967 and 1968, for example, INIA introduced four new potato varieties to Chile and began promoting their cultivation to the country's farming communities, stressing their high yields and "excellent culinary qualities." At the same time, INIA began trials on chemical herbicides, like Chloro IPC, to inhibit potato sprouting after cultivation.[66] In a quest to increase the production of domestic cooking oils, INIA scientists also experimented with two new varieties of sunflower, Armavirski-3497 and Peredovik. They quickly discovered that the new varieties, both of which originated in the Soviet Union, could increase per hectare cooking oil production by more than 20 percent. A Soviet lentil variety, Penzenskaja-14, showed similar promise, producing a larger, more disease-resistant harvest.[67]

Chile's Christian Democrats used new state agencies to promote other signature technologies of the Green Revolution as well. Consistent with the mandate of the country's first land reform law, passed two years before Frei's election, Frei used INDAP to facilitate small growers' access to fertilizers rich in nitrogen, phosphorous, potassium, and calcium, as well as pesticides, insecticides, and hybrid seeds.[68] According to a study of thirty-five small corn farmers on an agricultural settlement that had been created in 1964, between 1965 and 1966 use of insecticides increased by 30 percent, use of nitrogen fertilizers by 20.5 percent, and use of hybrid seeds by 57 percent.[69] Just a few years later, the Chilean government's decision to allow, for the first time ever, the importation of synthetic fertilizers led to a near-doubling in fertilizer usage around the country between 1967 and 1973, albeit at the expense of Chile's own storied nitrate industry.[70]

INDAP and other agrarian agencies also organized dozens of agricultural training courses. As part of these efforts, the Frei government dispatched newly trained development technicians to the countryside to teach agrarian reform beneficiaries best practices for seeding fields and preventing crops from succumbing to pests and inclement weather.[71] With the assistance of CORFO, agricultural experts also worked with newly formed cooperatives to instruct campesinos how to use and maintain heated chicken coops, mechanized tilling and harvesting equipment, and of course, tractors.[72] During just the first year of the Frei administration's tenure, total CORFO investment in the agricultural sector increased by more than 80 percent.[73]

Despite efforts at diversification, the area of Chile's agricultural economy that continued to receive the lion's share of state attention during this period was its beef industry, a subsector that remained largely in the hands of big landholders. Between 1964 and 1965, the state development corporation's total investment in beef production was estimated to have increased by an astounding 257 percent. Much of that money went toward creating a national network of beef slaughterhouses, a project that had begun under Frei's

Para cultivar grandes extensiones, a tiempo y en forma económica, conviene utilizar maquinaria.
La maquinaria es cara, pero se paga a 5 años plazo.
Los campesinos la compran entre todos. La pagarán con las mayores utilidades y se harán dueños de un importante capital.

FIGURE 8. An agrarian reform publication demonstrates the importance of modern farming technology. "To cultivate large areas in a timely, efficient manner, it's helpful to use machinery. Machinery is expensive but it can be paid for over a five-year period. Campesinos pool their resources to buy together. They will pay for it using their profits and will then be owners of an important capital investment." Land Tenure Center Files, Steenbock Memorial Library, University of Wisconsin, Madison.

predecessor Alessandri and which envisaged the construction of a modern, sanitary, and decentralized complex of more than a dozen processing facilities. By 1969 the government's state agricultural subsidiary, the Sociedad de Construcciones y Operaciones Agropecuarias (Corporation for Agricultural Construction and Operations, SOCOAGRO), had constructed five such facilities, each strategically located near some of the country's most populous consumer centers.[74] During the Frei presidency, state financial assistance also flowed toward other projects that preserved, and in some cases expanded, the interests of beef producers and processors—for instance, the building of at least four cured meat (*cecina*) factories in Santiago, Chillán, Temuco, and Valdivia.[75]

Following the production chain for beef illuminates the problematic nature of agricultural officials' sustained focus on animal production in general. As the Chilean state stressed the need to expand the production of domestic sources of protein—whether beef, chicken, or pork—it accelerated the transformation of Chile's available farmland into a feed source for animals rather than a source of direct human consumption. As a result, the distance between farm and table grew longer. The rapid rise in the production of corn and barley—key grains for the beef cattle, chicken, and hogs that increasingly lived in feedlot-style conditions—and the concurrent slow growth or stagnation for commodities like potatoes, beans, and wheat—all key staples in the human diet—illustrates the gradual industrialization of Chile's agricultural sector during agrarian reform. While Chile produced just over 1.76 million metric *quintals* of corn and just over 697,000 metric quintals of barley in 1963, by 1968 the country was producing over 3.2 million metric quintals of the former and 1.5 million metric quintals of the latter.[76] Over roughly that same period, total potato production declined, bean production flatlined, and wheat production grew only slightly—this despite the introduction of several new high-yield, bug-resistant wheat varieties.[77]

RESOURCEFUL CONSUMERS

As the final year of Frei's presidential term began, Chile's agricultural planning office sought to highlight the significance of agrarian reform for rural consumers by contrasting the total quantity of a variety of staple goods that a campesina could have purchased with her husband's average monthly salary in 1969 as opposed to the same average salary a half decade earlier. Whereas the average income for a rural family in 1964 was equivalent to the cost of 235 liters of fresh milk, 45 dozen eggs, 24 kilos of beef cazuela, 84 kilos of beans, 145 kilos of potatoes, or 98 kilos of bread, in 1969, the new average rural income equaled 375 liters of fresh milk, 60 dozen eggs, 54 kilos of beef cazuela, 144 kilos of beans, 505 kilos of potatoes, or 223 kilos of bread.[78] Such figures demonstrated a state of newfound economic and nutritional security in many rural homes. "We had plenty of food to eat in those years," one agrarian leader recalled, equating improved nutrition and access to warm clothing with a sense of rural dignity.[79]

But beneath such numbers and recollections lay a deep contradiction: at the same time that rural families saw their incomes and purchasing power rise, state officials actively promoted a message that rural restraint, sacrifice, and resourcefulness were virtues to be modeled and applauded. In that sense, the *asentamiento*, or settlement, system became a physical site through which agrarian reform beneficiaries were taught not just modern techniques for agricultural production but also the value of self-reliance and thrift.

Created under the Frei administration's more expansive 1967 Agrarian Reform Law (Law 16.640), which allowed the state to expropriate any estate that included more than eighty hectares of irrigated land or the land of land-owners who were not abiding by social legislation, the asentamiento was a form of territorial organization that comprised either the entirety of a once privately run rural estate or combined multiple smaller estates into a single administrative unit. All of the land that fell within the territorial boundaries of a given asentamiento would be legally controlled by the state for an interim period of time—usually between three and five years. After that point, land reform beneficiaries, known as *asentados*, would together decide whether to adopt an individual, cooperative, or collective land tenure arrangement on the property they worked.[80]

During the transitional period, state economists, agronomists, planning officials, and rural union leaders worked through the asentamiento system to set production schedules; organize their own productive endeavors; and transfer knowledge about crop rotation, animal vaccinations, and the use of fertilizers and pesticides.[81] Such guidance made the asentamiento "the best school imaginable" for rural workers, according to INDAP officials—a sort of training center in which campesinos entered with little or no formal agricultural education, acquired new know-how, and then exited with the ability to sustain themselves and their communities.[82] However, beyond simply improving the productivity of rural lands or bettering working conditions for rural workers, the asentamiento was also envisioned by the state as a site to promote new social and economic behaviors within peasant communities.

The model asentado, state officials argued, was someone who was simultaneously a productive laborer, an innovative *empresario* (business person), *and* a conscientious household consumer. For men, this meant foregoing antisocial behaviors like drinking and revelry, activities that recklessly squandered newly acquired wages and negatively impacted worker productivity.[83] To help asentados understand the importance of productivity and discipline, the Chilean state produced and distributed short, image-laden stories that explained, in simple narrative form, basic economic terms like "credit," "investment," and "debt."[84] In one such manual, two campesinos, Juan Farías and his neighbor Eduardo Pérez, earn some 4,000 escudos after becoming members of their asentamiento. Of that money, the two allocate more than half to paying off their debts. But what do to with the approximately 1,500 escudos that remained, the story's protagonists ask?[85] The two debate this question as they walk through the fields of their asentamiento. Laughing with delight, Pérez reveals his plan to go to town one evening to spend his remaining earnings. His wiser friend Farías quickly suggests that Pérez reconsider the idea. "In a short time this land will be handed over to us. And then we are going to have to pay for it," Farías reminds his neighbor. "What's more, we'll have to obtain everything we need to work the land well," Farías notes, stressing the social value of restraint and saving.[86]

When it came to rural women, the Frei government promoted narratives about female participation in agrarian reform that were even more firmly rooted in traditional notions of domestic sacrifice. In the conclusion to CORA's aforementioned illustrated parable, Juan Farías returns to his home, where the principles of thrift are applauded once again, this time in the household setting. After telling his wife, Rosa Elvira, that the money from the harvest has been safely deposited in the bank, Farías inquires if the family is lacking any essentials for their home or their children. Rosa Elvira's negative response both impresses and delights him. "We'll spend the least amount possible. There are other more important things," she tells her husband. "The most important thing is the land."[87]

When inflation and scarcity returned in the late 1960s, agrarian reform agencies reinforced the message that it was women's patriotic duty to sacrifice their own consumer experience for the sake of the larger good—even when rural incomes were rising. INDAP agents increasingly implored rural women to find high-protein alternatives for beef by raising their own small game, like rabbits, and purchasing protein substitutes, like fish.[88] They also taught these same communities how to prepare and preserve their own vegetables and dairy products. Finally, agrarian officials provided women with tutorials on how to maintain small family gardens and utilize household compost when larger agricultural operations siphoned off scarce fertilizers.[89]

Taken as a whole, state agencies' messaging to rural women emphasized that a woman's commitment to Chile's agrarian transformation, and therefore to the nation's economic well-being, was demonstrated through her resourcefulness at home. A woman who was committed to modernizing outdated structures of land tenure would be willing to embrace decidedly antimodern steps to aid the nation—for example, repurposing old jars as storage containers or using makeshift cooking devices in an effort to conserve the limited wages that her husband now earned.[90] With just four tin cans, one state-published instructional pamphlet noted, homemakers who lacked access to a real woodstove could construct a contraption that served the same function.[91] And with just a little bit of fabric and some old cardboard, a housewife could patch together an improvised shopping bag to carry to town on market days.[92]

The promotion of resourcefulness as a virtue in and of itself appeared to be more about the state's goal of ensuring urban consumers' needs and desires were still met during moments of scarcity than it was about extending dignity or equality to the countryside. The distribution of some seventy thousand sewing machines to rural women under the Frei government was perhaps the most iconic example of what might be called the modernity-sacrifice paradox that stood at the center of the Christian Democrats' approach to rural reform.[93] State-backed deliveries of sewing machines on the basis of credit that women received from their local Mothers' Centers (CEMAs), together with the proliferation of community sewing classes, gave rural women access to a vital durable appliance that saved time and energy in performing traditional domestic activities. The machines also gave women an opportunity to make a bit of cash, apart from whatever wages their husbands earned.[94] But at the same time, the sewing machine kept rural women out of the market for ready-to-wear clothing by making it easier for them to mend worn-out pants, shirts, and linens, and even produce their own clothing. In this way, the scarce fruits of consumer life—in this case, limited supplies of domestic textiles—would not be unintentionally redirected away from the still thin urban consumer marketplace.[95]

Ultimately, state narratives that had once promoted collective action and rural uplift sounded increasingly like advertisements for a sort of rugged rural individualism. As such, they worked at cross-purposes with many of the original communitarian goals of agrarian reform. In one news report about women's participation in agrarian reform, published by INDAP in 1968, state officials defined rural women's social role in notably narrow domestic terms: to oversee the health of their children, their husbands, and themselves.[96] In another piece published by that same magazine a few months later, the Frei administration similarly praised the example of a rural woman named Julia Román Calderón, suggesting that she embodied the ideal of rural womanhood. Describing Román Calderón as a supportive wife and mother of eight children, the piece focused on her tenacity and perseverance, epitomized in her daily routine. Each day, Román Calderón rose at seven in the morning and prepared breakfast for her husband and children. After her children departed for school and her husband for work in the fields, she quickly moved on to lunch preparations and laundry, then continued by making dinner and the snack, or *once*, that accompanied evening tea. In a time of crisis and rapid social and economic change, the bulletin argued that these everyday actions were the glue that held the reform process intact.[97] Few reform leaders acknowledged that they also reproduced gendered inequities within the home and spatial inequities between the city and countryside.

On the eve of the Second World War, Chile's agricultural exports surpassed the value of its agricultural imports by some US$13 million. However, as the global war began, those numbers began to flip. Food imports soared higher, reaching US$57 million as Chile contemplated breaking off relations with the Axis powers. Two decades later, Chile's food imports had surged to roughly US$160 million per year. Meanwhile, the country's agricultural exports fell for the first time in recent history, totaling just US$39 million in 1964.[98] It was in this context that economic experts identified Chile's agrarian economy as a—if not *the*—cause of a serious social and economic crisis. How Chile obtained its food exacerbated the country's bonds of economic dependence, to use the parlance of the era.

What had Chile's agrarian development efforts of the 1950s and 1960s done to undo this dependence? How had the livelihoods of Chile's rural and urban populations changed as a result? The answer to those questions was decidedly mixed. While technologies, like canning, and the establishment of new national industries, like the sugar industry, improved and regularized Chilean consumers' access to domestic food sources, political events and demographic trends of the 1950s suggested that they neither reduced the stresses of urban life nor created a more equitable relationship between city and country. During the 1960s, agrarian reform, which coupled the promotion of scientific agriculture with actual land redistribution, succeeded in many of the areas where earlier attempts to modernize and rationalize the food economy had come up short. During the first three years of Frei's presidency, real wages for agrarian workers increased almost fivefold. By 1967, it had become illegal for rural employers to pay their workers with in-kind payments rather than cash.[99] Both achievements were attributable to a wave of peasant strikes and petitions, which set the stage for more ambitious agrarian reform legislation in 1967, as well as a new law that promoted rural unionization. The latter landmark legislation opened the door to the creation of approximately thirty-five hundred union organizations and four large national rural labor confederations, which coordinated work between them.[100] Whereas just 1,658 rural workers belonged to unions in 1964, rural union membership had soared to nearly 102,000 by the end of Frei's presidential term.[101] By early 1970, more than 35,000 families were also members of over 230 agrarian cooperatives, a twentyfold increase in just a half decade.[102]

However, there were important caveats and qualifiers when it came to many of those accomplishments. Despite investments in high-yield crop varieties and fertilizers, agricultural production of key food crops often fell short of initial projections.[103] The Christian Democrats resolved neither the country's negative trade imbalance when it came to agricultural goods nor the problem of rural-to-urban migration. In fact, in the arena of trade, reported figures from the period suggested that Chile's imbalance had actually grown more, not less, severe under Frei's watch.[104] Most disappointing to rural workers was the fact that the number of peasants who received land during the Frei presidency came nowhere near the president's initial promise; while the Christian Democrats had promised that their reform project would create 100,000 new peasant farmers, only 20,000 of the country's projected 250,000 landless peasants had received land to farm for themselves by 1970. Nearly two-thirds of those individuals resided in the relatively well-off Central Valley.[105] Few policies symbolized the disappointment and shortcomings of the Christian Democrats' agrarian reform better than the government's decision to reinstitute much-abhorred beef-rationing policies at the end of Frei's term in office—this despite the many steps taken to mechanize agricultural production and modernize the supply chain.[106]

Nearly all observers could agree that the beginning of agrarian reform in the 1960s heightened the contradictions of Chile's social and economic systems. "I believe that social processes have a dynamic," the agricultural expert Jacques Chonchol noted as he reflected back on the successes and failures of the agrarian reform efforts he helped administer. "When they are beginning, they do not rouse too many aspirations, but if people see that things are working, [reforms] wake up expectations that things need to move more quickly and that, above all, they provide benefits to the interested parties."[107] Having been introduced to the possibility of becoming full political and economic citizens, rural food producers increasingly demanded that the state guarantee the same social and economic rights that their urban counterparts cherished.

Consider, for example, a letter sent from 283 rural workers on the Fundo San José del Carmen to Chile's Ministry of Agriculture in the winter of 1966. Addressing the government's notable exclusion of nonpermanent laborers from most agrarian reform initiatives, the group demanded that the state immediately incorporate them into the reform process as *obligados*—that is, supplementary laborers who assisted tenant farmers during harvest and planting season—and *voluntarios*, children of permanent resident workers. "The great majority of us were born and raised on this land, just like our fathers before us and our children after us, who continue to work for the Hacienda. We are campesinos who know agricultural work well, we have many years of experience, and we are filled with a love for the land and a desire to see it produce more," the group wrote. "We want the fruit of our labor to be for the benefit of our families, the education of our children, and the progress of this country." After citing, nearly to the word, the promises made to them by the Frei administration, as well as recent discussions they had had with CORA officials, the 283 peasants each signed their names. Next to each name, the workers sealed their signatures with an ink-stained thumbprint. For many, this process was likely the first time they had signed their names on a piece of paper of their own will, rather than under the orders of a hacienda foreman.[108] Chile's campesinos would no longer stand by idly, waiting for economic democracy and economic justice to arrive in the countryside.

In the prime of his career, Jorge Ahumada passed away unexpectedly in 1965. He was just forty-eight years old at the time, and the agrarian reform process for which he had long advocated had barely commenced. Although he would spend much of his final years outside Chile, advising other Latin American governments on their own development plans, Ahumada's ideas—from increasing the total area of the country dedicated to food production to improving campesinos access to agricultural technology—infused the Christian Democrats' push to reform and modernize the Chilean countryside.[109] Five years after Ahumada's passing, Salvador Allende, the country's former health minister and one of Chile's most outspoken socialist senators, pledged, like the Christian Democrats before him, to consider the inequities of the Chilean countryside on their own terms rather than in relation to the needs and desires of urban communities. But unlike Frei or Ahumada, land redistribution was envisioned by Allende as part of a much more capacious social and economic revolution.

Would Chile's new president succeed in breaking up large rural estates while at the same time ensuring that food production met the country's growing consumer needs? This would be among the most pressing questions of the early 1970s.

PART THREE

Recipes for Change

FIVE

When Revolution Tasted Like Empanadas and Red Wine

SOME OF NORA GÓMEZ'S most concrete memories of Chile's Popular Unity (UP) revolution involved finally earning a wage that allowed her to pay rent, secure a bit of savings for her future, buy new clothing for her children, and end what until 1970 had been a persistent fear: that from one week to the next, she might not be able to provide a decent meal for her family. "I had two children . . . and I can honestly say that I never went without," said Gómez, who was also employed at an electronics factory that was nationalized in the early months of the revolution. What's most notable about Gómez's account is how it implicitly counters the often repeated conservative characterization of the Chilean road to socialism as a drawn-out economic crisis defined by daily household struggles with food scarcity and preferential consumer treatment for the government's closest supporters. "Let me reiterate," she added, "I wasn't even part of the left . . . and still I lacked nothing."[1]

Nora Gómez's description of the UP can be read as a revisionist account of the thousand-day revolution that consumed Chile from the austral spring of 1970 through the middle of 1973. While memories of hyperinflation, partisan consumer distribution schemas, and perpetually long lines at local commercial establishments form the foundation of what historian Mario Garcés has called a "negative common sense" about Chile's socialist experiment, the concreteness of Gómez's recollections underscores an overlooked narrative about the UP period, one associated with newfound economic security and the sudden disappearance of economic want within many of Chile's working-class communities.[2] Indeed, for many Chileans the fullness of the early months of the revolution was literal. New refrigerators stuffed with previously scarce basic foodstuffs, store shelves reliably well stocked, and shopping arcades jam-packed with eager patrons are but a few of the most striking images that the archival record of the early UP period reveals. In the run-up to the Christmas holiday of 1970 and the New Year celebrations of 1971, Allende slashed the prices of household staples like eggs and bread as well as those of a few specialty items, like holiday chickens.[3] As a result, popular consumers became the beneficiaries of a genuine consumer bonanza—a fact that even those who would eventually become hardened opponents of the UP recognized and praised. "Sales this year," the director of Chile's small retailers' association observed in early March 1971, "are better than any other February in recent memory."[4] Highlighting the material culture of revolutionary consumption under the UP, a leader of another local business association in Santiago noted that same month that he had never before sold as much ham as he did in early 1971.[5]

One year after Allende's coalition government took office, that sense of abundance still revealed itself in the many shopping galleries that lined the streets of downtown Santiago. Upon visiting the commercial zone around Avenidas Bulnes, Ahumada, Estado, and Diagonal Cervantes, another Chilean journalist wrote in 1971 of pedestrians "passing by incessantly, their arms full of packages, as Christmas street retailers hawked their goods with loud yells." In consumer goods stores administered by Chile's Dirección de Industria y Comercio (Office of Industry and Commerce, DIRINCO), the revolution's revamped consumer watchdog agency, the same reporter asked retailers how their supply looked for that year's holiday season. The response of one merchant was revealing: a simple gesture toward the store's inventory of tricycles, toy trucks, batteries, and Christmas tree lights, which, the shopkeeper suggested, were still flying off the shelves.[6]

Placed in a broader historical context of persistent grassroots struggle to ensure popular access to basic consumer goods, late 1970 and early 1971 constituted an unparalleled period of plenty rather than a moment of struggle and sacrifice. This chapter recounts the causes, consequences, and lived experiences of this consumer rhapsody, which became a defining, though often forgotten, feature of Salvador Allende's first year in power.

TOWARD A SOCIALIST MODEL OF DEVELOPMENT

On the first Friday of September 1970, a narrow plurality of Chilean voters elected a longtime socialist senator to be the next president of the Chilean Republic.[7] After fending off attempts by domestic political opponents and the United States to block the ratification of his election, Salvador Allende assumed office in November of that year. In doing so, he reassured his supporters that his government would be the first anywhere in the world to forge an electoral path to socialism. But patience would be required, Chile's new president warned. The struggle ahead would be a long and difficult one. "We don't expect to achieve socialism overnight. . . . I have said this very clearly, you do not get socialism by decree," Allende reminded his fellow citizens.[8]

To begin cutting a revolutionary path, the sixty-two-year-old medical doctor rallied his broad electoral coalition, which included members of his own Socialist Party, the Chilean Communist Party (PCCh), a smattering of smaller middle-class reform parties, and militants from the country's dissident Catholic left, many of whom had split with the Christian Democratic Party over differences about the speed and purpose of Eduardo Frei's "revolution in liberty." The eclectic assemblage of movements that underwrote Allende's fourth bid for Chile's highest elected office resembled the Chilean Popular Front (FP) of the late 1930s. Indeed, like the FP, the UP promised to respect existing laws and rejected calls from some on the left for armed struggle or the creation of a single vanguard party.[9]

However, in contrast to aspiring political leaders of the late 1930s, Allende argued that, after decades of experimentation with various modes of state-led capitalist development, the time had come for Chile to pursue more far-reaching structural reforms. "[I]t should unquestionably be said . . . that the Popular Front is not the Popular Unity of today," Allende remarked shortly after his electoral victory had been confirmed.[10] While the FP had represented the "decision of the people's parties to be the left within the capitalist system," the UP's task in 1970 was to finally produce a "revolutionary transformation" and "open the road to socialism."[11]

At the center of UP's revolutionary road was the goal of constructing a more just, sovereign, and democratic national economy. Although the Frei administration had partially expanded the state's presence in the economy, many progressive intellectuals and policy makers argued that the social and economic welfare of Chile's popular majority remained subservient to the power of economic monopolies and foreign capital.[12] Commentators offered various data points from the 1960s to illustrate how this system distorted Chile's economy, thus offering Allende's government a justification for radical change. Just 17 percent of all firms owned 78 percent of all private assets. In the mining sector, three US-based multinationals managed all large mining operations and accounted for 60 percent of Chile's total exports. And in the realm of commercial distribution, twelve private companies controlled nearly half of all wholesale distribution activity.[13]

In response to these conditions, Chile's socialist coalition promised to place the country's social needs—things like health care, nutrition, education, and housing—above the economic interests of domestic monopolies, foreign corporations, private banks, and Chile's landowning class.[14] In his "First Forty Measures of a People's Government," Allende outlined his commitment to economic justice by focusing on the most quotidian spaces of social life. Among other things, he pledged more robust government transfers to poor and working-class families, a free school breakfast and lunch program for all elementary students, and the expansion of the country's childhood milk distribution initiative. The UP also called for the strict enforcement of rent controls, universal access to basic medical exams and medicines, the promotion of "popular tourism" options for poor and working-class families, and the establishment of a fair tax system, which included the abolition of regressive consumption taxes on things like basic foodstuffs.[15]

Simultaneously, Chile's new socialist government also committed itself to sweeping structural transformation. The coalition's leaders promised to nationalize Chile's mineral and metal deposits, starting with copper; socialize Chile's private financial system and its most vital domestic industries; and accelerate the agrarian reform initiative that Frei's Christian Democratic government had begun. In describing his hope that the UP would draw upon the firsthand knowledge of workers and other organic intellectuals as it pursued such revolutionary change, one supporter urged the UP to be bold with its policy proposals. Chile, he told the PCCh-run newspaper *El Siglo*, needs "Chuquicamata-size ideas," a reference to Chile's gargantuan open-pit copper mine that was at the center of Allende's nationalization program.[16]

In important ways, the micro revolutions that impacted daily life and the macro or structural changes that the UP proposed were synergistically linked; UP planners contended the fulfillment of the former would only be possible if the latter succeeded. Per Allende's vision, the state's gradual takeover of the country's most strategic industries—what the UP often referred to as the "commanding heights of the economy"—would provide the state access to a steady stream of revenue, thus underwriting the social and economic programs that would improve living conditions for tens of thousands of working-class Chileans.[17] Some in Allende's government used the term "socialist accounting" to describe this philosophy in which profitable enterprises, like mining, subsidized less profitable industries and programs dedicated to the common good.[18] Two UP-aligned economists, Sergio Bitar and Eduardo Moyano, used another, more powerful concept to describe the government's economic thought. Under the UP, the two wrote, the Chilean state would enshrine a "popular option" for development. The model they envisioned was one oriented toward producing identifiable, popular consumer goods that would not only generate a decent standard of living but also create cascading poles of economic growth in specific sectors of the national economy.[19]

In Allende's first six months in office, the UP made notable progress toward enacting its vision of socialist developmentalism. In late 1970, Allende put the final touches on the constitutional reform proposal to nationalize Chilean copper deposits; six months later, Chile's national congress adopted the measure.[20] To ring in the new year in 1971, the government announced its purchase of a controlling share of Chile's coal mining industry. It also set in motion plans to nationalize the extraction of iron ore, the country's only steel foundry, large portions of its private banking sector, and the few nitrate-processing facilities that remained in operation on the desert plains of the northern Atacama.[21]

Revolutionary actions continued with the establishment of a state-run economic sector, what the UP's economic officials called the Social Property Area (APS).[22] Then, using the powers of Decree Law 520, the same decree that had in 1932 established the hemisphere's first permanent national price control agency, the Allende administration began populating the APS by requisitioning those industries it deemed inefficient or considered vital to the economic well-being of the nation. By the end of 1971, seventy industries had come under state control.[23] In its first year, the UP also extended its reform efforts deep into the Chilean countryside, expropriating some thirteen hundred large estates on which an estimated sixteen thousand peasant families lived.[24]

The first political dividends of these policies were secured in April 1971 when the UP won a resounding victory in the country's municipal elections. Compared to September of the previous year, the coalition's vote share increased by a remarkable 13 percent.[25] In a speech that marked the end of the first year of his revolution, Allende proudly declared, "The people of Chile have recovered what belongs to them."[26]

DEMOCRACY IS *PAN Y LECHE*

The former AOAN organizer Carlos Alberto Martínez supported the election of Salvador Allende in 1970, and almost certainly did so without hesitation.

Having recently turned eighty-five years old when Allende assumed office, Martínez, like many UP supporters, would have found the socialist coalition's program attractive for many of the same reasons he and an earlier generation had marched against hunger and formed cost-of-living committees during the economic crisis of 1918–19 and again in the 1930s: life remained hard and expensive. Infant mortality, a metric deeply associated with a much younger Dr. Salvador Allende because of his early writings, still hovered around one hundred deaths for every one thousand live births in the mid-1960s; although infant death rates had begun to fall in the late-1960s, by most accounts, both childhood and infant mortality numbers actually increased slightly as Chileans headed to the polls in 1970.[27] Proper medical care remained hard to come by, particularly outside the capital.[28] Chronic malnutrition still afflicted around one-third of the country's adult population and as much as half of the country's youth.[29] As one particularly pessimistic 1970 study of working-class food consumption in Chile concluded, "an acceptable level of [human] development" was "unlikely to be reached" in a country, like Chile, where such a large part of the population still consumed a diet so deficient in protein.[30]

According to some indicators, the socioeconomic situation of many Chileans appeared to be objectively *worse* at the end of the 1960s than it was in the middle decades of the twentieth century, when Allende embarked on a career in politics. One Chilean economist estimated that the purchasing power of Chile's living wage, known as the *sueldo vital*, was significantly lower in 1970 than in 1950.[31] In a 1970 annual economic report, the government's national planning office revealed that almost one-half of Chile's formally employed population—more than 1.25 million individuals—lived on earnings that fell well below the minimum wage.[32] What's more, the severity of the situation appeared to be intensifying as inflationary pressures chipped away at purchasing power under the Christian Democrats, and agrarian productivity, which had initially surged in the mid-1960s, appeared to be stagnating by the end of the decade.[33] As evidence of the problem, local food markets had allegedly begun labeling basic food items, like pasta and rice, with superficial superlatives like "special" and "extra" to justify—and obfuscate—price markups.[34] It was unsurprising, then, that UP voters expressed particular enthusiasm for Allende's promise that inflation would be brought, once and for all, to a screeching halt under his watch.[35]

Responding to these economic concerns, UP economic advisers got to work immediately. Their first objective was to design and implement a series of policies that would reactivate economic growth while ensuring a more equitable distribution of national income. A widely circulated study conducted by Pedro Vuskovic, the CEPAL economist chosen by Allende to be the UP's first minister of economy, had found that the richest 1 percent of the Chilean population possessed an income that was sixty-nine times greater than that of the poorest 10 percent. Revolutionary policy makers therefore prioritized growing consumers' purchasing power and undoing distribution bottlenecks that hampered the exchange of basic consumer goods.[36]

In pursuit of this goal, the UP doubled down on the strict enforcement of consumer price controls. The Allende administration also implemented a significant wage increase for working-class wage earners. By late 1970, the government and Chile's national labor federation reached a settlement on a multitier wage system that enacted a 66 percent wage readjustment for Chile's lowest-paid wage earners, followed by increases of between 34 and 39 percent for workers who fell in higher-paying categories.[37] The UP wagered that providing workers with a quick infusion of new money would have an unprecedented stimulating effect on employment, since these populations represented an entirely undeveloped consumer market. As the eminent British historian Eric Hobsbawm noted after a short visit to the country in 1971, it should "never be forgotten that no more than 300,000 of the 9 million Chileans were the effective customers for industry" before Allende's election.[38]

The socialist government's quintessentially Keynesian policies had a profound short-term effect on Chile's economy. National GDP rose by 8 percent in 1971, the country's highest growth rate since 1950 and a figure significantly higher than the country's average growth rate of 4.4 percent during the 1960s.[39] During the UP's first year, industrial production grew by 12.1 percent, with the food economy posting some of the most impressive growth results of all. To cite a few of the most astonishing figures, between 1970 and 1972, domestic production of flour grew by more than 14 percent, sugar by nearly 17 percent, condensed milk by nearly 26 percent, cooking oil by more than 31 percent, pasta noodles by more than 81 percent, and coffee by more than 155 percent.[40] At the same time, unemployment fell precipitously. According to Chile's planning ministry, 146,000 more people were employed in 1971 than in 1970.[41] The decline in unemployment was most dramatic around metropolitan Santiago, where the rate dropped from 8.3 to 3.8 percent over the course of 1971.[42]

As the value of real wages rose by over 20 percent, inequality within the labor force was slashed.[43] The combination of rising wages and the government's strict enforcement of price ceilings for dozens of essential goods caused purchasing power to soar and inflation to be halved.[44] Taken together, such policies generated arguably the largest downward redistribution of income in Chile's twentieth century. In 1970, the share of labor in Chile's GDP amounted to just over 52 percent; just one year later it was estimated that labor's income share accounted for nearly 62 percent of national income.[45] In articulating the ethical principles behind what at first glance might have appeared to be run-of-the-mill economic populism, Allende argued that his government's purpose was more profound. The UP's economic policies, he said, were intended to "strengthen democracy and broaden liberty through . . . economic liberation."[46]

The state's concerted effort to redirect national productive capacities away from luxury products and toward the production of high-quality, basic consumer goods cemented ordinary Chilean consumers as the major recipients of the revolution's early bounty. The types of purchases that many low-income urban workers, rural peasants, and shantytown dwellers made in 1971 embodied the *fiesta* of that year, a term that the Chilean sociologist Tomás Moulian has used to describe the economic bliss of the revolution's early months.[47] Stories recounting poor and working-class encounters with everything from cotton linens and store-bought mattresses to new leather shoes filled the pages of popular newspapers and magazines. These accounts often appeared alongside advertisements that promoted the sale of housewares or features about grand openings for new restaurants and grocery stores.[48] "The string shopping bags of working-class housewives are bulging these days with food and household goods picked from supermarket shelves and street-market stalls," *New York Times* correspondent Juan de Onís wrote in a dispatch he published from Santiago in the Chilean fall of 1971.[49]

The ubiquity of basic household goods, both in commercial establishments and the homes of working people, became the unlikely iconography of Chile's early revolutionary progress. "Demand for coffee has doubled, and the same can be said of propane," a Radical Party politician told the popular women's magazine *Eva* on the first anniversary of the UP's inauguration. In contrast to earlier periods of growth, greater purchasing power was not confined to the country's *sectores acomodados* (well-to-do sectors). "Now," he added, "all who demand a right to eat and to find decent clothing are having that right respected."[50] Data collected by the economic historian Stefan de Vylder to approximate evolving food consumption habits between Allende's election and the second year of the revolution suggest that the only two food

TABLE 3 Apparent Consumption of Major Food Crops
and Livestock Products in Chile, 1970 and 1972
(in Kilos/Capita)[a]

Food	1970	1972	% Change
Wheat	152.7	178.1	16.6
Corn	54.1	64.0	18.3
Rice	9.7	11.8	21.6
Potato	51.6	55.8	8.1
Sugar	32.0	39.6	23.8
Cooking oils	7.0	7.6	8.6
Wine (in liters)	47.0	52.6	11.9
Beef and veal	17.4	15.4	−11.5
Lamb and mutton	3.5	2.8	−20.0
Pork	4.9	6.1	24.5
Poultry	6.4	7.6	18.7
Milk (in liters)	123.9	171.8	38.7
Eggs (in units)	93.0	117.3	26.1

SOURCE: Reproduced from Stefan de Vylder, *Allende's Chile: The Political Economy of the Rise and Fall of the Unidad Popular* (Cambridge, UK: Cambridge University Press, 1976), 203.

a. Apparent consumption = domestic production and imports, disregarding smuggling and hoarding.

items Chileans consumed less of in 1972 than in 1970 were beef and lamb. For several goods, like rice, pork, chicken, and eggs, estimated percentage increases in total consumption between those two years were somewhere between 21 percent (for rice) and 26 percent (for eggs).[51] Overall, the caloric availability in Chile during the first two years of the UP revolution was calculated by one nutrition researcher to be 8 percent greater than in the five-year period 1965–69.[52] Increases in total food consumption were even more remarkable. Chileans ate as much as 14 percent more food in 1971 than in the 1966–70 period. In 1972, they consumed an additional 12 percent more on top of that.[53]

Arguably no product became more deeply associated with the UP's early months than powdered milk. The Chilean government had operated a national milk distribution program for more than three decades when the UP took office, but the geographic scope of that program had remained limited to Chile's major urban centers. Almost immediately, Allende expanded the milk program. In the early months of his presidency, the country's national health system established a far-reaching network of approximately thirteen hundred state clinics that both helped distribute milk and promote child

FIGURE 9. A young boy poses with a bottle of milk, a symbol of the Chilean state's efforts to improve health outcomes for the country's children. Colección Museo Histórico Nacional, Santiago de Chile.

well-being. The UP's milk program itself eventually reached some 3.6 million children, transforming the calcium-rich liquid into the "symbol" of the UP's holistic approach to public health, in the words of the program's directors.[54] According to a survey of one thousand Santiago households in 1972, approximately 78 percent of families eligible for the program were participating in it. The amount of powdered milk distributed by the state increased from 13,700 tons in 1970 to 40,500 tons one year later.[55] Other estimates suggest that between 1970 and 1972, total consumption of milk in Chile increased by nearly 39 percent.[56]

The Allende government pursued parallel nutritional and food safety measures by embracing technical expertise and regulation. In the second week of December 1970, the UP inaugurated a series of meetings with food experts from around the country—what it called the *jornadas de control de alimentos* (food control workdays)—to reformulate the country's approach to food safety matters and demand strict adherence to existing public health regulations. Simultaneously, government officials established a four-city network of laboratories to test food quality around the country.[57] By the end of its first year, food engineers and scientists affiliated with Chilean universities had also started to experiment with new grains, like soybeans and bulgur wheat, to manufacture nutritious children's crackers and cookies, and eventually a low-cost, soy-based baby formula.[58] In Allende's Chile, "democracy is about *pan y leche*" (bread and milk), an editorial in the PCCh's newspaper declared.[59]

All of these experiences made concrete the UP's promise that the Chilean revolution would be flavored with the "taste of *empanadas y vino tinto*" (meat pies and red wine)—a slogan used by Allende to both denote the national character of the UP's revolutionary trajectory and emphasize the promise that material sacrifice could and would be avoided on Chile's road to socialism.[60] In even more ebullient language, the writer and longtime Communist militant Volodia Teitelboim described the first five months of the Allende government as "the most brilliant in Chilean history."[61]

REVOLUTION IN THE COUNTRYSIDE?

"[W]e weren't going to suffer anymore [after Allende's election]. . . . [W]e weren't going to lack food. . . . [T]here would be food for everyone's children." That's how a worker at one of Chile's largest food-processing plants described the first half of Chile's revolutionary experience several decades after Chile's military brought the UP experiment to a violent close.[62] But as those charged with implementing the country's socialist program soon realized, the material gains that many of Chile's urban working- and middle-class communities experienced in 1971 depended on the government's ability to increase, or at the very least maintain, production in the Chilean countryside. Redistributing tens of thousands of acres of fertile land to landless peasants and small farmers while simultaneously keeping urban consumers' growing appetite for food sated would be an especially difficult task.

The architects of UP's agrarian reform frequently maintained that the key difference between their administration's approach to rural reform and that of their predecessors was that the latter had pursued agrarian reform in isolation from structural reforms in other sectors of the economy, such as mining, finance, and manufacturing.[63] In a speech that he gave to a gathering of nitrate miners in the town of Pedro de Valdivia in 1971, Allende articulated his alternative vision of a deeply interconnected national economy. "We need . . . the nitrates [of Chile] to become the fertilizer of the small- and medium-sized farmer of Chile because we need the land to produce more." By laboring in the nitrate fields and processing plants of the rugged Atacama, Allende contended, the noble miners of the Norte Grande were not just resurrecting their own depressed industry but were also realizing a goal of agrarian reform: that "one day Chile would produce the food it needed."[64]

With that objective in mind, agrarian officials, led by Minister of Agriculture Jacques Chonchol, designed a new system of land tenure in which two new agrarian institutions would become the transitional pillars of a socialist agricultural sector.[65] The first, known as Centros de la Reforma Agraria (agrarian reform centers, CERAs), aimed to supplant the Frei government's asentamiento system by creating dozens of regionally organized, not-for-profit communal corporations throughout the countryside. Each CERA would be responsible for unifying production on the formerly private agrarian properties that had existed in a given parish. According to the terms of this new system, any rural worker in that municipality could be a member of the new collective and as such would pay minimal dues and a fixed rent to the communal corporation. In return, each member would gain easier access to state credit, farm implements, markets, and public services, as well as a portion of the CERA's collective profits.[66]

Allende's administration expected this arrangement to generate several beneficial changes. First, the CERA system would put an end to new forms of exclusion that had taken root on many asentamientos by extending participation beyond those tenant farmers who lived on a given expropriated hacienda; under the new model, membership would also be extended to itinerant laborers who worked the land seasonally. Second, the CERA system aimed to displace the outsized political influence that large landowners' trade associations continued to exert over the country's agricultural future. As the UP leadership envisioned it, the CERA system would be bolstered by new, parish-wide decision-making bodies in which all rural workers—men and women, migrant laborers and tenant farmers—were free to participate. Members of the communal corporation would meet regularly in regional council meetings to set a given community's production goals, coordinate planting schedules, and interface with the state's various agricultural promotion and credit providers, the latter of which disbursed financial assistance in accordance with the regular submission of production plans.[67]

UP planners maintained that, in the long run, the CERA system would assuage problems of rural economic insecurity, particularly rising levels of personal debt, that continued to restrain the mobility and well-being of a new class of small landholders even after Frei had begun his agrarian reform.

By linking what two historians of the reforms call "socialist morality" with "capitalist incentives," the CERA model guaranteed a minimum wage within all CERAs alongside a special "bonus system" that was tied to individual worker productivity.[68] At the same time, each family that participated in a CERA retained their own individual house and garden plot, so that they could continue to raise crops and small game for their personal consumption. The only new restriction was that the total amount of land dedicated to personal garden plots could be no more than one-fifth of the CERA's total arable land. This way, government planners hoped, subsistence production would never come at the expense of urban food needs, a problem that some agricultural officials suspected was occurring in the late 1960s.[69]

In parallel to the CERA, the UP government also opened the way for a second set of farming units, known as Centros de Producción (production centers, CEPROs). While CERAs aimed to satisfy basic regional consumer needs in a given geographic space, CEPROs would exist in those areas of the agricultural economy where special expertise or technical training was needed for efficient production—for example, in forestry development and livestock breeding. In contrast to the CERA, the expropriated lands on which a CEPRO operated would remain firmly under state control. But in the absence of a path toward private land ownership, farmworkers on state-run CEPROs would be guaranteed wages comparable to those of urban industrial workers, along with their own home and a garden plot to supplement household consumption.[70]

By most early accounts, the UP's early adjustments to Chile's agrarian reform project showed promise. By the end of 1971, twenty-five CERAs had been established across the Chilean countryside.[71] Real agricultural credit, much of which was channeled through state-run banks at low interest rates, had reportedly increased by 57 percent during the revolution's early months. Agricultural prices, meanwhile, outpaced the cost of required agrarian inputs, helping to win over the trust and support of many medium-sized farmers.[72] The reformed sector also benefited through improved access to new agricultural technologies. Between 1970 and 1972, tractor usage in Chile was estimated to have doubled from just ten thousand to over twenty thousand. Roughly 70 percent of those new tractors went directly to rural workers on expropriated lands.[73]

For the majority of food crops, 1971 and 1972 were some of the most bountiful years of agricultural production in recent memory. More wheat was harvested in Chile in 1971 than in any previous recorded year in Chilean

FIGURE 10. UP officials deliver a modern combine harvester to a rural community as part of the country's agrarian reform. Fundación Salvador Allende, Santiago de Chile.

agricultural history. Similarly impressive production numbers were recorded for Chilean staples like chickpeas, a crop that logged its highest ever yield in 1972, and beans, which registered its second highest yield ever that same year.[74] The same was true in much of the dairy and meat subsectors; although the domestic production of beef declined slightly in 1972, compared to the two previous years, production of pork, poultry, milk, and eggs was greater in 1972 than in 1970 or 1971.[75] Most impressively, perhaps, in the span of just two years the UP expropriated more than twice as many properties as the Frei government had during its entire six years in office. Rural workers' wages simultaneously shot up by 75 percent.[76]

THE MULTIPLICATION OF FISH

Speaking to rural workers at a gathering on agrarian reform in August 1971, Allende would declare that just as Chile's copper was now in Chilean hands—and thus was expected to be more productive—so too would Chile's land, now increasingly in the hands of Chilean peasants, be more effectively worked. It was farmworkers' responsibility to the nation, Allende said, to "ensure that there is enough bread for every mouth and every table."[77] But given the UP's desire to distinguish its agrarian reform policies from those of its predecessors, it was hardly surprising that Allende's government rarely acknowledged how its food and agricultural policies were intimately bound up with the past. In short, Allende's ability to boost food production would have been largely unthinkable without the political and economic foundation laid by previous administrations. Even as it assembled a new agenda to transform what, how, and for whom basic foodstuffs were produced in Chile, the UP often reaped what earlier governments had sown.

The UP's attempt to develop Chile's national hog and chicken industries—and thus diversify meat consumption away from beef—was one example of how Allende's agrarian reform rested on the Frei government's efforts to develop the agricultural sector through state-led economic planning. In 1968, Chile's Ministry of Agriculture reported its new aviculture enterprises had nearly tripled domestic broiler chicken production in just two years, from 8 million chickens in 1965 to 21 million in 1967.[78] That same year, the Frei government also backed the development of a twenty-four-member hog cooperative near the city of Talca, suggesting that this initiative be modeled after the successful chicken production efforts underway at the nearby Marchigüe Cooperative.[79] These previous investments made realistic the UP's ambitious promise to establish at least eighteen new hog farms, build a special pork-processing plant in metropolitan Santiago, and double domestic chicken production, all during its first two years in power.[80]

The UP's debt to years of economic planning by the Chilean state was perhaps nowhere clearer than on the nutrient-rich Pacific coastline. For decades, Chilean officials had imagined its coastal waters as an untapped nutritional "reserve."[81] Writing during the FP period, a nutrition expert working at Chile's Ministry of Development had declared that fish harvested from the Pacific's cold waters might one day supply the majority of the country's protein needs.[82] So captivating was this notion that when the Chilean diplomat and poet Pablo Neruda had organized asylum in Chile for over two thousand Spanish Republicans during the Spanish Civil War, he had pointed to the exiles' experience in that country's fishing industry as one important reason to welcome them to Chile. "We've been outlining plans for a diverse set of industries that [the Spanish refugees] might establish in Chile," Neruda wrote to Chile's Ministry of Foreign Relations from France in 1939 as he coordinated the group's departure to South America. Neruda even attempted to transport key infrastructural aspects of Spain's fishing industry to Chile, such as salting machines and fish-canning equipment, along with the exiles.[83]

One decade later, Spanish Civil War veteran Bibiano Fernández Osorio-Tafall left his temporary refuge in Mexico to join Chile's community of exiled Spanish Republicans. When he accepted a position as the head of the Food and Agriculture Organization's (FAO) new regional office in Santiago, Osorio-Tafall argued that exploiting Chile's Pacific fisheries offered the best hope for resolving hunger in Chile.[84] In the subsequent years, the FAO, under Osorio-Tafall's leadership, produced important scientific breakthroughs in commercial aquaculture. Beginning in the late 1950s, for example, the FAO backed experiments to produce a nutritiously rich, odorless, fish-based flour as a novel substitute for regular wheat-based flour.[85] Chilean manufacturers, meanwhile, opened dozens of new canning factories that utilized fish as one of their principal inputs. By 1947, nearly half of the country's roughly sixty canning factories were producing canned fish in one form or another.[86] Offering a window into the success of such initiatives, the FAO reported a 45 percent increase in fish consumption in parts of Santiago in the early 1950s.[87]

By the early 1960s, however, Chile's fish boom had begun to wane. While the aggregate amount of fish caught continued to climb, the amount of that fish that was intended for Chilean dining tables declined. In 1960, FAO numbers indicated that 16 percent of all fish caught in Chile was for immediate human consumption, but one year later that figure had fallen to just over 10 percent. Increasingly, the country's annual catch was diverted toward the more profitable, export-oriented fishmeal industry, and then on to factory-style farms to be used as animal feed.[88]

Allende's government sought to correct course by resurrecting the focus on human consumption that had been built into earlier economic planning while at the same time continuing to promote fishmeal and fish oil to foreign markets.[89] To sustain both of these goals, the UP got to work improving basic infrastructure at Chile's major fishing ports and forging technical exchange agreements with key international allies.[90] In April 1971, for example, one Chilean newspaper reported that scientific cooperation between Great Britain, Chile, and the Panama-based Central American Institute for Nutrition had finally created a first-of-its-kind process that transformed Chilean merluza into a high-protein concentrate that could be used to enrich popular beverages, crackers, and soups.[91] The Allende government also asked government product and logistics engineers to improve the efficiency and hygiene of transportation systems that moved fish from port to plate. One of the socialist government's most touted achievements was to invent a specially designed, easy-to-wash plastic fish crate to store and ship seafood to urban markets. The new crate quickly replaced the cumbersome and unsanitary wooden boxes that seafood distributors customarily used to transport their catch.[92]

The hallmark event in elevating the profile of the national fishing industry came in January 1972 when Chile's socialist president traveled to the port city of San Antonio to welcome a fleet of Soviet fishing ships into Chilean waters.[93] The three deepwater trawlers, the *Astronom*, the *Yantar*, and the *Sumi*, boasted some of the most modern fishing technologies available. According to an agreement the two countries had signed just a few months earlier, those technologies would be placed at the disposal of Chile's state-run fishing company to increase annual yields.[94] The cooperation would be complemented by the presence of two Soviet research vessels "capable of detecting the richest deposits of marine life" off the Chilean coast.[95] Working together, these two types of ships could harvest merluza and its close relative, pescada, at unprecedented oceanic depths, then clean and process their catch before returning to shore. The Chilean government projected that the Soviet ships' work in the Pacific would increase annual production of fish in Chile by 30 percent over the course of 1972.[96] The PCCh's daily newspaper emphasized that more than 70 percent of the bounty produced by the Soviet trawlers would go directly to Chilean consumers, rather than being ground into fishmeal for foreign export markets.[97]

Only a few months into the Chilean-Soviet collaboration, the head of distribution and sales at Santiago's central fish market confirmed the strikingly positive results of the accord. He claimed that daily sales of merluza in Santiago alone had already risen to approximately nine hundred kilos per day—an astounding 200 percent increase.[98] Other commentators verified the accomplishments of the collaboration by referencing two quantifiable measurements: protein content and foreign exchange. "The large numbers of consumers who have not incorporated fish into their normal diet must become aware of the fact that Chile imports 262 million dollars-worth of food each year, 120 million dollars of which is spent on bringing beef into the country," one pro-UP journalist wrote. What's more, the writer added, one hundred grams of fish provided nearly four grams more protein than its equivalent in beef.[99]

A writer for *El Siglo* sought out a more dramatic, biblical reference to underscore the fishing program's achievements. Under the headline "The

Multiplication of the Fish," the paper compared the technology transfer that stood at the center of the Chilean-Soviet fishing pact to the parable of Jesus transforming a basket of fish and bread into endless abundance. Technology, the editorialist maintained, would save the working Chilean family money and help the UP government achieve its "goal of providing food for thousands of homes."[100]

In his first presidential address, a speech that marked the one-year anniversary of the UP's rise to power, Salvador Allende underscored the feeling of plenty that defined Chile after one year on the road to socialism. His words illustrate a deep sense of pride and confidence, as well as an unwavering belief that the country's revolutionary experiment would continue to march forward without being forced to make a national appeal for material sacrifice. "We Chileans have done more during this year than was done during the first year of the Cuban revolution—and I say this without diminishing the Cubans," Allende contended during the presidential address that marked the end of his first year in office. "Also keep in mind that we have made our revolution without social costs. I can assure you that there is no other country in the world that has taken the revolutionary road with the [low] social costs of your People's Government."[101] During his weekslong visit to Allende's Chile in 1971, Cuba's revolutionary leader Fidel Castro appeared to agree with much of that statement. What Chile was experiencing was not so much a "socialist" revolution, Castro allegedly remarked, as it was a "revolution of consumption."[102]

Yet as Allende's second year in office commenced, a growing number of indicators suggested that the period of consumer euphoria was quickly drawing to a close. Already in 1971, certain high-demand foodstuffs, most notably beef, began to disappear from local markets. In some cases, the shortages were the result of exceptionally hard winter storms that disrupted food cultivation and transportation networks both within the country and between Chile and neighboring Argentina. In other cases, the problems reflected the UP's inability to increase consumer supply at the same rate as purchasing power.[103] There is little doubt that political opponents of the government, particularly large landowners, contributed to this disequilibrium. In the weeks and months after Allende assumed office, for example, many big cattle ranchers shipped between 160,000 and 200,000 head of cattle across the Andes to Argentina, claiming the UP's acceleration of land reform brought too much uncertainty.[104] Other landowners slaughtered their herds outright, fearing that either their cattle would be seized by the state or beef prices would eventually decline.[105] At the end of July 1971, a local Santiago newspaper reported that the only meat product *not* in short supply in Santiago markets that month was the "quite unappetizing option of horse meat."[106]

The situation grew more difficult when a major earthquake shook the Central Valley, halting food production for several days and postponing winter seeding of grains in the country's agricultural heartland.[107] According to a *New York Times* correspondent, some Chileans, still awash in purchasing power because of the UP's new wage rates, turned to expensive Danish and French poultry to satisfy their newfound appetite for high-protein foodstuffs.[108] Others sought out imported beef, no matter the cost. Of the nearly 86,000 tons of beef consumed in Greater Santiago in the year 1971, nearly 42 percent was imported—more than double the previous year's total.[109] While Chile's state-run food marketing firm, ECA, imported 13,038 tons of chilled and frozen beef in 1970, just one year later it was importing more than 28,800 tons.[110] At a time when global food prices were on the rise and the price of copper, Chile's most important export, declined, the country was quite literally eating up its currency reserves. In just one year, the US$95 million trade surplus that the government had inherited had turned into a trade deficit of US$90 million.[111]

As economic challenges built anew in the final months of 1971, a palpable sense of frustration and unease expanded from Chile's elites down into the country's middling economic sectors. The disquieting conditions that Allende had declared dead and over, like scarcity and inflation, had clearly not been vanquished for good; in fact, by late 1971 and into early 1972, some believed that such problems might actually have been exacerbated during the revolution's first year. "Daily we see that there is no meat, chicken, milk, noodles, and other essential items, and when we do find these products, we have to pay prices that are far beyond our resources," read a call to action issued by a group of anti-Allende women in late November 1971.[112] The announcement requested that women bring empty pots and pans with them to a public street demonstration against the UP in downtown Santiago on the first day of December, timed to correspond with the end of Fidel Castro's weekslong stay.

Astute observers began to wonder: Might the opposition be able to co-opt an issue, food consumption, that had turned tens of thousands of voters to the UP camp during the national election of 1970 and the municipal elections of 1971? Chile's road to socialism was about to become far rougher and far more conflictual.

SIX

A Battle for the Chilean Stomach

THE MANY ECONOMIC REFORMS and social programs that the Allende government set in motion during its first year in office were among the striking achievements of Chile's Popular Unity (UP) era. But for the tens of thousands of Chileans who both benefited from and sustained those initiatives, the most formative experiences of the country's thousand-day revolution were often less ceremonious affairs. Whether by volunteering to help construct affordable housing, organizing political demonstrations, or taking part in the occupation of rural lands and urban workplaces, the political communities who comprised the socialist coalition's grassroots base made sense of Chile's revolutionary experiment in the neighborhoods in which they resided, on the shop floors of the factories in which they worked, and through daily interactions with political allies and adversaries alike. The emergence of economic abundance during the UP's first year was one development that brought the feeling of revolution into some unlikely areas of daily life, including the marketplace, the traditionally private corners of the domestic sphere, and eventually the bellies of Chilean consumers themselves.[1]

As the UP entered its second year in power, Chileans demonstrated their commitment to the country's socialist experiment by participating in the struggle to maintain the nutritional security that had been achieved during the revolution's early months.[2] As a case in point, consider the abbreviated biography of Eduardo Flores Flores, a working-class man who lived much of his life in the southwestern Santiago parishes of Ñuñoa and La Reina and whose political militancy reflects the everyday nature of grassroots revolutionary resolve. Born in 1906, on the eve of a decade of working-class struggles that would shake Chile to its political and economic core, Flores's own political initiation came in the mid-1930s. During those years he participated in his first demonstration against the rising tide of fascism in Chile and around the world. Shortly thereafter, Flores joined a small pro-Soviet solidarity organization, though his political work quickly became more grounded in his immediate surroundings. To confront the shortages that he and his neighbors faced because of the Second World War, Flores served as the president of his neighborhood "cost-of-living committee" and on a community development council in his home parish of Ñuñoa. That same year, his organizing channeled him into the official ranks of the Chilean Communist Party (PCCh). When the worst of the early Cold War anti-communist repression ended, Flores eventually became a leader within Chile's national labor movement as it grew in strength throughout the 1950s and 1960s.

One could imagine that after Allende's election the longtime Communist militant, then in his midsixties, might have scaled back his political commitments, perhaps taking time to enjoy a life in political retirement. In a country where the organized left thrived on intergenerational bonds of solidarity, Flores had done his part to pass on his own firmly held political beliefs to a new legion of activists; of his twenty-nine grandchildren, several had joined Chile's Communist Youth movement by the time the UP took office. But complacency was not a feeling Flores knew well. When shortages and inflation returned in early 1972, he recommitted himself to political work, helping to establish one of the first *juntas de abastecimiento y precios* (supply and price control boards, JAPs) in the middle-class neighborhood of La Reina. For Flores, as for many other Chileans, the political and economic fights to ensure food availability were as much a culminating moment in a decades-long march to socialism as they were the birth of something entirely new and unfamiliar.

The citizen-run consumer committee that Flores helped to establish monitored prices for basic goods in local stores and improved the distribution of scarce household products. Per Flores's account, the results of such actions were felt immediately. Meat supplies at the community's local butcher shop stabilized because the consumer committee directly facilitated coordination with the country's state-run meat distributor. Six merchants from the neighborhood, each of whom specialized in the sale of nonperishable goods, soon agreed to work directly with state distribution firms to secure similar supply guarantees for their shops. Within weeks, this JAP's success had inspired others to create consumer committees in their own neighborhoods. The community's mobilization also put in motion plans to open a special, state-run yardstick store in the neighborhood, where official prices were maintained even as inflationary pressures returned.[3]

This chapter explores how the sort of consumer activism in which Eduardo Flores was engaged became a crucible for developing and showcasing grassroots political power. By reconstructing the history and significance of the food distribution initiatives that emerged during the UP revolution's second year—in particular the work of the JAPs and the various informal offshoots that they spawned—it surveys the actions of local actors who sought to remedy the contradictions of the UP's early economic policies by assuming a more active role in everyday economic activities. Grassroots activists insisted that it was only with the participation of the communities committed to revolutionary change that Chile's socialist government would overcome both the shortsightedness of state economic planners and the acts of sabotage that the revolution's opponents executed.

Over time the JAPs became a deeply contested space not only between Allende and his conservative detractors but also between the UP and the most radical members of its base, many of whom were determined to expand the scope and speed of Chile's transition to socialism. By rethinking how an essential activity like food distribution operated, local revolutionaries enacted their vision of a more democratic economy—and whom it would serve. In the wake of a counterrevolutionary offensive against the UP in the Chilean spring of 1972, joint worker-consumer control of the food economy revealed the potential of radical democracy, while simultaneously breeding intense disdain among the revolution's foes.[4]

JUST MARKETS

As had been the case with the popular mobilizations that marked Chile's entry into the Cold War era more than two decades earlier, it started with bread. Tomás Moreno Beiza, a deputy secretary within Chile's national bakery workers' union, was among the first to bring the matter of bread to the attention of the new UP government just a few days before Salvador Allende's inauguration in November 1970. According to the union leader, Chile's new socialist government would be wise to appoint a group of bakers from his union as unofficial state inspectors within their respective places of employment. Such an initiative, in the union's view, would ensure that bakery owners placed basic standards of hygiene and economic fairness ahead of profit, thus safeguarding the physical and financial health of bakers and working-class consumers alike. Bakery proprietors were widely suspected of using inaccurate scales that cheated consumers, and Moreno Beiza himself even alleged that managers regularly forced their workers to gather up each day's spilled flour in order to reuse it in the next day's breads. Giving workers the power to report such infractions would finally subject bakeries to the most "strict control" possible. What's more, transferring inspection powers to those who labored in bakery kitchens, day in and day out, would relieve DIRINCO, the country's overtaxed consumer protection agency, of a small share of its heavy workload. "We workers are confident that for the first time we will also be the government," Moreno Beiza expectantly declared.[5]

The petition of the bakery workers' union was indicative of broader popular discord that continued to surround basic consumer products like bread as the UP assumed power. At the same time, the Allende government's response to the bakers' union demonstrated an acute awareness that everyday concerns about food production and provisioning needed to be addressed fully and directly to contain popular discontent. To that end, the UP took one of its first actions against unscrupulous bread producers in the first months of 1971 when it entrusted bakery inspections to select groups of consumers, most of them women who received special training from DIRINCO about properly monitoring the price and quality of bread being sold around Santiago. According to one of the women who organized these early vigilance efforts, Chile's nationwide network of mothers' centers, a bastion of support for the Frei administration during the 1960s, also stood ready to coordinate targeted consumer boycotts of any bakery that was suspected of engaging in speculative or unhygienic practices.[6]

Inspectors' reports on price and supply "irregularities" at multiple Santiago bakeries justified the state's requisition of six bakeries in the early months of the revolution. Inspections also triggered the government to deploy additional monitoring teams to observe production and exchange processes and scrutinize the sales records of some 180 other bread-making facilities across the country.[7] Among the auditors' most significant duties would be enforcing the UP's January 1971 decree stipulating a fixed price for a single, high-quality loaf of bread at all bakeries around the country.[8] "DIRINCO is no longer an organization that consumers distrust, but is instead a regulatory agency that carries out its actions for the benefit of all," Minister of Economy Pedro Vuskovic declared shortly after the new decree went into place.[9] Offering additional praise for the exemplary collaboration between the state, workers, and consumers, writers at *El Siglo* argued that such efforts demonstrated that neither consumers nor the state would tolerate the "classist division between first- and second-class Chileans" any longer.[10]

Citizens' efforts to maintain the price and quality of bread around Santiago presaged the establishment of locally run consumer committees in neighborhoods across the city, including the one that Eduardo Flores helped organize in La Reina. At a July 1971 gathering held in Santiago's Estadio Chile, Vuskovic first publicly urged female supporters of the UP to take the lead in building a parallel system of consumer inspection. He even pledged to create a special office within his own ministry to deal exclusively with the country's supply problems.[11] Within weeks, grassroots actors heeded the economy minister's call, with the PCCh often spearheading the various consumer organizing campaigns that sprouted up in the capital.[12]

Over the next six months, the neighborhood consumer watchdog committees known as JAPs became one of the most recognizable features of the revolution in the urban sphere as they monitored prices and supply chains and denounced economic monopolies.[13] In many of their earliest instantiations, JAPs utilized the existing infrastructure of unions, mothers' centers, and community boards to train hundreds of local activists as "honorary consumer inspectors." As unofficial representatives of the state's consumer protection agency, citizen inspectors had the power to audit suspicious economic activities in their communities. In extreme cases, DIRINCO even permitted consumer activists to seize and redistribute essential goods that private distributors or retailers were intentionally holding off the market.[14]

Although the state-sanctioned extension of inspection and expropriation powers to ordinary citizens may have seemed radical to some, it was a move that had the initial support of both the working poor and many small merchants. In the municipality of Colina, a few dozen kilometers north of Santiago's city limits, Manuel Araya San Martín, a retailer and proud member of Chile's Christian Democratic Party (PDC), argued that the JAPs had universal appeal to both groups in his community. He even went so far as to claim that the basic idea of the JAP was something that his preferred presidential candidate, the Christian Democrat Radomiro Tomic, had supported in his 1970 run against Allende. When asked what accounted for the committees' allure, Araya San Martín responded by observing that "kitchen table problems are the same for everyone. Hoarding makes a communist, a *gremialista* [a member of the anti-Allende movement consisting largely of white collar workers and small business owners], and a Christian Democrat all suffer in the same way." The JAPs were "not part of any one party"; on the contrary, they were an institution that "belonged to all Chileans," Araya San Martín insisted.[15]

Over time, JAPs took on new and often more expansive roles. As the UP's second year in power approached, JAP activists directed their energy toward formalizing existing relationships between popular consumers and ad hoc distribution centers that marginal communities had relied upon for years to fulfill their basic social and economic needs. Family-run grocery stores, women's centers, neighborhood community boards, local labor halls, and participating butcher shops became the principal nodes of this system, serving as de facto sites of exchange for things like beans, sugar, flour, tea, rice, cooking oil, and especially chicken and beef. Working with state distribution firms, JAPs also increasingly engaged in the regulated sale of essential non-foodstuffs, including fabric, detergent, matches, and sewing yarn.

In this way, revolutionary food activism at once reflected a reencounter with the Popular Front (FP) era, when local consumers had spearheaded neighborhood consumer watchdog committees to denounce speculators, and an extension of the various practices of economic solidarity that had taken hold on Santiago's urbanizing periphery during the interceding postwar era.[16] In La Granja and La Cisterna, two working-class neighborhoods on the southern edge of Greater Santiago, the first JAP committees reportedly emerged out of a special food program that began during the first months of the revolution. Run by the state's agricultural marketing company, ECA, the initiative helped distribute products like potatoes and onions from nearby farms to shantytown consumers.[17] One of the most concrete examples of the collaboration that anticipated the JAPs occurred in the neighboring communities of Santa Rosa Chena de Peñaflor, a relatively poor but rapidly urbanizing community southwest of Santiago, and Los Campesinos, an agrarian reform settlement. There, just a few months before the UP's 1970 election, residents of the two communities—one increasingly urban and the other largely rural—put the finishing touches on an accord that previewed the workings of many JAP committees. The agreement stipulated that urban consumers would be granted exclusive access to the agricultural bounty harvested on the cooperatively run properties of Los Campesinos. The peasant farmers of the rural settlement also obtained a permanent market for their produce.

Victoria Flores, an urban community activist, and Raul Figueroa, a member of the agricultural cooperative, led the effort to consolidate this first-of-its-kind system. Both spoke approvingly of how the pact linked the country's land redistribution efforts to a defined market of low-income consumers who resided on the margins of the national consumer economy. "We've signed this agreement to show . . . that Agrarian Reform can also serve the poor people of the city," Flores declared in an interview. She pointed out that consumers in their community would pay a third to a quarter of current produce prices after the agreement went into effect. Figueroa concurred, vocalizing his dream that this type of direct food distribution would soon spread across the entire Santiago periphery.[18]

Although direct distribution was one element of the UP's approach to the food economy, more often the JAPs themselves constituted the end point in a restructured system of nationalized food producers and state distribution firms. Before Allende's election, food distribution in Chile tended to be organized as a three-tiered pyramid. Atop the pyramid were a handful of large import firms, many of them owned by foreign nationals, which had a firm grip on the wholesale distribution of domestically produced and imported foodstuffs. In the middle lay an intermediate grouping of semi-wholesalers, most of whom sold their food products in Santiago's Vega Central and at a handful of large supermarkets that existed around the capital. Finally, at the bottom of the pyramid sat the small neighborhood markets that most consumers relied upon to meet their basic daily needs, but which in most cases were dependent on the Vega Central for their stock.

In an attempt to both reduce the time it took for essential products to work their way through the aforementioned supply chain and contain the cost that consumers paid at the end of the chain, the Allende government sought to chop up the distribution pyramid. First, by nationalizing the companies atop the pyramid and consolidating their assets into a single state-run company, known as the Chilean National Distribution Company (DINAC), the state aimed to assume control over the most vital component of the supply chain: wholesale distribution. Then, by creating alliances with small retailers at the bottom of the pyramid—in essence, turning butchers, bakers, small bodega-style dry goods purveyors, and neighborhood produce sellers into JAP affiliates—the state could gradually cut out the need for the middle section of the food distribution pyramid.[19]

During the first half of the revolution, Chileans embraced new modes of state-mediated exchange, not just out of ideological affinity with the UP but also because it appeared that such a system would, in fact, ease enduring economic hardships. In La Cisterna, the shopkeeper Hernán Nuñez was among those who organized one of that community's first JAP committees in his neighborhood of Clara Estrella. In an interview he gave to *El Siglo*, Nuñez noted that among the community's thirty or so small retailers and food purveyors, twenty-three had joined the JAP in the first two months after its founding. "Its benefits are well-known to everyone," he maintained, noting that residents of La Cisterna were "able to buy everything" after the JAP began enlisting members. Nuñez remarked that after he affiliated with the JAP his own store started receiving as many as four hundred chickens per week through new state-run distribution channels, all at official wholesale prices. That figure, he told the paper, represented a fourfold increase in his chicken supply when compared to life before the JAP.[20] "This is the first time . . . that [the needs of] both *pobladores* and small merchants have been taken into consideration," another JAP supporter noted in a newspaper report that described unscrupulous middlemen as a common enemy of both groups.[21]

Early media accounts of the JAPs within pro-UP publications went to great lengths to emphasize the economic confidence that the early JAP network inspired. One report contrasted the effectiveness of DINAC with the unpredictability of Chile's private wholesale firms. The report quoted a Santiago baker who noted that it often took a private distributor more than two weeks to deliver needed merchandise to his bakery. What's more, when merchandise finally arrived, it was often at prices well above state-mandated price ceilings. "The most important thing is food," the baker said. "The first people that the Government should go after are the big distribution monopolies. . . . The big guys (*los grandes señores*) are the ones who starve the people," he maintained, demonstrating a clear preference for local economic control of the distribution chain and antipathy for monopoly capitalism.[22]

During the second half of 1971 and into early 1972, small merchants, particularly those located in the urbanizing periphery of Santiago, looked to the JAPs to resolve the problems of supply scarcity and unpredictable delivery schedules that, for them, constituted a daily encounter with economic injustice. At one price and supply committee meeting in Santiago, a frustrated merchant noted that for three Wednesdays in a row, his butcher shop had received no chickens from the private distributor who typically supplied his business. He demanded that the state, through DIRINCO, detail a public plan of action to remedy this unacceptable problem.[23] Similarly, a report in *El Siglo* used the story of a small beverage retailer in the community of José María Caro to demonstrate how local merchants would benefit from the JAPs. Big drink distributors had for months limited their sales of beer and

FIGURE 11. A UP poster encourages consumers and small merchants to join their local consumer supply committees. Fundación Salvador Allende, Santiago de Chile.

soda to small retailers in marginal *poblaciones* around the capital, preferring instead to sell to just a handful of larger commercial establishments where prices were higher and demand was assumed to be more reliable. A new JAP outpost in José María Caro curbed such discrimination, since small, previously excluded merchants could now pool their purchases from private distributors to create economies of scale that diluted the risk for both small merchants and distributors.[24]

While the work of the JAPs built political bridges in the mold of the FP, the popularity of the grassroots network also reflected consumers' and small merchants' shared desire to extend the principles of economic democracy beyond the factory floor. Put differently, for many *japistas* (JAP activists), joining neighborhood consumer committees was about reimagining the boundaries of political participation in everyday economic life. JAP meetings became forums to debate everything from the concept of a "just price" to where the line should be drawn between the proper regulation of commercial exchange and unwarranted state "harassment" of small business owners.[25] Quite often these debates reflected in miniature discussions taking place on the global stage at the very same moment, such as when the Allende government articulated its conception of "just profit" to foreign mining corporations or presented its historic "Charter of Economic Rights and Duties of States" to the membership of the United Nations Conference on Trade and Development (UNCTAD).[26] While the charter demanded equitable trade relations for the commodity-dependent economies of the Global South, the JAPs demanded equitable relations of exchange in the everyday economy.

UP supporters' use of food to demonstrate an ethical commitment to the principle of equality was widely visible in the periphery of Santiago in early December 1971. Just days after contingents of mostly upper-class women marched through the streets of the capital, banging empty pots and pans, the revolutionary women of Campamento "Che Guevara" staged a community potluck to counter images of food scarcity that their opponents were broadcasting. As they invited their well-to-do neighbors in parishes like Providencia to visit the peripheral neighborhoods of the capital, pro-UP women advertised a four-course menu at a community potluck in their own working-class community—one that began with a light consommé and nutritious lettuce salad topped with chicken, olives, and avocado and was then followed by chicken cazuela and a special dessert, plus coffee. "All of the foodstuffs that the poor *momias* [the term used by UP supporters to attack the revolution's wealthy opponents] have apparently not seen in a great while were acquired by the pobladores and shopkeepers of the campamento," *El Siglo* reported in its tongue-in-check description of the event. There would even be bathrooms and private parking available: "all free of charge, quite naturally."[27]

POLITICIZING PROTEIN

The JAP gained official legal status as an institutionalized appendage of Chile's Ministry of Economy in the fall of 1972. Across Chile, but particularly in Santiago, a proliferating number of JAPs gradually transformed the consumer economy into an arena for collective political formation.[28] In a report presented to the PCCh's Central Committee in the early spring of 1972, one of the party's chief economic thinkers, José Cademártori, provided a series of figures that underscored the growing participation of Chilean consumers in UP-backed JAPs during the revolution's first two years. Some 1,200 such consumer committees were up and running in towns and neighborhoods across Chile by September 1972, Cademártori noted, just a few dozen shy of the goal the UP had set for itself at the beginning of that year.[29] Of those, an estimated 720 operated in Greater Santiago, while another 500 existed in provinces beyond Santiago.[30] In Santiago province alone, approximately 7,000 small- and medium-sized merchants had created agreements with their neighborhood JAPs to ensure that state distribution and marketing agencies adequately supplied their shelves with goods that were tagged with official prices.[31] According to a report published in the pro-UP magazine *Chile Hoy*, as of late May 1972, state-run firms, which supplied the JAPs, controlled the distribution of around 85 percent of all meat in Chile; 60 percent of all sugar; 50 percent of all fish and seafood; and between a fifth and a quarter of the country's supplies of pasta, cooking oil, rice, tea, crackers, and canned goods.[32]

But as economic challenges swelled and both domestic and international opposition to Allende's government consolidated, the role of the JAPs in the UP's revolutionary experiment evolved. Instead of offering a positive vision of a socialist future, over the course of 1972 the JAPs increasingly assumed a defensive posture that seemed punitive and partisan to the UP's opponents as well as many middle-class Chileans who had initially supported the coalition. While Allende remained committed to the ambitious campaign promises he had laid out during the 1970 election campaign, this cresting wave of disillusionment forced the UP to recalibrate its political and economic agenda.

As a PCCh militant and active japista in the Santiago parish of La Cisterna declared amid a brewing counteroffensive by Chile's anti-communist right, the JAPs' rootedness in local community life made it an especially "powerful weapon in the fight against the enemies of the people."[33] Like many other UP-backed organizations and state agencies, the JAP thus became a redoubt against counterreform and reaction.

It was in this context that the JAPs, and especially japista women, assumed a leadership role in what would become one of the UP era's signature consumer campaigns: encouraging the public to consume alternatives to scarce red meat. In this regard, one of the less conventional spaces of revolutionary activity that took hold in the early months of 1972 was the state-sponsored, neighborhood fish fry, known colloquially as a *fritanga*. Envisioned by the UP as a way of turning a growing supply of high-protein fish that emerged from the 1971 Soviet-Chilean fishing pact into a new line of consumer demand, the JAPs and their various constituent organizations led an effort to celebrate what would become known as "Fish Days."[34] At such gatherings, a fixture of community life in UP strongholds during early 1972, elected officials, activists from local mothers' centers, japistas, and at times members of the national police and military, gathered to prepare and consume fresh seafood and other domestically produced foods that the Allende government made available at little or no cost.[35]

One of the most notable efforts in popular fish promotion occurred in late April 1972 when a cluster of communities north of downtown Santiago hosted an event that became known as Operation Merluza. The program included a weeklong cooking exposition led by DIRINCO functionaries, nutrition experts, public health officials, and social workers from more than a dozen Santiago health outposts. After the expo concluded, female participants returned to their home communities with thirty "easy and economical recipes" for preparing frozen merluza that could be shared with their neighbors.[36]

The ultimate objective of these unlikely examples of revolutionary praxis was to bring more poor and working people into contact with a nationally produced food product that was, at least in the popular imagination, still associated with elite consumption habits. In so doing, the "substitution economy" aimed to boost domestic consumption of protein-packed alternatives to scarce, prohibitively expensive beef. Patricio Palma, the director of DIRINCO for much of the Chilean revolution, remembers that in the first few months of 1972, there was hardly a weekend that went by in which he and

FIGURE 12. Salvador Allende participates in a local community potluck during the revolution. Fundación Salvador Allende, Santiago de Chile.

his staff did not accompany UP politicians to Santiago poblaciones or out to the provinces to eat fried merluza and bear witness to the popular-front-style collaboration that undergirded the revolution.[37] Allende himself highlighted the connection between women, fish, and revolutionary patriotism during his 1972 May Day address. "We are going to replace the protein from beef with protein from fish, and merluza is the symbol of the initiative of Chile's women," he declared.[38] The consumption of protein-rich, domestically produced merluza was such a significant icon of the UP's commitment to a socialist future that the popular pro-Allende folk band Quilapayún dedicated an entire song to the fish in 1972. "How are you going to say that merluza is no good," the musicians asked listeners, if merluza filled Chileans with "the happiness of life"?[39]

GENDERED MILITANCY

For a time, some of Allende's political opponents reluctantly endorsed the government's fish campaign in an effort to diversify consumption patterns. In early 1972, for example, the popular women's magazine *Eva*, a publication that would soon become an important outlet for the anti-Allende women's movement, used its regular recipes section to promote fish consumption, providing its readership with dozens of ways to prepare domestically caught fish and seafood. "In the absence of beef, there's no choice but to turn toward the sea," the magazine's editors wrote in the summer of 1972.[40] But as the UP revolution marched forward, a growing number of consumers saw the government's fish campaign as a form of revolutionary discipline that bordered on coercive.[41] The substitution economy—and the politicization of food upon which it was built—reproduced social roles from the top down, none more so than the gendered division of labor within domestic life.

The words of JAP promoter Eduardo Flores are instructive in that they show where a commitment to revolutionary egalitarianism ran into trouble. "As a working-class activist, I'm conscious of the needs of the urban poor, who've struggle[d] for so many years against scarcity, against low wages, against food shortages, and against the lack of the basic necessities of life," Flores told *El Siglo* in early 1972, explaining what motivated his activism in the JAPs. "I think the largest burden in all of this has fallen on our women, who must confront speculation, hoarding, [and] long lines to buy just bit of meat.... This is the primary reason to keep fighting.... [A]iding our women is of utmost importance."[42] In Flores's reading, it was a man's duty to participate in the political struggle against scarcity to rescue his distressed female partner—and in turn, the traditional family structure—from domestic hardship.[43] Echoing the same gendered conceptualizations of female vulnerability and familial victimization, another left-leaning Chilean publication would write that "it's the *pobladora* [urban poor woman] who has on her shoulders the weight of feeding her family, it's the female laborer who must watch over the health of her children, and it's the housewife who must wake up early to obtain bread for her family."[44] Such words speak to the relative marginalization of women within the JAPs; although consumer committees had been set up to better integrate women into the revolutionary process, the fact that men often held positions of leadership within them restricted women's own political horizons.

The Allende government's equation of women's militancy with what historian Michelle Chase, in the context of the Cuban Revolution, has called a discourse of "revolutionary austerity" underscored the increasingly tenuous bond between many Chilean women and the UP starting in the revolution's second year.[45] The state's enlistment of women to disseminate a message of domestic sacrifice also came to represent a political weakness of the JAP model. Rather than being seen as a source of female economic emancipation, the JAPs increasingly symbolized the confined space within which women were allowed to express their political desires. In this fraught context, female support for Chile's socialist coalition slowly fractured.

For some women, disillusionment stemmed from the growing sense that JAP committees were becoming vehicles for dietary policing and surveillance. In an interview conducted by the historian Margaret Power, one resident of a peripheral neighborhood northwest of Santiago recalled how her neighborhood JAP was an instrument for doling out favors based upon partisan affiliations.[46] A common anti-JAP slogan used by the PDC in 1972 underscored that feeling. "The food your family depends on," the party maintained, "should not depend on the politics of your most sectarian neighbor."[47] Some of the revolution's most conservative critics even accused the JAPs of replicating Cuba's Comités para la Defensa de la Revolución (Committees for the Defense of the Revolution)—the neighborhood boards that enforced party discipline during Castro's revolution. The most extreme charges came from conservative media outlets, like the vociferously anti-Allende *El Mercurio*. Under the headline "Communists to Control the Chilean Food Supply," the paper contended that the PCCh was forcing consumers to take loyalty pledges before granting access to basic goods that party leaders, through the JAPs, held off the market.[48] In its political materials, the right-wing National Party even took to replacing the "J" in "JAP" with a Soviet hammer and sickle.[49]

Such sentiments inevitably created hard-to-shake feelings of isolation and resentment, even among women who continued to be active JAP members. More than three decades after the revolution, one Santiago japista remembered working from sunrise to sunset in her consumer committee. The experience was "terrible," though, because neighbors rarely appreciated her tireless efforts.[50] In an interview with a Chilean historian in 2011, Sonia Paz Jiménez, a resident of the southern Santiago población of La Victoria and a former JAP activist, similarly described the process through which the JAPs became discredited as an economic boom turned into a bust. "The first year was good, so good. Everyone had money, you bought what you wanted. . . . But then things started to disappear and things got more difficult," Paz Jiménez recalled. "Many people that were for Allende started to turn against him because they lacked things. You went to buy a kilo of rice at the store and were told 'there's none,' A liter of oil: 'there's none.' There was nothing. . . . And the shop owners went around telling the people 'It's because of the JAP, *poh*.' And so we became their enemies."[51]

Over time, the UP's reproduction of a gendered division of labor through the JAPs even led some Chileans who occupied the UP's far-left flank, particularly supporters of the Revolutionary Left Movement, or MIR, to question the UP's commitment to a notion of equality that went beyond rigid classifications of class and party. In a thinly veiled criticism of PCCh economic thought, one female activist told *El Rebelde*, the paper of record for the MIR, that a truly revolutionary woman had an obligation to "shake off bourgeois lies and myths" that suggested a woman's proper place was "in the home, caring for children and preparing food."[52] While the MIR and other leftist groups did not reject the important economic work that JAP activists were engaged in, many did suggest that the model needed to give the residents of local communities greater political say in how and where food distribution centers were run.

A NEW RECIPE FOR REVOLUTION?

Confronted with a fractious base of support and an increasingly aggressive opposition, in June 1972 Allende called together the leaders from the various parties in his coalition to assess the depth of the country's political and economic crisis and chart a new path forward. The Lo Curro conclave was the second of two meetings held among top UP leaders in the first half of that year, and it would confirm the existence of two competing strategies within Allende's governing coalition.[53] One faction, led by the PCCh, argued that in the face of mounting conflict, the time had come for the UP to consolidate its economic gains and seek compromise with the most moderate elements of the opposition. According to top PCCh leaders, the UP needed to extend an olive branch to the Christian Democrats, in particular, if for no other reason than to prevent an alliance between the country's middling sectors and the more extreme elements of the anti-UP opposition.

The second position, espoused by Chile's Socialist Party and a growing number of individuals associated with the Catholic left, argued that more than at any other time during the first year and a half of the revolution, the UP needed to align itself with its mobilized grassroots base, including the MIR. As historian Peter Winn writes, the Socialist Party's strategy would have meant placing the state "at the head of the revolution from below."[54] Chile's Popular Unity experiment stood at a political crossroads as it traveled the road toward socialism: Would Allende's government accelerate its revolutionary agenda and side with the coalition's grassroots base to turn back the tide of economic crisis and anti-UP countermobilization? Or would the government seek a rapprochement with the country's political center to preserve the gains that had been made to date?

Confronted with this strategic conundrum, Allende vacillated.[55] On the one hand, the Chilean president called on officials within his coalition to restart negotiations with the country's Christian Democrats as a last-ditch effort to ease worsening tensions between the executive branch and the opposition-controlled national legislature and judiciary. As an initial act of good faith, Allende promised to temporarily halt all nationalizations by decree. The UP simultaneously sought to reduce the growing disequilibrium between supply and demand through a series of incremental price ceiling adjustments for both nonessential and essential goods. Then, in August 1972, the government announced an initial currency devaluation. Both policies were intended to halt rising inflation, but in the short term they unleashed a rapid rise in prices and a subsequent spike in social unrest.[56]

On the other hand, UP officials scurried to stanch the organized political left's growing discontent with Allende. In an interview he gave to the pro-UP newspaper *Chile Hoy*, DIRINCO chief Palma, who in 1972 had become not-so-affectionately known as the country's "Price-Hike Man," promised that he would work tirelessly to realign his agency's mission of consumer protection with the growing demands of workers and pobladores, even as prices rose.[57] The government, Palma told the paper, was in the process of "changing the focus of DIRINCO completely" by making his office more responsive to grassroots organizations. According to Palma, this meant changing the perceived "paternalism" of DIRINCO and ensuring it was instead an agent of popular empowerment.[58]

But events quickly moved beyond the Allende administration's control as representatives of the country's progressive social movements and many members of the organized Chilean left seized the opportunity to push the revolution forward. During the winter of 1972, in the western Santiago parish of Maipú, workers at Perlak, one of Chile's largest food-processing plants, went on strike, occupied their workplace, and set the foundation for Chile's first *cordón industrial*, a regionally organized "belt" of worker-run industries.[59] Shortly thereafter, workers seized five other canning factories around the capital. MIR sympathizers, meanwhile, occupied a state-controlled distribution warehouse in the southern parish of La Granja to demand that the UP prioritize the construction of what became known as *almacenes populares*—literally, "popular supermarkets"—in communities where the JAPs had little presence.[60] This agitation peaked in late July 1972 when representatives from all of Chile's left political parties, with the notable exception of the PCCh, gathered in the southern city of Concepción to a hold a national popular assembly and chart a new, more participatory path toward a socialist future. The event, which followed the publication of a joint manifesto by the most radical parties of the UP and the MIR, was the most resounding display of popular revolutionary fervor to date.[61]

In this context, a preliminary accord that had been hashed out between the UP and the PDC collapsed when the ascendant conservative wing of the PDC rejected its terms. Instead, the PDC announced its decision to throw its support behind a newly created, anti-Allende political front. Known as the Confederación de la Democracia (Confederation of Democracy, CODE), the coalition was the brainchild of Chile's far-right National Party and *gremio* movement, the conservative guild of mostly white-collar professionals and business owners. CODE's establishment put Chile on a political crash course.[62] Having failed to create a new political center, Allende entered the spring of 1972 standing atop an increasingly unstable base of political support.

CAPITAL STRIKE OR DISTRIBUTION REVOLUTION?

During the month of October 1972, the power of Chile's anti-Allende opposition exploded with force and fury. Responding to a rumor that the UP was about to make good on its threat to nationalize the private transportation sector, truckers affiliated with the country's national trucking federation parked their vehicles on the sides of major thoroughfares and in open fields, turned off their engines, and effectively shut down the distribution of basic goods in the country for nearly a month.[63] What began as a transportation strike reverberated through the anti-UP opposition as small shop owners, industrialists, and middle-class professionals closed shop or called in sick.[64]

Chile's food economy was hit hard by the coordinated job action. According to a government analysis of the strike, more than ten million liters of milk were destroyed because of the transportation stoppage alone. An incalculable amount of agricultural seed and fertilizers also never arrived in the Chilean countryside, setting the stage for agricultural disaster and even more dire food shortages.[65] In 1973, production of potatoes fell by 15 percent, production of beans by more than a fifth, and production of garbanzos by more than half compared to 1972. One of the most dramatic economic declines occurred in wheat; total production fell by more than 37 percent in 1973—the most significant single-year percentage decline for the subsector since the late nineteenth century.[66] Given that wheat was a crop whose production remained largely in the hands of large landowners, such a precipitous drop suggests that the food crisis that overwhelmed Chile in 1973 often began on land that UP's most strident opponents still controlled.[67]

Hundreds, perhaps thousands, of retail stores and other commercial establishments shuttered their doors for much of the month, pushing an already struggling economy over the precipice. Halfway through the strike, which became commonly referred to as the October Bosses' Strike, Santiago's *La Tercera de la Hora* newspaper provided a dramatic account of conditions in and around the Chilean capital: "The scarcity of food and lack of gasoline were yesterday the most critical matters confronting the population as a result of the strike.... Shortages were palpable for beef, fish and seafood, chicken, milk, eggs, and vegetables, among other foodstuffs. For its part, the distribution of bread has also been seriously affected by a lack of flour and lack of fuel to heat the ovens of bakeries. In Santiago's Vega Central market, as in local farmers' markets, peripheral markets, and neighborhood grocery stores, the absence of food was nearly complete."[68] By directly assailing the distribution of basic consumer goods in order to forge oppositional unity, anti-Allende forces bet that making the country's consumer crisis even more acute would have marginal short-term political cost while offering great medium- and long-term returns.

In an attempt to end the strike and restore distribution activities around the country, Allende granted a series of concessions to his opponents, including the appointment of three moderate military officials to key cabinet posts.

Shortly thereafter, he selected a fourth retired military official, General Alberto Bachelet, to lead a new state-run, but less overtly political, consumer distribution agency and removed a major private distribution firm from the government's list of enterprises to be nationalized.[69] A few months later, the UP revoked the honorary price inspector status of dozens of local consumer price control activists as well, thus acceding to the Chilean right's claim that activists were acting recklessly during their inspections of small retailers.[70] If there had been doubts about Allende's strategic impulses during the winter of 1972, the moves reaffirmed Allende's position that the Chilean revolution needed to be consolidated before radicalizing itself further.

The country's mobilized revolutionary left objected to all of this. Indeed, no event more directly ignited revolutionary movements' belief that they deserved a more prominent voice in charting the country's socialist path than the October Bosses' Strike.[71] As Chilean social scientist Arturo Valenzuela has written, it was the "countermobilization of the petite bourgeoisie" in October 1972 that, in true "dialectical fashion," produced the most "significant and autonomous mobilization" of the country's working class to date.[72] On the political left, "nobody rested" for an entire month, DIRINCO director Palma later recalled. Workers, women, and students all flooded into the streets to keep the food economy running. Some commandeered delivery trucks that had been abandoned by their drivers and delivered undistributed goods to JAP outposts and state distribution centers. Others got to work devising plans to build new popular supermarkets.[73] A group of socialist women, calling themselves the Frente Patriótico de Mujeres (Patriotic Front of Women), even advocated that female UP sympathizers create their own informal health brigades to decrease the public health implications of hunger, which were exacerbated by the closure of private medical offices.[74] "Keeping the supply chain running is an economic game, but it's clearly political as well," Palma remembered thinking at the time.[75]

The case of a SOPROLE dairy factory in Santiago, a major source of milk and other dairy products for Santiago residents, was exemplary of the sort of "popular power" (poder popular) that eventually broke the Bosses' Strike from below. Although many workers in the plant had been clamoring for the factory's socialization for months, the treasurer of the SOPROLE workers' union, Fernando Troncoso, told one reporter that it was only because of the October strike that the 250 blue-collar workers employed at his factory— together with some 30 white-collar workers who refused to take part in the monthlong work stoppage—pursued real revolutionary action. The workers seized the factory "at a moment when most of us weren't even really think-ing about doing so," Troncoso remarked. "In the first days [of the takeover], we were forced to do extra shifts to replace those who did not show up." Soon the factory's occupiers were joined on the plant floor by members of the community's JAP as well as many students. Because of this radical move, the occupied factory continued churning out milk, cheese, and butter for the duration of the strike.

The problem of distribution was resolved by borrowing trucks belonging to state agencies and trade unions. "The very same workers who made the milk, the cheeses, the ricotta, the *manjar* [dulce de leche], and other products immediately became responsible for also delivering those very same products to consumers in the various neighborhoods of Santiago," the labor leader remarked. Troncoso told a reporter that he himself went nine straight days without rest that October. At night, he camped out with his comrades to protect the factory from sabotage. Then, around five o'clock each morning, he would go out with his fellow workers to deliver the goods that had been produced and packaged the day before to JAP committees around the city.[76]

Given the importance of protecting working-class people's ability to find basic foodstuffs, it came as little surprise that some of the most visible actions to end the strike—and then retroactively sanction those who had participated in it—occurred at grocery stores like the one operated by Chile's first major supermarket franchise, ALMAC.[77] On the second Wednesday of November 1972, several hundred community members gathered outside a branch of the local grocery store chain, located in the southwestern Santiago neighbor-hood of Santa Julia. Citing the store owners' participation in the lockout, the protesters pried open the store's doors, hauled out its merchandise, and commenced a system of popular distribution, with fixed prices, of seventeen scarce consumer essentials.[78] According to many left-wing activists, the sale of these ad hoc *canastas populares* (popular baskets) was the first step in restor-ing nutritional security to poor and working-class Santiago neighborhoods.[79] During the first month of 1973, the possession of JAP membership cards and the heavily regulated distribution of fixed "baskets" of consumer essentials became an increasingly common—although not entirely state-backed—means of rationing scarce goods in neighborhoods throughout Santiago and beyond.[80] According to an early 1973 survey of ninety homemakers from six Santiago poblaciones, nearly two-thirds of women supported the use of ration cards to deal with the problem of shortages. As evidence that popular trust lay primarily in local political institutions, the survey also found that pobladores preferred having the JAP or local neighborhood boards administer a rationing program, rather than the national government, military, or someone who did not otherwise have close ties to the community itself.[81]

REVOLUTION AT THE MARKET

The direct action that left-wing groups took to resist the strike quickly became the basis for new modes of community-based regulation and distribution that ran parallel to the state but went beyond the traditional scope of the JAPs. In early 1973, *Punto Final*, another publication affiliated with the MIR, recounted one such experiment in popular consumer democracy that emerged on the periphery of the upscale Santiago neighborhood of Las Condes. According to the magazine, militants on the left first organized a supply and distribution network within a small, working-class section of the parish sometime in late 1972. A short while later, the group temporarily seized control of a provisions warehouse controlled by the state distribution company DINAC, in order to begin distributing basic goods to poor and working-class consumers on their own terms. On the day of the citizens' takeover, members of the network held a secret-ballot election to elect a leadership committee, and a resident of the community, rather than a state-appointed official, was selected to head the new organization alongside a council of twenty-four other individuals. "If capitalism can be used in such a way that it benefits us, we'll use it. If not, we'll take another route," Luis Cáceres, the newly elected president of the consumer committee, told *Punto Final*. Leftist activists dubbed the experiment Chile's "first soviet for basic consumer provisioning."[82]

To be sure, in presenting their work as an alternative to the sometimes vertical structure of the PCCh–run JAPs, the activists who in early 1973 organized and expanded Chile's network of *almacenes del pueblo*, or people's stores, as well as various types of autonomous supply committees, known as *comités de abastecimiento popular* (popular supply committees, CAPs), did not see their actions as being in opposition to the UP.[83] Rather, in the wake of the October Bosses' Strike, they portrayed their work as an alternative mechanism for restoring the JAPs' original promise of economic democracy in the consumer marketplace.[84]

This was what happened in the neighborhood of Nueva Habana, a self-built neighborhood formed just prior to the revolution in the parish of La

Florida. In late 1972 and into 1973, the work of food distribution embodied revolutionary action in Nueva Habana as grassroots leaders demanded that all private producers of basic foodstuffs be socialized and food provisioning be handed over to locally run communal councils.[85] After the October strike, the community's leaders, among them the prominent MIR activist Alejandro Villalobos, built an economic architecture that cut out private distributors and, in large part, the state itself. Local residents selected a delegate from each block in Nueva Habana to identify the basic needs of every household in the community. The local consumer delegates then issued each family one of three color-coded ration cards—yellow, red, or white, depending on family size—and instructed residents to present their cards to the community's new "people's store" to receive a set number of weekly goods at a fixed price.[86]

Some of the most dramatic enactments of a more participatory, more equitable food economy occurred in the western Santiago parish of Maipú. A site of profound revolutionary fervor since the formation of the Cerrillos-Maipú industrial belt and the worker-led takeover of the food-processing company Perlak, the community mobilized against the possibility that socialized companies within the parish might be returned to their former owners or placed in a comanagement arrangement with the state to ease tensions after the October strike. Maipú residents also sought to lay the groundwork for a new alliance between workers, local consumers, and small agricultural producers who inhabited the surrounding rural areas. The climax of such efforts came in June 1973 when the leadership of Cordón Cerrillos-Maipú pursued arguably their most radical action to date: the coordinated seizure of thirty-nine privately owned farms in the area and popular expropriation—and conversion—of the community's old municipal slaughterhouse into a new at-cost, community-run food market.[87] Meeting outside the doors of Perlak on June 19 of that month, workers and residents of the area filed onto buses and hopped on tractors to begin the land occupation. In parallel, a second group of activists, many of them women, took control of Maipú's municipal slaughterhouse. Within hours the occupiers had transformed the space into a site of direct food distribution.

Identifying herself as "an old woman, who is exploited from five in the morning until midnight" and "lives on a humble pension," a domestic worker expressed her glee about the new market to a journalist roughly one week after the popular takeover had succeeded. "In this *mercado popular* [popular market] everything is five or six times cheaper," she noted with great pleasure.[88] Another Maipú resident expressed similar excitement about the June actions. Through collective action, the community had demonstrated that "if we are united with one another, we are capable of resolving the problem of shortages on our own," the resident proudly maintained. "[G]oing forward we'll be able to confront many other types of issues."[89]

The words of Rosa Ríos and María Farías Godoy, two residents of Nueva Habana who actively participated in their own community's citizen-run distribution program, capture the centrality of food justice organizing to Chile's radical left. At the same time, Ríos and Farías Godoy underscore the tenuous relationship between women and the revolution, a relationship that grew increasingly complicated starting in the second year of the UP's socialist experiment. Speaking to reporters in early 1973, Ríos maintained that the most important accomplishment of her community's new exchange system was its success in ending long lines at local markets, thus providing poor women like herself some semblance of economic stability.[90] Farías Godoy responded to a journalist's question about popular attitudes toward rationing by noting that her community welcomed such a system because she and her neighbors had, in the young woman's words, "always lived rationed" by dismally low wages. "I know what rationing feels like, and I'm not alone; every worker knows what rationing feels like! Now, for the first time, it's the rich who will experience rationing," the pobladora contended.[91] By excluding private interests from the food economy, women consumers, acting in concert with the state, would not only be provided a minimal nutritional guarantee; even more important, food security itself would also open up the time and space for women to begin participating in the revolution in ways that extended beyond their traditional domestic roles.

In taking stock of Chile's national consumer crisis after the October strike, Bosco Parra, a leader within the progressive Catholic Party, Izquierda Cristiana (Christian Left, IC) offered comparable views about the new ethics of consumption that emerged out of many leftist circles during the most trying days of Chile's socialist transition. In the short term, Parra argued, supporters of the revolution needed to disabuse themselves of the idea that "abundance," "opulence," and a modern "consumer society" were possible in Chile. Parra questioned whether such conditions were even desirable. "The person who promises abundance without limits, the person who promises that in just five years we are going to have a country on the brink of becoming a high consumption society, is lying," the IC leader said. What *was* possible, however, was the creation of a society that, in Parra's words, "extracts dignity from scarcity." In tackling the challenges that confronted the UP during its second year in power, the task of the revolutionary was to present socialism as a "method of organization" for repairing decades of injustice against Chile's poor and working-classes.[92]

As the comments of people like Ríos, Farías Godoy, and Parra exemplified, the creation of alternative mechanisms for distributing food altered the cultural, political, and ideological horizons of those who were committed to a more just national economy. But just as such views were being articulated, Chile's right-wing opposition was beginning to construct its own vision of how a national economy should function. In the process, counterrevolutionary forces began to disfigure—often beyond recognition—one of the most widely accepted tenants of midcentury citizenship in Chile: that it was the state's duty to guarantee its citizens' access to a decent and dignified standard of living, starting at the kitchen table.

SEVEN

Barren Plots and Empty Pots

AT FIRST BLUSH, Carmen Sáenz does not typify an individual poised to assume a leading role in a counterrevolution. Though she was undoubtedly a member of Chile's upper crust, the Sáenz family had, at least until the 1960s, been associated with the less reactionary tendencies of the country's landed elite. The progressive political views of her own father, an entrepreneurial agriculturalist who popularized new farming technologies and seed varieties on his southern frontier wheat fields, had made him the first politician to win a national election as a candidate for Chile's Popular Front (FP): in 1936, voters elected Cristóbal Sáenz to represent the rural provinces of Bío-Bío and Cautín in the national senate.[1] Although Carmen Sáenz drifted into more conservative circles after the Second World War, her disagreements with those to her left rarely spilled beyond the institutional boundaries of decorous debate. Later in life, Sáenz even recalled that her family's relationship with Salvador Allende himself was amicable, despite clear ideological differences.[2]

Digging just below the surface, however, one sees that Carmen Sáenz's emergence as a prominent voice within Chile's conservative movement seems more predictable, even probable, than is suggested by a cursory review of her family biography or one of the many curated interviews she gave in her later years.[3] Starting in the 1960s, as Sáenz began to identify with more hard-line currents on the political right, she and her husband, the then-congressman Patricio Phillips, played an active role in building the power of the upstart Chilean National Party (PN). By the time of Allende's election, the PN had become the standard-bearer of a more insurgent conservatism—one that Sáenz's husband hailed as a counterweight to the 1959 Cuban Revolution.[4]

By the time Sáenz made her very public entry into protest politics in late 1971, she embodied the most uncompromising elements of Cold War anti-communism. That was the moment when Sáenz helped rally thousands of Chilean women to the streets of Santiago in what was by most accounts the first significant street demonstration against Chile's leftist coalition. The timing of the protest highlighted elite discontent with Fidel Castro's weeks-long visit to the country. But it was the demonstrators' chosen protest instrument, an empty casserole pot, that came to symbolize the opposition's claims about where their country's socialist experiment had failed most dramatically. Allende had initially promised a revolution of plenty, not sacrifice. But one year into the Chilean revolution, his opponents asserted that government economic policies were leaving kitchen pantries across the country empty.[5]

This chapter chronicles the rise of Chile's anti-Allende political right, of which Carmen Sáenz was a notable member. Beginning in late 1971, the Allende government's inability to maintain the material abundance that it had delivered during its first year, coupled with both foreign and homegrown efforts to sabotage the country's consumer economy, galvanized key sectors of Chile's middle and upper classes against the Popular Unity (UP) revolution. Confronted with more aggressive state-led efforts to redistribute land, agriculturalists decried declining domestic production of staples like beef and wheat. As problems of food scarcity reemerged in urban areas, shopkeepers attacked the state's growing participation in the distribution and marketing of food essentials, maintaining that such actions overstepped the line separating public and private life. Similarly, conservative women fought against what they perceived as state intrusion into one of the most personal spaces of the domestic sphere: the kitchen. In sum, frustrations over how food was produced, distributed, and consumed united into a singular oppositional bloc three distinct social groups that, before the early 1970s, shared few political values with one another.[6]

The long-term impacts of the anti-Allende opposition's political actions were significant. As landowners, small shop owners, and conservative housewives disrupted and delegitimized long-standing political and ethical beliefs about the importance of state economic intervention in the national economy, they opened space, intentionally or otherwise, for a small but well-connected cohort of conservative economists to wield new influence. Rather than articulating basic nutrition as a fundamental right of citizenship, which the state had a duty to guarantee and protect, key economic thinkers on the emergent anti-Allende right advocated for the provisioning of food to be treated like all other consumer goods—that is, as a process that market forces should determine. In the decades that followed Allende's overthrow, the notion that the state had an obligation to safeguard the sanctity of the open marketplace outweighed the burdens that a largely unregulated economy imposed on poor and working-class Chileans. In turn, the food economy—and the consumer economy, more generally—showcased the radical free-market project known first in Chile and then around the world as "neoliberalism."[7]

LANDHOLDERS AGAINST REFORM

The first mass mobilizations against the UP did not occur until more than a year into Allende's presidency. However, conservative efforts to contain reformers' pursuit of major social and economic change in Chile had begun to gather momentum even before the UP's 1970 election. Given the political circumstances of the 1960s, it was hardly surprising that the epicenter of opposition to early structural reforms was the Chilean countryside. There, large agricultural landholders pointed to productive stagnation to make the case that redistributive polices imperiled not only the livelihoods of rural producers but also domestic food security.

The Frei administration's decision to expand the legal basis for state-led land expropriations had put landholders in an especially uncomfortable position. The passage of Agrarian Reform Law 16.640 in 1967, in particular, expanded the scenarios under which the state could seize agricultural lands. Under the new law, latifundistas who ignored social legislation, as well as those with properties whose size state assessors deemed counterproductive to the social and economic development of the countryside, became subject to increased scrutiny, irrespective of the productive status of the lands in question.[8] The threat of expropriation, together with a wave of peasant-led land occupations, produced uncertainty and antipathy among the landholding elite. Recounting a speech that Jacques Chonchol gave sometime during the late 1960s or early 1970s, Carmen Sáenz remembered the intense disdain she felt when the country's leading voice on agricultural matters suggested that from that point forward "the peasants would be in charge" of the countryside. Even decades later, Chonchol's words evoked resentment. "What started to predominate was violence," Sáenz told one interviewer. The Chilean state's expropriation of agricultural lands, which had often been in the same family's hands for generations, was, in the conservative activist's words, simply "brutal."[9]

The benefits of historical distance reveal that Sáenz's memories about both campesino violence and state overreach were often grounded in an incomplete accounting of the past. In his assessment of rural land seizures, the historian Peter Winn notes that peasant *tomas* (occupations) in Chile were largely peaceful, in great contrast, for example, to agrarian reform in early-twentieth-century Mexico or Bolivia after its revolution in 1952. Only rarely, Winn maintains, did Chilean peasant groups destroy formerly private agricultural properties. Instead, the new possessors of such estates wanted to "preserve" all that was taken for their own collective exploitation.[10]

Nevertheless, landholders' anxieties about agrarian reform were real, and they stretched across an increasingly broad cross section of Chile's rural population.[11] Some of the earliest beneficiaries of agrarian reform efforts in the early and mid-1960s—mostly male tenant farmers, many of them with ties to Chile's Christian Democratic Party (PDC)—constituted by the late 1960s a small but relatively well-off class of landholders. These newcomers to the propertied class interpreted the extension of land titles and credit to less established rural communities as a political and economic threat. Citing their new status as small agrarian capitalists, the members of the twenty-seven local committees that made up the Association of Small Agriculturalists of Lanco, located in the province of Valdivia, asked President Frei in November 1968 to halt new lines of credit to small peasants who, mired in debt, would almost certainly be unable to repay state loans. Any group that continued to receive credit from the state without first repaying at least 90 percent of its liabilities to the state was "openly harming those who, with great sacrifice, had paid back their acquired debts," the petitioners argued.[12] Such stratification among different categories of rural workers foreshadowed ideological divisions that would emerge within the broader rural labor movement after the UP's election in 1970.[13]

Latifundistas responded to this environment of uncertainty in various ways. Starting in the late 1960s, many landowners fired workers whom estate foremen discovered participating in rural organizing efforts.[14] They also publicly denounced urban state officials for intruding in the affairs of what landowners claimed was an otherwise peaceful countryside. In a 1969 editorial that attacked the growing presence of idealistic city folk in rural life, the leadership of Chile's large landowners' association, the SNA, maintained that the source of campesino strife originated outside the countryside itself.[15]

By 1968 it was clear that landowners were the ones embracing more overt forms of violence to maintain their hold over the rural economy. In June of that year, the rural union leader Guillermo Atúnez Arriagada became one of the first victims of such violence when a foreman on the privately held Santa Ana fundo, located just east of Talca, shot and killed Atúnez Arriagada for allegedly organizing rural workers on the estate.[16] Earlier in the year, another latifundista who resided near the rural city of Colchagua had pulled a gun on the agronomist Hugo Vidal, a leading figure in the development of the much-heralded Marchigüe chicken cooperative.[17] In October, a group of ten large landowners near the southern town of Llanquihue attacked an INDAP official and a rural worker as the two men left a meeting about agrarian reform matters in the region.[18] In August 1969, two journalists working for the conservative Santiago-based newspaper *El Mercurio* were even threatened by a group of more than two dozen landowners who suspected the men were, in fact, officials from one of Chile's agrarian reform agencies.[19]

Few families more aptly represented landowner intransigence than the Benavente family of Linares. Regarded as local power brokers across the southern edge of the Central Valley, in January 1968 the family's eldest son, Gabriel Benavente Palma, shot—and left partially paralyzed—a young INDAP official named Guillermo Quinteros. Quinteros had traveled to the Benaventes' Cuñao Bajo property to meet with a tenant farmer who was active in the area's rural union movement.[20] In the months that followed, violence on and near the Benavente family's properties became a recurring feature of life in Linares. In May 1968, for example, a group of peasants loyal to the prominent landholding family confronted a competing group of campesinos who had demanded that the state break up another Benavente property in the wake of the 1967 agrarian reform law. The physical confrontation that ensued between Benavente loyalists and pro-reform peasants left nine people hospitalized.[21]

One year later, in early September 1969, Benavente reappeared in the public eye when he staged an armed occupation of CORA's regional headquarters in Linares.[22] The action, which came just one day after the state finalized an order to expropriate yet another Benavente property, was a prelude to arguably the most dramatic instance of counterreform violence during the Frei years: the murder of CORA's regional director, Hernán Mery. A thirty-year-old agronomist who had worked for the state's development agency before joining CORA in 1965, Mery had only recently been tapped to head CORA's agrarian reform operations in Linares and Maule when he and a delegation of state officials and members of the Chilean national police arrived at a Benavente estate to enforce a state-mandated expropriation order in late April 1970.[23] Amid a confrontation between pro- and anti-reform groups that occurred at the property's locked gates, a club-wielding Benavente loyalist struck and killed the young agrarian official.[24]

Allende's election in 1970 provided an unexpected respite from the tensions of the last two years of the Frei presidency. Although he promised to deepen agrarian reform while on the campaign trail, Chile's new socialist president initially struck a more conciliatory tone with the country's agricultural associations and trade groups after assuming office. In turn, many landowners adopted a cautious wait-and-see attitude.[25] An article published in the SNA's monthly bulletin, *El Campesino*, expressed optimism, for example, that the country's expanding chicken industry—a key part of the broader effort to develop domestic sources of protein—would thrive under Allende.[26]

SNA president Benjamín Matte's decision to lead a trade delegation to Cuba in December 1970 represented a key moment in the thaw between the UP and Chile's rural oligarchy. Although he was criticized by some members of the Chilean right for participating in the mission, Matte maintained that the opening of new international markets for Chilean beans, onions, garlic, and timber products was vital to his country's economic future. The SNA spokesperson also underscored the benefits that would accrue to Chilean consumers by importing Cuban tobacco, shrimp, seafood, and the organic compound urea, a vital additive to agricultural fertilizers and animal feed.[27] For many landowners, the UP's approach to agricultural development did not, at least initially, seem incompatible with the promises of a "green revolution."[28]

Although select sectors of Chile's landed elite benefited handsomely from UP food and agriculture policies, a lasting truce between the UP and Chile's large landholders proved chimeric. Events that dominated headlines in late December 1970 anticipated clashes to come. Just days before the Christmas holiday, a coalition of indigenous groups and rural workers in the southern province of Cautín seized the sprawling Rucalán estate, an iconic frontier property controlled by the area's powerful Landarretche family. The occupiers effectively controlled the estate for four days before its former owners reclaimed the property by force.[29]

In the end, the late December mobilizations compelled Allende to take a decisive stand on behalf of Chile's rural poor. Citing the Landarretches' role in the violent counteroffensive against the peasant occupation, Chile's national police arrested the patriarch of the family, along with one of his adult sons, on Christmas Day 1970. In the weeks that followed, state officials formally transferred Rucalán to the same community of Mapuche activists who had preemptively occupied it. "Since we took nothing with us, the State sent us people from INDAP, and they were our ambassadors," remembered Don Heriberto Ailío, one of the leaders of both the original occupation and the new agrarian settlement that emerged from it.[30]

A short while later, in February 1971, Allende relocated the headquarters of Chile's agrarian reform efforts, including the offices of Agriculture Minister Jacques Chonchol himself, to Cautín. Peasants in the area interpreted the move as a show of support and a green light to accelerate land seizures.[31] By the spring of 1971, the UP and Chile's large landowners stood at loggerheads with one another.[32]

PRODUCTION TROUBLES

Carmen Sáenz said that it was not long after the seizure of Rucalán that the Chilean state set in motion the expropriation of Calatayud, one of the rural properties that she and her husband had inherited from her family. The seizure of the wheat-producing estate, located just outside Traiguén, a rural hamlet equidistant between the cities of Los Angeles and Temuco, was largely "political," in Sáenz's view.[33] Given the fact that so much of her family's land was covered by rivers and uncultivatable lowland areas, the eighty-hectare— roughly two-hundred-acre—private property threshold that the Allende government sought to enforce in the countryside made little sense in her family's case, the anti-Allende militant claimed.[34]

Another Allende critic, Hernán Millas, would later use the expropriation of the Sáenz family's properties as a parable for the economic recklessness of the UP's agrarian reform. During the mid-twentieth century, the Traiguén estate had become a model of agricultural modernization, Millas wrote. Prior to the UP's election, the farm had been producing around 35,000 quintals of wheat per year—roughly 3.5 million kilos. It had regularized the use of some of the highest-quality varieties of hybrid seeds in all of Chile. What's more, it became home to one of the country's most coveted herds of Dutch dairy cattle. In the estate's ultramodern, *azulejo*-tiled milking facilities, cows reportedly listened to peaceful melodies to improve milk production. So exemplary was the farm that students from agronomy programs at the nearby Universidad Austral de Valdivia and the Universidad de Chile visited it regularly to learn about best agricultural practices.[35]

But this idyllic situation ended when the Chilean state took control of the aforementioned lands—at least that was the claim popularized by Allende opponents like Sáenz and Millas. In the wake of the Traiguén-based farm's expropriation, wheat production was said to have declined by roughly 90 percent. Annual milk production dropped precipitously as well, falling by more than a third, from 800,000 liters to 260,000 liters. Moreover, opponents of the expropriation argued that the short-term goals of state intervention irreversibly altered the area's once-pastoral landscape. For example, dozens of old-growth trees were chopped down to make room for new hog pens. In describing the haphazard methods that rural peasants and agrarian reform advisers embraced as part of their joint management of the farm, Millas maintained that it was only "logical that months later the scourge of hunger would appear throughout Chile."[36]

Opposition leaders held up the expropriation of the Sáenz family's lands as a symbol of the UP's decision to push forward with land redistribution, no matter its social or economic costs. Indeed, as Chile's march toward socialism advanced, the state's inability to couple redistributive efforts, on the one hand, with steady improvements in agricultural productivity, on the other, became one of the landholding community's key rhetorical attacks against the revolution.[37] In June 1972, one year after the UP first unveiled its plans for a "battle of production" in the Chilean countryside, Matte pointed out that Chile was on pace to spend US$455 million on food imports that year, a figure that was three times more than what the UP government had originally anticipated at the beginning of the year. While Chile fell short of that unnerving number in 1972, importing US$318 million worth of food instead, just one year later food imports far surpassed that figure as Chile brought in foreign food valued at US$512 million to make up for domestic shortfalls.[38]

SNA leaders underscored the fact that many of the goods being imported—like milk and beef—were ones that Chile had the capacity to produce itself.[39] In the event Allende infringed upon landowners' right to retain eighty hectares of individual property, Matte contended, the government would be committing a "crime against the consumer."[40] A special SNA commission formed in 1973 to assess the declining state of popular nutrition in the country contended that agricultural production levels for many key foodstuffs were similar, if not inferior, to those registered in 1936—a thirty-five-year *retroceso* (regression), in the commission's words.[41]

For one widely consumed crop, wheat, that assertion proved quite accurate. Although economic experts maintained that consumer demand for bread, the primary comestible for which wheat was utilized, was relatively inelastic—meaning that improved purchasing power only marginally affected demand—domestic wheat production plummeted in the final two years of the revolution. In 1973, Chile would produce just under 7,467,000 metric quintals—a precipitous decline from the 13,679,740 metric quintals it harvested in 1971 and a number that was even less than the roughly 8,659,000 metric quintals that the country produced when the famed wheat grower Cristóbal Sáenz was elected to national office in 1936.[42]

To make up for domestic underperformance, wheat imports soared. In 1970, Chile had imported four million tons of wheat from abroad, but by 1972, it was importing around seven million tons. According to analysts at the Linares-based newspaper *El Heraldo*, the only explanation for this disconcerting surge was the "indiscriminate and politicized" nature of the UP's agrarian reform program.[43] As further evidence of substandard production, a 1972 government decree mandated that Chilean millers produce eighty-eight kilos of wheat flour from every one hundred kilos of raw wheat—an increase of ten kilos over the previous standard. As a result, Chilean consumers encountered noticeably less flavorful loaves of bread—what one anti-Allende paper referred to as *pan de guerra*, or wartime bread.[44]

MAKING MILITANT MERCHANTS

In an interview in early 1973 with SNA's monthly bulletin, Matte offered some preliminary thoughts about why he believed Allende's agrarian reform—and ultimately the UP's socialist experiment, more generally—was failing. When it came to Chile's agricultural woes, the former SNA spokesperson blamed the socialist coalition's unwillingness to reform the system of economic controls and regulations that kept food prices artificially low for urban consumers. Such a system, he argued, offered no incentives for rural producers to modernize their operations. Although agrarian reformers in both Frei's and Allende's governments claimed that they would end the long-standing division between city and country, geographic inequity between urban and rural space remained, in Matte's words, "the root of the problem" in 1973, just as it had been decades before.[45]

Matte's critique would have undoubtedly resonated with many small and medium-sized Chilean farmers after the Second World War. However, the rural leader's words failed to account for one of the greatest political storylines of early 1970s Chile: the emergence of a strong and increasingly unified urban bloc that demanded an end to the same sorts of state intervention in the urban food economy that agriculturalists had denounced for decades. Put differently, a coalition of city-dwelling Chileans, which included food pur-veyors and many consumers, began to articulate, for arguably the first time in twentieth-century Chilean history, a parallel argument to that of their landholding counterparts. The very regulatory policies that the government had long promoted to actually protect city consumers and small retailers from predatory distribution and import firms and absentee landowners, were, in the view of nearly all members of a nascent anti-Allende coalition, also to blame for everyday economic problems like scarcity. As doubts emerged about the UP's ability to maintain the gains achieved during the revolution's early months, women and members of Chile's petit bourgeoisie thus became unlikely allies of one another, and of Chile's rural landowning class.

Similar to what had transpired with large landowners, the Allende government had made overtures to various elements of the Chilean middle class in the lead-up to the 1970 presidential election and throughout the early months of the revolution. In analyzing the UP's electoral victory, a *New York Times* reporter called Chile's middling sectors a "willing force" in the coun-try's move left. "The theory that a growing middle class guarantees capitalist stability in Latin America has been undermined by the democratic election of a Marxist President in Chile," the US paper argued, pointing out that a sizable cross section of the roughly 30 percent of Chileans who might reasonably be identified as "middle class" had supported a socialist candidate.[46] In the months that followed, the material successes of the UP economy seemed to consolidate middle-class support for Allende. Indeed, no single event pro-vided clearer evidence of the leftward march of the country's middling sectors than Chile's April 1971 municipal elections, in which UP-affiliated candidates secured an unprecedented majority of all votes cast.[47]

The Confederación del Comercio Detallista (Small Retailers' Confedera-tion), one of Chile's largest organized constituencies representing middle-class interests, was one of the groups that offered its tacit support to Allende and his coalition at multiple moments during the UP's first year in office. According to the association's leadership, retailers and small business owners had promoted "tranquility" among their membership base after Allende's 1970 electoral victory, promoting what confederation leadership called "active collaboration, constructive criticism . . . and frank dialogue" with the socialist government.[48] During the first half of 1971, the white-collar guild had continued to maintain a cooperative relationship with the coalitional government—this despite the fact that, as a single economic bloc, small retailers believed they were "the only sector of the workforce" that did not see their incomes rise significantly in the early months of the UP. Price-fixing policies and other state-imposed economic measures reduced profit margins on most retail goods. Nevertheless, the economic calculations of the retailers' association suggested that such policies could be tolerated so long as rising purchasing power eventually generated enough volume in sales to offset shrinking margins.[49]

The waning of Chile's consumer boom called into question the durability of small business owners' pact with the government. The PN's presentation of an impeachment claim against Minister of Economy Pedro Vuskovic constituted an initial shot across the bow in this regard. In the winter of 1971, isolated food shortages began to emerge across the country. The attempt to pin the responsibility for these shortages on the UP's chief economic policy maker was central to the Chilean opposition's attempt to turn small merchants against state interference in the food economy. While the measure failed in its short-term objective—it did not succeed in removing a top Allende cabinet official from office—it triumphed in the longer-term mission of driving a wedge between the small merchant community and the UP.[50] In a note sent to Vuskovic shortly after the PN's failed action, members of Chile's small business community denounced the government's repeated claim that the speculative actions of small merchants had fueled shortages.[51]

In the months that followed, Chile's food economy became a crucible of political struggle. The UP's push to build a parallel system of consumer distribution at the neighborhood level became the most identifiable target of retailer frustration. During a three-hour meeting with Chile's minister of economy, held in late October 1971, the president of the Confederación del Comercio Detallista, together with more than two dozen leaders from regional business owners' associations, expressed their uneasiness over the state's expanded presence in the previously private arena of consumer distribution and exchange. Such actions, the retailers maintained, would ultimately imperil merchants' ability to access the inventory they needed to restock merchandise holdings.[52]

Conflicts between the UP and small retailers over the most effective way of approaching distribution in a socialist economy grew more intense after the confederation and three other small business owners' guilds acquired a controlling stake in the Compañía Distribuidora Nacional (National Distributor Company, CODINA), one of Chile's most important private distribution companies. While the UP and small retailers shared disdain for large

TABLE 4 Select Foodstuffs Distributed by State-Run
Distributors in Chile (as of Mid-1973)

Product	Percent of Total Distribution Controlled by State-Run Firms
Flours and starches[a]	86.5
Meat, fish, and seafood[b]	87.27
Cooking oils, processed meats, and fats[c]	82.95
Dairy products and eggs[d]	69.65
Fruits and vegetables[e]	8.49
Sugars and other sweets[f]	79.47
Canned goods and concentrates[g]	58.24
Caffeinated beverages and other drinks[h]	58.11
Alcoholic beverages[i]	17.92
Food and drink consumed outside the home[j]	61.24

SOURCE: *El Mercurio*, July 8, 1973, cited and originally reproduced in José Garrido Rojas, "Origen y alcances de la crisis alimenticia," in Pablo Baroana et al., *Fuerzas armadas y seguridad nacional* (Santiago: Ediciones Portada), 192.

a. 22 products, including rice, wheat flours, corn starch, mote, noodles, beans, chickpeas, lentils, bread, and crackers

b. 23 products, including cuts of beef, lamb, pork, and chicken; also common types of fish and seafood

c. 8 products, including cooking oils, lard, ham, margarine, mortadella, and sausages

d. 8 products, including cream, eggs, milk, butter, and cheese

e. 12 products, including garlic, peas, onion, lettuce, potatoes, cabbage, carrots, lemons, oranges, and bananas

f. 8 products, including sugars, hard candies, chocolates, quince jam, apricot jam, jellies, and ice cream

g. 13 products, including Nescafe, Milo, broth, canned fruits and vegetables, canned fish and seafood

h. 13 products, including teas, yerba maté, coffee, salt, pepper, peach nectar (*huesillo*), Coca-Cola, Orange Crush, ginger ale, and Cachantún

i. 6 products, including wine, beer, pisco, and vermouth

j. 7 products, including complete lunches (*almuerzos completos*), à la carte dishes (*platos sueltos*), bottles of Coca-Cola and Orange Crush, fruit juices, breakfast dishes, and beer

distribution firms, retailer owners believed they could sideline both the state and private middlemen from the distribution chain by turning CODINA into a corporate entity whose operations guild members controlled.[53] But not long after the purchase of CODINA, quarrels between gremio shareholders and the UP about the future of the distribution chain grew more public. In May 1972, talks about the role that now "ex-CODINA" would play in Allende's Chile broke down when, according to the confederation's leadership, the government granted its state-run distribution company, DINAC, exclusive control of domestically produced sugar.[54] The action, together with a UP proposal to use DINAC to create as many as one hundred new state-run supermarkets in peripheral communities, was interpreted by small merchants as a direct affront to the existence of private grocers around the country.[55] The great specter haunting Chile, according to the retailers' confederation, was a future in which establishments that were supplied by the state became the only places consumers could readily acquire essential goods.[56] By 1973, figures published by *El Mercurio* painted such a picture. According to the conservative newspaper, by July of that year, state-run distributors had taken control of more than half the total domestic distribution for eight different categories of food and drink. For some goods, like flour- and starch-based foods, meat, fish, cooking oils, and processed meats, the state controlled more than 80 percent of the supply chain.

PANTRY POLITICS

From the late Chilean fall and into the winter of 1972, conflicts between retailers and the key food-related agencies of the UP state became ubiquitous. In late May, as rumors swirled about a potential state expropriation of part or all of the country's private trucking industry, the state's independent comptroller office took the provocative action of briefly suspending Patricio Palma, the chief of Chile's national consumer agency, for allegedly failing to provide independent auditors with sufficient information about a series of state expropriations that were executed that month.[57] Shortly after his return to DIRINCO, Palma escalated the conflict by temporarily requisitioning multiple Santiago establishments that had closed their doors to both celebrate Chile's National Commerce Day and protest the UP's interference in the economic lives of private retailers.[58]

In June and July, a series of scandals involving DIRINCO inspectors continued to rock the agency. In one case, the head of DIRINCO's regional operations in the northern city of Arica, an active Communist Party (PCCh) militant, was arrested for allegedly channeling seized contraband goods directly to Communist-run JAPs in the city for eventual resale.[59] A month later, the head of DIRINCO's offices in Valdivia, a Socialist Party member, faced similar scrutiny from the comptroller's office after issuing what the auditing agency suggested were arbitrary fines to local bakers. The official was also accused of encouraging butchers in the area to sidestep the state's beef distributor, SOCOAGRO, in favor of a local slaughterhouse with which DIRINCO officials had personal ties.[60] In August 1972, conflict between the state and small retailers came to a head when a grocer in Punta Arenas died shortly after he tried to prevent DIRINCO officials from expropriating his privately owned store. The exact circumstances of the shopkeeper's passing were murky; according to reports, Manuel Aguilar García suffered a heart attack, though opponents of the UP claimed the cardiac episode was brought on by the sixty-year-old merchant's detention at the hands of state authorities. Regardless of how his death happened, Chile's petit bourgeoise had their first martyr, and in the days that followed, tens of thousands of small retailers around the country protested by closing their doors to customers.[61]

Knowing full well that retail closures would exacerbate the country's economic turbulence, merchants wagered that consumers would blame state overreach, rather than the actions of merchants themselves, for short-term economic inconveniences. This was a risky gamble, to be sure. As several decades of political history suggested, consumers—and particularly women consumers—had rarely allied themselves with Chile's merchant and small business community. On the contrary, in fact. As survey takers affiliated with the Confederación del Comercio Detallista had discovered shortly before Chile's economic boom began to falter, on the whole Chilean women continued to blame small retailers, not the state, for problems like shortages and inflation. Consumers, past and present, viewed merchants as "hoarders, who didn't help anybody and who lived only to make money," the confederation's leadership noted with disappointment in reaction to the survey's results.[62]

But by the end of 1971 and into 1972, a sizable bloc of consumers put aside feelings of animosity toward retailers to forge the unlikeliest of alliances. In short, an important segment of the Chilean women's movement stopped emphasizing the state's role as a guarantor of collective consumer health and material well-being and instead began to stress the importance of allowing individual consumers to act in the marketplace without limitation or restraint, when and how they desired.[63] Scarcity and inflation—two issues that, as this book has shown, had long contributed to the checkered economic history of twentieth-century Chile—would become a call to arms against, rather than for, state intervention in the consumer economy. The leadership of Chile's merchants' gremio had won their wager.

This shift in many women's political allegiances was at least a decade in the making. Most historians of twentieth-century Chile point to the early 1960s as the pivotal moment when an important segment of the Chilean women's movement surged toward the political right. While Chilean women had played an active role in episodes of right-wing reaction in the past—for example, joining anti-communist organizations like the Association of Housewives in the late 1940s—it was not until the early 1960s that women became leading protagonists in a national conservative movement. Most notably, during Chile's 1964 presidential election, women had acted as central players in the US-funded "scare campaign" that derailed Salvador Allende's third—and ultimately unsuccessful—presidential bid. At the heart of that campaign was the claim, promoted by the PDC of the early 1960s, that the socialist politician's policies were an affront to the essential domestic roles of Chilean women, in particular their identities as loyal wives and providing mothers.[64] In one of the more dramatic anti-Allende radio ads, Juana Castro, the outspoken anti-communist sister of Fidel and Raúl Castro, could be heard on Chilean radio stations, admonishing mothers that their children would be "taken" from them and "sent to the Communist bloc" should Allende be elected. "Remember your families. Remember your children," Castro cautioned Chilean women as they headed to the polls that year.[65]

Between Allende's September 1970 electoral victory and the Chilean Congress's ratification of that victory six weeks later, conservative contingents of anti-Allende women reactivated the old networks that had mobilized against Allende in 1964. Working through Chile's far-right PN and the more centrist PDC, women assumed a leading role in a spate of public demonstrations that questioned the legitimacy of Allende's narrow electoral victory. Images of women clad in black invoked conservative "mourning" for Chilean democracy.[66] However, women's inability to block Allende's inauguration led most female activists to temporarily retreat from the public stage, and for the first year of the Chilean revolution, women offered little organized opposition to the new UP government.

The March of the Empty Pots and Pans was arguably the first organized mass response to the Allende government after its rise to power. Coordinated by well-to-do women like Carmen Sáenz, thousands of protestors converged on Santiago's Plaza Italia—the unofficial boundary between the city's upper-class *barrio alto* neighborhoods and the more hardscrabble downtown areas of the capital—in the early evening hours of December 1, 1971.[67] From there, the mostly female contingent began an orderly march west down Santiago's principal thoroughfare, provocatively flanked by uniformed members of the far-right militia group, Patria y Libertad (Fatherland and Liberty, PL). The organizers intended for the march to conclude with a small rally in front of Chile's National Library, but that plan never materialized. When UP youth brigades heckled, jeered, and in some cases physically assaulted the female demonstrators, clashes broke out between them and the PL commandos who had assembled to provide security to the marchers.[68] As street fights between the two groups escalated, the Allende government deployed state security forces to break up the conflicts. With little hesitation, the Allende government also declared a temporary state of emergency, thus turning public security in the city over to a Santiago-based military unit under the command of a still little-known general named Augusto Pinochet.[69]

In the weeks that followed the march, the empty pot became a symbol of anti-Allende sentiment, emblazoned on the mastheads of opposition newspapers and donned in lapel-pin form on women's sweaters and blouses. As the rhythmic drumming of metal pots on apartment balconies became the soundtrack of feminine responsibility, the luxury designer Cartier was even said to have created a miniature gold likeness of a cooking pot, which some wealthy Chilean women remember wearing to publicly display their opposition to the Allende government. (Anti-UP women of lesser means possessed similar cooking-pot-shaped pins, but they tended to be made of copper.)[70]

A sympathetic journalist who covered the nascent anti-Allende women's movement reflected on the events of December by praising the female marchers as the "only sector of Chilean society" that was not "plagued by hatred." That same writer went on to argue that it would be imperative for Chilean women to commit to never "abandoning their future, the future of their children, and the future of their grandchildren" when confronted with the economic challenges of rising prices and shortages or the political challenges of ever-intensifying sectarian polarization.[71]

From a strategic perspective, the December march dispersed the site of struggle against the UP away from congressional committees and trade association meeting rooms and toward less formal political spaces like the city street, newspaper columns, and grocery storefronts.[72] It was there that women emphasized how food shortages and rising food prices cut across social class divisions. When the first anti-Allende umbrella organization, the Frente Nacional del Área Privada (National Front for Private Enterprise, FRENAP), emerged after the march, it immediately incorporated women into positions of leadership and consumer concerns into its agenda. Under the direction of Gabriela Oyarzun de Loccy, FRENAP was one of the first organizations to present consumers, small merchants, and large producers as a single political bloc with shared economic interests.[73] In a series of newspaper advertisements that it placed in major newspapers like *La Tercera de la Hora* in early 1972, FRENAP profiled the specific types of actors in this budding alliance—everyone from small shopkeepers and taxi drivers to white-collar professionals and homemakers. The advertisements presented these groups as united in their belief that state intervention in the economy no longer protected their interests but instead stigmatized them as culpable for the country's economic woes.[74]

In early 1972, several of the original organizers of the December anti-UP march established Poder Femenino. Organized to "defend" Chilean women from state policies that limited their ability to provide for their families, the nonpartisan but highly political organization planned neighborhood marches against the UP, collective pot-banging gatherings, anti-Allende leaflet drops, boycotts of pro-UP retailers, and a crusade against a government proposal to create a social service program that would have required women to serve as volunteers in state-run day care and medical facilities.[75] One of its most successful initiatives—and according to historian Margaret Power, the first on which Poder Femenino, as an organization, issued a public statement of support—sought to block the UP's nationalization of the prominent Chilean paper company, the Compañía Manufacturera de Papeles y Cartones, or La Papelera, Chile's largest producer of newsprint.[76] Working with a committee of female paper factory workers and wives of male plant workers, Poder Femenino used the fight against La Papelera's nationalization to demonstrate the varied class character of the anti-Allende opposition.

Few events better exemplified the convergence between female consumers and small merchants, particularly those who earned their living selling foodstuffs, than the consumer-merchant campaign against frozen merluza. When traditional sources of protein, like beef, began to disappear from butcher counters in early 1972, important women's magazines like *Eva* initially heeded the government's call to reduce red meat consumption by offering readers recipes that included easier-to-access ingredients, like fish and chicken.[77] But as the supply situation grew more dire, the UP's political adversaries maintained that the existence of the substitution economy constituted an attempt by the leftist coalition to dictate domestic meal planning. According to an editorial that appeared in the Santiago daily *La Tercera de la Hora*, President Allende's insinuation that, as reforms to the country's food economy took hold, Chileans would need to adjust their craving for meat for perhaps as long as a decade, was the "most unpopular and impolitic measure" that any government had adopted in recent memory. What's more, the proposition belied the UP's claim that material sacrifice would be avoided on the road to socialism.[78]

The source of deepest consumer frustration was connected to the question of what would take beef's place on the dinner plate. While surveys from the mid-1960s suggested that approximately three-quarters of Chilean consumers would accept fresh fish as a substitute for beef, Allende's proposal that consumers replace beef with what opponents referred to as *merluza rusa* (Russian hake) or *pesca soviética* (Soviet fish)—that is, frozen merluza caught by Soviet fishing ships—offended producers, merchants, and consumers alike.[79] According to Chilean fishermen, the Soviets' use of deepwater industrial fishing boats threatened their ability to make a living catching fish in shallower waters. Fishmongers also attacked the Soviet-harvested fish's growing presence in fish terminals, arguing that the state's gratis distribution of fish to state-backed community potlucks and fish fries depressed their own sales.

Women, however, expressed the greatest displeasure with frozen merluza. Well-off homemakers, the only cross section of the consuming class who had purchased fish and seafood with any regularity before the UP's rise to power, expressed a particularly strong aversion to cooking with frozen fish. According to the aforementioned 1966 consumer survey, around 60 percent of individuals in the two highest socioeconomic brackets said it would be "difficult" or "very difficult" to accept frozen fish as an alternative to fresh beef, citing the fact that it became a soupy and often inedible mush when thawed and cooked.[80] But that same food survey showed that an antipathy toward frozen fish cut across Chile's rigid social class divisions. While strong majorities of consumers from the lowest socioeconomic stratum of Chilean society said their families would "easily accept" eating chicken, pork, fresh fish, and fresh seafood if there was not enough beef, frozen fish was the only proposed beef substitute that majorities of consumers from every socioeconomic background, including the least well-off, said would be "difficult" or "very difficult" to integrate into their families' culinary repertoires.[81]

OCTOBER COUNTERREVOLUTIONARIES

Despite the opposition's accusations, the UP was hardly the only party responsible for the economic drama that consumed Chile during the democratic revolution's second and third years. Foreign actors, in particular the United States, played an equal, if not greater, role in fomenting economic chaos. Following the US president's directive in 1970 that US intelligence services should make the Chilean economy "scream," the United States, at

President Richard Nixon's urging, restricted Chile's access to credit from the Export-Import Bank, the powerful US government lending institution that had loaned the country over US$600 million in the twenty-five years prior to the UP's election. The United States also reduced Chile's access to economic assistance from the US Agency for International Development (USAID), which had aided Frei's rural reform and food production efforts in the 1960s.[82]

Beyond the monies they controlled directly, Nixon and his top foreign policy officials engaged in a far-reaching lobbying and disinformation campaign that limited Chile's access to private sources of credit and blocked most international loans and development assistance. As a result, between Allende's election in 1970 and November 1972, private credit extended to Chile by US banks declined from $219 million to just $32 million.[83] At the same time, international lending from organizations like the World Bank and the Inter-American Development Bank (IDB) slowed to a trickle. The IDB had granted a total of fifty-nine loans to the country, totaling $310 million, between 1960 and 1970, but released just two small loans, totaling just $2 million, during Allende's thousand-day presidency.[84] The "invisible blockade" of Chile, as UP supporters dubbed the US-led economic war being waged against them, greatly exacerbated distortions that resulted from the government's economic decisions by choking Chile's import-dependent consumer economy.[85]

The October 1972 Bosses' Strike marked the convergence between the international campaign against the Allende government and the domestic war on Chile's consumer economy. As discussed in the previous chapter, Chilean truck drivers, affiliated with Chile's gremio movement and drawing significant covert financial assistance from US intelligence agencies, precipitated the anti-government uprising in the early spring of that year when they brought overland distribution of essential goods in the country to a near standstill.[86] Within days the protest had spread far beyond the country's truckers' syndicate. Many white-collar professionals—including doctors and lawyers—stayed home from work. Small business owners similarly closed up shop, while members of far-right paramilitary groups, like PL, acted as shock troops, roaming city streets to intimidate those who did not adhere to the strike.[87] Reports on the right-wing work stoppage published by the pro-UP newspaper *Puro Chile* in late October 1972 highlighted instances of violence that ranged from bombings of government offices to the destruction of farm equipment on agrarian reform settlements.[88] In one of the more dramatic instances of sabotage, one anti-Allende butcher reportedly took two hundred kilos of pork out to the street and set it ablaze—a provocative act of public opposition to Allende's food policies that enraged UP sympathizers.[89]

Discussing the coalition-building work that went on behind oppositional lines, anti-Allende militants interviewed in the mid-1970s recalled the notable role that Poder Femenino activists played during the strike. In many cases, conservative women went door to door in reliably anti-Allende neighborhoods to collect provisions for Chile's striking truckers. Reports also highlight the work of Poder Femenino activists who organized anti-UP watchdog committees to guard private retail stores from state expropriation or popular seizure.[90] Some women took an active part in more confrontational and provocative actions. To cite one example, anti-Allende informants interviewed by one scholar in the 1970s told of anti-Allende women's groups running improvised manufacturing centers that produced three-pronged steel tacks, known as *miguelitos*. Opposition groups spread the spikes across roadways to shred the rubber tires of delivery vehicles that were not respecting the trucking syndicates' transportation stoppage.[91] Women, one prominent anti-Allende writer contended in an article that *Eva* published amid the October strike, represented the quintessential foot soldiers in a clandestine, "guerrilla-style" struggle against the Chilean revolution.[92]

In the aftermath of the October strike, the opposition ramped up its attacks on those revolutionary institutions that were most closely associated with the production, distribution, and sale of food. In this respect, no organization became more intensely vilified by right-wing forces than the JAP.[93] In the working-class población of Villa Ecuador, anti-Allende merchants laid the groundwork for a countervailing alternative to the JAP. According to the merchant Orlando Alarcón, a cofounder of what one paper referred to as a *comité de comerciantes*, or merchants' committee, around five hundred retailers in the area forged ahead with their own form of merchant-consumer collaboration amid the chaos and confusion of late 1972. What consumers and retailers shared, according to Alarcón, was a desire to end the partisan food distribution strategies that residents increasingly associated with the JAP.[94]

A declaration, issued by a group of organizations that had backed the October Bosses' Strike a few weeks after the shutdown had ended, provided a damning assessment of cresting consumer frustration. "For the first time in Chile's history," consumers needed to be in the "good graces of the state" to access food, the statement read. "Faced with the impossibility of conquering the consciousness of the *pueblo*, Marxism has tried to take it over through hunger," the statement's authors added.[95] For some in the opposition, the absence of food became a hyperbolic metonym for creeping UP totalitarianism. The government seeks to "use everyday food as a tool of domination and subjugation in order to finish off the liberties Chileans enjoy," the leadership of CODE, the anti-Allende coalition that bridged divisions between the rightist National Party and the more centrist PDC, pronounced in early January 1973. "The country must be very aware that not only is the right to subsistence at risk here but so too is the right to disagree with the Government, to criticize it, and to try to alter the wrong-headed path that has brought us to the dangerous point of today," the coalition declared.[96]

TOWARD A (SUPER) MARKET ECONOMY?

As the October strike drew to a close, *Eva*, a publication that now stood firmly in the anti-Allende camp, depicted the Chilean consumer and the private supermarket as the two primary victims of Chile's socialist revolution. Under the provocative headline "Will Our Supermarkets Survive?," Carmen Puelma, one of the so-called trench journalists who had chronicled women's participation in the anti-UP protests of the previous year, argued that the autonomy of privately owned grocery stores, as well as consumers' ability to patronize such establishments, needed to be defended at all costs. All over the world, rich and poor consumers alike had greeted the supermarket with "excitement"—and they did so because the new economic institution embodied fundamental liberal principles, like freedom and equality, she maintained. In contrast to butcher shops or small mom-and-pop-style corner markets—two spaces of exchange where others "directed, and sometimes even decided, what a given consumer could and could not buy"—in the commercial supermarket "everyone can buy" and "everyone waits in the same line to pay, without special privileges." Although commercial supermarkets were still a relatively novel part of Chile's economic landscape in the early 1970s, such establishments were seen by opponents of the revolution as one of the few spaces where individual choices could at once be expressed and fulfilled without political interference. The experience of walking "up and down the aisles, freely and comfortably," made the consumer feel, in Puelma's words, like she was "in her own home pantry, reviewing and selecting the exact products that she needs."[97]

This way of conceptualizing freedom, equality, and personal contentment in relation to the absence of the state would have surely puzzled the many

Chileans who had witnessed or participated in the consumer mobilizations of earlier decades. Indeed, in a country like Chile, where ideas about democracy and the economy had been so deeply forged by and with the active hand of the state, regulation of the consumer marketplace seemed an almost unquestioned feature of everyday life. But such sentiments were shifting as segments of the consuming public turned the food economy into a battleground against the state.

The economist Álvaro Bardón was intrigued with this radically new way of thinking about where in economic life the hand of the state should and should not exist. A longtime Christian Democrat, Bardón, like Puelma, had grown wary of state economic intervention during the 1960s while working at Chile's Central Bank. Such feelings only intensified as he completed postgraduate studies in economics at the University of Chicago, an incubator for free-market economic thought.[98] Of greatest interest—and concern—to the longtime Christian Democrat was the state's approach to inflation. In fact, even amid the boom months of the early UP revolution, Bardón maintained that consumer prices in the country were on the verge of exploding because of the Allende government's uninhibited expansion of the money supply to meet budget shortfalls. Such an approach to fiscal policy was reckless, Bardón insisted. In one of his first newspaper columns on the topic, published in late May 1971, the Chicago-trained economist claimed that the amount of money in the hands of businesses and private individuals had increased by an astounding 100 percent over the course of a single year. That one-year figure was 30 percent greater than at any other one-year period in recent Chilean history. If Chileans thought the mid-1950s—the prior recordholder when it came to monetary expansion—were challenging, then 1972, 1973, and the years beyond would be nightmarish, he predicted.[99] When the essential character of scarce goods rendered price hikes a moot and ineffective option, consumers could expect a combination of long lines and rationing cards, Bardón maintained.[100]

Bardón had little interest in analyzing the political costs that the Allende government might have incurred had it not engaged in vigorous pump priming. Nor did he consider the culpability of Chile's political opposition—either foreign or domestic—in creating the conditions for the crisis. But the economist's analysis of the forces driving inflation was nonetheless notable in that it directly challenged the prevailing economic wisdom of his day.[101] At a time when most Chilean economists, including those from his own PDC, saw inadequate food supply as a primary cause of inflation, Bardón argued that the rate at which a country's Central Bank grew its money supply was far more significant. In the years that followed, this view would come to be hegemonic among economists of nearly all political persuasions.[102]

Soaring inflation numbers appeared to vindicate Bardón and his intellectual contemporaries. In 1972, inflation reached 260.5 percent; one year later, it surpassed 600 percent.[103] The printing of new money became a symbol of what another leading anti-Allende voice, Bardón's fellow Chicago-school colleague Sergio de Castro, would refer to as the hyper-politicization of the Chilean economy under Allende. At the same time, calls for monetary stability provided a unifying economic message for critics of the government. In his stridently anti-Allende tone, de Castro amplified Bardón's more measured message, arguing that Chile's ever-expanding system of price controls and the alternative channels of food distribution that expanded in 1972 and 1973 represented a government attempt to obtain "total power" by holding the stomachs of Chilean consumers hostage to JAP activists and state food distributors.[104]

The period after the October Bosses' Strike was critical in turning what de Castro referred to as "notarial documentation" of the UP's policy shortcomings—that is, descriptive claims about the UP's economic missteps—into the beginnings of a new economic prescription.[105] Appealing to public anxiety about food shortages after a month of unrest, Bardón noted that the strike made clear, as no event before it had, that the Chilean economy required "clear rules of the game," and that such rules needed to be consistently and equitably applied to all economic sectors, whether blue-collar laborers, business owners, or public employees.[106] Such a view, which subsumed substantive claims about material equality within formal claims about the law and equality of opportunity, would form the bedrock upon which Bardón, de Castro, and their ilk fashioned their own economic program for a post-Allende Chile. For many in this group that became known as the Chicago Boys, the fight against democratic socialism presented an opportunity to undo state agencies and economic assumptions that, in their view, had disfigured economic liberalism for nearly half a century.[107]

As the fall of 1973 turned to winter in Chile, the PDC unofficially "declared war" on the JAPs, adopting the same sort of hard-line position that the far more conservative PN had been advocating for nearly a year. As an alternative, the newly chosen directorate of the PDC's National Committee of Pobladores proposed in a May press conference that the JAPs' powers be returned to the local neighborhood councils, known as *juntas de vecinos*, which the Christian Democrats had created in the 1960s. In those communities where the JAPs had a monopoly on food distribution, PDC activists prepared to colonize JAP committees themselves and use them for their own ends. "Today, desperation is spreading like never before due to a lack of foodstuffs," the committee maintained. It concluded that UP policies were creating a situation in which soon there would "really be nothing left to eat in Chile."[108]

In the weeks that followed, other opponents of the UP shamed the government over deteriorating conditions as well. In some cases, their actions also served to exacerbate the severity of the crisis. By staging a series of hunger marches and rallies, consumers in mostly middle-class neighborhoods, and increasingly working-class communities as well, denounced the state's excessive interference in the production and distribution of food.[109] At the same time, agricultural workers affiliated with the PDC-aligned Triunfo Campesino rural workers' confederation called upon their fellow unionists to hold a forty-eight-hour strike to protest a government decree that forced campesinos to sell select products, like wheat and potatoes, to the state as a precondition for obtaining new lines of state credit.[110] Three decades after FP president Pedro Aguirre Cerda had first promised "bread, shelter, and a warm overcoat" to all Chileans, another leader of Chile's PDC lamented that the UP had created a situation in which none of these three basic needs were regularly fulfilled. As a winter of shortages loomed on the horizon, this feeling of desperation encapsulated what the Allende critic called Chile's worst crisis since the Great Depression.[111]

While large landowners, merchants, and female consumers destabilized the UP by directly attacking the state's role in producing, distributing, and selling food, intellectual and military opponents of the UP moved into alignment with one another behind the scenes. Their common goal was to oust the democratically elected Allende government from power.[112] A meeting between retired Chilean marine and prominent businessman Roberto Kelly and his close friend, the naval commander and eventual *golpista* (coup plotter) José Toribio Merino, just weeks after the October 1972 Bosses' Strike, represented a turning point in this regard. Cognizant of the fact that, whenever and however Allende left office, the Chilean opposition would be handed an economy in tatters, Kelly and Toribio Merino concurred that any measure taken by anti-Allende forces needed to be coupled with a set of proposals to resuscitate the Chilean economy. With that objective in mind, Kelly contacted an old friend, the Chicago-trained economist and cofounder of the conservative weekly *Qué Pasa,* Emilio Sanfuentes. Sanfuentes, in turn, called upon de Castro, who at the time had been named the new editor of the economics page at the magazine. It fell to de Castro to gather a group of young conservative economists to begin drafting a sweeping set of recommendations that might remedy Chile's economic ills in some still-to-be determined post-Allende future.

Starting in the final months of 1972 and continuing into early 1973, the gatherings of this incipient economic advisory committee were "constant," according to de Castro, emanating an air of apolitical, scientific expertise but all the while tied up with the highly political goal of ending Chile's socialist revolution. While some of the participants, like Bardón, were members of opposition parties, de Castro has long maintained that most of those who participated in the group were "independent" of partisan politics. What united them, he has argued, was a "profound dismay" that Chile was "falling into an abyss."[113]

In this way, the men's self-presentation as apolitical agents of change mirrored Chile's right-wing women's movement and elements of the gremio movement. However, while the anti-Allende women's movement and the gremialistas relied on the ability to turn out Chile's far-right opposition to the streets, the Chicago Boys' success would ultimately depend upon their ties with members of Chile's old political and economic guard—and over time, the political demobilization of Chilean society. In the Chilean fall of 1973, for example, de Castro recalled the significance of being summoned to a congressional finance committee meeting, chaired at the time by Carmen Sáenz's husband and prominent PN leader Patricio Phillips. De Castro had been asked to testify about Chile's economic crisis, and the hearing presented one of the first opportunities for the anti-Allende advisory group to publicly articulate its economic findings and proposals. Not long after, the first chapters of the group's long-awaited report on what a post-Allende economy might look like were delivered for review to Toribio Merino and other pro-coup forces within the Chilean military. The opposition prepared to land its final blow against Chile's socialist revolution.

Epilogue

COUNTERREVOLUTION AT THE MARKET

MIGUEL WOODWARD was an early victim of Chile's 1973 military coup. A Catholic priest, member of Chile's Movimiento de Acción Popular Unitario (Popular Unity Action Movement, MAPU), and proponent of the social-justice-oriented Catholicism known as "liberation theology," Woodward had worked tirelessly to sustain Chile's democratic revolution in Población Progreso, the Valparaíso shantytown in which he lived and served. In the face of counterrevolutionary advances, Woodward's role as a coordinator of one of Valparaíso's most active JAPs occupied much of his time in late 1972 and early 1973. Residents remember that when basic goods grew scarce in those months, Father Woodward made great efforts to secure foodstuffs for his neighbors. Each week at sunrise, the priest led a contingent of community residents and Popular Unity (UP) activists to a state distribution site to pick up whatever goods were available. The group then proceeded to deliver the coveted bounty, which often included meat that had been imported from China, to JAP outpost No. 93. Woodward insisted that staples be distributed fairly; all 570 JAP members in the community would receive an equal amount of rationed meat, community members recalled, typically around a quarter kilo per week.[1]

This vital work endeared Miguel Woodward to the working-class residents of Valparaíso. But the leadership role that he assumed within the JAP also provoked the ire of some local merchants, who refused to join Progreso's consumer committee and attributed a decline in their own profits to the JAP's existence. Disdain for Woodward's commitment to economic justice ultimately precipitated his brutal murder. Just a few days after the September 1973 military coup, a local merchant with whom Woodward had allegedly had a dispute aided a group of Chilean naval officers as they searched for the "red priest" in the hills above Valparaíso. Unable to locate him, the military staked out the area around his neighborhood, awaiting his eventual return home. When the reverend finally abandoned the temporary refuge he had taken at a friend's house, military officials quickly detained him.

The details of the events that followed are not entirely clear, but reports indicate that Woodward spent several days locked up as a political prisoner on a Chilean naval ship, the *Esmeralda*, which was docked near Valparaíso. The testimonies of other UP activists with whom the priest was held suggest that he was interrogated, tortured repeatedly, and eventually killed aboard the ship. More than a week and a half after the coup, Woodward's battered, lifeless body was discovered outside a nearby naval hospital. The military, which by that point firmly controlled the government, gave no explanation for how his body arrived there. The only information that it released about the death was that it had occurred *en vía pública*—the vague, passive turn of phrase used by the military to describe an undefined public space wherein an individual had been killed after a supposed encounter with state security forces.[2]

The military coup that toppled Salvador Allende's government began in earnest during the early morning hours of Tuesday, September 11, 1973. The conspiracy came on the heels of yet another truckers' strike, which pushed Chile's food economy over the precipice in the middle of the cold months of winter.[3] As the distribution of staple goods throughout the country was brought to a standstill—this time from late July through August—thousands of small retailers once again adhered to the strike by closing their own shop doors for days, and in some cases for weeks.[4]

The end goal of the shutdown was lost on no one. Even the anti-Allende newspaper *La Tercera de la Hora* noted that it was "essential" to separate "two concrete situations" from one another when assessing the causes of Chile's food shortages. Prior to the 1973 distribution strike there already existed an "acute scarcity of primary necessity goods like cooking oil, sugar, rice, milk, among others," the paper declared, adding that the UP's economic policies were largely to blame for such problems. But editorial writers at the daily also acknowledged a second, indisputable fact: the latest truck drivers' action had pushed the country's supply problems to their breaking point.[5] The situation was so dire that state distributors were reportedly planning to distribute five hundred tons of Mexican horsemeat in a last-ditch attempt to ensure Chilean consumers had at least a few pieces of meat for their traditional Independence Day celebrations on September 18.[6]

The palpability of the crisis forced Salvador Allende to make the most difficult choice of his political career: give up power peacefully or ride out a violent onslaught by elements of his own military inside the presidential palace. In the end, he opted for a version of the latter. In his last radio broadcast, the Chilean president thanked supporters for their commitment to his coalition's socialist project. At its most fundamental level, the experiment had sought to fulfill ordinary Chileans' "great yearnings for justice," he noted. "Workers of my country, I have faith in Chile and its destiny. Other men will overcome this dark and bitter moment when treason seeks to prevail," Chile's socialist president told his fellow citizens one final time before signing off.[7]

Shortly after that speech, Hawker Hunter fighter jets belonging to Chile's national air force and manned by Chilean pilots soared low over downtown Santiago, bombarding the country's neoclassical-inspired presidential palace, La Moneda. There remains some debate about whether the bombing itself killed Allende or the Chilean president committed suicide before the first bombs fell, though most evidence points to the second scenario. No matter; the events of that day brought Chile's democratic road to socialism to an end. Given that the counterrevolutionary opposition pointed to hyperinflation as part of the justification for the coup, there was a dark irony in the fact that the building the military destroyed had originally been used to mint the country's coinage.[8]

In the days and weeks that followed the coup, Chile's military worked night and day to locate and detain key members of the UP government, as well as prominent sympathizers of the coalition. Some top Allende government officials fled into exile with the assistance of welcoming foreign embassies.[9] Many others were arrested and sent to detention camps, such as Dawson Island, a secluded military outpost in Tierra del Fuego. Among the prisoners held at the remote Patagonia facility were UP economic advisers Sergio Bitar and Fernando Flores and the constitutionalist Brigadier General Alberto Bachelet of the air force, who had worked with Flores to break bottlenecks in the supply chain for basic consumer goods, especially food, after the October 1972 Bosses' Strike. While Bitar and Flores were eventually released from prison and allowed to go into foreign exile, Bachelet passed away in 1974, just a few weeks shy of his fifty-first birthday; his death was the result of the repeated physical torture to which he was subjected by Pinochet's forces.[10]

Countless others, many of them less recognizable activists, community leaders, and trade unionists—people like Miguel Woodward—were also arrested, held without charge, and tortured. The most reliable numbers suggest that roughly 13,500 people were detained in the weeks immediately following the coup. Of those, some 1,500 were never seen again. Around 3,000 people in total were murdered by the regime during its more than a decade and a half in power (1973–90). The fate of many of the dictatorship's victims remained unknown for years, as bodies disappeared into unmarked graves or were thrown into the deep waters of the Pacific.[11]

Marta Ugarte, a Chilean Communist Party (PCCh) militant and former director of the regional body that coordinated consumer activities between the various neighborhood-based JAP committees in the province of Santiago, was one notable victim of state terror. Detained by Chile's secret police in August 1976, then tortured at the infamous Villa Grimaldi concentration camp on the periphery of Santiago, Ugarte's remains eventually surfaced on a beach near Valparaíso, providing one of the first confirmations to Chilean human rights workers of the fate of Chile's *desaparecidos* (disappeared persons). Of her death, Ugarte's friend, Communist comrade, and DIRINCO collaborator, Patricio Palma, later maintained that her murder at the hands of the state should be understood in terms of the important positions she held within the Central Committee of the PCCh and the JAP. "There's no doubt that those who killed [Marta Ugarte] knew exactly the role she had played and that reveals just how much the JAP generated the ire of the counter-revolution," Palma said.[12]

Roberto Kelly, the unofficial intermediary between Chile's cadre of Chicago-trained economists and the military, remembered arriving at the conservative publishing house, Editorial Lord Cochrane, as military jets terrorized the residents of Santiago. In his hands Kelly carried the completed text of the economic report the Chicago Boys had been working on for more than half a year. The final version of the document had been completed shortly before the September coup, and the former military officer turned businessman ordered the group of economists who joined him at the Providencia-based office to make mimeographed copies as fast as possible. Those present remember the mimeograph machine breaking down temporarily as a result of the day's furious activities. But the group of young counterrevolutionaries persisted, and they eventually handed over to Kelly several copies of the thick report, reproduced on low-quality paper. Kelly, in turn, delivered the group's economic plans, dubbed "El Ladrillo" (The Brick) because of the report's hefty size and shape, to the military leaders who had executed the coup.[13]

Reading El Ladrilllo in its entirety produced an epiphany for Kelly. "As a marine, I had always thought that [Chile's] presidents were honorable people, with good intentions, for whom the nature of national politics, most prominently the necessity of making political compromises, had impeded the materialization of their proposals," Kelly later noted. However, in the Chicago Boys' analysis Kelly found what he believed was a "concrete exit" from the economic problems that had long plagued the Chilean economy.[14] Kelly was convinced that if the state guaranteed free-market principles would always supersede the social considerations that had previously been so central to economic development efforts in the country, Chile's economy could be transformed for the better.[15]

One night after the ouster of Allende, Chilean intelligence officials picked up Rafael Cumsille. On orders from the new military regime, the young leader of Chile's small retailers' guild was shuttled to the coup government's temporary command center. However, unlike Father Miguel Woodward or Marta Ugarte, Cumsille had little reason to fear for his safety. As a leading spokesperson for Chile's conservative gremio movement, he had been a constant voice of opposition to the Allende government throughout 1972 and 1973. His leading role during the Bosses' Strike of 1972, which had briefly landed him prison, made him a hero to Chile's political right. Now, military leaders wanted to draw upon Cumsille's connections and experience as they sought to restart the production and distribution of basic goods throughout the national economy. As Cumsille describes it in his memoirs, that process began in his initial meeting with General Oscar Bonilla, one of the new regime's principal leaders.[16]

In the days that followed his first talks with Chile's top military brass, Cumsille worked with the new dictatorship to dismantle many Allende-era economic policies, starting with the country's system of price controls and state-run distribution networks. His initial target was a UP mandate that required all truckers to receive a special government permit before moving consumer goods within Chile. From there the coup government issued dictatorial decrees that recognized private retailers as the only legal "consumer distribution channel" in the country, dissolved the state-run Secretaría General de Distribución, disbanded local JAP committees, and revoked the "honorary" price inspector status of citizen price monitors who were otherwise unaffiliated with the state's consumer protection agency.[17] While DIRINCO remained in operation as a state agency, its authority to actively intervene in the economy on the behalf of consumers of modest means was largely disabled. In this way, a key demand of small shopkeepers, merchants, and distributors helped open the door to Chile's neoliberal future.

Cumsille's near-messianic sense of purpose and resolve after the military coup—his belief that he was doing right by the Chilean economy and Chilean consumers, in particular—is inescapable in his recounting of the dictatorship's early days. "The State never was and never will be the best administrator and distributor," the anti-Allende leader forcefully argued in his published memoirs, adding that "the passage of time" only "vindicated" that view.[18] Per Cumsille's accounting, the culpability for shortages and hyperinflation during the Allende years lay with state-run distribution companies and the JAPs, which community leaders like Miguel Woodward, Eduardo Flores, Rosa Ríos, María Farías Godoy, Marta Ugarte, and thousands of others had worked tirelessly to build during Chile's thousand-day revolution.

Reflecting on the various constituencies that had applauded the dictatorship's economic reforms, Cumsille claimed that "happiest of all" were Chile's housewives, because they no longer had to contend with long lines and the uncertainty of consumer scarcity.[19] The gremio boss's observation simplifies how political and class polarization divided Chilean women into pro- and anti-UP camps, especially during the final year of the revolution. However, such views have long been repeated by many upper- and middle-class women, who on the whole reacted to the 1973 coup with approbation. "I was overjoyed when Allende fell. I remember drinking an entire bottle of champagne by myself," Carmen Sáenz recounted years later.[20] In another interview that the Poder Femenino leader gave immediately after the coup, she identified September 11, 1973, as the day she gave up her public political militancy and returned to her traditional domestic role. "I feel like a newly unemployed person, but one who is happy"; "those she love[d]"—her husband and children most of all—were alive and well because of the military's intervention, Sáenz told the women's magazine, *Eva*.[21]

The economic pain that would soon torment poor and working-class Chileans was completely lost on Sáenz and others who rapidly regained their economic privileges in the months after the coup. In Sáenz's case, the Pinochet dictatorship returned the agrarian properties that the Allende government had seized as part of an agrarian counterreform. Dairy production once again became the center of agricultural operations on the family's Calatayud estate.[22] Beyond returning expropriated properties to their former owners, the dictatorship's reversal of a decade of agrarian reform included the implementation of short-term policies designed to reanimate agricultural productivity—for example, importing forty thousand tons of German-produced synthetic fertilizers and several thousand tons of high-quality barley and potato seeds.[23]

Additionally, the military developed longer-term policies that marginalized any rural worker who had supported agrarian reform and decoupled agricultural production from Chile's domestic food needs.[24] In Pinochet's Chile, "natural economic advantage based on market determination of prices" would dictate the nature and terms of rural production, one foreign observer wrote in 1980. This meant Chile would begin prioritizing agricultural goods for which it could "compete effectively" in the global market.[25] The dictatorship also removed the state from the domestic marketing and sale of agricultural products. Finally, the dictatorship began privatizing Chile's vast food storage, processing, and commercialization network, as well as the physical infrastructure that sustained it: trucks, silos, warehouses, and packaging facilities, among other things.[26] In Pinochet's Chile, food security—the ability of a nation to fulfill its citizens' dietary needs—would be violently delinked from the idea of food sovereignty: the notion that all people have the right to consume healthy food and to exert democratic control over the agricultural system that produces such food.[27]

The economic reality that the new regime's policies produced was far more complicated and contradictory than Cumsille and other coup supporters would ever admit. For example, despite the fact that some Chilean women had supported Allende's ouster, the economic situation of many middle- and working-class families hardly improved. If anything, policies of privatization and austerity made conditions far worse in the immediate wake of the coup. Purchasing power declined for several years after the coup; in 1974, inflation in Chile reached nearly 400 percent, arguably the highest rate anywhere in the world at that time.[28] According to IMF statistics, real national income in Chile dropped by as much as 26 percent in 1975. Unemployment soared; by 1976, between one-fifth and one-quarter of all working-age Chileans were jobless.[29]

Those who retained their jobs in factories that the military took over were often subjected to increasingly precarious workplace conditions. The new labor regime that was instituted in Chile's national beef company, SOCOAGRO, was illustrative. Although SOCOAGRO remained in public hands for a few years after the coup, military leaders authorized private security forces to operate freely in processing plants around the country in order to squash dissent against the new military regime. The dictatorship also declared the terms of existing labor contracts at SOCOAGRO null and void, ended automatic wage adjustments, and unilaterally increased the standard workweek to forty-five hours.[30] In an effort to cut costs and discipline the labor force, the military even forced workers at the country's meat-processing plants to pay for their own boots and uniforms, which they were required to wear while on the job.[31]

When workers returned home, the situation was rarely any easier. The end of consumer price controls caused the prices of basic goods, like bread, to rise by as much as 1,000 percent.[32] Nutritional intake plummeted as a result. In a study of the two Santiago shantytowns José María Caro and Lo Hermida, the researcher Mariana Schkolnik found that by the end of the 1970s, nearly three-quarters of the residents of the first community and two-thirds of the members of the latter community consumed less than the internationally recommended 2,319 calories per day. In both communities, respondents indicated that somewhere between 75 and 80 percent of those calories were derived from nutrient-poor foods like flour, oils, fats, and sugar.[33] "Look, before there was more work and we ate well," one housewife in José María Caro told Schkolnik, contrasting her own family's current economic situation with the pre-Pinochet period. The pobladora went on: "[W]e never ate *pan pelado* (plain bread) like we do now; we had rolls with butter that were cheaper . . . avocado. Before you could buy milk, the kids drank the milk for breakfast, we ate meat more often. . . . [N]ow you just see bones. . . . Before, we made meatballs, we made pasta, and added in some meat. . . . [N]ow we don't even have eggs because they're so expensive. . . . Fruit, to be frank, we almost never eat."[34]

Policies of liberalization, privatization, and austerity—three key prongs of the new neoliberal economic order in Chile—deepened inequalities, and conditions like those described by residents of José María Caro became more common, despite the fact that Chile was slowly being inundated with non-essential consumer imports. In her book *Buying into the Regime*, historian Heidi Tinsman relates an anecdote that a rural woman she once interviewed told her about the differing economic experiences of the Allende and Pinochet eras. During Allende's presidency, the woman said, we had "so much [money] we could wallpaper the house but there was nothing to buy." In contrast, under Pinochet, there were consumer goods everywhere but "no money," thus making it nearly impossible to buy many of the new imported goods that filled Chilean stores.[35] By participating in hunger marches, organizing neighborhood potlucks, and sewing *arpilleras*—patchwork tapestries

FIGURE 13. Arpilleras created during the dictatorship memorialize Allende's half liter of milk program and the work of the JAPs. Fundación Salvador Allende, Santiago de Chile.

that Pinochet opponents produced to document life before and after the 1973 coup—UP sympathizers memorialized a lost era when access to milk had been a basic social right of all children, and poor and working-class communities had exercised their own democratic control over their local consumer economy. For most, those experiences and memories surely felt more distant and out of reach than ever before.

Rafael Cumsille was not alone in his steadfast defense of the new economic order that Pinochet promoted. When Roberto Kelly's biographer asked him about the human rights violations of the Pinochet era—specifically, if he regretted anything that had occurred after the 1973 coup—he replied that his only lament was "not having had more time to do more and better things" for Chile. Chile had been a "country without a future" before Pinochet, he argued.[36] As evidence of the regime's success, he reminded his interviewer that the democratic governments that succeeded the dictatorship had done little to alter the economic model that Pinochet installed. Chicago Boy Sergio de Castro's response to another interviewer's question about any regrets he had, knowing that Chile's economic counterrevolution was predicated on unconscionable violence, is even more revealing of the political right's maniacal sense of purpose. "There are no corrective measures that are painless," the economist said. "They don't exist. There is always someone who will be harmed."[37] When assessing the history of the Pinochet dictatorship through the voices of the Chicago Boys, the beginning of Chile's neoliberal moment appears diametrically opposed to everything that preceded it.

However, the persistence into post-1973 Chile of certain economic discourses associated with the country before the dictatorship point to a more complicated picture, one riven by both violent ruptures and unsuspecting continuities. In many respects, one can see in the Pinochet era how fragments of the old battles waged by popular consumers prior to 1973 lived on, their meanings appropriated and disfigured, to be sure, but their essence not entirely discarded. In a July 1985 editorial published in the *Revista del Consumidor*, the bulletin of the dictatorship's restructured consumer protection office, state officials declared that Chile was well on its way to becoming a country of "twelve million consumers"—a figure forty times greater than the one that leftist historian Eric Hobsbawm bemoaned after visiting Chile in the early 1970s. What's more, Pinochet's consumer agency pointed out that, throughout the country, consumers were using the courts to bring claims against "dishonest merchants" and "refund those consumers who had purchased goods in poor condition." As early as nursery school, in fact, teachers were instructing Chilean schoolchildren to check the expiration dates on their packaged foods before indulging. Adults were instructed how to "compare prices, examine the terms and conditions of one's purchases when buying on credit, and avoid making purchasing decision[s] under the pressure of a seller."[38] Detached from any political context, one could envision any number of state agencies peddling similar guidance to Chilean consumers from the 1930s forward. Indeed, the ideal of a society shaped by consumer awareness and consumer plenty had been fundamental to nearly all progressive visions of a more just, fair, and democratic economy during much of the twentieth century.

But the new consumer culture that emerged in Pinochet's Chile carried a subtext antithetical to how the economy and society had been understood in Chile before 1973. As Chile's *Revista del Consumidor* put it in that same 1985 editorial, Chileans, "for the first time in history," realized that when they embraced the narrow identity of "consumer," they were finally acting as "guardians and defenders of their own interests." By "shaking off" the "lethargy produced by the statist system," the magazine concluded, individual consumers were, at long last, assuming the responsibility that "until present times had been held by the state."[39] Or, as another editorial in the same bulletin would declare, Chilean citizens, "acting as consumers," had become responsible for "the welfare and adequate fulfillment" of society's most "basic needs."[40] Whereas a right to subsistence had previously been a defining feature of economic citizenship and a source of collective action, the neoliberal Chilean state turned consumption into a narrow, individual economic act. To eat well was not a basic economic right that the state ensured by intervening at the point of production, distribution, or exchange. Instead, it was an activity that was dictated by an individual's time and ability to navigate the market.

Calling consumption the "most important personal freedom," Chicago Boy Álvaro Bardón captured the new economic common sense that the state promoted in post-Allende Chile. In a newspaper column he published a little more than a year after DIRINCO declared Chile a "country of twelve million consumers," Bardón maintained that individual consumption—and the confidence that the currency one used to participate in the consumer economy was stable and abundant—fueled modern capitalist development. The simple desire to consume motivated individuals to work hard and keep producing. "What does one work for and make sacrifices for if money doesn't have any purchase? Have we already forgotten about the Popular Unity period, when it didn't matter if one did or did not have money because the scarcity was so profound?" Bardón asked.[41] Amid the economist's words lay the mangled remnants of the sort of citizenship that poor and working-class Chileans had fought for during the twentieth century, the broken dreams about what the state could and should provide for all of its citizens.

Nearly four decades later, Chileans are pushing back against the market-based assumptions of the Pinochet era harder than at any point in recent memory. As a young demonstrator wrote on her protest placard during the unprecedented social uprising that erupted in Chile in October 2019, neo-liberalism was "born in Chile" but would "die" there as well.[42] As activists work to bury the old, a growing number of Chileans have made the task of building a state that once again guarantees essential goods and services as fundamental social and economic rights of citizenship their political mission. The question of whose needs the national economy should serve remains as vital today as ever.

KEY ACRONYMS AND TERMS
IN CHILEAN FOOD HISTORY

ACEITE Cooking oil

ADC Association of Housewives, a women's organization formed in 1947 by President Gabriel González Videla to, among other things, teach women proper food consumption habits and counter Chile's more progressive women's movement

ALIMENTACIÓN Literally "nutrition" or "sustenance"; distinct from "eating" (*comer*) in that it most often refers to those forms of nourishment that sustain physical health and well-being

ALMACENES POPULARES/ALMACENES DEL PUEBLO Ad hoc distribution centers for staple goods, established in urban shantytowns during the Popular Unity revolution and supplied by state-run distribution companies

ALMACENES REGULADORES State-run "yardstick" stores, first created during the Popular Front era to provide staple goods to urban consumers at fixed prices and thus incentivize private retail stores to lower their own prices

AOAN Workers' Assembly for National Nutrition, a cross-class social movement formed in 1918 by Chile's labor movement to fight rising prices, particularly the cost of food in Santiago and other cities

ASENTAMIENTO Literally "settlement"; refers to the transitional institution established during Eduardo Frei's agrarian reform in the mid-1960s to integrate formerly landless campesinos into the rural economy

BARES LÁCTEOS State-run "milk bars" that sold an array of calcium-rich dairy products at fixed prices; established under Chile's Popular Front governments

CANASTA POPULAR/CANASTA BÁSICA Literally "popular" or "basic basket"; refers to a fixed bundle of staple goods distributed to poor and working-class consumers by the Chilean state during the Popular Unity era

CAZUELA Typical Chilean soup most often consisting of a chunk of meat, potatoes, and vegetables cooked in broth

CENADECO National Organizing Committee for Consumer Defense, an urban consumer organization formed after World War II in which Communist Party activists played an outsized role

CEPROS Production centers; state-run agricultural farms created during the Popular Unity revolution in sectors of the agricultural economy where special expertise or technical training was needed for efficient production, for example in forestry and livestock breeding

CERAS Agrarian reform centers; a key institution of Chile's land reform efforts during the Popular Unity revolution and the successor to the asentamiento system; intended to extend participation in agrarian reform beyond the tenant farmers who lived on expropriated haciendas

CHARQUICÁN Potato-heavy casserole mixed with onions, peppers, and pieces of beef or horsemeat

CNA National Nutrition Council, the state agency established in the mid-1930s to devise national nutrition policies

COCHAYUYO Nutrient-rich kelp harvested along the Chilean coastline

COMISARIATO Chile's national price control and consumer protection office, established by decree in 1932

COMISIONES DE VIGILANCIA Citizen-run consumer watchdog committees, first created in the 1940s; antecedent to similar grassroots efforts to monitor markets in the early 1970s

COMITÉS DE ABASTECIMIENTO POPULAR Literally "popular supply committees"; community organizations created by Chile's radical left in the final months of the Popular Unity revolution to administer the distribution of staple goods; created as a more participatory alternative to the JAPs

CONSERVAS Canned goods

DINAC Chilean National Distribution Company, a state-run distribution company that was created through the nationalization of several private distribution firms during the Popular Unity revolution

DIRINCO Office of Industry and Commerce, established in the 1960s as the retooled successor to the country's first consumer protection agency, the Comisariato

ECA Agricultural Trading Company, a state agency created in the 1960s to streamline the marketing of key agricultural commodities

EMPANADA DE PINO Traditional Chilean hand pie made with beef, onions, raisins, olives, and a hard-boiled egg

FERIAS LIBRES Community farmers' markets established in urban areas for the direct exchange of fresh produce; first institutionalized during the Popular Front era

FICHAS Company scrip used to pay workers on the nitrate plains and large rural estates

FRITANGA Community fish fry; promoted during the Popular Unity revolution to popularize the consumption of domestically caught fish, particularly hake

GREMIOS Professional guilds or associations, comprised largely of white-collar workers and professionals; a key component of the conservative opposition to Allende in the early 1970s

INDAP Institute for Agrarian Development, a state-run agency created to train and assist beneficiaries of Chile's agrarian reform process starting in the 1960s

INIA National Institute for Agricultural Research, a state agricultural research office established during Chile's agrarian reform in the 1960s

JAPS Literally "price and supply boards"; community-led consumer monitoring committees and distribution centers created during the Popular Unity revolution

LATIFUNDIO Chile's large agricultural estate system; also known as the "hacienda"

MEMCH Movement for the Emancipation of the Chilean Woman, Chile's progressive women's movement, established in the mid-1930s

MERLUZA Hake

OFICINA Nitrate processing center in Chile's northern Atacama desert

PAN Bread

PANTRUCAS Inexpensive bone-broth noodle soup with onions; a substitute for the more delectable cazuela

PEQUENES Hand pies filled with onions; a less expensive substitute for the empanada de pino

PODER FEMENINO Conservative women's organization formed in the early 1970s to oppose the Popular Unity government

POROTOS Beans

PULPERÍA Name given to the company store in nitrate communities or on large rural estates

REGATONES Small retailers who engaged in the practice of purchasing vital consumer goods to then resell at marked-up prices

RESTAURANTES POPULARES Literally "popular restaurants"; state-run dining halls that served low-cost, nutrient-rich meals during the Popular Front era

SALITRE Nitrates; most commonly processed into agricultural fertilizers but also gunpowder

SOCOAGRO Corporation for Agricultural Construction and Operations, a state agricultural company most often associated with the modernization of Chile's beef industry in the late 1960s and early 1970s

SUBSISTENCIA Literally "subsistence"; used to refer to essential or staple goods, including food, shelter, and clothing

VEGA CENTRAL Chile's main wholesale food and produce market in Santiago

VINO TINTO Red wine

NOTES

INTRODUCTION

1. "Dicen pescadores chilenos: 'Queremos aprender,'" *El Siglo*, January 20, 1972; "San Antonio de fiesta: Hoy reciben barcos soviéticos," *El Siglo*, January 26, 1972; "Faena de pesqueros soviéticos aumenta 30% producción de merluza," *El Siglo*, February 11, 1972; and Rubén Moore, "La multiplicación de los peces," *El Siglo*, February 16, 1972. On the UP's merluza campaign, see also Francisca Espinoza Muñoz, "'La Batalla de la Merluza': Política y consumo alimenticio en el Chile de la Unidad Popular (1970–1973)," *Historia* 51, no. 1 (2018): 31–54.

2. On the meaning of the "empanadas and red wine" slogan, see Peter Winn, "Furies of the Andes: Violence and Terror in the Chilean Revolution and Counter-revolution," in *A Century of Revolution: Insurgent and Counterinsurgent Violence during Latin America's Long Cold War*, ed. Greg Grandin and Gilbert M. Joseph (Durham, NC: Duke University Press, 2010), 240.

3. See, for example, "Pesca soviética en Chile," *El Mercurio* (Santiago), February 2, 1972; "Hacia el consumo dirigido," *El Mercurio* (Santiago), February 8, 1972; and "Escasez de merluza fresca," *El Mercurio* (Santiago), February 21, 1972. As historian Mario Garcés writes, scarcity and rising prices for a growing list of essential goods produced a sense of social crisis that proved difficult for the UP coalition to shake. See Mario Garcés D., "Construyendo 'las poblaciones': El movimiento de pobladores durante la Unidad Popular," in *Cuando hicimos historia: La experiencia de la Unidad Popular*, ed. Julio Pinto Vallejos (Santiago: LOM Ediciones, 2005), 57–79.

4. Salvador Allende, "Public Health Program in Chile," April 6, 1942, National Archives and Records Administration II (NARA II), Record Group (RG) 229, box 84, folder 24, Diseases.

5. See Paul W. Drake, *Socialism and Populism in Chile, 1932–52* (Urbana: University of Illinois Press, 1978). For use of the term "creole socialism" and its relation to food, see Arnold J. Bauer, *Goods, Power, History: Latin America's Material Culture* (Cambridge, UK: Cambridge University Press, 2001), 197.

6. "Se inició avalanche de pescado de los barcos soviéticos," *El Siglo*, January 20, 1972.

7. "Croquetas a base de merluza: Listas para la venta al público," *El Siglo*, March 2, 1972.

8. Joshua Frens-String, "Communists, Commissars, and Consumers: The Politics of Food on the Chilean Road to Socialism," *Hispanic American Historical Review* 98, no. 3 (2018): 471–501.

9. "Gran fiesta de la merluza ayer en el barrio Chacabuco," *El Siglo*, March 17, 1972, cited in Frens-String, "Communists, Commissars, and Consumers," 490–491.

10. Joaquín Lavín, *Chile, revolución silenciosa* (Santiago: Zig-Zag, 1987). The association of consumption with conservatism and free-market capitalism has been echoed by critics of the Pinochet regime as well. See, for example, Tomás Moulian, *El consumo me consume* (Santiago: LOM Ediciones, 1998). See also Patricio Silva, "Modernization, Consumerism, and Politics in Chile," in *Neoliberalism with a Human Face? The Politics and Economics of the Chilean Model*, ed. David E. Hojman (Liverpool, UK: Institute for Latin American Studies, University of Liverpool, 1995), 118–132.

11. Heidi Tinsman, *Buying into the Regime: Grapes and Consumption in Cold War Chile and the United States* (Durham, NC: Duke University Press, 2014), 15–16. See also Camilo D. Trumper, *Ephemeral Histories: Public Art, Politics, and the Struggle for the Streets in Chile* (Oakland: University of California Press, 2016), esp. ch. 1, "Of Spoons and Other Political Things: The Design of Socialist Citizenship," 17–42. Tinsman and Trumper's positions also stand in contrast with how an earlier generation of social and political historians interpreted the rise of mass politics, the emergence of an organized political left, and the consolidation of developmental welfare states around Latin America. In works that emphasized struggles over labor conditions, workers' rights, and the terms of industrial production as the "main events" in the history of the left, earlier scholars interpreted consumer mobilization as a largely "prepolitical" form—that is, a mode of mobilization that was ancillary to workplace organization. For examples, see Eric Hobsbawm, *Primitive Rebels: Studies in Archaic Forms of Social Movement in the 19th and 20th Centuries* (New York: W. W. Norton, 1965), 108–125; and George Rudé, *The Crowd in the French Revolution* (London: Oxford University Press, 1959). E. P. Thompson's work on the moral economy began to move beyond this more orthodox view of food riots by emphasizing their deeply political nature. See "The Moral Economy of the English Crowd in the Eighteenth Century," *Past and Present* 50 (1971): 76–136.

12. Meg Jacobs, "'How about Some Meat?' The Office of Price Administration, Consumption Politics, and State Building from the Bottom Up, 1941–1946," *Journal of American History* 84, no. 3 (December 1997): 911–912, cited in Frens-String, "Communists, Commissars, and Consumers," 474. See also Meg Jacobs, *Pocketbook Politics: Economic Citizenship in Twentieth-Century America* (Princeton, NJ: Princeton University Press, 2005).

13. Eduardo Elena, *Dignifying Argentina: Peronism, Citizenship, and Mass Consumption* (Pittsburgh, PA: University of Pittsburgh Press, 2011); Rebekah Pite,

Creating a Common Table in Twentieth-Century Argentina: Doña Petrona, Women, and Food (Chapel Hill: University of North Carolina Press, 2013); Natalia Milanesio, *Workers Go Shopping in Peronist Argentina: The Rise of Popular Consumer Culture* (Albuquerque: University of New Mexico Press, 2015); and Jennifer Adair, *In Search of the Lost Decade: Everyday Rights in Post-Dictatorship Argentina* (Oakland: University of California Press, 2019).

14. Jeffrey M. Pilcher, *Que Vivan los Tamales! Food and the Making of Mexican Identity* (Albuquerque: University of New Mexico Press, 1998); Enrique C. Ochoa, *Feeding Mexico: The Political Uses of Food since 1910* (Wilmington, DE: SR Books, 2000); and Sandra Aguilar-Rodríguez, "Cooking Modernity: Nutrition Policies, Class, and Gender in 1940s and 1950s Mexico City," *Americas* 64, no. 2 (October 2007): 177–205. Similar arguments have been made in the Peruvian context. See Paulo Drinot, "Food, Race, and Working-Class Identity: Restaurantes Populares in 1930s Peru," *Americas* 62, no. 2 (October 2005): 245–270.

15. Brodwyn Fischer, "The Red Menace Reconsidered: A Forgotten History of Communist Mobilization in Rio de Janeiro's Favelas, 1945–1964," *Hispanic American Historical Review* 94, no. 1 (2014): 1–33.

16. Alejandro Velasco, *Barrio Rising: Urban Popular Politics and the Making of Modern Venezuela* (Oakland: University of California Press, 2015), esp. chs. 5 and 6.

17. On this distinction between consumerism and consumption politics, see Meg Jacobs, "State of the Field: The Politics of Consumption," *Reviews in American History* 39 (2011): 561–573. See also Lizabeth Cohen, "The Class Experience of Mass Consumption: Workers as Consumers in Interwar America," in *The Power of Culture: Critical Essays in American History*, ed. Richard Wightman Fox and Jackson Lears (Chicago: University of Chicago Press, 1993), 135–160. See also Frens-String, "Communists, Commissars, and Consumers," 474.

18. Nick Cullather, *The Hungry World: America's Cold War Battle against Poverty in Asia* (Cambridge, MA: Harvard University Press, 2010); and Jeffrey M. Pilcher, *The Sausage Rebellion: Public Health, Private Enterprise, and Meat in Mexico City, 1890–1917* (Albuquerque: University of New Mexico Press, 2006).

19. Amy Bentley, *Eating for Victory: Food Rationing and the Politics of Domesticity* (Urbana: University of Illinois Press, 1998); Michelle Chase, *Revolution within the Revolution: Women and Gender Politics in Cuba, 1952–1962* (Chapel Hill: University of North Carolina Press, 2015); Julie Guard, "A Mighty Power against the Cost of Living: Canadian Housewives Organize in the 1930s," *International Labor and Working-Class History* 77 (2010): 27–47; Jacobs, "'How about Some Meat?'"; and Lana Dee Povitz, *Stirrings: How Activist New Yorkers Ignited a Food Justice Movement* (Chapel Hill: University of North Carolina Press, 2019).

20. Arjun Appadurai, "How to Make a National Cuisine: Cookbooks in Contemporary India," *Comparative Studies in Society and History* 30, no. 1 (January 1988): 3–24; and Louis A. Pérez Jr., *Rice in the Time of Sugar: The Political Economy of Food in Cuba* (Chapel Hill: University of North Carolina Press, 2019). See also Daniel Bender and Jeffrey M. Pilcher, "Editors' Introduction: Radicalizing the History of Food," *Radical History Review* 110 (2001): 1–7.

21. Jason W. Moore, *Capitalism in the Web of Life: Ecology and the Accumulation of Capital* (New York: Verso Books, 2015). See also Jason W. Moore and Raj Patel, *A History of the World in Seven Cheap Things: A Guide to Capitalism, Nature, and the Future of the Planet* (Oakland: University of California Press, 2017).

22. Sidney W. Mintz, "Food and Eating: Some Persisting Questions," in *Food Nations: Selling Taste in Consumer Societies*, ed. Warren Belasco and Philip Scranton (New York: Routledge, 2002), 27–28, cited in Frens-String, "Communists, Commissars, and Consumers," 475.

23. On the concept of "culinary modernism"—that is, the role that the modern, frequently industrialized food economy has played in producing different forms of equality and economic liberation—see Rachel Laudan, "A Plea for Culinary Modernism: Why We Should Love Fast, Modern, Processed Food (with a New Postscript)," in *Food Fights: How History Matters to Contemporary Food Debates*, ed. Charles C. Ludington and Matthew Morse Booker (Chapel Hill: University of North Carolina Press, 2019), 262–284.

24. This book follows important work in environmental history that has sought to overcome the divide between urban and rural history. See, for example, William Cronon, *Nature's Metropolis: Chicago and the Great West* (New York: W. W. Norton, 1991). See also, Andrew Needham, *Power Lines: Phoenix and the Making of the Modern Southwest* (Princeton, NJ: Princeton University Press, 2014). It also builds on historian Barbara Weinstein's call for historians to not cede explorations of material inequality to the social sciences. As Weinstein writes, historians working after the "linguistic" or "cultural turn" have the ability to "imagine how political power and cultural representations shape economic forces and combine to lubricate a process of economic divergence with its attendant spatial inequality." See Weinstein, "Developing Inequality," *American Historical Review* 113, no. 1 (February 2008): 14.

CHAPTER 1. WORLDS OF ABUNDANCE, WORLDS OF SCARCITY

1. José Miguel Varas, *Chacón* (Santiago: Impresora Horizonte, 1968), 26–27. For other biographical accounts of Chacón and his political life, see "Juan Chacón, hombre y comunista," *El Siglo*, February [day illegible], 1968, International Institute of Social History (IISH), Marcelo Segall Rosenmann Collection (MSR), folder 29; "Chacón Corona: Ejemplar vida de un comunista," *El Siglo*, February 16, 1965, IISH, MSR, folder 29; and "Juan Chacón Corona," *El Siglo*, March 11, 1962, IISH, MSR, folder 31.

2. Varas, *Chacón*, 38–39.

3. Armando de Ramón, *Santiago de Chile (1541–1991): Historia de una sociedad urbana* (Madrid: Editorial MAPFRE, 1992), 174–202, 245. See also Edward Murphy, *For a Proper Home: Housing Rights in the Margins of Urban Chile, 1960–2010* (Pittsburgh, PA: University of Pittsburgh Press, 2015), 41–50.

4. Simón Castillo Fernández, *El Río Mapocho y sus riberas: Espacio público e intervención urbana en Santiago de Chile (1885–1918)* (Santiago: Universidad Alberto Hurtado, 2014).

5. Peter DeShazo, *Urban Workers and Labor Unions in Chile, 1902–1927* (Madison: University of Wisconsin Press, 1983), 5–7; Richard Walter, *Politics and Urban Growth in Santiago, Chile, 1891–1941* (Stanford, CA: Stanford University Press, 2005), 1–7; and de Ramón, *Santiago de Chile*, 245.

6. Arthur Ruhl, "Santiago: The Metropolis of the Andes," *Scribner's Magazine*, February 1908, 139–155, cited in Walter, *Politics and Urban Growth*, 18.

7. Between 1905 and 1925, the number of industrial establishments in Santiago increased slightly, from 954 to 1,147. However, the number of individuals who worked in such industries told a more dramatic story of urban working-class growth: industries that had employed just 16,500 workers at the turn of the century employed nearly 34,500 just two decades later. Elizabeth Quay Hutchison, *Labors Appropriate to Their Sex: Gender, Labor, and Politics in Urban Chile* (Durham, NC: Duke University Press, 2000), 21–22, 27–28. See also DeShazo, *Urban Workers*, 16.

8. Arnold Bauer, *Chilean Rural Society from Spanish Conquest to 1930* (Cambridge, UK: Cambridge University Press, 1975), 76.

9. Bauer, *Chilean Rural Society*, 76–77.

10. Bauer, *Chilean Rural Society*, 77–78.

11. Robert McCaa, ed., *Chile: XI Censo de población (1940); Recopilación de cifras publicadas por la Dirección de Estadísticas y Censos* (Santiago: Centro Latinoamericano de Demografía, 1972), 450–451. Between 1872 and 1915 the total geographic space that was located within the capital city's limits also doubled in size. See Bruce H. Herrick, *Urban Migration and Economic Development in Chile* (Cambridge, MA: MIT Press, 1965), 47–50; 54. See also Ann Louise Hagerman, "Internal Migration in Chile to 1920: Its Relationship to the Labor Market, Agricultural Growth, and Urbanization" (PhD diss., University of California-Davis, 1978), 386–393, 442–479.

12. Gabriel Palma, "Trying to 'Tax and Spend' Oneself Out of the 'Dutch Disease': The Chilean Economy from the War of the Pacific to the Great Depression," in *An Economic History of Twentieth-Century Latin America*, vol. 1, *The Export Age*, ed. Enrique Cárdenas, José Antonio Ocampo, and Rosemary Thorp (London: Palgrave Macmillan, 2000), 217–264.

13. Edward D. Melillo, "The First Green Revolution: Debt Peonage and the Making of the Nitrogen Fertilizer Trade, 1840–1930," *American Historical Review* 117 (2012): 1028–1060.

14. Cited in Charles W. Bergquist, "Exports, Labor, and the Left: An Essay on Twentieth-Century Chilean History," Wilson Center Latin America Program Working Papers 97 (1981), 5. According to Melillo, California farmers alone "doubled their annual consumption of imported fertilizer, increasing it from 36,000 tons to 71,364" between 1913 and 1923, with Chilean nitrogen serving as the "key ingredient" in such soil conditioners. Edward D. Melillo, *Strangers on Familiar Soil:*

Rediscovering the Chile-California Connection (New Haven, CT: Yale University Press, 2015), 105.

15. Alejandro Soto Cárdenas, *Influencia británica en el salitre: Origen, naturaleza y decadencia* (Santiago: Editorial Universidad de Santiago, 1998).

16. Maurice Zeitlin, *The Civil Wars in Chile (or the Bourgeois Revolutions That Never Were)* (Princeton, NJ: Princeton University Press, 1984), 92–95.

17. Enrique Reyes Navarro, *Salitre chileno, mercado mundial y propaganda (1889–1916): Labor del Fiscal don Alejandro Bertrand* (Iquique: Centro de Investigación de la Realidad del Norte, 1986), 18.

18. Reyes Navarro, *Salitre chileno*, 22–23.

19. William S. Myers, "The Position of Nitrogen in Agriculture, Our Leading Industry: An Address Delivered to the American Railway Development Association at Their Annual Meeting in San Antonio, Texas," May 13, 1925, Archivo Nacional Histórico (ANH), Fondo Salitre (FSAL), Chile Nitrate Corporation Limited, vol. 639.

20. Chilean Nitrate of Soda Educational Bureau, "The Increase in Nitrate of Soda as a Fertilizer," 1910, ANH, FSAL, Chile Nitrate Corporation Limited, vol. 639.

21. Chilean Nitrate of Soda Educational Bureau, "Nitrate Letter No. 5," January 1925, ANH, FSAL, Chile Nitrate Corporation Limited, vol. 905; and Chilean Nitrate of Soda Educational Bureau, "Nitrate Letter No. 7," March 1925, ANH, FSAL, Chile Nitrate Corporation Limited, vol. 639.

22. Chilean Nitrate of Soda Educational Bureau, "Nitrate Letter No. 5"; and Chilean Nitrate of Soda Educational Bureau, "Nitrate Letter No. 7."

23. E. Semper and E. Michels, *La industria del salitre en Chile* (Santiago de Chile: Imprenta Barcelona, 1908), 330–331.

24. Michael Monteón, "The *Enganche* in the Chilean Nitrate Sector, 1880–1930," *Latin American Perspectives* 6, no. 4 (1979): 66–79. See also Lawrence A. Stickell, "Migration and Mining: Labor in Northern Chile in the Nitrate Era" (PhD diss., Indiana University, 1979), 70–81.

25. Monteón, "The *Enganche*," 67; and Stickell, "Migration and Mining," 71–72.

26. Stickell, "Migration and Mining," 75.

27. Bergquist, "Exports," 44, 69–70.

28. Bergquist, "Exports," 19.

29. Bergquist, "Exports," 22–24.

30. Bergquist, "Exports," 23.

31. Varas, *Chacón*, 22–23.

32. For a detailed discussion of the refining process that Chacón likely would have witnessed, see Bergquist, "Exports," 22–23. According to historian Sergio González Miranda, many of the major technological advances that lessened the physical stress on nitrate miners were not introduced until the first and second decades of the twentieth century. These included diesel engines to generate electricity in select nitrate oficinas (1904); conveyor belts (1910); machines that mechanically sifted and separated nitrate from other, less useful materials (1911); crushing

and grinding machines (1912); and mechanical front hoes and shovels to aid in the extraction of caliche (1917). González Miranda, *Matamunqui: El ciclo de expansión del nitrato de Chile; La sociedad pampina y su industria* (Santiago: RIL Editores, 2016), 78.

33. Varas, *Chacón*, 23.

34. Varas, *Chacón*, 23–24

35. González Miranda, *Matamunqui*, 507–543.

36. Stickell, "Migration and Mining," 70–71.

37. Miguel Calvo Rebollar, "Dinero no veían, solo fichas: El pago de salarios en las salitreras de Chile hasta 1925," *De Re Metallica* 2 (2009): 9–30; and Marcelo Segall, "Biografía social de la ficha salario," *Mapocho* 2 (1964): 97–131.

38. Nitrate workers frequently faced two options: either migrate between nitrate oficinas to resist the layoffs and wage cuts that accompanied falling nitrate sales or accept the depressed wage rates that accompanied an often saturated labor market. See Bergquist, "Exports," 17–19.

39. As of 1927, 60 percent of those hired by the nitrate industry were illiterate. That number was likely substantially higher earlier in the century, making the role of labor advocates and "scribes" critical to worker mobilization and petitioning. Bergquist, "Exports," 31.

40. Manuel Salas Lavaqui, *Trabajos y antecedentes presentados al Supremo Gobierno de Chile por la Comisión Consultiva del Norte* (Santiago: Imprenta Cervantes, 1908). For more on food struggles and popular politics on the nitrate pampa, see "Memorias de Julio Valiente," 1960, IISH, MSR, folder 272.

41. "Manifiesto de los gremios obreros de la provincia de Tarapacá al supremo Gobierno," in Salas Lavaqui, *Trabajos y antecedentes*, 562.

42. William Howard Russell, *A Visit to Chile and the Nitrate Fields of Tarapacá* (London: J. S. Virtue, 1890), 144.

43. William A. Reid, *Nitrate Fields of Chile*. 4th ed. (Baltimore, MD: Sun Book and Job Printing Office, 1935), 13–15, cited in Melillo, *Strangers on Familiar Soil*, 102.

44. Melillo, *Strangers on Familiar Soil*, 106.

45. Melillo, "First Green Revolution," 1050.

46. Enriqueta de Carpio, "Colaboración de Provincia: Los alimentos cada día escasean más en los hogares humildes," *La Mujer Nueva*, October 1936.

47. For a classic literary representation of poverty in midcentury Chile, see Alberto Romero's novel *La viuda del conventillo* (Buenos Aires: Biblo Editorial, 1930). See also Nicomedes Guzmán, *La Sangre y la esperanza* (Santiago: Orbe, 1943).

48. Walter, *Politics and Urban Growth*, 84. On public health matters in urbanizing Santiago, see also Hugo Alberto Maureira, "'Los culpables de la miseria': Poverty and Public Health during the Spanish Influenza Epidemic in Chile, 1918–1920" (PhD diss., Georgetown University, 2011), esp. 145–151.

49. Quoted in Walter, *Politics and Urban Growth*, 18–20.

50. "Memorial al alcalde de Santiago, después del comicio de noviembre de 1918," *El Mercurio* (Santiago), November 23, 1918, reprinted in Patricio Maestri de Diego, Luis Peña Rojas, and Claudio Peralta Castillo, *La Asamblea Obrera de Alimentación*

Nacional: Un hito en la historia de Chile (Santiago: Academia de Humanismo Cristiano, 2002), 239.

51. Walter, *Politics and Urban Growth*, 3–4. On street vending culture, see Gabriel Salazar V., *Ferias libres: Espacio residual de soberanía ciudadana* (Santiago: Ediciones Sur, 2003).

52. Cited in DeShazo, *Urban Workers*, 56–64. The comuna of Santiago was far and away the most populous in the twenty-four-parish department of Santiago.

53. Carlos Barroilret, "Trabajo y pan," *El Mercurio* (Valparaíso), August 23, 1914.

54. Daniel Palma Alvarado, "De apetitos y de cañas: El consumo de alimentos y bebidas en Santiago a fines del siglo XIX," *Historia* 37, no. 2 (2004): 399.

55. Palma Alvarado, "De apetitos y de cañas," 397–401. For more on the traditional diet of a typical working-class family in Santiago, see Jorge Errázuriz Tagle and Guillermo Eyzaguirre Rouse, *Estudio social: Monografía de una familia obrera de Santiago* (Santiago: Barcelona, 1903), 24–27. On the rise of mass tea consumption in Chile—and its relation to a decline in regionally produced consumption of yerba maté—see José Gabriel Jeffs Munizaga, "Chile en el macrocircuito de la yerba mate: Auge y caída de un producto típico del Cono Sur americano," *Revista Iberoamericana de Viticultura, Agroindustria y Ruralidad* 4, no. 11 (2017): 148–170. According to one early study of nutrition habits, around half of a typical Chilean's daily caloric intake came from wheat products, in particular bread. See Eduardo Cruz-Coke, "Los equilibrios alimenticios y la alimentación del pueblo chileno," *Revista Médica de Chile* (Santiago) 56.4 (June 1928): 533.

56. See, for example, Lucía Larraín Bulnes, *Manual de cocina: A beneficio de Lourdes* (Santiago: Imprenta Claret, 1913), 3–7. See also Duquesa Martell, *Cocina de Cuaresma*, 2nd ed. (Santiago: Guillermo E. Miranda, 1904), 25–26, 46. On beef consumption, see Bauer, *Chilean Rural Society*, 76–77. Bauer notes elsewhere that in the late nineteenth century, not only did elite menus feature imported French foodstuffs, but the menus themselves were also frequently written in French. Bauer, *Goods, Power, History*, 197.

57. Benjamin Orlove and Arnold J. Bauer, "Chile in the Belle Epoque: Primitive Producers, Civilized Consumers," in *The Allure of the Foreign: Imported Goods in Postcolonial Latin America*, ed. Benjamin Orlove (Ann Arbor: University of Michigan Press, 1997), 130. On the chasm between elite and popular consumption patterns in mid-nineteenth- and early twentieth-century Chile, see also Arnold J. Bauer, "Industry and the Missing Bourgeoisie: Consumption and Development in Chile, 1850–1950," *Hispanic American Historical Review* 70, no. 2 (May 1990): 227–253.

58. Julio Subercaseaux, *Reminiscencias* (Santiago: Editorial Nascimiento, 1976), 276, cited in María Angélica Illanes Oliva, *En el nombre del pueblo, del estado y de la ciencia: Historia social de la salud pública, Chile 1880–1973 (Hacia una historia social del Siglo XX)* (Santiago: Ministerio de Salud, 2010), 27.

59. Raymond B. Craib, *The Cry of the Renegade: Politics and Poetry in Interwar Chile* (New York: Oxford University Press, 2016), 21.

60. On the emergence of the "social question" in Chile, see Manuel Bastías Saavedra, "Intervención del estado y derechos sociales: Transformaciones en el

pensamiento jurídico chileno en la era de la cuestión social, 1880–1925," *Historia* 48, no. 1 (2015): 11–42; Vicente Espinoza, *Para una historia de los pobres de la ciudad* (Santiago: Ediciones Sur, 1988); Julio Pinto Vallejos, *Desgarros y utopías en la pampa salitrera: La consolidación de la identidad obrera en tiempos de la cuestión social (1890–1923)* (Santiago: LOM Ediciones, 2007); and Juan Carlos Yáñez Andrade, *La intervención social en Chile, 1907–1932* (Santiago: RIL Editores, 2008).

61. Thomas C. Wright, *Landowners and Reform in Chile: The Sociedad Nacional de Agricultura, 1919–40* (Urbana: University of Illinois Press, 1982), 101–105.

62. Wright, *Landowners and Reform in Chile*, 103.

63. For discussion of the construction of the "villainous landlord" trope, see Wright, *Landowners and Reform*, 31–37.

64. For primary accounts of the 1905 protests, see "Los Desórdenes en Santiago," *El Ferrocarril*, October 23, 1905; and "Llegada de Huelgistas," [month and day illegible], 1905, IISH, MSR, folder 10. For an interesting analysis of 1905 protests written during the first year of the UP revolution, see "La sangre del pueblo," *Qué Pasa*, October 22, 1971, IIHS, MSR, folder 11. Scholarly accounts of the protests include Gonzálo Izquierdo Fernández, "Octubre de 1905: Un episodio en la historia social chilena," *Historia* 13 (1976): 55–96. See also Benjamin Orlove, "Meat and Strength: The Moral Economy of a Chilean Food Riot," *Cultural Anthropology* 12, no. 2 (1997): 234–268.

65. Orlove, "Meat and Strength," 239–241. See also Espinoza, *Para una historia*, 29.

66. "La actitud de la juventud," *El Ferrocarril*, October 23, 1905.

67. "Los Desórdenes en Santiago"; "Continúan los desórdenes," *El Ferrocarril*, October 24, 1905; and "Reestablecimiento del orden público," *El Ferrocarril*, October 25, 1905. In Izquierdo's meticulous accounting of the event, he highlights the class character of the popular violence by noting that those who attacked commercial establishments specifically avoided destroying property of those they perceived as members of the working class. When they realized that a kiosk was owned by a person of modest means, for example, they would write "belongs to a poor worker" and move on to a new target owned by a more well-off individual. Izquierdo Fernández, "Octubre de 1905," 62.

68. Edward Alsworth Ross, *South of Panama* (New York: Century Company, 1917), 375–376.

69. "Reestablecimiento del orden público." The figure of three hundred killed comes from Ramón Subercaseaux, *Memorias de ochena años* (Santiago: Editorial Nascimento, 1936), 135. Murphy maintains that between two and three hundred were killed. See Murphy, *For a Proper Home*, 51. For an additional scholarly account of the 1905 meat riots, see Brian Loveman, *Chile: The Legacy of Hispanic Capitalism* (New York: Oxford University Press, 2001), 166–167.

70. Loveman, *Chile*, 166–167.

71. Wright, *Landowners and Reform*, 109.

72. Espinoza, *Para una historia*, 39–45.

73. Yáñez Andrade, *La intervención social*, 31–37.

74. Yáñez Andrade, *La intervención social*, 117–119.

75. For a discussion of the strikers' demands and the memory of the subsequent massacre, see Lessie Jo Frazier, *Salt in the Sand: Memory, Violence, and the Nation-State in Chile, 1890 to the Present* (Durham, NC: Duke University Press, 2007), 117–157.

76. The scholarly literature on the December 1907 Santa María School massacre is extensive. Key recent works and primary source collections include Sergio González Miranda, *Ofrenda de una massacre: Claves e indicios históricos de la emancipación pampina de 1907* (Santiago: LOM Ediciones, 2007); Sergio González Miranda, ed., *A 90 años de los sucesos de la Escuela de Santa María de Iquique* (Santiago: LOM Ediciones, 1998); and Pedro Bravo Elizondo, *Santa María de Iquique 1907: Documentos para su historia* (Santiago: Ediciones del Litoral, 1993).

77. Cited in Frazier, *Salt in the Sand*, 115.

78. Atilano Oróstegui, "Cómo se vive en la pampa salitrera," 1934, 7–12, Biblioteca Nacional de Chile (BNC), Sección Chilena (SC).

79. Julián Cobó, *Yo vi nacer y morir los pueblos salitreros* (Santiago: Editorial Quimantú, 1971), 17.

80. Frazier, *Salt in the Sand*, 115.

81. Luis Emilio Recabarren, *Ricos y pobres a través de un siglo de la vida repúblicana* (1910; repr., Santiago: LOM Ediciones, 2010), 45–46.

82. Recabarren, *Ricos y pobres*, 48–51.

83. Recabarren, *Ricos y pobres*, 46.

84. Cited in Pinto Vallejos, *Desgarros y utopías*, 138–139.

85. Julio Pinto Vallejos, "Socialismo y salitre: Recabarren, Tarapacá y la formación del Partido Obrero Socialista," *Historia* 32 (1999): 348.

86. *El Nacional*, March 20, 1911, cited in Pinto Vallejos, "Socialismo y salitre," 341.

87. Pinto Vallejos, "Socialismo y saltire," 354.

88. James Vernon, *Hunger: A Modern History* (Cambridge, MA: Belknap Press of Harvard University Press, 2007), 273.

89. Pinto Vallejos, *Desgarros y utopías*, 183.

90. Pinto Vallejos, *Desgarros y utopías*, 157–158.

91. See Vaclav Smil, *Enriching the Earth: Fritz Haber, Carl Bosch, and the Transformation of World Food Production* (Cambridge, MA: MIT Press, 2004).

92. "Visitando la hospedería," *El Chileno*, November 8, 1914.

93. Varas, *Chacón*, 26–41.

94. Varas, *Chacón*, 27.

CHAPTER 2. RED CONSUMERS

1. On the life of Carlos Alberto Martínez, see Congreso Nacional de Chile, "Carlos Alberto Martínez Martínez," in *Historia Política Legislativa del Congreso Nacional de Chile*, http://historiapolitica.bcn.cl/resenas_parlamentarias/wiki

/Carlos_Alberto_Mart%C3%ADnez_Mart%C3%ADnez. For other discussions of Martínez and his political activities, see Sergio Grez Toso, *Historia del comunismo en Chile: La era de Recabarren (1912–1924)* (Santiago: LOM Ediciones, 2011). For letters written by Recabarren and Martínez, see an important collection of correspondence between the two men: "Cartas de Luis Emilio Recabarren a Alberto Martínez," Fondos varios, ANH, Santiago. For an interview with Martínez when he served as minister of land and colonization in 1931, see "Dos Palabras con el Ministro de Tierras y Colonización, Don Carlos Alberto Martínez," *Sucesos*, October 22, 1931, 17–19, IISH, MSR, folder 24.

2. "El gran comicio público de ayer," *El Diario Ilustrado*, November 23, 1918; and "La carestía de los artículos de consumo," *El Mercurio* (Santiago), November 23, 1918.

3. "El gran comicio público de ayer." See also coverage in *El Mercurio* (Santiago), November 23, 1918, as cited in Maestri de Diego, Peña Rojas, and Peralta Castillo, *La Asamblea*, 75 and Craib, *The Cry of the Renegade*, 23.

4. Craib, *The Cry of the Renegade*, 21. In the war's wake, consumer prices for many food staples more than doubled in Chile, with estimates suggesting that the average Chilean wage earner was forced to spend upwards of three-quarters of his/her income just to meet subsistence needs.

5. Santiago Labarca, "Memorias de Santiago Labarca—La Asamblea Obrera de Alimentación Nacional," *Claridad* 1, no. 9 (1920).

6. Carlos Alberto Martínez, "Discurso de Presidente de la AOAN, en el Teatro Municipal, a propósito del proyecto de una Administración Nacional de Subsistencias," *La Opinión*, December 21, 1918, reprinted in Maestri de Diego, Peña Rojas, and Peralta Castillo, *La Asamblea*, 247–249. The Chilean historian Gabriel Salazar maintains that the AOAN organized its calls for more direct forms of political participation around basic economic concerns. According to Salazar, the AOAN ultimately aimed to create a "Popular Legislative Assembly" in Chile—that is, a new deliberative legislative body, capable of "colegislating" on behalf of Chilean workers. Gabriel Salazar V., *Del poder constituyente de asalariados e intelectuales (Chile, siglos XX y XXI)* (Santiago: LOM Ediciones, 2012), 43–48. For accounts of the AOAN, see the various newspaper clippings about the AOAN in the Marcelo Segall Rosenmann Collection at Amsterdam's International Institute of Social History, especially folders 13 and 14. Examples are "De hace medio siglo," *El Mercurio* (Santiago), December 19, 1919, IISH, MSR, folder 13; "De hace medio siglo," *El Mercurio* (Santiago), March 11, 1919, IISH, MSR, folder 13; "De hace medio siglo," *El Mercurio* (Santiago), October 26, 1919, IISH, MSR, folder 13; and "Potpourri," 1918, IISH, MSR, folder 13.

7. "Invitación a los gremios para organizar un Comité pro-abaratamiento de los precios de los artículos alimenticios," *La Opinión*, October 7, 1918, reprinted in Maestri de Diego, Peña Rojas, and Peralta Castillo, *La Asamblea*, 225–226.

8. "Al pueblo del país," *La Opinión*, October 22, 1918, reprinted in Maestri de Diego, Peña Rojas, and Peralta Castillo, *La Asamblea*, 227–229.

9. Letters exchanged by Martínez and Recabarren in the late 1910s reveal this geographic role reversal, in which workers on the nitrate plains followed the

actions of urban workers. See, for example, Recabarren (Antofagasta) to Martínez (Santiago), July 31, 1919, ANH, Cartas de Luis Emilio Recabarren a Carlos Alberto Martínez, Correspondencia, 1918–1920.

10. On the association of meat with masculine strength, see Pilcher, *Sausage Rebellion*, 24. See also Natalia Milanesio, "Food Politics and Consumption in Peronist Argentina," *Hispanic American Historical Review* 90, no. 1 (February 2010): 84–85.

11. "Al pueblo del país."

12. "Segundo memorial al Presidente de la República," *El Mercurio* (Santiago), February 8–9, 1919, reprinted in Maestri de Diego, Peña Rojas, and Peralta Castillo, *La Asamblea*, 257–271.

13. "Manifiesto al pueblo de Chile," *La Opinión*, February, 10, 1919, reprinted in Maestri de Diego, Peña Rojas, and Peralta Castillo, *La Asamblea*, 275–282.

14. "Primer memorial al Presidente de la República," *El Mercurio* (Santiago), November 23, 1918, reprinted in Maestri de Diego, Peña Rojas, and Peralta Castillo, *La Asamblea*, 231–237.

15. "Segundo memorial al Presidente de la República."

16. Martínez, "Discurso de Presidente de la AOAN."

17. *El Mercurio* (Santiago), April 20, 1919, cited in Wright, *Landowners and Reform in Chile*, 107.

18. Craib, *The Cry of the Renegade*, 24–25.

19. On repression against the AOAN, as well as internal disputes within the movement, see Igancio Rodríguez Terrazas, "Protesta y soberanía popular: Las marchas del hambre en Santiago de Chile, 1918–1919" (undergraduate thesis, Pontificia Universidad Católica de Chile, 2001), 88–92, 99–103, 128–141.

20. Quoted in Jorge Barría Cerón, "Chile: La cuestión política y social en 1920–1926," *Annales de la Universidad de Chile* 116 (1959): 59.

21. Varas, *Chacón*, 35–36. "Reca" is a reference to POS founder Luis Emilio Recabarren, who ran for president in 1920.

22. Sergio Grez Toso, "La Asamblea Constituyente de Asalariados e Intelectuales, Chile, 1925: Entre el olvido y la mitificación," *Izquierdas* 29 (September 2016): 1–48; and Salazar V., *Del poder constituyente*, 76–93.

23. "Enseñanzas de la lucha," *Sucesos*, 1925, IISH, MSR, folder 21; "La candidatura Salas," IISH, MSR, folder 22; and José Santos Salas, speech presented in Santiago, October 11, 1925, IIHS, MSR, folder 168.

24. Wright, *Landowners and Reform in Chile*, 107–109. For a complete summary of food and consumer measures adopted by the national government in the 1920s, see Guillermo Torres Orrego, "El Comisariato General de Subsistencias y Precios de la República" (undergraduate thesis, University of Chile, 1947), 18–24.

25. M. C. Mirow, "Origins of the Social Function of Property," *Fordham Law Review* 80, no. 3 (2011): 1183–1217. For a critique of the state's use of the 1925 constitution to expand economic intervention, see Enrique Brahm García, *Propiedad sin libertad: Chile, 1925–1973: Aspectos relevantes en el avance de la legislación socializadora* (Santiago: Universidad de los Andes, 1999).

26. Gabriel Palma, "From an Export-Led to an Import-Substituting Economy, Chile 1914–1939," in *Latin America in the 1930s: The Role of the Periphery in World Crisis*, ed. Rosemary Thorp (London: Palgrave Macmillan, 1984), 55–56.

27. Banco Central de Chile, *Sexta memoria anual presentada a la superintendencia de bancos: Año 1931* (Santiago: Banco Central, 1932), 11.

28. Cited in Fredrick B. Pike, *Chile and the United States, 1880–1962: The Emergence of Chile's Social Crisis and the Challenge to U.S. Diplomacy* (South Bend, IN: University of Notre Dame Press, 1963), 208–209.

29. For a detailed look at the policy measures taken by Alessandri in the face of the crisis of the 1930s, see Joaquín Fermandois, *Abismo y cimiento: Gustavo Ross y las relaciones entre Chile y los Estados Unidos, 1932–1938* (Santiago: Ediciones Universidad Católica de Chile, 1997). On the Great Depression's impact on labor, see Ángela Vergara, "Chilean Workers and the Great Depression, 1930–1938," in *The Great Depression in Latin America*, ed. Paulo Drinot and Alan Knight (Durham, NC: Duke University Press, 2014), 51–80. See also Michael Monteón, *Chile and the Great Depression: The Politics of Underdevelopment, 1927–1948* (Tempe: Center for Latin American Studies, Arizona State University, 1998).

30. Rodrigo Henríquez Vásquez, *En "estado sólido": Políticas politización en la construcción estatal, Chile 1920–1950* (Santiago: Ediciones UC, 2014), 220–224. See also Loveman, *Chile*, 202–203. Statistics gathered by Chile's industrialists' association in the mid-1940s suggest that one of the most significant issues in the mid-1930s was the growing fraction of average annual income that went toward food purchases. See Mauricio Hartard Ebert, "Indice del costo de la vida en Santiago," *Industria* 63, no. 10 (October 1946): 587–589.

31. "El pueblo se muere de hambre," *Frente Popular*, September 14, 1936.

32. "El pueblo se muere de hambre." See also "La alimentación popular y los salarios," *Frente Popular*, September 30, 1936. In the 1930s, basic food provisioning became an important state function. Dozens of state-funded soup kitchens served an estimated 100,000 meals per day at the peak of the crisis. In Santiago alone, twenty-seven soup kitchens provided more than half of those meals—around 60,000 per day in mid-1932. See "Ollas comunes para alimentar cesantes," *Zig-Zag*, July 2, 1932.

33. "El pueblo se muere de hambre."

34. "Culpable de la carestía de la vida, *Frente Popular*, September 25, 1936.

35. "Contra la especulación se coaliga el Pueblo," *Frente Popular*, September 14, 1936.

36. "Organiza la lucha contra la vida cara," *Frente Popular*, September 29, 1936.

37. "Marcha de hambre," *Frente Popular*, October 9, 1936; and "Violentemente disuelta manifestación de hoy," *Frente Popular*, October 12, 1936.

38. "Se formarán comisiones de vigilancia contra los acaparadores de víveres," *Frente Popular*, October 2, 1936.

39. "Mujeres fueron apaleados," *Frente Popular*, October 12, 1936.

40. "El pueblo se muere de hambre."

41. See, for example, "Trust del pan," *La Mujer Nueva* (June 1936), 2; "Por qué es cara la vida?" *La Mujer Nueva* (August 1936), 4; and Temma Kaplan, "Female

Consciousness and Collective Action: The Case of Barcelona, 1910–1918," *Signs* 7 (1982): 545–566.

42. "Que bajen las papas!," *La Mujer Nueva* (October 1936), 3.

43. "Un pequeño triunfo del MEMCH," *La Mujer Nueva* (July 1937), 1–2. For more on MEMCh activism in consumer issues, see Corinne Antezana-Pernet, "Mobilizing Women in the Popular Front Era: Feminism, Class, and Politics in the *Movimiento Pro-Emancipación de la Mujer Chilena* (MEMCh), 1935–1950" (PhD diss., University of California, Irvine, 1996), 182–183, 234–235, 351–352.

44. "Alza de las subsistencias preocupa al Frente Popular," *Frente Popular*, October 7, 1936.

45. On the electoral history of the FP, see Drake, *Socialism and Populism*.

46. See, for example, "Junta de vigilancia a intendente de Santiago," February 17, 1939, ANH, Fondo Intendencia de Santiago (FIS), vol. 1014.

47. Decree-Law (DL) 520, Santiago, August 30, 1932, www.leychile.cl/Navegar ?idNorma=6157. On the precedent of Ibáñez's original attempt to create price controls, see Wright, *Landowners and Reform in Chile*, 109.

48. Torres Orrego, "El Comisariato General," 36–37.

49. Fred Francisco Facusse Orellana, "La fijación de los precios en el comercio interno de Chile" (undergraduate thesis, Pontificia Universidad Católica de Chile, 1964), 64.

50. Brahm García, *Propiedad sin libertad*, 77–78.

51. "Nómina de los artículos declarados de primera necesidad o de uso o consumo habitual clasificados por Decreto Supremo (Hasta el 28 de Febrero de 1945)," *Boletín del Comisariato General de Subsistencias y Precios* 2 (March 1945): 30–35. On the state's role in regulating staple goods and its social and economic impact, see Elías Nehgme Rodriguez, *La economía nacional y el problema de las subsistencias en Chile* (Santiago: Imprenta Condor, 1943).

52. Henríquez Vásquez, *En "estado sólido"*, 219–220.

53. While the average Chilean consumed far more tea than coffee, the inclusion of the latter may have been a gesture toward consumer trends in Europe and the United States. The presence of vegetables and fish on such lists underscored the emergence of what nutritionists of the era called "protective foods"—that is, vitamin-rich goods that would protect the body from diseases like scurvy and rickets. For more on Chile's engagement with midcentury nutrition science, see chapter 3.

54. On the work of the Comisariato under the FP, see Henríquez Vásquez, *En "estado sólido"*, 224–235. See also Marcelo Cavarozzi, "The Government and the Industrial Bourgeoisie in Chile: 1938–1964" (PhD diss., University of California-Berkeley, 1975), 169, 177–182. In reviewing the Comisariato's archives, it is difficult to estimate exactly how much the workforce of the agency grew under the FP. During one month (January) in 1944, however, some 165 new hires were made by the agency. See "Decreto 98," January 15, 1944, Archivo Nacional de la Administración (ARNAD), Ministerio de Economía (MECO), Fondo Servicio Nacional del Consumidor (FSERNAC), vol. 3. See also Departamento de Contabilidad, "Decretos 716, 717, and 718," March 20, 1944, ARNAD, MECO, FSERNAC, vol. 5. By 1946,

the agency employed more than 175 individuals. See "El derecho a la subsistencia" (editorial), *Boletín Oficial del Comisariato General de Subsistencias y Precios* 11 (January 1936): 350–351.

55. Volodia Teitelboim, *Un hombre de edad media (Antes del olvido II)* (Santiago: Editorial Sudamericana, 2000), 165–166, 174, 242. Upon assuming office in 1939, the FP added housing to its list of controlled "goods," leading to a particularly active housing justice campaign by the FP in the early 1940s that included a freeze on evictions. See Espinoza, *Para una historia de los pobres*, 185–224.

56. Comisariato General de Subsistencias y Precios—Departamento de Fiscalía, "Decreto No. 536," March 24, 1943, ARNAD, MECO, FSERNAC, vol. 1; and Comisariato General de Subsistencias y Precios—Departamento de Fiscalía, "Decreto No. 568," March 30, 1943, ARNAD, MECO, FSERNAC, vol. 1.

57. In a 1943 profile piece, the *New York Times* declared Contreras de Schnake the "only woman to ever rule one of the world's major capital cities as Mayor." See "Triumph Achieved by First Woman to Serve as Mayor [of] a Large City," *New York Times*, January 30, 1943.

58. Walter, *Politics and Urban Growth*, 224; and Salazar V., *Ferias libres*, 79–85.

59. "Triumph achieved by First Woman to Serve as Mayor."

60. Salazar V., *Ferias libres*, 83–84.

61. Walter, *Politics and Urban Growth*, 230–231.

62. On social Catholicism and nutrition, see chapter 3.

63. "Acción popular contra los especuladores," *El Siglo*, September 24, 1946; "El pueblo se apoderó de té acaparado," *El Siglo*, September 29, 1946; "Obligaron a vender alimentos," *El Siglo*, September 30, 1946; and "El pueblo hace justicia con sus propias manos," *El Siglo*, September 30, 1946. Data compiled by Chile's industrialists' association highlights the surge in the price of cooking oil (especially imports), the majority of which appears to have been soy-based oil imported from neighboring Argentina. The total amount of money that Chile spent on cooking oil imports in 1947 was an astounding forty-three times greater in 1946 than it was in 1947. In addition, the wholesale price of soy-based oil in 1947 was more than double the price in 1946, according to data published in *Industria*. See Mauricio Hartard Ebert, "Importación de Productos de Industrias Alimenticias," *Industria* 65, no. 5 (May 1948): 309–311; and Mauricio Hartard Ebert, "Precios de Algunos Productos Industriales," *Industria* 65, no. 11 (November 1948): 731–732.

64. "El pueblo se apoderó de té acaparado."

65. "El pueblo hace justicia con sus propias manos."

66. "Surgen nuevos comites contra el hambre," *El Siglo*, October 2, 1946; "Quince mil personas adquieron aceite y azúcar," *El Siglo*, October 3, 1946; "A formar comites contra el hambre!," *El Siglo*, October 4, 1946; "Continúa acción popular contra especulación," *El Siglo*, October 8, 1946; and "Se han repartido 38 mil 600 litros de aceite para la población de Santiago," *El Siglo*, December 7, 1946. For more on these events, see Frens-String, "Communists, Commissars, and Consumers," 480.

67. Thompson, "Moral Economy of the English Crowd," 78–79.

68. "El terror comunista sigue llevando al hambre a numerosas familias obreras," *La Opinión*, November 21, 1946; "Ofrecen en venta vales para adquirir aceite solo a quienes ingresen al Partido Comunista," *La Opinión*, November 24, 1946; "Más de un millón de pesos semanales ganan comunistas con la venta de cupones de aceite," *La Opinión*, November 27, 1946; "Comunistas están revendiendo cupones para comprar aceite," *La Opinión*, December 1, 1946; "Aceiteras," *La Opinión*, December 12, 1946; and "Venta ilegal de vales y robo de mercaderías," *La Opinión*, December 12, 1946. For the PCCh's response to Bautista Rossetti's campaign against the party, see "Emplazamos a 'La Opinión,'" *El Siglo*, December 8, 1946; and "Rossetti y el aceite," *El Siglo*, December 8, 1946.

69. "Que se suprima el Comisariato y se cree la Dirección General De Subsistencias," *La Opinión*, December 16, 1946.

70. PCCh members played an especially active role in housing justice campaigns after the FP's 1938 election. See Espinoza, *Para una historia de los pobres*, 185–237. See also Jorge Rojas Flores, "La lucha por la vivienda en tiempos de González Videla: Las experiencias de las poblaciones Los Nogales, Lo Zañartu y Luis Emilio Recabarren en Santiago de Chile, 1946–1947," *Izquierdas* 39 (April 2018): 1–33.

71. "La cárcel para los especuladores," *Frente Popular*, October 9, 1936.

72. "El pueblo debe pasar a la ofensiva al fascismo y la vida cara," *El Popular* (Antofagasta), December 7, 1941. On consumer-related demands of pampa residents, see Servicio de Investigaciones, Identificación y Pasaportes, "Memorandum No. 13," March 22, 1938, Archivo Regional de Tarapacá (ART), Fondo Intendencia de Tarapacá (FITAR), vol. 1711.

73. So closely had the party become associated with consumer mobilization that in the late 1940s a US State Department official, labor attaché Daniel Horowitz, was accused by some of his North American colleagues of being a sympathizer of the party because of the friendship that he and his wife had established with a Santiago-based consumer organizer, Graciela Mandujano. Daniel L. Horowitz, oral history conducted by Herbert Weiner, Association for Diplomatic Studies and Training Foreign Affairs Oral History Project Labor Series, May 27, 1994, Library of Congress, Washington, DC, http://memory.loc.gov/cgi-bin/query/D?mfdip:1:./temp /~ammem_NxHC.

74. See Jody Pavilack, *Mining for the Nation: The Politics of Chile's Coal Communities from the Popular Front to the Cold War* (University Park: Pennsylvania State University Press, 2011), 129–131. Similar frustrations were expressed at the Teniente copper mine, where rising food prices led to the formation of local cost-of-living committees in early 1941. See Thomas Miller Klubock, *Contested Communities: Class, Gender, and Politics in Chile's El Teniente Copper Mine, 1904–1951* (Durham, NC: Duke University Press, 1998), 229.

75. Daniel Horowitz, "No. 13,417: Labor and Social Developments in Chile— November 25, 1945 to January 15, 1946," January 31, 1946, NARA II, RG 59, box 5365, folder 3.

76. On the Chilean labor movement's restraint during the war, particularly its decision to contain strike actions, see Andrew Barnard, "Chile," in *Latin America*

Between the Second World War and the Cold War, 1944–1948, ed. Leslie Bethell and Ian Roxborough (Cambridge, UK: Cambridge University Press, 1992), 69–72. See also Pavilack, *Mining for the Nation,* 176–207.

77. On Chilean workers' refusal to load nitrates and copper for Axis countries, see "Sigue nuestro salitre y cobre llegando a potencias del Eje," *El Siglo,* January 29, 1943. On the actions against Mustakis, see Pascual Barraza, "Contenido de la lucha por la rebaja de las subsistencias," *Principios* 27 (September 1943): 9–10.

78. "El hambre y los lanzamientos será el acto de hoy en el Caupolicán," *El Siglo,* May 26, 1946; "Los grandes monopolios tienen pase libre para especular," *El Siglo,* June 4, 1946; "Monopolio obtuvo alza en el precio del arroz," *El Siglo,* June 5, 1946; and "10 millones de pesos en productos acaparados tiene la Firma Menichetti," *El Siglo,* June 6, 1946. In 1973, the conservative anti-Allende paper *El Mercurio* republished an old article attacking CENADECO in an attempt to draw parallels with the PCCh's role in consumer mobilization during the Popular Unity era. "La 'CENADECO' es una institución inventada y controlada por elementos comunistas," *El Mercurio,* January 18, 1973, IIHS, MSR, folder 141.

79. Luis Reinoso, "La solución de los problemas nacionales a través de la movilización de las masas—Enseñanzas del XIII Congreso," *Principios* 56–57 (February–March 1946): 15–19.

80. On the history of female-led kitchen shutdowns, or *cocinas apagadas,* see González Miranda, *Matamunqui,* 507–542.

81. "Da cuenta de paro ilegal que afecta faenas salitreras," January 17, 1946, ART, FITAR, vol. 1839; "Proporciona nuevos antecedentes sobre paro ilegal en la pampa," January 18, 1946, ART, FITAR, vol. 1839; and "Da cuenta para momentaneo de obreros en Campamento 'La Santiago,'" March 27, 1946, ART, FITAR, vol. 1839. The strikes over rising food prices at La Santiago in January 1946 set off a series of coordinated actions at over half a dozen other nitrate offices. See "Refiérese a huelga en la pampa salitrera," January 21, 1946, ART, FITAR, vol. 1839; "Sobre paralización de faenas en el Campamento 'San Jose,'" March 12, 1946, ART, FITAR, vol. 1839; and "Da cuenta de huelga ilegal en la Oficina salitrera 'Santa Laura,'" May 4, 1946, ART, FITAR, vol. 1849.

82. See Carlos Huneeus, *La guerra fría chilena: Gabriel González Videla y la ley maldita* (Santiago: Debate, 2009), 109–110. The PCCh had been just the seventh largest party in the country's broad electoral field in 1944.

83. Pavilack, *Mining for the Nation,* 249–255.

84. Cited in Karin Alejandra Rosemblatt, *Gendered Compromises: Political Cultures and the State in Chile, 1920–1950* (Chapel Hill: University of North Carolina Press, 2000), 118–119.

85. Varas, *Chacón,* 124.

86. Varas, *Chacón,* 125–126.

87. See Pavilack, *Mining for the Nation,* 259–265.

88. Pavilack, *Mining for the Nation,* 259–265. For González Videla's take on the bread crisis of 1947, see his *Memorias* (Santiago: Editora Nacional Gabriela Mistral, 1974), 1: 629–633.

89. Pavilack, *Mining for the Nation*, 259–262.

90. Pavilack, *Mining for the Nation*, 283–288.

91. Pavilack, *Mining for the Nation*, 292.

92. Huneeus, *La guerra fría chilena*, 240–241.

93. "Correspondencia recibida y despachada por la Oficina de la Mujer," November 2–5, 1947, ANH, Fondo Gabriel González Videla (FGGV), vol. 18.

94. On the early history of the Asociación de Dueñas de Casa, see Raquel Yanulaque Garrido, "Asociación Nacional de Dueñas de Casa," Memoria de prueba (Santiago: Universidad de Chile, 1950), ANH, FGGV, vol. 132. See also chapter 3 of this book. For an example of González Videla's attack on the PCCh for its role in consumer matters, see Gabriel González Videla, "Discurso en Osorno," November 3, 1949, ANH, FGGV, vol. 101. On the ADC and its depoliticization of female consumers, see Rosa M. de González Videla, "Cartilla de Consumidor," 1950, ANH, FGGV, vol. 131.

95. Rosemblatt, *Gendered Compromises*, 119–120.

CHAPTER 3. CONTROLLING FOR NUTRITION

1. For Volodia Teitelboim's reflections on Eduardo Cruz-Coke, see Eduardo Cruz-Coke and Marta Lagos Cruz-Coke, *Testimonios* (Santiago: Procultura Fundación, 2015), 397.

2. On Cruz-Coke's role in the formation of Chile's social welfare state, see Carlos Huneeus and María Paz Lanas, "Ciencia política e historia: Eduardo Cruz-Coke y el estado de bienestar en Chile, 1937–1938," *Historia* 35 (2002): 151–186. See also David Vásquez V. and Felipe Rivera, eds., *Eduardo Cruz-Coke Lassabe: Política, ciencia y espíritu, 1899–1974* (Santiago: Biblioteca el Congreso Nacional, 2013).

3. For example, Eduardo Cruz-Coke, "Creación de capitales nacionales: Discurso pronunciado en la sesión del Senado," September 15, 1941, reprinted in Cruz-Coke, *Discursos: Política, economía, salubridad, habitación, relaciones exteriores agricultura* (Santiago: Editorial Nascimento, 1946), 17–44.

4. Huneeus, *La guerra fría chilena*, 120–121; and Pavilack, *Mining for the Nation*, 259–265.

5. Huneeus, *La guerra fría chilena*, 240–241.

6. Huneeus, *La guerra fría chilena*, 230.

7. William Prout, "On the Ultimate Composition of Simple Alimentary Substances," *Philosophical Transactions of the Royal Society of London* 117 (1827): 255–388. See also Michael Pollan, *In Defense of Food: An Eater's Manifesto* (New York: Penguin Books, 2008), 19–22.

8. Smil, *Enriching the Earth*, 5–12. Emerging as part of a broader socioscientific movement to identify the social and environmental determinants of public health, the findings of Prout, Liebig, and others soon became tools for public officials and enterprising philanthropists to confront the social demands of Europe's growing urban working-class population through medicine. On the emergence of social

medicine and its importance in Latin America and Chile in particular, see Adam Gaffney, *To Heal Humankind: The Right to Health in History* (New York: Routledge, 2017), 63–68, 137–144.

9. Cullather, *Hungry World*, 15.

10. Nick Cullather, "The Foreign Policy of the Calorie," *American Historical Review* 112, no. 2 (April 2007): 341–342.

11. Cullather, "Foreign Policy of the Calorie," 343. For an important Latin American portion of this story about energy, science, and diet, see Stefan Pohl-Valero, "La Raza Entra Por La Boca: Energy, Diet, and Eugenics in Colombia, 1890–1940," *Hispanic American Historical Review* 94, no. 3 (2014): 455–486.

12. Vernon, *Hunger*, 89–90.

13. Vernon, *Hunger*, 83–84, 90. The same year that Hobson made these comments, British researcher Seebohm Rowntree used caloric intake as a way to measure poverty in Great Britain. One of the first major social surveys of popular nutrition to be conducted in the country, Rowntree's research highlighted the cost and quantity of calories necessary for an individual in the city of York to remain a "healthy and productive member of society." Between 1885 and 1910, social scientists and nutritionists in the United States carried out more than five hundred similar surveys to evaluate the eating habits of a wide range of social groups, including workers, the urban poor, and indigenous communities. See Cullather, "Foreign Policy of the Calorie," 343.

14. On the origins of "nutrition science," see Harvey Levenstein, *Revolution at the Table: The Transformation of the American Diet* (New York: Oxford University Press, 1988), 44–46. See also League of Nations, *The Problem of Nutrition: Interim Report of the Mixed Committee on the Problem of Nutrition* (Geneva: League of Nations, 1936), 1: 32.

15. On the history of the vitamin, see Rima D. Apple, *Vitamania: Vitamins in American Culture*. (New Brunswick, NJ: Rutgers University Press, 1996). See also Catherine Price, *Vitamania: How Vitamins Revolutionized the Way We Think about Food* (New York: Penguin Press, 2015). A brief history of this moment in nutrition science can also be found in Pollan, *In Defense of Food*, 21–22.

16. "Tablas de alimentación," *Boletín del Ministerio de Higiene, Asistencia, Previsión y Trabajo* 2 (June 1927): 6–8.

17. See Juan Carlos Yáñez Andrade, "Los pobres están invitados a la mesa: Debates y proyectos transnacionales de alimentación popular en América del Sur, 1930–1950," *Historia Crítica* 71 (2019): 77.

18. "La alimentación según las profesiones," *Boletín del Ministerio de Higiene, Asistencia, Previsión y Trabajo* 3 (July 1927): 6–8.

19. Peter Hakim and Giorgio Solimano, *Development, Reform, and Malnutrition* (Cambridge, MA: MIT Press, 1978), 33–34. See also Patricio Valdivieso F., *Dignidad humana y justicia: La historia de Chile, la política social y el cristianismo, 1880–1920* (Santiago: Ediciones Universidad Católica de Chile, 2006), 290–291.

20. League of Nations, *Problem of Nutrition*, 17–18.

21. Dr. E. Prado G., "La alimentación del trabajador," *Industria* 66, no. 4 (April 1949): 259–262. Rosemblatt notes that although Chile did not establish a national

minimum wage until 1956, experiments setting "living wages" in select sectors of the economy reinforced the notion that a wage should reflect the cost of basic subsistence goods. See Rosemblatt, *Gendered Compromises*, 60–62. As survey after survey showed, throughout the early twentieth century the most prominent subsistence good in the typical working-class budget (in terms of the amount of money spent) was food. In 1935, food accounted for an astounding 71 percent of the total household budget. See Jorge Mardones Restat, "El problema de la alimentación en Chile," *Revista de Medicina y Alimentación* 1, no. 6 (January 1935): 367–378. See also Robert Morse Woodbury, *Food Consumption and Dietary Surveys in the Americas: Report Presented by the International Labour Office to the Eleventh Pan American Sanitary Conference, Rio de Janeiro, 7–18 September 1942* (Montreal: International Labour Office, 1942), 6.

22. Roberto Barahona and Osvaldo Sotomayor, *El problema de la tuberculosis en Chile* (Santiago: Liga Social de Chile, 1935), 5, 8–10.

23. Barahona and Sotomayor, *El problema de la tuberculosis*, 8. In describing the broader impact of social diseases on Chile's economy, Dr. Salvador Allende claimed that 20 percent of Chile's economically active population was "removed from the workforce" by such ailments. According to the young socialist physician, this situation was tantamount to one-fifth of all workers in the country going out on strike. See Salvador Allende Gossens, *La realidad médico-social chilena* (1939; repr., Santiago: Editorial Cuarto Propio, 1999), 278.

24. Allende Gossens, *La realidad médico-social chilena*, 3, 20.

25. Mardones Restat, "El problema de la alimentación en Chile," 367. Upon visiting Chile and other Southern Cone countries in 1927, one of the world's preeminent nutrition scientists of the era, the Japanese doctor Tadasu Saiki, similarly connected the threat of TB in his home country to poor dietary regimens. See Tadasu Saiki, "Necesidad de estudiar la nutrición," *Revista de la Sociedad Médica de Valparaíso* 1, no. 8 (September–October 1927): 513–514.

26. Carlos Casassus, *El flagelo de la tuberculosis* (Santiago: Sección Bienestar de los Ferrocarriles del Estado, 1935), 22.

27. Casassus, *El flagelo de la tuberculosis*, 12.

28. Plutarco Padilla, "Influencia sobre la tuberculosis en Chile," *Revista de la Sociedad Médica de Valparaíso* 1, no. 3 (November–December 1926): 137–142.

29. Jadwiga E. Pieper Mooney, *The Politics of Motherhood: Maternity and Women's Rights in Twentieth-Century Chile* (Pittsburgh, PA: University of Pittsburgh Press, 2009), 19.

30. Allende Gossens, *La realidad médico-social chilena*, 3.

31. Allende Gossens, *La realidad médico-social chilena*, 10.

32. "El Ministro de Salubridad y el problema de la desnutrición," *Boletín del Ministerio de Salubridad, Previsión y Asistencia Social* (July 1939): 1.

33. Allende Gossens, *La realidad médico-social chilena*, 277.

34. María Soledad Zárate, "Alimentación y previsión biológica: La política médico-asistencial de Eduardo Cruz-Coke," in *Medicina Preventiva y Medicina Dirigida/Eduardo Cruz-Coke L.*, ed. Rafael Sagredo Baeza (Santiago: Cámara de la

Construcción, Pontificia Universidad Católica de Chile, Dirección de Bibliotecas, Archivos y Museos, 2012), xxviii.

35. See, for example, "Primer Congreso de Alimentación Popular—Sesión Inaugural," *Revista de la Alimentación Popular* 1, nos. 4–5 (January–February, 1931): 8–17. See also Julio Santa Maria, "Alimentación científica del pueblo," *Revista de Asistencia Social* 5, no. 1 (March 1937): 1–29.

36. Juan Carlos Yáñez Andrade, "El problema de la alimentación: Un enfoque desde las encuestas de nutrición; Chile, 1928–1938," *América Latina en la Historia Económica: Revista de Investigación* 24, no. 1 (2017): 69.

37. Yáñez Andrade compares this early data collection work to that of the nineteenth-century French social scientist Frédéric le Play. See Yáñez Andrade, "El problema de la alimentación," 69. On le Play's own work, see Dana Simmons, *Vital Minimum: Need, Science, and Politics in Modern France* (Chicago: University of Chicago Press, 2015), 69–73.

38. Raquel Reyes, "Encuesta de nutrición a partir de censos agropecuarios y de población" (undergraduate thesis, Universidad de Chile, 1933).

39. Julio V. Santa Maria, *La alimentación de nuestro pueblo* (Santiago: Talleres San Vicente, 1935).

40. Ramón González, "Como se alimenta la familia obrera en Santiago," *Revista de Medicina y Alimentación* 2, no. 1 (October 1935): 15–25. Although there is little evidence to suggest what Chilean nutrition researchers were reading, it should be noted that similar discussions about social diseases and diet dominated public health discussions in the US South during this same period. On those studies, see Elizabeth W. Etheridge, *The Butterfly Caste: A Social History of Pellagra* (Westport, CT: Greenwood Publishing Company, 1972). I thank historian Audra Wolfe for pointing me toward this parallel history.

41. Mardones Restat, "El problema de la alimentación en Chile," 369. See also Inés Torres Moncada, "Alimentación de las clases populares" (undergraduate thesis: Universidad de Chile, 1938); and Ángel Rodas S. "Algunos aspectos de la alimentación popular en Chillán," *Revista de Medicina y Alimentación* 2, no. 6 (January 1937): 272–276.

42. See Yáñez Andrade, "El problema de la alimentación," 89–90. See also Neghme Rodríguez, *La economía nacional*, 53–54.

43. "Extracto del informe Burnet-Dragoni a la Liga de las Naciones y al Gobierno Chileno sobre la alimentación popular en Chile," *Revista de Asistencia Social* 5, no. 1 (March 1937): 111–124.

44. See the reproduction of Burnet and Dragoni's results in Neghme Rodríguez, *La economía nacional*, 73–74.

45. "Extracto del informe Burnet-Dragoni," 118–119.

46. Victor Grossi, "Programa de Nutrición," *Boletín del Ministerio de Salubridad, Previsión y Asistencia Social* (June–August 1937): 1.

47. For a succinct yet comprehensive summary of Cruz-Coke's early life and work, see Zárate, "Alimentación y previsión biológica," ix–xvi.

48. Zárate, "Alimentación y previsión biológica,"xi.

49. Eduardo Cruz-Coke, "Los equilibrios alimenticios y la alimentación del pueblo," *Revista Médica de Chile* 56, no. 4 (June 1928): 524–525.

50. Huneeus and Paz Lanas, "Ciencia política e historia," 13–16; and Zárate, "Alimentación y previsión biológica," xliv–xlviii. See also Jorge Mardones Restat, *Efectos sociales de la Ley de Medicina Preventiva* (Santiago: Empresa Editora Zig-Zag, 1937); and Jorge Mardones Restat, *Aspecto médico de la aplicación de la Ley de Medicina Preventiva* (Santiago: Imprenta Universo, 1937).

51. Juan Carlos Yáñez Andrade highlights the establishment of similar nutritional councils in Argentina and Uruguay between the mid-1930s and early 1940s. See his "Los pobres están invitados a la mesa," 69–91. On Mexico's creation of a national nutrition council, see Ochoa, *Feeding Mexico*.

52. Decreto Supremo No. 80, February 12, 1937, cited in Huneeus and Paz Lanas, "Ciencia política e historia," 11.

53. On the collaboration between the CNA and one prominent nutrition journal, see "El Consejo Nacional de Alimentación," *Revista de Medicina y Alimentación* 2, no. 7 (April 1937): 317; and A. Macchiavello, J. Mardones Restat, and C. Maldonado B., "Nutrición y alimentación humana," *Revista de Medicina y Alimentación* 3, no. 5 (October 1938): 204–207.

54. Aníbal Alfaro O., "Organización de los restoranes populares en las diversas ciudades de la República," *Boletín Municipal de la República* 8, no. 90 (January 1938): 7–10; Aníbal Alfaro O., "Organización de los restoranes populares en las diversas ciudades de la República," *Boletín Municipal de la República* 8, no. 91 (February 1938): 14–18; Aníbal Alfaro O., "Organización de los restoranes populares en las diversas ciudades de la República," *Boletín Municipal de la República* 8, no. 92 (March 1938): 10–13; Aníbal Alfaro O., "Organización de los restoranes populares en las diversas ciudades de la República," *Boletín Municipal de la República* 8, no. 93 (April 1938): 12–16; Aníbal Alfaro O., "Organización de los restoranes populares en las diversas ciudades de la República," *Boletín Municipal de la República* 8, no. 94 (May 1938): 8–11; and Aníbal Alfaro O., "Organización de los restoranes populares en las diversas ciudades de la República," *Boletín Municipal de la República* 8, no. 95 (June 1938): 9–14.

55. "Las municipalidades y algunas de sus funciones de carácter económico social," *Boletín Municipal de la República* 8, no. 102 (January 1939): 3–4; "Curso de Nutrición," *Boletín Municipal de la República* 8, no. 102 (January 1939): 46–50; "Curso de Nutrición," *Boletín Municipal de la República* 8, no. 103 (February 1939): 41–60; and Julio Santa María, "Aplicaciones prácticas del curso de higiene de la alimentación," *Boletín Municipal de la República* 8, no. 105 (April 1939): 47–65.

56. Jorge Mardones Restat, "A propósito del enriquecimiento de los alimentos," *Revista de Medicina y Alimentación* 5, nos. 5–6 (October 1942–January 1943): 190–194.

57. "Informaciones Técnicas," *Revista de Medicina y Alimentación* 8, nos. 1–3 (January, April, June 1948): 112; and "Sopal Sanitas," *Revista de Medicina y Alimentación* 8, nos. 4–6 (October 1948, January 1949, April 1949).

58. C. Leyton, G., "Contenido mineral de la leche y el queso de la producción nacional y de la relación de éste con el forraje y el suelo," *Revista de Medicina y Alimentación* 6, nos. 7–8 (October–December 1945): 295–299.

59. "INACO expone los aspectos principales de su gestión," *Panorama Económico* 188 (March 1955): 123–125. Intrigued by Great Britain's enrichment of bread with vitamin B during the Second World War, Eduardo Cruz-Coke advocated for enriching bread in Chile to increase access to essential nutrients while not disrupting basic consumer habits. See Zárate, "Alimentación y previsión biológica," xxxvi–xxxvii.

60. Jorge Mardones Restat and Ricardo Cox, *La alimentación en Chile: Estudios del Consejo Nacional de Alimentación* (Santiago: Imprenta Universitaria, 1942).

61. Mardones Restat and Cox, *La alimentación en Chile*, 269, 274–275.

62. Mardones Restat and Cox, *La alimentación en Chile*, 274–277.

63. Eduardo Cruz-Coke, *Plan de gobierno de Chile para mejorar la alimentación del pueblo* (Santiago: Consejo de Alimentación, 1937); and Zárate, "Alimentación y previsión biológica," xxix–xxx.

64. Huneeus and Paz highlight the fact that the CNA's leadership included nine individuals. The CNA's founding statute mandated that one member be a representative from the Facultad de Medicina, one hail from the Junta de Exportación Agrícola, and one be an official from the Comisariato. The remaining six were freely chosen by the executive branch. Huneeus and Paz Lanas, "Ciencia política y historia," 11.

65. Cruz-Coke, *Plan de gobierno*, 5.

66. Cruz-Coke, *Plan de gobierno*, 5. See also Francisco Landa Perroni, *El problema de la leche en relación con la alimentación popular en Chile* (Santiago: Imprenta y Litografía Universo, S.A., 1939), 21–46.

67. Cruz-Coke, *Plan de gobierno*, 5. Key excerpts from the report were published and discussed in March 1937 in the *Revista de Asistencia Social*. See Aurora Rodríguez B., "El Consejo Nacional de Alimentación y su Plan de Alimentación Popular," *Revista de Asistencia Social* 5, no. 1 (March 1937): 46–74.

68. For an excellent recent examination of the Comisariato during this period, see Henríquez Vásquez, *En "estado sólido"*, 207–243. On the CSO, see Rosemblatt, *Gendered Compromises*, 126–135.

69. Alfaro O., "Organización de los restoranes populares en las diversas ciudades de la República," *Boletín Municipal de la República* 8, no. 90 (January 1938): 9–10. See also Jorge Mardones Restat and Lidia Contreras, *Regímenes alimenticios para restaurantes económicos de adultos* (Santiago: Imprenta Leblanc, 1939).

70. *La Prensa del Tercer Distrito*, August 15, 1936, 32. Cited in Juan Carlos Yáñez Andrade, "'Alimentación abundante, sana y barata': Los restaurantes populares en Santiago (1936–1942)," *Cuadernos de Historia* 45 (December 2016): 131.

71. Cited in Zárate, "Alimentación y previsión biológica," xxx.

72. Eduardo Cruz-Coke, "Discusión proyecto de ley de fomento a la industria lechera, discurso pronunciado en el Senado el 13 de septiembre de 1944, con ocasión de discutirse el proyecto de ley sobre fomento de la industria lechería," in Cruz-Coke,

Discursos, 289; and Illanes Oliva, *En el nombre del pueblo*, 205. As Karin Rosemblatt notes, the CSO's takeover of the Central de Leche was part of a larger effort by the agency to control basic parts of the economy that affected public health. Other areas in which the CSO played a growing role included the pharmaceutical and clothing industries, as well farming and ranching enterprises. See Rosemblatt, *Gendered Compromises*, 133. For more on state intervention in the milk economy, see Nicolás Carmona C., "La Central de Leche 'Chile': Un caso de industrialización estatal fallido (1935–1960)" (undergraduate thesis, Universidad de Chile, 2008).

73. Armando Rojas Richard, "Memoria—Central de Leche 'Chile,' S.A., 1939–1941," Biblioteca Nacional de Chile—Santiago (BNC), Sección de Revistas (SR).

74. Illanes Oliva, *En el nombre del pueblo*, 333, 350–351.

75. Rojas Richard, "Memoria—Central de Leche 'Chile' S.A., 1939–1941," 30–31.

76. Illanes Oliva, *En el nombre del pueblo*, 306. According to Illanes Oliva, the Central de Leche also handed out some twenty thousand chocolate milk rations in the wake of the state's takeover of milk pasteurization.

77. Alfredo Riquelme Barriga, "Abastecimiento de proteínas de la nación," *Revista de Medicina y Alimentación* 7, no. 8 (December 1947): 71.

78. See Cruz-Coke, "Discusión proyecto de ley de fomento de la industria lechera," 277, cited in Zárate, "Alimentación y previsión biológica," xxxii.

79. Allende, "Public Health Program in Chile," NARA II, RG 229, box 84, folder 24.

80. "Nuestro porvenir está cimentado en la Carta del Atlántico," *El Siglo*, March 9, 1943.

81. Moisés Poblete Troncoso, *El subconsumo en América del Sur: Alimentos, vestuario y vivienda* (Santiago: Editorial Nascimento, 1946), 12–13.

82. See Henry Wallace, *Century of the Common Man* (New York: Reynal & Hitchcock, 1943), cited in Poblete Troncoso, *El subconsumo*, 13. Poblete translated Wallace's "quart" to the roughly equivalent metric form, the liter. On Wallace's historic 1943 visit to Chile, a landmark event for the Chilean left and the FP, see Pavilack, *Mining for the Nation*, 181–187.

83. Salvador Allende Gossens, *La contradicción de Chile: Régimen de izquierda, política económica de derecha* (Santiago: Talleres Gráficos, 1943).

84. On the state of wages in Chile from 1940 to 1948, see Juan Crocco Ferrari, "El standard de vida de la población," in *Geografía Económica de Chile*, ed. Corporación de Fomento de la Producción (CORFO) (Santiago: Imprenta Universitaria, 1950), 2: 217.

85. Allende Gossens, *La contradicción de Chile*, 28–29.

86. Allende Gossens, *La contradicción de Chile*, 36–37.

87. For a summary of the FP's shortcomings, see Loveman, *Chile*, 208–217.

88. Julio V. Santa María, "Características de nuestros hábitos alimentarios," *Revista de Medicina y Alimentación* 8, nos. 4–6 (October 1948, January 1949, April 1949): 117.

89. M. Tamblay, J. V. Santa María, and L. C. de Saavedra, "Programa de educación y encuesta alimentaria de la Unidad Sanitaria de Quinta Normal," *Revista*

Chilena de Higiene y Medicina Preventiva 9, no. 2 (1947): 83–109; Minerva Malic L., Julio V. Santa Maria, and Lidia C. Saavedra,"Programa de educación y encuestas alimentarias de la Unidad Sanitaria de Quinta Normal, II—Tendencias en el consumo de alimentos," *Revista Chilena de Higiene y Medicina Preventiva* 10, no. 3 (1948): 159–170; and Silvia Rosas B., Julio V. Santa María, and Lidia C. Saavedra, "Programa de educación y encuestas alimentarias de la Unidad Sanitaria de Quinta Normal (1945–1956), III—Aspectos económicos de la alimentación," *Revista Chilena de Higiene y Medicina Preventiva* 10, no. 3 (1948): 171–180.

90. On the construction of the "unfit mother," see Pieper Mooney, *Politics of Motherhood*, 14–15, 19–21. On the ADC, see again Yanulaque Garrido, "Asociación Nacional de Dueñas de Casa," ANH, FGGV, vol. 132.

91. Gladys Garretón, "La Asociación de Dueñas de Casa a través de la República," *Fiel* 1, no. 1 (September 1949): 11–12; and "Educación del Consumidor," *Fiel* 1, no. 3 (November 1949): 6–7.

92. Crocco Ferrari, "El standard de vida de la población," 241.

93. Gabriel González Videla, "Mensaje al Congreso—1947" (Santiago: n.p., 1947), xxvii, cited in Albert O. Hirschman, "Inflation in Chile," in *Journeys toward Progress: Studies of Economic Policy Making in Latin America* (New York: Greenwood Publishing, 1968), 161.

94. For a brief history of the evolution in Chile's price control and consumer protection efforts, see Jorge Giusti, "Participación popular en Chile: Antecedentes para su estudio; Las JAP," *Revista Mexicana de Sociología* 37, no. 3 (1975): 767–768.

95. Rosemblatt, *Gendered Compromises*, 147.

96. Hakim and Solimano, *Development, Reform, and Malnutrition*, 11.

97. Riquelme Barriga, "Abastecimiento de proteínas de la nación," 71.

98. In emphasizing Cruz-Coke's interest in resolving Chile's urban problems, his daughter Marta Cruz-Coke writes that for her father, "politics was about 'caring for the city.'" See Cruz-Coke and Lagos Cruz-Coke, *Testimonios*, 340.

CHAPTER 4. CULTIVATING CONSUMPTION

1. Pedro Milos, *Historia y memoria: 2 de abril de 1957* (Santiago: LOM Ediciones, 2007).

2. Jorge Ahumada, *En vez de la miseria* (Santiago: Editorial del Pacífico, S.A., 1958), 20. A comprehensive biography of Ahumada, which I draw upon in this chapter, can be found in Hilary Burger, "A Different *Cepalino*: Jorge Ahumada," in "An Intellectual History of ECLA Culture, 1948–1964" (PhD diss., Harvard University, 1998), 142–188.

3. Burger, "Different *Cepalino*," 147–153.

4. Burger, "Different *Cepalino*," 153–163. Shortly after Cuba's 1959 revolution, Ahumada would also spend some time in Cuba advising the Castro government on its development plans.

5. The literature on Chile's agrarian reform is vast. Some of the most valuable secondary works are José Bengoa, *Historia rural de Chile central: Crisis y ruptura del poder hacendal* (Santiago: LOM Ediciones, 2015); José Garrido, ed., *Historia de la reforma agraria chilena* (Santiago: Editorial Universitaria, 1988); Thomas Miller Klubock, *La Frontera: Forests and Ecological Conflict in Chile's Frontier Territory* (Durham, NC: Duke University Press, 2014); Brian Loveman, *Struggle in the Countryside: Politics and Rural Labor in Chile, 1919–1973* (Bloomington: Indiana University Press, 1976); Heidi Tinsman, *Partners in Conflict: The Politics of Gender, Sexuality, and Labor in the Chilean Agrarian Reform, 1950–1973* (Durham, NC: Duke University Press, 2002); and Peter Winn and Cristóbal Kay, "Agrarian Reform and Rural Revolution," *Journal of Latin American Studies* 6, no. 1 (1974): 135–159.

6. Ahumada, *En vez de la miseria*, 95–104. On the competing structuralist and monetarist interpretations of inflation in the postwar period, see Werner Baer, "The Inflation Controversy in Latin America: A Survey," *Latin American Research Review* 2, no. 2 (Spring 1967): 3–25.

7. "Asamblea Obrera de Alimentación Nacional al País," *Federación de Obreros de Imprenta* 1, no. 8 (November 2, 1918).

8. Thomas C. Wright, "Origins of the Politics of Inflation in Chile, 1888–1918," *Hispanic American Historical Review* 53, no. 2 (May 1973): 258. On the long history of state-supported colonization of Chile's southern frontier, see Hagerman, "Internal Migration in Chile to 1920," 299–332.

9. Evaristo Rios, *Socialismo y algunas fases de su doctrina* (Santiago: Imprenta el Progreso, 1919), 6, 11, 14.

10. Carlos Keller, *Cómo salir de la crisis* (Santiago: Editorial Nascimento, 1932), 24–29. See also Vergara, "Chilean Workers and the Great Depression," 58–61.

11. Loveman, *Struggle in the Countryside*, 146–151. See also Thomas Miller Klubock, "Ránquil: Violence and Peasant Politics on Chile's Southern Frontier," in *A Century of Violence: Insurgent and Counterinsurgent Violence during Latin America's Long Cold War*, ed. Greg Grandin and Gilbert M. Joseph (Durham, NC: Duke University Press, 2010), 121–159.

12. Loveman, *Struggle in the Countryside*, 151–158.

13. Carlos Alberto Martínez, "Conferencia por radio el viernes 18 de Agosto," in *Hacia la reforma agraria* (Santiago de Chile: Caja de Colonización Agrícola 1939), 43.

14. "Dos Palabras con el Ministro de Tierras y Colonización, Don Carlos Alberto Martínez," *Sucesos*, October 22, 1931, 17–19, IISH, MSR, folder 24. See also Carlos Alberto Martínez, "Discurso pronunciado en el congreso de aspirantes a colonos del sur de Chile, verificado en Temuco," in *Hacia la reforma agraria* (Santiago de Chile: Caja de Colonización Agrícola 1939), 55.

15. Martínez, "Discurso pronunciado en el congreso de aspirantes a colonos del sur," 54–55.

16. Tinsman, *Partners in Conflict*, 87; and Loveman, *Struggle in the Countryside*, 118–119, 164–170.

17. For a biographical summary of Santa Cruz's professional achievements, see Eduardo Saouma, "Special Representative for the FAO World Conference on Agrarian Reform and Rural Development," FAO Director's General Bulletin, No. 77/53, September 29, 1977, Archivo Histórico del Ministerio de Relaciones Exteriores (ARREE), Fondo Hernán Santa Cruz (FHSC), vol. 4.

18. Hernán Santa Cruz, "Discurso del Embajador Hernán Santa Cruz sobre la creación de la Comisión Económica Latinoamericana, pronunciado en el Consejo Económico y Social," Lake Success, NY, August 1, 1947, ARREE, FHSC, vol. 5. For similar views that emphasized improving production methods over land redistribution to meet Chile's food needs, see Hugo K. Sievers, "Aporte de la ganadería a la alimentación en Chile," in *Chile: Su futura alimentación*, Ciclo de conferencias organizadas por la Dirección General de Bibliotecas, Archivos y Museos (Santiago: Editorial Nascimento, 1963), 92–132.

19. On canning and the "triumph over seasonality" in the late nineteenth and early twentieth centuries, see Katherine Leonard Turner, *How the Other Half Ate: A History of Working-Class Meals at the Turn of the Century* (Oakland: University of California Press, 2014), 28–29, 33–36.

20. Sergio Vergara, "Realidad y porvenir de la industria de conservas de Chile," *Panorama Económico* 7 (September–October 1947): 25–27; and "Chile acaba de descubrir las conservas," *Panorama Económico* 100 (May 1954): 294. For more on Chile's canning industry, see Interdepartmental Committee on Nutrition for National Defense, *Chile: Nutrition Survey, March–June 1960* (Washington, DC, April 1961), 50–60.

21. "Chile acaba de descubrir las conservas."

22. "En la industrialización de la producción agropecuaria nacional, sobresale la Compañía Chilena de Productos Alimenticios, S.A.I.," *Panorama Económico* 7 (September–October 1947): 28–29.

23. Interdepartmental Committee on Nutrition, *Chile: Nutrition Survey*, 64.

24. On food provisioning in the Norte Grande, see Martin I. Glassner, "Feeding a Desert City: Antofagasta, Chile," *Economic Geography* 45, no. 4 (October 1969): 339–348.

25. "INACO expone los aspectos principales de su gestión."

26. CORFO, *Cinco años de labor, 1939–1943* (Santiago, 1944), 160–162.

27. CORFO, *Cinco años de labor*, 178. See also Alfonso Quintana Burgos, "La mecanización agrícola saldará el déficit en producción de alimentos," *Panorama Económico* 15 (September–December 1948): 19–20; and "Usted siembra trigo y nosotros, acero!," *Panorama Económico* 92 (December 1953): 844.

28. CORFO, *Cinco años de labor*, 130–132.

29. Interdepartmental Committee on Nutrition, *Chile: Nutrition Survey*, 66.

30. Cited in K.H. Silvert, "The State of Chilean Agriculture," American Universities Field Staff Reports, (July 1, 1957): 11–12, University of Wisconsin-Madison (UWM), Steenbock Memorial Library (SML), Land Tenure Center Files (LTCF), CH 7 S4.

31. CORFO and Ministerio de Agricultura, *Plan Agrario* (n.p., 1954), 2–4, cited in Silvert, "State of Chilean Agriculture," 12.

32. Silvert, "State of Chilean Agriculture," 12–13. On Plan Chillán, see also Melillo, *Strangers on Familiar Soil*, 158. On planners' comparisons of the TVA and Plan Chillán, see William San Martín, "Nitrogen Revolutions: Agricultural Expertise, Technology, and Policy in Cold War Chile" (PhD diss., University of California, Davis, 2017), 75. On the expansion of integrative rural development plans to other parts of Chile in the 1960s, see Ministerio de Agricultura, "Programa Mundial de Alimentos de las NN.UU. y F.A.O.—Desarrollo de las comunidades del Estero de Punitaqui," April 1963, 1–9, ARNAD, Fondo Ministerio de Agricultura (FMA), vol. 1617; and Ministerio de Agricultura, "Plan Pase," 1964, 3–4, ARNAD, FMA, vol. 1565.

33. Alejandro Hales, "Desarrollo agrícola y desarrollo industrial," *Panorama Económico* 99 (May 7, 1954): 236–237.

34. Hales, "Desarrollo agrícola y desarrollo industrial," 236–237.

35. "IANSA y campesinos 'endulzan' a Chile," *Quiubo Compadre* (second half of April 1967): 2.

36. "IANSA y campesinos 'endulzan' a Chile."

37. Roberto Aliaga Sánchez, *Cultivo de remolacha azucarera en Chile: Aspectos generales y su desarrollo en el país* (Santiago: IANSA, 1973), 53–55.

38. Klubock, *La Frontera*, 179–181.

39. Herrick, *Urban Migration*, 44–47.

40. Robert R. Kaufman, *The Politics of Land Reform in Chile, 1950–1970* (Cambridge, MA: Harvard University Press, 1972), 221–228.

41. Milos, *Historia y memoria*; and Espinoza, *Para una historia*, 239–261.

42. Ahumada, *En vez de la miseria*, 13–14.

43. "Property and Production: A Pamphlet Promoting Christian Democracy's Agrarian Reform," in *The Chile Reader: History, Culture, Politics*, ed. Elizabeth Quay Hutchison et al. (Durham, NC: Duke University Press, 2014), 358.

44. Tinsman, *Partners in Conflict*, 1–2.

45. Waldo S. Rowan, "Chile Launches Agrarian Reform," *Foreign Agriculture* 6, no. 6 (February 5, 1968), UWM, SML, LTCF, CH 3 R69. See also Carlos Keller, "Cómo triplicar la producción agrícola," in *Chile: Su futura alimentación*, 133–170.

46. Agricultural officials emphasized the fast rate of reproduction and growth for both chickens and pigs, in contrast to beef cattle, when making the case for greater production of the former. Ricardo Costabal E., "Hacia un plan avícola (I)," *Agricultura Técnica* 26, no. 2 (April–June 1966): 45–69, BNC, SC; "La criadora de pollos," *Quiubo Compadre* 11 (second half of November 1965): 14; and Gonzálo Castro, "Manual de producción porcina," *Boletín Divulgativo* 1 (1969). BNC, SC.

47. "Aprovechemos nuestros chanchos," *Quiubo Compadre* 3 (second half of July 1965): 13; "Con el pie derecho partió la crianza de cerdos en Cooperativa Chancho," *Quiubo Compadre* 72 (first half of June 1968): 4–5; and "Campesinos piden centralizar en sus manos la producción y comercialización del cerdo," *Quiubo Compadre* 93 (second half of April 1969): 7.

48. On the goal of raising rural income, see Ahumada, *En vez de la miseria*, 107–110.

49. "Un buen negocio: Críe pollitos," *Quiubo Compadre* 5 (second half of August 1965): 13. For more on chicken farming during agrarian reform, see "Acción coordinada para el progreso de la comunidad," *Quiubo Compadre* 32 (first half of October 1966): 6–7.

50. "Política nacional avícola," *Quiubo Compadre* 87 (second half of January 1969): 12.

51. "Aves y huevos para mejorar la dieta," *Quiubo Compadre* 53 (second half of August 1967): 3.

52. "Cultívelos bien: Los repollos se los agradecerán," *Quiubo Compadre* 12 (second half of December 1965): 13; "Cultivo de la zanahoria," *Quiubo Compadre* 13 (second half of December 1965): 10; "Capitalice sus papas," *Quiubo Compadre* 18 (first half of March 1966): 12; and "Chile tras el aumento de su producción de papas," *Quiubo Compadre* 59 (second half of November 1967): 7.

53. "Noticiario Campesino," *Quiubo Compadre* 37 (second half of December 1966); and "Inaugurada Planta Conservera de Chol Chol," *Quiubo Compadre* 36 (first half of December 1966): 10.

54. "Los huertos de San Pedro," *Quiubo Compadre* 17 (second half of February 1966): 15.

55. Frances M. Foland, "Chile's Agricultural Food Supply (No. 1)," June 27, 1968, 1–3, UWM, SML, LTCF, CH 7 F65, vol. 1.

56. Empresa de Comercio Agrícola, *Estudio de la comercialización de los productos alimenticios en la región geoeconómica del Bío-Bío: Antecedentes generales de la región del Bío-Bío* (Santiago: n.p., 1967), 2, BNC, SC.

57. Hernán Gómez Montt and Iván Berger J., "El desarrollo de la cuenca del Río Maule," *Desarrollo Económico* 3, nos. 3–4 (1966): 15–19, UWM, SML, LTCF, CH 79 G65.

58. "Proyecto crea Corporación de Desarrollo Agro Industrial de la Región," *El Heraldo* (Linares), September 23, 1971. The proposed bill was eventually defeated in Chile's Senate in 1972.

59. "Un plan realista para el desarollo agrícola de Chile," *Quiubo Compadre*, suplemento (first half of April 1969): 1–8. For more on regional development, see Gamaliel Carrasco and Andrés Vergara, *Programa de fomento pecuario y desarrollo campesino de las colonias y asentamientos de la Corporación de la Reforma Agraria* (Santiago: CORA, 1970), BNC, Colección José Arguedas (CJA).

60. William C. Thiesenhusen, "Current Status of Agrarian Reform in Chile," *AID Spring Review*, May 1, 1970, 10, in *Land Tenure Center Annual Report*, 1969–70, pt. 3, UWM, SML, LTC Annual Reports (LTCAR).

61. "Un plan realista para el desarrollo agrícola de Chile."

62. Jacques Chonchol, *El desarrollo de América Latina y la reforma agraria* (Santiago: Editorial del Pacífico, S.A., 1964), 110–112.

63. Manuel Elgueta Guerin, *Memorias de vida: 1902–1983* (Santiago: n.p., 1986). BNC, SC.

64. Instituto Nacional de Investigación Agrícola (INIA), *Primera memoria anual del Instituto de Investigaciones Agropecuarios, 1964–1965* (Santiago: Ministerio de Agricultura, 1965), 5–6, BNC, SR.

65. INIA, *Primera memoria anual*, 5. For a good summary of the Green Revolution in global historical perspective, see Benjamin Siegel, "Whither Agriculture? The Green Revolution @ 50," *Public Books*, January 14, 2019, www.publicbooks.org /whither-agriculture-the-green-revolution-50/.

66. INIA, *Cuarta memoria anual del Instituto de Investigaciones Agropecuarios, 1967–1968* (Santiago: Ministerio de Agricultura, 1968), 14, BNC, SR.

67. INIA, *Primera memoria anual*.

68. "Las plantas tienen HAMBRE," *Quiubo Compadre* (second half of June 1965): 13; and "Abonar la tierra . . . es recibir más," *Quiubo Compadre* (first half of June 1966): 5.

69. San Martín, "Nitrogen Revolutions," 137.

70. San Martín, "Nitrogen Revolutions," 145–147. As San Martín notes, even before the passage of the 1967 law that allowed synthetic fertilizers to be imported, fertilizer usage in Chile had begun to increase, rising from just 7,300 metric tons in 1951 to 38,200 metric tons in 1967. San Martín also notes that the most common fertilizers imported after 1967 were ammonium nitrate, ammonium phosphate, and urea.

71. "Diez consejos para la siembra de trigo," *Quiubo Compadre* (second half of June 1965): 13; "Use buenas semillas," *Quiubo Compadre* (first half of September 1965): 10; and "La Lombriz: Una colaboradora silenciosa," *Quiubo Compadre* (second half of October 1965): 10.

72. "La criadora de pollos," *Quiubo Compadre* (second half of November 1965): 14; "Servicio Agrícola y Ganadero: Gran impulsor de la Reforma Agraria," *Quiubo Compadre* (first half of March 1969): 13; and "El maíz híbrido es . . . pura plata," *Quiubo Compadre* (first half of September 1967): 14. See also CORFO, "Agricultural and Industrial Progress Report: 1965–1966," 4, UWM, SML, LTCF, CH 31 C67.

73. Luis Ortega Martínez et al., *Corporación de Fomento de la Producción: 50 años de realizaciones, 1939–1989* (Santiago: Departamento de Historia, Facultad de Humanidades, Universidad de Santiago de Chile, 1989), 189. During the early years of the Frei government, two major CORFO projects were the creation of a state-backed farm implement manufacturing company, the Servicio de Equipos Agrícolas Mecanizados (Mechanized Agricultural Equipment Service, SEAM), and a national seed company, the Empresa Nacional de Semillas. Ortega Martínez et al., *Corporación de Fomento de la Producción*, 183, 192–193.

74. Arturo Mackenna S. to Armando Jaramillo L., "Programa Nacional de Desarrollo Ganadero y Su Política de Mataderos," October 16, 1962, ARNAD, Archivo de la Corporación de Fomento de la Producción (CORFO)—Empresas CORFO (ECORFO), Fondo SOCOAGRO (FSOCOAGRO), vol. 304; and SOCOAGRO, "Memoria y balance al 31 de diciembre de 1969," ARNAD, CORFO-ECORFO, FSOCOAGRO, vol. 312. See also Miguel Ponce, *La industria de la carne en Chile, 1955–2005: Medio siglo de modernización* (Santiago: Editorial Puerto de Palos, 2005).

75. Ortega Martínez et al., *Corporación de Fomento de la Producción*, 189–193.

76. See Juan Braun et al., *Economía chilena, 1810–1995: Estadísticas históricas*, Documento de Trabajo no. 187 (Santiago: Pontificia Universidad Católica de Chile–Instituto de Economía, 2000), 41. According to a 1966 estimate by the INIA, between 65 and 90 percent of all corn produced in Chile should go toward supplying the feed needs of Chile's chicken industry. Ricardo Costabal E., "Hacia un plan avícola (I)," *Agricultura Técnica* 26, no. 2 (April–June 1966): 45–69, BNC, SC.

77. Costabal E., "Hacia un plan avícola (I)." Total potato production fell from just over 8.4 million metric quintals in 1963 to 7.2 million metric quintals in 1968. Total bean production, which registered 641,300 metric quintals in 1963, only increased slightly, to 650,500 metric quintals, in 1968. In 1969, total bean production fell to 467,530 metric quintals. Total wheat production grew slightly, from just over 11 million metric quintals in 1965 to just under 12.2 million metric quintals in 1968. See Braun et al., *Economía chilena, 1810–1995*, 41. On the Frei government's focus on animal feed, see also, Ricardo Costabal, E., "Una formula eficiente para engorda de pollos broilers," *Investigación y Progreso Agrícola* (Santiago) 1 (1967): 31; Jaime Devilat B., "Ensilaje de trébol rosada significa más carne," *Investigación y Progeso Agrícola* (Santiago) 1 (1967): 30; and Manuel Elgueta G., "El concurso del maíz," *Investigación y Progreso Agrícola* (Santiago) 1 (1967): 1–3.

78. "Cómo llena la canasta la dueña de casa?," *Quiubo Compadre* 106 (second half of December 1969): 7.

79. Gonzálo Tapia Soko, ed., *El derecho de todo ser: Testimonio biográfico del dirigente campesino Manuel Oliveros* (Santiago: Programa Interdisciplinario de Investigaciones en Educación, 1990), 45. Florencia Mallon shows that for many indigenous communities, plentiful subsistence production, rather than abundant production of cash crops, was equated with agricultural prosperity during the agrarian reform. Mallon, *Courage Tastes of Blood: The Mapuche Community of Nicolás Ailío and the Chilean State, 1906–2001* (Durham, NC: Duke University Press, 2005), 124, 130. I thank Nathan Stone for pointing me to this citation.

80. For detailed discussion of the asentamiento system, see Frances M. Foland, "Chile's Agrarian Reform in Operation," July 6, 1968, UWM, SML, LTCF, CH 3 F65. See also Tinsman, *Partners in Conflict*, 174.

81. "La rotación de cultivos asegura mejores cosechas," *Quiubo Compadre* (first half of August 1965): 13; "Un pasto contra la sequía," *Quiubo Compadre* (first half of November 1965): 2; and "Los campesinos se interesan por las leyes de su país," *Quiubo Compadre* (first half of January 1966): 10. For more about INDAP's work, see Tinsman, *Partners in Conflict*, 103.

82. "La mejor escuela: Los asentamientos," *Quiubo Compadre* (second half of February 1966): 10.

83. "Curados, enfermedad nacional," *Quiubo Compadre* (second half of August 1965): 2. See also "El sueño de Juanito," *Quiubo Compadre* (second half of June 1965): 14; and "Aprovechar el tiempo libre," *Quiubo Compadre* (second half of June 1965): 14.

84. Corporación de Reforma Agraria, *Qué sería del campesino sin su mujer?* (Santiago: CORA, 1968), BNC, SC. See also various articles that were published

in *Quiubo Compadre*; for example, "Los compromisos hay que cumplirlos," *Quiubo Compadre* (second half of May 1968): 3.

85. CORA, Departamento de Desarrollo Campesino, "Capitalización Campesina," 1967, UWM, SML, LTCF, CH 23 C34.

86. CORA, Departamento de Desarrollo Campesino, "Capitalización Campesina." The Frei administration's willingness to incorporate rural Chileans into agrarian reform largely stopped with male *inquilinos* (tenant farmers)—men like the fictional Pérez and Farías—who might someday own their own land. *Afuerinos*, the mostly single men who moved around the countryside as seasonal workers, had limited access to the asentamiento. Long described as unreliable, untrustworthy rabble-rousers by large landowners, migrant laborers made up as much as a quarter of all paid agricultural workers and often hailed from indigenous communities. Tinsman, *Partners in Conflict*, 24–25.

87. CORA, Departamento de Desarrollo Campesino, "Capitalización Campesina."

88. "El conejo Angora: Un cuento que *no* es un cuento," *Quiubo Compadre* (second half of September 1965): 13.

89. "Prepárela en casa: Salsa de tomato," *Quiubo Compadre* (first half of February 1966); "Prepare mantequilla en casa," *Quiubo Compadre* (second half of December 1967): 12; and "Con la huerta casera surten a sus familias," *Quiubo Compadre* (first half of June 1968): 7.

90. "Aproveche sus tarros vacíos," *Quiubo Compadre* (second half of June 1965): 12.

91. "Con cuatro latas, hágase un práctico horno," *Quiubo Compadre* (first half of August 1966): 14.

92. "Un bolso práctico," *Quiubo Compadre* (second half of October 1965): 10.

93. Verónica Oxman V., "La participación de la mujer campesina en organizaciones: Los centros de madres rurales," Academia de Humanismo Cristiano (September 1983), 45, UWM, SML, LTCF, CH 69.2 095. On one of the first deliveries of sewing machines by INDAP, see "Noticiario Campesino," *Quiubo Compadre* (second half of August 1965).

94. Oxman V., "La participación de la mujer campesina," 45–48.

95. "Tejámosle a la guagua," *Quiubo Comprade* (second half of July 1965): 12; and "Cómo hacer un lindo costuerero," *Quiubo Compadre* (second half of August 1965): 10.

96. "La Mujer: Principal responsable de la salud de su familia," *Quiubo Compadre* (first half of October 1968): 13.

97. Cuando las cosas hay que hacerlas se hacen . . . y listo!," *Quiubo Compadre* (first half of May 1969): 5. See also the state's encouragement that women band together to form consumer cooperatives in an effort to save money: Corporación de Reforma Agraria, *Qué sería del campesino*.

98. Los seis años de Reforma Agraria—Lo que había el 64," *Quiubo Compadre* (second half of August 1970): 2.

99. Tinsman, *Partners in Conflict*, 104.

100. Tinsman notes that more than two thousand petitions were submitted by rural workers to the Ministry of Agriculture between 1964 and 1967. Another two thousand petitions were submitted in 1968 alone. Tinsman, *Partners in Conflict*, 103.

101. "Desarrollo social: Poderoso motor de promoción," *Quiubo Compadre* (September 1970): 4–5.

102. "Desarrollo social," 4–5.

103. Thiesenhusen, "Current Status of Agrarian Reform in Chile," 15.

104. Thiesenhusen writes that Chile had a negative trade balance for its agricultural products of US$96 million in 1967. In 1968, that figure grew to US$141 million. All signs suggested it would be even higher in 1969. With respect to migration, Thiesenhusen observed that urban unemployment continued to rise under Frei, reaching at least 7.1 percent in Greater Santiago in 1969 (up from 5.9 percent in 1968). This was at least in part due to the continuation of rural to urban migration and the inability of the urban sector to adequately absorb new arrivals. See Thiesenhusen, "Current Status of Agrarian Reform in Chile," 15, 19–20.

105. Winn and Kay, "Agrarian Reform and Rural Revolution," 136–137; and Thiesenhusen, "Current Status of Agrarian Reform," 2, 3.

106. See Arturo Palma and Juan Varas, *Efecto de la política de restricciones de carne de vacuno en el consumo y producción de sustitutos* (Santiago: Servicio Agrícola y Ganadero, 1968). See also Cristián Birchmeier Salgado, "'Habrá carne para toda la población': El consumo de carnes como herramienta de igualación social en el proyecto de la Unidad Popular. Santiago, 1970–1973" (undergraduate thesis, Universidad Alberto Hurtado, 2012).

107. Claudio Robles Ortiz, *Jacques Chonchol: Un Cristiano revolucionario en la política chilena del siglo XX* (Santiago: Ediciones Universidad Finis Terrae, 2016), 223.

108. "Trabajadores del fundo San José del Carmen al Ministro de Agricultura, Hugo Trivelli," July 5, 1966. ARNAD, FMA, vol. 1709.

109. Burger, "Different *Cepalino*," 143.

CHAPTER 5. EMPANADAS AND RED WINE

1. Nora Gómez, interview, quoted in Sandra Castillo Soto, *Cordones industriales: nuevas formas de sociabilidad obrera y organización política popular (Chile 1970–1973)* (Santiago: Escaparate, 2009), 57.

2. Garcés D., "Construyendo 'las poblaciones,'" 77.

3. "Bajarán los precios de pollos y huevos," *El Siglo*, December 24, 1970; "Un pan mejor y más barato," *El Siglo*, December 25, 1970; and "A Firme: 2700 el kilo de pan; El Presidente Allende firma hoy el decreto," *El Siglo*, December 27, 1970.

4. "Nunca en un mes de febrero se había vendido tanto," *El Siglo*, March 8, 1971.

5. "Nunca en un mes de febrero se había vendido tanto."

6. "Calles de Santiago repletas de compradores y vendedores," *El Siglo*, December 22, 1971.

7. Allende won 36.2 percent of all ballots cast in 1970, narrowly defeating National Party candidate Jorge Alessandri (34.9 percent) and Christian Democratic candidate Radomiro Tomic (27.8 percent). The Chilean Congress ratified his election on October 24, 1970, after an intense attempt by the Chilean right, the United States, and conservative elements in the Chilean military to block Congress's formal approval. See Peter Kornbluh, *The Pinochet File: A Declassified Dossier of Atrocity and Accountability* (New York: New Press, 2013), 1–79.

8. On comparisons between the FP and UP governments, see Allende's interview with journalist Saul Landau, "An Interview with Allende: 'You Don't Get Socialism Overnight,'" January 30, 1971, in *New Chile*, 2nd ed., ed. North American Congress on Latin America (New York: NACLA, 1973), 16–19.

9. For a political history of the organized left from the FP to the UP, see Tomás Moulian, *Fracturas: De Pedro Aguirre Cerda a Salvador Allende, 1938–1973* (Santiago: LOM, 2006).

10. On the differences between the FP and the UP, see Salvador Allende's speech to the convention of the Chilean Radical Party in July 1971. The speech was reprinted in *El Siglo* on July 31, 1971, and republished later as "Radicalism and Bourgeois Sectors," in *The Chilean Road to Socialism*, ed. Dale L. Johnson (New York: Anchor Books, 1973), esp. 285–286.

11. Peter Winn, *Weavers of Revolution: The Yarur Workers and Chile's Road to Socialism* (Oxford: Oxford University Press, 1986), 57.

12. See, for example, Américo Zorilla, "La crisis del capitalismo chileno," November 27, 1970, in *El pensamiento económico del Gobierno de Allende*, ed. Gonzalo Martner (Santiago: Editorial Universitaria, 1971), 11–22.

13. Patricio Meller, *The Unidad Popular and the Pinochet Dictatorship: A Political Economy Analysis* (London: Palgrave Macmillan, 2000), 27.

14. One of the clearest articulations of the UP's new priorities and early economic philosophy can be seen in Pedro Vuskovic Bravo, "Chile: Toward the Building of Socialism," in Johnson, *Chilean Road to Socialism*, esp. 424. For more analysis and discussion of how economic conditions in the late 1960s influenced the UP's economic vision, see Joshua Frens-String, "A 'Popular Option' for Development? Reconsidering the Rise and Fall of Chile's Political Economy of Socialism," *Radical Americas*, forthcoming in 2021.

15. For a full, translated list of the UP's "40 Measures," see "The Forty Measures," in Johnson, *Chilean Road to Socialism*, 170.

16. "Por primera vez el pueblo chileno tiene una oportunidad," *El Siglo,* November 8, 1970. The reference is to the world's largest open-pit copper mine, Chuquicamata, located in the north of Chile.

17. In their comprehensive assessment of the UP's political economy, Barbara Stallings and Andy Zimbalist provide a slightly different schematic for thinking about the dual goals of UP socialism, arguing that the coalition simultaneously pursued "structural changes" and "economic development objectives." Stallings and Zimbalist, "The Political Economy of the Unidad Popular," *Latin American Perspectives* 2, no. 1 (1975): 70–71.

18. Peter Winn, *La revolución chilena* (Santiago: LOM Ediciones, 2013), 96.

19. Sergio Bitar and Eduardo Moyano, "Redistribución del consumo y transición al socialismo," *Cuadernos de la Realidad Nacional* 11 (January 1972): 31–32. See also Stefan de Vylder, *Allende's Chile: The Political Economy of the Rise and Fall of the Unidad Popular* (Cambridge, UK: Cambridge University Press, 1976), 114–116; Frens-String, "Communists, Commissars, and Consumers," 483; and Frens-String, "A 'Popular Option' for Development?".

20. Salvador Allende, "La nacionalización del cobre: Por qué se nacionaliza," December 1970, in Martner, *El pensamiento económico*, 127–147; and Allende, "Informe al pueblo sobre la nacionalización del cobre," July 11, 1971, in Martner, *El pensamiento económico*, 148–168.

21. Gonzalo Martner and Pablo Bifani, "La nueva política del hierro," July 1, 1971, in Martner, *El pensamiento económico*, 207–216; and Pedro Vuskovic, "Necesidad de estatizar el sistema bancario," January 1971, in Martner, *El pensamiento económico*, 251–253.

22. Salvador Allende, "El área de propiedad social," March 4, 1971, in Martner, *El pensamiento económico*, 32–36.

23. Salvador Allende Gossens, "The Chilean Revolution One Year In," in Hutchison et al., *Chile Reader*, 402.

24. Allende Gossens, "Chilean Revolution One Year In," 402.

25. Juan de Onís, "Allende Is Given a Mandate by Vote," *New York Times*, April 6, 1971.

26. Allende Gossens, "Chilean Revolution One Year In," 401.

27. Hakim and Solimano, *Development, Reform, and Malnutrition*, 11; and Consejo Nacional para la Alimentación y Nutrición (CONPAN), *Chile: Estadísticas básicas en alimentación y nutrición; 1969–1978* (Santiago: Ministerio de Salud, 1980), 6.

28. On the poor state of health care in Chile when the UP took office, see María Angélica Illanes Oliva, "'El cuerpo nuestro de cada día': El pueblo como experiencia emancipatoria en tiempos de la Unidad Popular," in *Cuando hicimos historia: La experiencia de la Unidad Popular*, ed. Julio Pinto Vallejos (Santiago: LOM Ediciones, 2005), 127–145.

29. Richard E. Feinberg, *The Triumph of Allende: Chile's Legal Revolution* (New York: New American Library, 1972), 81.

30. On protein consumption in Chile at the beginning of the 1970s, see María Angélica Tagle, "La calidad y el valor proteico de la dieta del proletariado chileno," *Revista Médica de Chile* (August 1970): 562.

31. de Vylder, *Allende's Chile*, 7–9.

32. ODEPLAN, *Informe económico anual 1970* (Santiago, Editorial Universitaria, 1971), cited in Franck Gaudichaud, *Chile 1970–1973: Mil días que estremecieron el mundo* (Santiago: LOM Ediciones, 2016), 54.

33. In 1969, production of numerous agricultural crops declined, including wheat, corn, barley, beans, potatoes, and peas. See Braun et al., *Economía chilena*, 40–41.

34. Pedro Vuskovic, "Así Saldremos Adelante" (Santiago: Consejería de Difusión de la Presidencia de la República, 1971), 4–5, cited in Feinberg, *Triumph of Allende*, 81; and Francisco Ciudad, "Sobre la inflación y algo más," *El Siglo*, December 1, 1970.

35. Robles Ortiz, *Jacques Chonchol*, 226.

36. de Vylder, *Allende's Chile*, 53.

37. Walden Bello, "The Roots and Dynamics of Revolution and Counterrevolution in Chile" (PhD diss., Princeton University, 1975), 411–414. As Bello notes, the UP wage policy for Chile's middle-income bracket was, in actuality, even more generous than these official figures suggest. He writes: "Government statistics on the remuneration of public sector employees—the large bureaucratic middle class—in 1971 show that employees who were earning up to a living wage in 1970 received an average increase in income of 55.5 percent, far above the 39.9 percent projected by the decree" (413–414).

38. Eric Hobsbawm, "Chile: Year One," September 1971, reprinted in Hobsbawm, *Viva la Revolución: Hobsbawm on Latin America* (London: Little, Brown 2016), 379.

39. Patricio Meller, *Un siglo de economía política chilena (1890–1990)* (Santiago: Editorial Andrés Bello, 1996), 118–119. Chile experienced an even weaker growth rate of 3.6 percent just one year before Allende's election.

40. These government figures were reprinted in "Abastecimiento en cifras," *Chile Hoy* 1, no. 30 (January 5–11, 1973): 14–15.

41. Cited in de Vylder, *Allende's Chile*, 70–71. According to Chile's Office of Planning (ODEPLAN), 89,000 of the 146,000 newly employed individuals were new entrants into the labor force, while around 57,000 were formerly unemployed persons who reentered the labor force in 1971.

42. Meller, *Un siglo de economía política chilena*, 119.

43. Meller, *Un siglo de economía política chilena*, 119.

44. Gaudichaud, *Chile 1970–1973*, 97. Between late 1970 and late 1971, inflation was estimated to have fallen from an annual rate of well over 30 percent to somewhere between 15 and 20 percent.

45. Meller, *Unidad Popular*, 33–34. Meller notes that the share of labor in GDP averaged just 48.4 percent from 1960 to 1969. For additional analysis of these figures, see also Frens-String, "A 'Popular Option' for Development?".

46. Allende Gossens, "Chilean Revolution One Year In," 402.

47. Tomás Moulian, "La Unidad Popular: fiesta, drama y derrota," in *La forja de ilusiones: El sistema de partidos (1932–1973)* (Santiago: Universidad ARCIS-FLACSO, 1993).

48. "Inundarán mercado con televisores populares," *La Tercera de la Hora*, May 13, 1971. On the ubiquity of nationally produced bed linens in 1971, see Winn, *La revolución chilena*, 81. For more on the prevalence of shoe and mattress purchases, as well as purchases of more expensive items like refrigerators, in the early days of the revolution, see Luis Corvalán, *El Gobierno de Salvador Allende* (Santiago: LOM Ediciones, 2003), 24; also Frens-String, "Communists, Commissars, and Consumers," 483–484. Daily newspapers were replete with advertisements for things like bed

mattresses, television sets, and housewares in 1971. For example, see prominent ads for new dishware and mattresses in the pages of *La Tercera de la Hora* in mid-May 1971.

49. "Government's Price Freeze and Wage Rises Send Chileans on a Buying Spree," *New York Times*, May 13, 1971.

50. "A 3 bandas," *Eva*, November 5–11, 1971, 44. Although the *fiesta de consumo* (consumer party) was most clearly seen in urban spaces, the Chilean countryside felt the impact of the consumer boom as well. In the province of Aconcagua, for example, the percentage of homes with gas stoves nearly doubled from just 35 percent in 1970 to 60 percent by 1973, the year Allende's revolution was brought to a violent end. See Tinsman, *Buying into the Regime*, 74.

51. De Vylder, *Allende's Chile*, 203. De Vylder estimated "apparent consumption" of several key foodstuffs by adding together domestic production figures with total import figures. His figures did not account for any smuggling or hoarding of goods that might have occurred, though such practices were almost certainly greater in 1973 than in the revolution's first two years.

52. María Angélica Tagle et al. "Disponibilidad alimentaria: Chile 1970, 1971, 1972," Departamento de Nutrición, Facultad de Medicina, Universidad de Chile, Sede Santiago Norte, Publicación 54/73 (1973), cited in Hakim and Solimano, *Development, Reform, and Malnutrition*, 25.

53. Solón Barraclough and Almino Affonso, "Diagnóstico de la reforma agraria," *Cuadernos de la Realidad Nacional* (April 1973): 74–75, cited in Hakim and Solimano, *Development, Reform, and Malnutrition*, 25. See also Frens-String, "Communists, Commissars, and Consumers," 484.

54. Juan Carlos Concha, "Presentación de Juan Carlos Concha," in *Chile 1971: El primer año del Gobierno de la Unidad Popular*, ed. Pedro Milos (Santiago: Ediciones Universidad Alberto Hurtado, 2013), 65–68.

55. Hakim and Solimano, *Development, Reform, and Nutrition in Chile*, 38; "Hay que salvar a 25 mil niños que mueren anualmente por desnutrición," *El Siglo*, December 20, 1970; and "La leche salvará a mis hijos," *El Siglo*, January 6, 1971.

56. De Vylder, *Allende's Chile*, 203.

57. "Partieron las jornadas de control de alimentos," *El Siglo*, December 12, 1971.

58. "Tratan de fabricar galletas con porotos," *La Tercera de la Hora*, November 15, 1971; and "Con nuevo alimento infantil combatirán la desnutrición," *La Tercera de la Hora*, May 23, 1973.

59. "Pan y leche," *El Siglo*, December 10, 1970.

60. See Winn, "Furies of the Andes," 240.

61. Cited in Winn, *La revolución chilena*, 59.

62. Cited in Renzo Henríquez Guaico, "Industria Perlak: 'Dirigida y controlada por los trabajadores'; Desalieanción obrera en los tiempos de la Unidad Popular, 1970–1973," *Izquierdas* 20 (September 2014): 58.

63. "Chonchol explica la nueva Reforma Agraria," *El Siglo*, September 22, 1970; and "Reforma Agraria inseparable de la Revolución," *Poder Campesino* 14 (first half of August 1971): 8–9.

64. Salvador Allende, "Salitre: Historia trágica; Discurso en la Oficina Salitrera Pedro de Valdivia," February 6, 1971, www.marxists.org/espanol/allende/1971/febrero06.htm.

65. On the inefficiencies of the asentamiento, see Food and Agriculture Organization (FAO), *Evaluación preliminar de los asentamientos de Reforma Agraria de Chile: Aspectos socio-económicos* (Santiago: FAO, ICIRA, 1967).

66. "Centros de Reforma Agraria: Otro camino para asegurar la conquista de la tierra," *Poder Campesino* 15 (second half of August 1971): 8.

67. "Centros de Reforma Agraria." Gender equality remained limited in the CERA system. While women were granted the right to vote for campesino leadership within each CERA's "welfare" and "control" committees, they were only allowed to vote and participate on the CERA's "production" committee if they actively worked cooperative lands. On additional shortcomings of female political participation within the CERA structure, see Tinsman, *Partners in Conflict*, 241–243. See also Winn and Kay, "Agrarian Reform and Rural Revolution," 146–148.

68. Winn and Kay, "Agrarian Reform and Rural Revolution," 146–147.

69. Winn and Kay, "Agrarian Reform and Rural Revolution," 146–147.

70. Winn and Kay, "Agrarian Reform and Rural Revolution," 147.

71. Winn and Kay, "Agrarian Reform and Rural Revolution," 148.

72. Winn and Kay, "Agrarian Reform and Rural Revolution," 155.

73. De Vylder, *Allende's Chile*, 191–192.

74. Braun et al., *Economía chilena*, 40–41; "Dos años de Reforma Agraria del Gobierno Popular," UWM, SML, LTCF, Ch3 B166, 5. Winn and Kay write that "despite dislocations inherent in such a drastic transformation in land tenure, agrarian production grew slightly" during the first part of the UP revolution. See "Agrarian Reform and Rural Revolution," 155.

75. De Vylder, *Allende's Chile*, 201; and Frens-String, "A 'Popular Option' for Development?".

76. Winn and Kay, "Agrarian Reform and Rural Revolution," 153; and "Dos años de Reforma Agraria del Gobierno Popular."

77. Salvador Allende Gossens, "Discurso sobre la propiedad agraria," August 23, 1971, www.marxists.org/espanol/allende/1971/agosto023.htm.

78. "Sustitutos de carne de vacuno, *El Heraldo* (Linares), January 28, 1968; and "NO MÁS importaciones de carne de ave," *Quiubo Compadre* (second half of February 1968): 7.

79. Comisión para el estudio de propuestas para 'Matadero Procesador de Aves en Santiago,'" November 1963/April 1964, ARNAD, CORFO-ECORFO, FSOCOAGRO, vol. 305; and "Con el pie derecho partió la crianza de cerdos en Cooperativa de Chanco," *Quiubo Compadre* (first half of June 1968): 4–5. On the Marchigüe cooperative, see "Política nacional avícola," *Quiubo Compadre* (second half of January 1969): 12; "La Cooperativa de Marchigüe en cifras," *Quiubo Compadre* (first half of March 1969): 7; and Carrasco and Vergara, *Programa de fomento pecuario*. For additional information on the Frei government's efforts

to boost production of pork, see "The University of Minnesota Project in Chile: An Experiment in Production Education," October 1971, UWM, SML, LTCF, CH 5.5 M38.

80. Birchmeier Salgado, "'Habrá carne para toda la población,'" 99. On UP efforts to boost chicken and hog production, see "Decisivo aumento en producción de aves," *Poder Campesino* (January 1972): 16–17. At the Marchigüe chicken cooperative, the UP estimated that 150,000 chickens could be produced monthly in 1972. "El Plan Avícola 1972 prevé duplicar producción de pollos," *El Siglo*, February 22, 1972. See also Armando Fuenzalida Bunster, "No. 88: Requisa establecimiento industrial de alimentos para aves y cerdos," February 17, 1972, ARNAD, CORFO-ECORFO, FSOCOAGRO, vol. 878. The UP's goal of doubling chicken production proved overly ambitious, but poultry production did increase significantly under the Allende government, rising from 62,000 tons of meat in 1969–70 to 81,000 tons two years later. Pork production grew at a slightly slower pace, increasing from 48,000 tons in 1969–70 to 50,000 tons in 1971–72. See de Vylder, *Allende's Chile*, 201.

81. "Los pescadores y el desarrollo del país," *Quiubo Compadre* (first half of October 1965): 15, cited in Frens-String, "Communists, Commissars, and Consumers," 487.

82. Rodolfo Ravanal L. to Ministerio de Fomento, "Informa Proyecto de Fomento Pesquero de la Corporacion de Fomento de la Produccion," May 20, 1940, ARNAD, Fondo Ministerio de Fomento (FMFO), vol. 1717. See also Pedro Luis González. "La industria de la pesca," *Industria* 55, no. 11 (November 1938): 711–712.

83. Pablo Neruda to Ministry of Foreign Relations in Chile, "Inmigración Española," Memorandum, June 3, 1939, ARREE, Fondo Histórico (FH), vol. 1571. See also D. Carlos Madariaga P., "Inmigración Española." *Industria* 56, no. 6 (June 1939): 383. Numbering seventy-six individuals in total, fishermen represented the second largest group of refugees (organized by profession) that arrived on the *Winnipeg*, according to statistics published in the monthly bulletin of Chile's industrialist society. See "Refugiados Españoles Ofrecidas Para Servir en las Industrias," *Industria* 56, no. 8 (August 1939): 524.

84. See Kristin Wintersteen, "Protein from the Sea: The Global Rise of Fishmeal and the Industrialization of Southeast Pacific Fisheries, 1918–1973," DesiguALdades.net Working Paper Series, no. 26 (Berlin: Freie Universität, 2012), 1.

85. Wintersteen, "Protein from the Sea," 3, 7–8, 13–15.

86. Sergio Vergara, "Realidad y porvenir de la industria nacional de conservas de Chile," *Panorama Económico* 7 (September–October 1947): 25–27.

87. Wintersteen, "Protein from the Sea," 7.

88. Ministerio de Agricultura—Departamento de Pesca y Caza, "Memoria Anual," 1961, ARNAD, FMA, vol. 1573. Annual per capita fish consumption also fell in these years, from 6.66 kilos/year in 1960 to 5.59 kilos in 1961. On Chile's inability to significantly increase domestic fish consumption, see also Fernando Giménez, "Industria Pesquera," *Panorama Económico* (September–October 1947): 32–34.

89. "Chile vende más harina y aceite de pescado." *La Tercera de la Hora*, June 15, 1971. The report cites Chilean Central Bank figures, which showed that sales of fishmeal rose from 23,338 tons in 1970 to 54,765 tons one year later. Sales of fish oil similarly rose from 3,692 tons to 7,626 tons during this same period. New markets for these goods included Cuba, Korea, and the Philippines.

90. "Setecientas toneladas de pescado para Semana Santa," *La Tercera de la Hora*, April 8, 1971; and "Nuevas instalaciones portuarios duplicarán producción pesquera," *El Siglo*, February 10, 1972.

91. "Pescados colaborarán en lucha contra desnutrición," *La Tercera de la Hora*, April 24, 1971. According to Kristin Wintersteen, efforts to use fish in the production of what scientists called a "multiple protein complex" never fully got off the ground in Chile before the 1973 coup. Wintersteen, "Protein from the Sea," 15.

92. Hugo Palmarola Sagredo, "Productos y socialismo: Diseño Industrial Estatal en Chile," in *1973: La vida cotidiana de un año crucial*, ed. Claudio Rolle (Santiago: Planeta, 2003), 278.

93. "San Antonio de Fiesta: Hoy reciben barcos soviéticos," *El Siglo*, January 26, 1972.

94. Espinoza Muñoz, "'La Batalla de la Merluza,'" 39.

95. Espinoza Muñoz, "'La Batalla de la Merluza,'" 40.

96. "Faena de pesqueros soviéticos aumenta 30% producción de merluza," *El Siglo*, February 11, 1972, cited in Frens-String, "Communists, Commissars, and Consumers," 487.

97. "No hay perjuicio para pescadores artesanales," *El Siglo*, February 11, 1972.

98. "La merluza," *El Siglo*, August 20, 1972.

99. Gloria Alarcón, "Una solución alimenticia específicamente nacional," *El Siglo*, March 3, 1972.

100. Rubén Moore, "La multiplicación de los peces," *El Siglo*, February 16, 1972.

101. Allende Gossens, "Chilean Revolution One Year In," 404.

102. Castro's remark about Chile's revolution being a "revolution of consumption" is cited in Paul N. Rosenstein-Rodan, "Why Allende Failed," *Challenge* (May–June 1974): 10. He writes: "Fidel Castro correctly pointed out that 'Marxism is a revolution of production; Allende's was a revolution of consumption.'"

103. "Amplían prohibición para consumir vacuno," *La Tercera de la Hora*, July 9, 1971; "Santiago quedó sin carne ni pollos," *La Tercera de la Hora*, July 19, 1971; "Incidentes en el Matadero por la falta de abastecimientos," *La Tercera de la Hora*, July 23, 1971; and "La broma en vida," *La Tercera de la Hora*, July 27, 1971.

104. "No subirá la carne," *El Siglo*, May 8, 1971, cited in Frens-String, "Communists, Commissars, and Consumers," 485.

105. Hobsbawm, "Chile: Year One," 381.

106. "Santiago quedó sin carne ni pollos," *La Tercera de la Hora*, July 10, 1971; and "Incidentes en el matadero por la falta de abastecimientos," *La Tercera de la Hora*, July 23, 1971.

107. "Temporal hizo desaparecer pollos en Mercado Central," *La Tercera de la Hora*, July 15, 1971.

108. "Chile Is Increasing Her Imports to Offset a Shortage of Meat," *New York Times*, July 23, 1971.

109. SOCOAGRO—Departamento Estudios Económicos, "Consumo de carnes en el Gran Santiago," 1972, ARNAD, CORFO-ECORFO, FSOCOAGRO, vol. 316.

110. "Abastecimiento en cifras."

111. Meller, *Unidad Popular*, 35. Between 1970 and 1972, the total value of Chile's total imports (in millions of US dollars) increased from 956 to 1,103, while the total value of Chile's total exports decreased from 1,112 to 849. At the same time, food imports as a percentage of total imports (again measured in millions of US dollars) increased from just over 14 percent in 1970 to nearly 29 percent in 1972. Meller, *Un siglo de economía política chilena*, 127.

112. See *El Mercurio* (Santiago), November 29, 1971, cited in Margaret Power, *Right-Wing Women in Chile: Feminine Power and the Struggle against Allende, 1964–1973* (University Park: Pennsylvania State University Press, 2002), 150.

CHAPTER 6. A BATTLE FOR THE CHILEAN STOMACH

1. On the everyday nature of the revolution, see Marian Schlotterbeck, *Beyond the Vanguard: Everyday Revolutionaries in Allende's Chile* (Oakland: University of California Press, 2018), 6. See also chapter 5 of Winn, *La revolución chilena*.

2. In this chapter, I follow Schlotterbeck's observation that, starting in the early months of 1972, "access to foodstuffs and basic consumer goods was the front line of revolutionary struggle in Chile." *Beyond the Vanguard*, 116.

3. Flores narrated this biography to a journalist from the PCCh's daily, *El Siglo*, in early 1972. See "Las JAP: Arma mortífera contra el desabastecimiento y especulación," *El Siglo*, March 21, 1972, cited and discussed in Frens-String, "Communists, Commissars, and Consumers," 488–489. On SOCOAGRO and the JAP, see "SOCOAGRO en la Batalla de la Producción," November 3, 1972, ARNAD, CORFO-ECORFO, FSOCOAGRO, vol. 342.

4. Given the important public role of the JAP, there are still relatively few histories of it. For exceptions, see Boris Cofré, "La lucha por 'el pan' y la defensa del 'gobierno popular': las Juntas de Abastecimiento y Control de Precios en la vía chilena al socialismo," *Izquierdas* 41 (August 2018): 224–249; Giusti, "Participación popular en Chile"; Leonardo Melo Contreras, "Las Juntas de Abastecimiento y Precios: Historia y memoria de una experiencia de participación popular; Chile, 1970–1973" (undergraduate thesis, Universidad Academia de Humanismo Cristiano, 2012); Frens-String, "Communists, Commissars, and Consumers"; and Ernesto Pastrana and Monica Threlfall, *Pan, techo y poder: El movimiento de pobladores en Chile (1970–1973)* (Buenos Aires: Ediciones SIAP, 1974), 88–105. For an excellent local

view of JAP and its work in Concepción during the October 1972 Bosses' Strike, see Schlotterbeck, *Beyond the Vanguard*, 115–133.

5. "El pueblo comerá buen pan y no se le robará en el peso," *El Siglo*, October 30, 1970.

6. "Centros de Madres fiscalizarán el precio y calidad de pan," *El Siglo*, January 6, 1971.

7. "Obreros panificadores colaboran con DIRINCO en el control del pan," *El Siglo*, January 7, 1971; "Gobierno intervino 4 panaderías," *El Siglo*, January 8, 1971; and "Dos nuevas panaderías intervenidas por DIRINCO," *El Siglo*, January 10, 1971. The newspaper *El Siglo* reported on the immediate improvements that were made at several of the requisitioned bakeries a week after their seizure. See "Sí, se puede producir pan mejor y más barato, dice la DIRINCO," *El Siglo*, January 17, 1971.

8. "El pan único," *El Siglo*, January 8, 1971; and "Sí, se puede producir pan mejor y más barato."

9. "No más alzas," *El Siglo*, January 13, 1971.

10. "Pan y leche."

11. Pedro Vuskovic, "Conversation with the Women of Chile," July 29, 1971, reprinted in Johnson, *Chilean Road to Socialism*, 472.

12. "Pobladores, autoridades y comerciantes luchan unidos por el control de precios," *El Siglo*, August 9, 1971; "Comités de abastecimientos en todas las poblaciones," *El Siglo*, September 25, 1971; and "Corvalán: Llamado a vencer dificultades del abastecimiento," *El Siglo*, October 20, 1971. For a good review of the JAP's early history, see Gustavo González and Jorge Modinger, "Las JAP: Poder de la dueña de casa," *Chile Hoy* 1, no. 3 (June 30–July 6, 1972): 13–17.

13. Pastrana and Threlfall, *Pan, techo y poder*, 92–93.

14. "Antecedentes de la JAP," *Chile Hoy* 1, no. 3 (June 30–July 6 1972): 19. For an early mention of the role that mothers' centers played in the JAP, see "Comerciantes y pobladores crean Juntas de Abastecimiento," *El Siglo*, October 29, 1971.

15. "Las JAP son así," *El Siglo*, March 26, 1972.

16. On early precedents for the JAP, see Pastrana and Threlfall, *Pan, techo y poder*, 90–91. See also "Antecedentes de la JAP." In the fall of 1971, DIRINCO began working with the Ministry of Housing to create "popular grocery stores" (*almacenes populares*) in newly constructed working-class neighborhoods. "Almacenes populares para las poblaciones," *El Siglo*, May 9, 1971. See also "Almacenes populares de DIRINCO," *La Tercera de la Hora*, May 9, 1971.

17. "Mujeres participarán en la lucha contra especulación y acaparamiento," *El Siglo*, July 30, 1971.

18. "Unión pobladores-asentados derrota a intermediarios," *Quiubo Compadre* (second half of July 1970): 12–13.

19. Jacobo Schatan, "El desabastecimiento: La conspiración de EE.UU. que derrotó a la UP," in *Salvador Allende: Presencia en la ausencia*, ed. Miguel Lawner, Hernán Soto, and Jacobo Schatan (Santiago: LOM Ediciones, 2008), 210–211.

20. "Ya nadie compra patas de pollo," *El Siglo*, January 14, 1972.

21. "Pobladores, autoridades y comerciantes luchan unidos por el control de precios," *El Siglo*, August 9, 1971.

22. "Los monopolios distribuidores son los que hambrean al pueblo," *El Siglo*, October 24, 1971. On small retailers' support for the nationalization of big distributors, especially those that controlled the beef supply, see "El paso al Área Estatal de las empresas de distribución es positivo," *El Siglo*, December 13, 1971; and "El Gobierno requisó CODECAR para mejorar abastecimiento de carne," *El Siglo*, December 19,1971.

23. Gustavo González and Jorge Modinger, "Las JAP: Poder de la dueña de casa," *Chile Hoy* 1, no. 3 (June 30–July 6, 1972): 13–17.

24. "Las JAP contra la especulación," *El Siglo*, January 14, 1972.

25. See reporting on the discussions within one JAP assembly in mid-1972 in González and Modinger, "Las JAP: Poder de la dueña de casa." See also Frens-String, "Communists, Commissars, and Consumers," 489.

26. On the "just profits" idea, see Salvador Allende, "Speech to the United Nations (excerpts)," New York, December 4, 1972, www.marxists.org/archive /allende/1972/december/04.htm. On UNCTAD and the Charter of Economic Rights and Duties, see "Grave estancamiento en la Comisión de Productos Básicos," *La Tercera de la Hora*, May 11, 1972.

27. "'Olla común' con estacionamiento y baños para momios hambrientos," *El Siglo*, December 5, 1971.

28. Ministerio de Economía, Fomento y Reconstrucción, DIRINCO, Resolución 112, April 4, 1972, cited and discussed in Giusti, "Participación popular," 772–773. See also Cofré, "La lucha por 'el pan,'" 229–230.

29. José Cademártori, "Con las masas organizadas a derrotar el mercado negro y la especulación—Informe al pleno del Comité Central del Partido Comunista," *El Siglo*, September 29, 1972, reprinted in *La izquierda chilena (1969–1973): Documentos para el estudio de su línea estratégica*, ed. Victor Farías (Santiago: Centro de Estudios Públicos, 2000), 5:3153; and "1,224 Juntas de Abastecimiento se formarán este año en el país," *El Siglo*, January 29, 1972.

30. The first official JAP in the Chilean countryside was apparently not created until February 1972. See "Comienza la pelea contra especulación en el sector rural," *El Siglo*, February 6, 1972. See also "Empiezan a multiplicarse Centros de Abastecimiento Rural," *El Siglo*, March 13, 1972.

31. Cademártori, "Con las masas organizadas." For a visual and quantitative representation of the JAP's reach by 1973, see Cofré, "La lucha por 'el pan,'" 238–240.

32. "Antecedentes de la JAP."

33. "JAP: Formidable arma de combate contra los enemgios del pueblo," *El Siglo*, March 18, 1972. See also articles in *El Siglo* published after the legal codification of the JAP in early April 1972. The PCCh regularly refers to the JAPs as a political and economic "weapon." "Las JAP, armas del pueblo," *El Siglo*, April 7, 1972. See also "Tenemos que vencer también la contrarevolución en el abastecimiento," *El Siglo*, October 1, 1972.

34. "Día del pescado," *El Siglo*, February 21, 1972.

35. For a description of a typical community fish fry gathering, see "Santiago se cuadra con el consumo masivo de merluza," *El Siglo*, April 10, 1972. To celebrate International Women's Day in March 1972, the UP even ensured that a crate of merluza be provided to every mothers' center in the country, free of charge, for the community's enjoyment. See "Un cajón de merluza para centros de madres," *El Siglo*, March 6, 1972. The role of women in such activities was facilitated by the fact that UP supporters won control of the ten-thousand-member Communal Union of Mothers' Centers in March 1972, thus displacing the influence that the Christian Democrats had over the organization. See "Unidad Popular ganó elección de Centros de Madres," *El Siglo*, March 6, 1972.

36. "Operación Merluza en área norte de Santiago," *El Siglo*, May 2, 1972; and "Croquetas a base de merluza; listas para la venta al público," *El Siglo*, March 2, 1972. See Frens-String, "Communists, Commissars, and Consumers," 490.

37. Patricio Palma, interview by Franck Gaudichaud, November 28, 2001, reprinted in *Poder popular y cordones industriales: Testimonios sobre el movimiento popular urbano, 1970–1973*, ed. Franck Gaudichaud (Santiago: LOM Ediciones, 2004), 406.

38. Salvador Allende, "Trabajadores y participación: Discurso en ocasión de celebrarse el Día del Trabajador," May 1, 1972, www.marxists.org/espanol/allende /1972/mayo01.htm.

39. Quilapayún, "A comer merluza," (Dicap, 1972).

40. "Productos del mar," *Eva*, January 7–13, 1972, 80–83. See also "Cocina sin carne," *Eva*, January 7–13, 1972, 84–85; and "Aun tenemos mariscos y frutas," *Eva*, February 4–10, 1972, 84–85.

41. See, for example, the role of the JAPs in encouraging consumer discipline, as described by a writer for *El Siglo* in September 1972. Percival Phillips, "Sobreconsumo y disciplina revolucionaria," *El Siglo*, September 14, 1972.

42. "Las JAP: Arma mortífera," cited in Frens-String, "Communists, Commissars, and Consumers," 489.

43. In his study of the homes that homeless peoples' committees built after land occupations in Santiago, historian Edward Murphy observes that "neighborhood designs were similar to those in place with low-income government housing programs." This included a kitchen that was separated from the living space, rather than a "communal kitchen and eating area." Citing the words of one neighborhood leader, Murphy notes that this gendered layout was intended to preserve the "integrity of the home and private life." Murphy, "In and Out of the Margins: Urban Land Seizures and Homeownership in Santiago, Chile," in *Cities from Scratch: Poverty and Informality in Urban Latin America*, ed. Brodwyn Fischer, Bryan McCann, and Javier Auyero (Durham, NC: Duke University Press, 2014), 89.

44. "JAP para avanzar," *El Rebelde*, October 30–November 4, 1972, cited in Frens-String, "Communists, Commissars, and Consumers," 490.

45. Chase, *Revolution within the Revolution*, 142–143, cited in Frens-String, "Communists, Commissars, and Consumers," 490.

46. Beatriz Campos [pseud.], interview by Margaret Power, February 3, 1994, excerpted and cited in Power, *Right-Wing Women*, 194–195. See also Alison J. Bruey, *Bread, Justice, and Liberty: Grassroots Activism and Human Rights in Pinochet's Chile* (Madison: University of Wisconsin Press, 2018), 36.

47. "Los alimentos de su familia dependerán al más sectario de sus vecinos," *La Tercera de la Hora*, January 14, 1973.

48. "El comunismo y las JAP," *El Mercurio* (Santiago), April 8, 1972.

49. "Ojo con las JAP," *La Tercera de la Hora*, May 10, 1972.

50. Eliana Parra, edited transcript of interviews by Edward Murphy, July 23, 2002, and September 4, 2002, in Murphy, *Historias poblacionales: Hacia una memoria incluyente* (Santiago: CEDECO: World Vision, 2004), 35. On political tensions in the JAPs, see also Tinsman, *Partners in Conflict*, 67–69.

51. Sonia Paz Jiménez, interview by Leonardo Melo Contreras, March 6, 2011, cited in Melo Contreras, "Las Juntas de Abastecimiento y Precios," 60.

52. "Liberación de la mujer," *El Rebelde*, May 2, 1972, cited in Frens-String, "Communists, Commissars, and Consumers," 492.

53. Sergio Bitar, *Chile, 1970–1973: Asumir la historia para construir el futuro* (Santiago: Pehuén, 1995), 142–143, 164.

54. In the parlance of the day, the UP had to decide whether it should *avanzar consolidando*—move forward by first consolidating—or *consolidar avanzando*—consolidate the revolution by pushing ahead with the UP's original agenda. See Winn, *Weavers of Revolution*, 233–234.

55. Bitar, *Chile*, 142–143.

56. Bitar, *Chile*, 164–167. On the economic missteps taken by the UP after Lo Curro, see Stallings and Zimbalist, "The Political Economy of the Unidad Popular," 79. Among the important Allende officials who resigned in the wake of Lo Curro was Jacobo Schatan, the director of DINAC. "Renunció a su cargo el gerente de DINAC," *La Tercera de la Hora*, July 1, 1972.

57. Marta Harnecker and Jorge Modinger, "Patricio Palma: Dirinco debe apoyarse en aparatos de masas," *Chile Hoy* 1, no. 12 (September 1–7, 1972): 32, 30.

58. Harnecker and Modinger, "Patricio Palma," 32, 30.

59. On the Perlak takeover, see Santos Romeo G., "El caso 'Perlak,'" *Chile Hoy* 1, no. 6 (June 21–27, 1972): 11; "Los trabajadores de Industrias Perlak intervenida a la opinión pública," *La Tercera de la Hora*, July 23, 1972, 10; and Jorge Modinger, "El esfuerzo nutritivo en el Área Social," *Chile Hoy* 1, no. 28 (December 22–28, 1972): 14–15. See also Henríquez Guaico, "Industria Perlak," 52–53.

60. "Control popular sobre los precios," *El Rebelde*, July 18, 1972; and "En 'operación comando' obreros ocuparon 5 fábricas conserveras," *La Tercera de la Hora*, July 12, 1972.

61. Schlotterbeck, *Beyond the Vanguard*, 109.

62. "Marchemos contra el fracaso," *La Tercera de la Hora*, September 12, 1972.

63. Truckers were also frustrated because of shortages of spare parts to repair failing vehicles and a decision by the government in late September to suspend imports of beef and butter. On the UP's suspension of foreign imports of beef and butter, see "Chile Stops Beef Imports," *The Times* (London), September 28, 1972.

64. For more on the October Bosses' Strike and the right-wing groups that carried it out, see chapter 7.

65. Robinson Rojas Sanford, *The Murder of Allende and the End of the Chilean Way to Socialism*, trans. Andree Conrad (New York: Harper & Row, 1975), 123–124.

66. Braun et al., *Economía chilena*, 38–41.

67. According to at least one assessment, peasant participation in the October strike was relatively limited. While the leadership of peasant unions aligned with the Christian Democrats and other anti-Allende parties proclaimed their support for the strike, few farms actively halted production, scholar Judith Astelerra noted. In fact, pro-UP peasant "commandos" made sure that most small-scale farming activities continued during the strike. Astelerra, "Land Reform in Chile during Allende's Government" (PhD diss, Cornell University, 1975), 345–346.

68. "Dramática escasez de alimentos y combustibles," *La Tercera de la Hora*, October 16, 1972.

69. "Allende Names Three Military Men to Cabinet in Move to Order," *New York Times*, November 3, 1972; "MIR pronunció contra gabiente cívico-militar," *La Tercera de la Hora*, November 9, 1973; and Gustavo González, "Los militares en la distribución," *Chile Hoy* 1, no. 33 (January 26–February 1, 1973): 5.

70. Salvador Allende Gossens, "Palabras del Presidente de la República, Compañero Salvador Allende Gossens, refiriéndose a las Juntas de Abastecimiento y Control de Precios," Santiago, February 19, 1973, BNC, SC; and "Allende: Los inspectores ad honores," *Chile Hoy* 1, no. 36 (February 16–22, 1973): 17.

71. For the MIR's opposition to the military's involvement in distribution, see "La Distribución: ¿Tarea de masas o de las FF.AA?," *Punto Final* 182 (April 24, 1973).

72. Arturo Valenzuela, *The Breakdown of Democratic Regimes: Chile* (Baltimore, MD: Johns Hopkins University Press, 1978), 79, cited in Eden Medina, *Cybernetic Revolutionaries: Technology and Politics in Allende's Chile* (Cambridge, MA: MIT Press, 2011), 147.

73. "Partido Socialista y Partido Comunista: Propósitos de ofensiva política," October 1972, reprinted in Farías, *La izquierda chilena*, 5:3310–3311.

74. "Partido Socialista (Comité Central): Comité Central Informa; Informe a los militantes sobre el paro patronal; Documento confidencial interno," October 19, 1972, reprinted in Farías, *La izquierda chilena* 5:3346–3347.

75. Patricio Palma, oral presentation at Seminario "Chile 1972" (Universidad Alberto Hurtado, Santiago, December 6, 2012), cited in Frens-String, "Communists, Commissars, and Consumers," 493.

76. "Requisaron SOPROLE, CODINA, Mellafe y Salas y otros," *Puro Chile*, October 11, 1972; and "SOPROLE: Sin pelos en la leche," *Chile Hoy* 1, no. 23 (November 17–23, 1972): 13. On the response of the UP base to the strike, see also

Faride Zeran, "La fuerza del pueblo," *Chile Hoy* 1, no. 20 (October 27–November 2, 1972): 7.

77. On the rise of ALMAC as Chile's first modern supermarket, starting in the late 1950s, see Peter D. Bennett, *Government's Role in Retail Marketing of Food Products in Chile* (Austin: University of Texas Press, 1968), 38–40.

78. The popular seizure of the Santa Julia ALMAC followed DIRINCO's seizure of other locales. See, for example, "Requisaron ALUSA y Los 'Almac,'" *Puro Chile*, October 20, 1972. For the goods in the *canasta popular* or *canasta básica* (basic basket), see "Centros de Abastecimiento Rural," *Poder Campesino* 28 (1972).

79. "El ALMAC Santa Julia será recuperado," *El Rebelde*, January 2–9, 1973; "El Almac Santa Julia en manos del pueblo," *El Rebelde*, January 9–15, 1973; "Almac de la discordia puede causar conflicto de poderes," *La Tercera de la Hora*, January 3, 1972; and "El despojo al Almac de Población Santa Julia," *La Tercera de la Hora*, January 4, 1973, as cited in Frens-String, "Communists, Commissars, and Consumers," 472.

80. On the growing prevalence of rationing schemas, see Marta Harnecker, "La distribución en el banquillo," *Chile Hoy* 1, no. 31 (January 12–18, 1973): 14–15. See also "Fernando Flores: Hoy, el racionamiento no es una medida ultra," *Chile Hoy* 1, no. 31 (January 12–18, 1973): 32, 29.

81. José Bengoa, "Racionamiento para los ricos, abastecimiento para los pobres," *Chile Hoy* 1, no. 32 (January 19–25, 1973): 5.

82. "Los trabajadores y el poder popular," *Punto Final*, May 8, 1973. See also Gaudichaud, *Chile 1970–1973*, 311–315.

83. One of those involved in building the revolution's "people's stores" system was future Chilean diplomat Heraldo Muñoz. He recounts his role as a national supervisor of such efforts in his biography. See Muñoz, *The Dictator's Shadow: Life under Augusto Pinochet* (New York: Basic Books, 2008), 1, 48–49. Another active leader in the "people's store" movement was the Peruvian revolutionary Marcos Rojas Turkowsky. See "Acta: Supermercados Monserrat, S.A.C.—Testimonio de la Escritura," August 10, 1973, IISH, Marco Rojas Turkowsky Files (MRT), folder 2; and "Pobladores respaldan almacenes populares," IISH, MRT, folder 2.

84. "Mejorar la acción de las JAP," *El Rebelde*, January 16–22, 1973; and "Distribución: Tarea del pueblo," *El Rebelde*, January 23–29, 1973; and "Mujeres le salen al paso a los camioneros chuecos," *Puro Chile*, October 26, 1972, cited in Frens-String, "Communists, Commissars, and Consumers," 494. See also, Bruey, *Bread, Justice, and Liberty*, 35–36.

85. Boris Cofré, "Historia de los pobladores del campamento Nueva Habana durante la Unidad Popular (1970–1973)" (undergraduate thesis, Universidad ARCIS, 2007), 211.

86. "Distribución: Tarea del pueblo," *El Rebelde*, January 23–29, 1973. Marta Harnecker, "La distribución en el banquillo," *Chile Hoy* (January 12–18, 1973): 14–15, cited in Frens-String, "Communists, Commissars, and Consumers," 494–495. For parallel efforts by Nueva Habana women to fight the consumption of

controlled substances, particularly alcohol, see Colin Henfry and Bernardo Sorj, *Chilean Voices: Activists Describe Their Experiences of the Popular Unity Period* (Hassocks, UK: Harvester Press, 1977), 99–100.

87. For a comprehensive account of both the land seizure and the seizure of Maipú's slaughterhouse, see Renzo Henríquez Guaico, *El poder del campo: Los campesinos de Maipú durante el gobierno de Allende* (Santiago: Londres 38 Espacio de Memorias, 2014), 63–82. The rural land occupations are immortalized in Patricio Guzmán's documentary film *La Batalla de Chile: La lucha de un pueblo sin armas.*

88. "Así se hace," *La Aurora de Chile*, June 28, 1973, cited in Henríquez Guaico, *El poder del campo*, 74.

89. "El Cordón Cerrillos: Los trabajadores, sus organizacións, el Gobierno," *Tarea Urgente* 1, no. 6 (June 23, 1973): 4, cited in Henríquez Guaico, *El poder del campo*, 79.

90. "Racionamiento sí... ¡Pero, para los ricos!," *El Rebelde*, January 23–29, 1973.

91. "María Farías Godoy, 'Siempre hemos vivido racionados,'" *Chile Hoy* 1, no. 32 (January 19–25, 1973), cited in Frens-String, "Communists, Commissars, and Consumers," 472–473.

92. Bosco Parra, "Es posible extraer dignidad de la escasez y transformar a la pobreza en dignidad," in "La izquierda hace su balance: Foro de la izquierda sobre la situación política realizado el 24–26 de octubre de 1972," *Punto Final*, December 5, 1972, reprinted in Farías, *La izquierda chilena*, 5:3379–3380.

CHAPTER 7. BARREN PLOTS AND EMPTY POTS

1. Cristóbal Sáenz also served in the cabinet of Aguirre Cerda and as an adviser to various state welfare agencies, including the Caja de Seguro Obligatorio and Chile's popular housing fund. For a short biography, see Biblioteca del Congreso Nacional de Chile, "Cristóbal Sáenz Cerda," www.bcn.cl/historiapolitica/resenas _parlamentarias/wiki/Crist%C3%B3bal_S%C3%A1enz_Cerda.

2. Carmen Sáenz Terpelle, "Quichamahuida y Calatayud," interview by Angela Cousiño Vicuña and María Angélica Ovalle Gana, July 24, 2012, in *Reforma Agraria Chilena: Testimonios de sus protagonistas* (Santiago de Chile: Memoriter, 2013), 338.

3. In multiple interviews conducted after the Pinochet dictatorship, Sáenz retold elements of her personal history. See, for example, Patricia Arancibia Clavel and Andrea Novoa Mackenna, *Una mujer de la frontera: Carmen Sáenz Terpelle* (Santiago: Editoral Biblioteca Americana, 2006); and Sáenz Terpelle, "Quichamahuida y Calatayud," 336–343. See also "Women Lead the Opposition to Allende: Interview with Carmen Sáenz," in Hutchison et al., *Chile Reader*, 406–409.

4. On Sáenz and her involvement in conservative politics, see Arancibia Clavel and Novoa Mackenna, *Una mujer de la frontera*, 125. See also Lisa Baldez, *Why Women Protest: Women's Movements in Chile* (Cambridge, UK: Cambridge University Press, 2002), 64–65. On the new right and the PN, including Patricio Phillips's

claim that the party offered a conservative response to the Latin American Solidarity Organization (OLAS) that emerged in Havana in 1967, see Verónica Valdivia Ortiz de Zárate, *Nacionales y gremialistas: El "parto" de la nueva derecha política chilena, 1964–1973* (Santiago: LOM Ediciones, 2008), 173.

5. On the December 1971 March of the Empty Pots and Pans, see Baldez, *Why Women Protest*, 76–83; and Power, *Right-Wing Women in Chile*, 147–168. See also "Women Lead the Opposition to Allende," 406–409.

6. For an excellent analysis of Chile's "insurrectionary middle class" during the early 1970s, see Marcelo Casals, "The Insurrection of the Middle Class: Social Mobilization and Counterrevolution during the Popular Unity Government, Chile, 1970–1973," *Journal of Social History* (November 2019): 1–26, https://doi.org/10.1093/jsh/shz110.

7. The literature on neoliberalism is vast. For recent works that consider neoliberalism's emergence out of the remnants of midcentury left developmentalism, see Johanna Bockman, *Markets in the Name of Socialism: The Left-Wing Origins of Neoliberalism* (Palo Alto, CA: Stanford University Press, 2011). See also Amy Offner, *Sorting Out the Mixed Economy: The Rise and Fall of Welfare and Developmental States in the Americas* (Princeton, NJ: Princeton University Press, 2019). For an early analysis of Chile as a laboratory for neoliberal restructuring, see Andre Gunder Frank, *Economic Genocide in Chile: Monetarist Theory versus Humanity* (Nottingham, UK: Spokesman Press, 1976). For later historical analyses of Chile and neoliberalism, see Peter Winn, ed., *Victims of the Chilean Miracle: Workers and Neoliberalism in the Pinochet Era, 1973–2002* (Durham, NC: Duke University Press, 2004). My approach to thinking about neoliberalism in Chile is rooted in the circumstances of its creation—namely as a response to democratic socialism. I follow Corey Robin's observation that a key task of socialism is to convert "hysterical misery into ordinary unhappiness" by guaranteeing basic social and economic rights. I thus view neoliberalism as its antithesis—that is, as a system that marketizes formerly guaranteed social and economic entitlements, making the process for obtaining them ever more burdensome and tied to existing social and economic hierarchies. See Corey Robin, "Converting Hysterical Misery into Ordinary Unhappiness," *Jacobin*, December 10, 2013, www.jacobinmag.com/2013/12/socialism-converting -hysterical-misery-into-ordinary-unhappiness/.

8. A PDC proposal in 1969 sought to force landowners of more than eighty hectares to submit an annual accounting of their agricultural productivity to CORA. This was an attempt by the state to monitor what lands were not being fully utilized and by whom. See "Proyecto de parlamentarios demócratacristianos hace tiritar a los latifundistas," *Quiubo Compadre* (second half of July 1968): 2.

9. Arancibia Clavel and Novoa Mackenna, *Una mujer de la frontera*, 123–124.

10. Winn, "Furies of the Andes," 248.

11. See the critical post-Allende assessment of the UP by economist Paul N. Rosenstein-Rodan, "Why Allende Failed," 11.

12. Asociación de Pequeños Agricultores to Eduardo Frei Montalva, "Sobre problemas de pequeños agricultores," November 23, 1968, ARNAD, FMA, vol. 1829.

13. On divisions within the rural labor movement, particularly those that emerged under the UP, see Tinsman, *Partners in Conflict*, 254–266.

14. For example, "La sangre no llegó al río," *Quiubo Compadre* (first half of September 1966). "Unidad campesina debe frenar la persecución sindical," *Quiubo Compadre* (second half of August 1968): 4–5.

15. "Ante la violencia," *El Campesino* (September 1969): 20–21.

16. "Capataz asesinó a dirigente sindical," *Quiubo Compadre* (second half of June 1968): 16.

17. "Latifundista de Colchagua le puso el revolver al pecho al impulsor de Marchigüe," *Quiubo Compadre* (first half of September 1968): 16.

18. "Acción matonesca de latifundistas sureños," *Quiubo Compadre* (first half of November 1968): 19.

19. "Fueron agredidos dos periodistas," *Quiubo Compadre* (second half of August 1969): 20. For a list of violent acts against agrarian reformers and rural campesinos during 1968 and 1969, see "Calendario de violencia anti-Reforma Agraria," *Quiubo Compadre* (May 1970): 11.

20. On the Benavente family and local politics, see the obituary on the family's patriarch published in Linares's principal newspaper: "Don Gabriel Benavente Benavente," *El Heraldo*, January 28, 1968. See also "Dueños de Fundo baleó a funcionario de INDAP," *El Heraldo*, January 24, 1968; "Criminal atentado contra un funcionario de INDAP," *Quiubo Compadre* (first half of February 1968): 16; and "Noticiario campesino," *Quiubo Compadre* (second half of February 1968): 5. In the wake of the shooting, the Benavente family retained lawyer and fellow Radical Party member Raúl Rettig. See "Juicio contra INDAP," *El Heraldo*, February 17, 1968. After the Pinochet dictatorship, Rettig was the lead author of Chile's truth commission report.

21. "Graves incidentes en La Primera de Longaví," *Quiubo Compadre* (second half of May 1968): 16.

22. "Grupos agricultores se tomó oficinas de CORA en Linares," *El Heraldo*, September 3, 1969; "Latifundista prepotente se apoderó de oficina de CORA," *Quiubo Compadre* (first half of September 1969): 2; and "Matonesca ocupación de oficinas CORA,"*Quiubo Compadre* (second half of September 1969): 10. A few months later, another CORA office in Linares, located in the town of Parral, was torched along with two INDAP automobiles. See "Criminal atentado contra oficinas de INDAP en Parral," *Quiubo Compadre* (April 1970): 10.

23. Secretaría de Consejo de la CORA, "No. 92—La Piedad," August 29, 1969, Expedientes de Expropiación, "La Piedad," ficha 140, carpeta 66, nos. 92–95, Archivo Servicio Agrícola y Ganadero (SAG), Archivo de la ex-Corporación de Reforma Agraria (Ex-CORA); and CORA, "Acuerdo 750," August 29, 1969, Expedientes de Expropiación, "La Piedad," ficha 140, carpeta 66, nos. 121–121, Archivo SAG, Archivo ex-CORA.

24. "La oligarquía es la culpable," *Quiubo Compadre* (May 1970): 8–9; "Cómo lo mataron?," *Quiubo Compadre* (May 1970): 9; and "La gran causa de Hernán Mery: Luchar por la reforma agraria," *Quiubo Compadre* (May 1970): 16. The state's public

accounts of its confrontations with the Benavente family frequently mention payments that were given to loyalists to "buy" support. Such bribes included special plots of land for campesinos who rejected rural unionization efforts, so they could grow their own crops. See "'Pese a las amenazas,' seguiremos con una reforma agraria sin violencias," *Quiubo Compadre* (second half of September 1969): 11.

25. On landowners' early attempts to coexist with the UP, see "Nuestra revolución constructiva," *El Campesino* (August 1971): 14–15; and "Necesidad de definir las reglas del juego," *El Campesino* (November 1970): 16–17. See also Oscar Oszlak, *La trama oculta del poder: Reforma agraria y comportamiento politico de los terratenientes chilenos, 1958–1973* (Santiago: LOM Ediciones, 2016), 268.

26. Ricardo Costabal E., "La cria-engorda del pollo broiler," *El Campesino* (December 1970): 48–75.

27. "La SNA en Cuba," *El Campesino* (January 1971): 14–17.

28. Tinsman notes that in 1972, "a year of record labor strikes and land seizures," Chile actually exported "record tons of fruit, more than at any other time in its history." Tinsman, *Buying into the Regime*, 43–44.

29. "The Mapuche Land Takeover at Rucalán: Interviews with Peasants and Landowners," in Hutchison et al., *Chile Reader*, 386–392; and "Fundo Rucalán, fue puesto en marcha por los campesinos," *Poder Campesino 2* (second half of January 1971): 14.

30. "Mapuche Land Takeover at Rucalán," 391.

31. "Defiant Chilean Peasants Are Seizing More Farms," *New York Times*, February 18, 1971.

32. The rapprochement between Chile's rural elite and the Allende government broke in the spring of 1971 when Allende refused, at the eleventh hour, to participate in Chile's Feria Internacional de Santiago (Santiago International Fair, FISA), the annual agricultural exposition that the SNA and other agricultural trade groups organized to celebrate the agrarian sector. In the wake of this public dustup, the SNA actively pursued a more confrontational position toward the Allende government. See Oscar Oszlak, *La trama oculta del poder: Reforma agraria y comportamiento politico de los terratenientes chilenos, 1958–1973* (Santiago: LOM Ediciones, 2016), 286–287.

33. Sáenz Terpelle, "Quichamahuida y Calatayud," 340.

34. Sáenz Terpelle, "Quichamahuida y Calatayud," 340.

35. Hernán Millas, *Anatomía de un fracaso: La experiencia socialista chilena* (Santiago: Empresa Editora Zig-Zag, 1973), 81–83.

36. Millas, *Anatomía de un fracaso*. Sáenz also describes the process of expropriation in her interview with Arancibia Clavel and Novoa Mackenna. See *Una mujer de la frontera*, 131–132.

37. Arancibia Clavel and Novoa Mackenna, *Una mujer de la frontera*, 130–131.

38. Meller, *Un siglo de economía política chilena*, 127.

39. On the rollout of Chile's yearlong "battle of production," see "La batalla de 1971: Aumentar la producción," *Poder Campesino* (second half of March 1971): 4–5.

See also "Compromiso para producir más firmaron campesinos y gobierno," *Poder Campesino* (second half of March 1971): 6. On food import numbers in the Chilean fall of 1972, see "Espectacular aumento de importaciones alimenticias," *La Tercera de la Hora*, June 2, 1972. Many of the products mentioned by Matte were the same ones Allende himself had invoked as symbols of Chile's overdependence on foreign foodstuffs. "Chile cannot continue as a country that must import each year $160 million worth of meat, wheat, lard, butter and vegetable oils, when there is enough good land to feed twice our population," Allende told the *New York Times* shortly after his 1970 victory. See "The Chileans Have Elected a Revolution," *New York Times*, November 1, 1970.

40. "'Habrá producción de alimentos si la paz vuelve a los campos,'" *La Tercera de la Hora*, August 24, 1972. While large landowners affiliated with associations like the SNA attacked the UP for its inability to boost production, Brian Loveman notes that significant opposition to the UP's approach to agrarian reform also emerged within some peasant and small landowner communities. Loveman, "Unidad Popular in the Countryside: Ni Razón, Ni Fuerza," *Latin American Perspectives* 1, no. 2 (Summer 1974): 154.

41. Consejo Nacional de Alimentación, "Alimentación para Chile: Drama y soluciones," *El Campesino* (August 1973): 7. Estimated agricultural production figures compiled by the Chilean agricultural historian José Garrido Rojas in 1973 suggest that production levels in 1972–73 were lower than in 1971–72 for twelve of fourteen key food crops. José Garrido Rojas, "Origen y alcances de la crisis alimenticia," in *Fuerzas armadas y seguridad nacional*, ed. Pablo Baroana et al. (Santiago: Ediciones Portada, 1973), 174.

42. Braun et al. *Economía chilena*, 40–41.

43. "Las cifras de importación de trigo," *El Heraldo*, November 26, 1972.

44. Cited in Pablo Baroana Urzúa, Martín Costabal Llona, and Álvaro Vial Gaete, *Mil días, mil por ciento: La economía chilena durante el gobierno de Allende* (Santiago: Universidad Finis Terrae, 1993), 81.

45. "Entrevista gremial: Benjamín Matte," *El Campesino* (April 1973): 17.

46. "Chile's Middle Class a Willing Force in Move to Left," *New York Times*, October 26, 1970.

47. Winn, *La revolución chilena*, 59.

48. "Carta abierta al señor Ministro de Economía," August 31, 1971, reprinted in *Revista Oficial del Comercio Detallista y de la Pequeña Industria de Chile* (August–September 1971): n.p. This letter was also reprinted in its entirety in the memoirs of Rafael Cumsille Zapapa, the then-president of the small retailers' association. See Cumsille Zapapa. *Recordando . . . Mi vida: De Don Arturo Alessandri Palma a Don Ricardo Lagos Escobar* (Santiago: Editorial Publival, 2005), 69–74. As evidence of the amicable early relationship between the UP and the small business community, see Cumsille Zapapa's discussion of collaboration between UP officials and merchants in commemorating Chile's "Día Nacional del Comercio" in June 1971. "Discurso pronunciado por el Presidente de la Confederación del Comercio

Detallista y la Pequeña Industria, don Rafael Cumsille Z.," *Revista Oficial del Comercio Detallista y de la Pequeña Industria de Chile* (June–July 1971): 1–2.

49. "Carta abierta al señor Ministro de Economía."

50. Victor González V., "Los abastecimientos," *La Tercera de la Hora*, August 14, 1971; "Nacionales presentaron la acusación contra Vuskovic," *La Tercera de la Hora*, September 9, 1971; "Rechazada acusación contra P. Vuskovic," *La Tercera de la Hora*, September 16, 1971; and "Jefes de minoristas parten en gira del sur," *La Tercera de la Hora*, September 17, 1971.

51. "'Detallistas' piden que se defina Pedro Vuskovic," *La Tercera de la Hora*, September 2, 1971.

52. "Comerciantes plantearon inquietudes a Vuskovic," *La Tercera de la Hora*, October 21, 1971.

53. "La importancia de la Central Nacional de Abastecimiento y Distribución," *Revista Oficial del Comercio Detallista y de la Pequeña Industria de Chile* (November 1971–January 1972): 27–29. See also Schatan "El desabastecimiento," 210–211.

54. "El comercio detallista rompe con el Gobierno," *La Tercera de la Hora*, April 20, 1972. See also "Comerciantes denuncian presiones de la DINAC," *La Tercera de la Hora*, April 27, 1972. On the formation and purpose of DINAC, see Jacobo Schatan W., "La Empresa Nacional de Comercialización y Distribución DINAC, S.A.," *Revista Oficial del Comercio Detallista y de la Pequeña Industria de Chile* (August–September 1971): n.p.

55. "El comercio detallista rompe con el Gobierno." See also "La ECA y DINAC," *Revista Oficial del Comercio Detallista y de la Pequeña Industria de Chile* (November 1971–January 1972): 26.

56. "Alerta a los consumidores y al comercio establecido," *La Tercerca de la Hora*, May 3, 1972.

57. "La Contraloría suspendió de su cargo a jefe de DIRINCO," *La Tercera de la Hora*, May 20, 1972; and "Camioneros discuten su paro nacional," *La Tercera de la Hora*, May 25, 1972.

58. "Requisados varios negocios céntricos," *La Tercera de la Hora*, June 8, 1972. See also Cumsille Zapapa, *Recordando . . . Mi vida*, 93–103. Chile's "Día Nacional de Comercio" is celebrated every June 6 to honor the life of the nineteenth-century Chilean statesman and small businessman Diego Portales on the day of his death in 1837.

59. "Incomunicado jefe de DIRINCO en Arica," *La Tercera de la Hora*, June 13, 1972.

60. "Investigan irregularidades de un jefe de DIRINCO en Valdivia," *La Tercera de la Hora*, July 19, 1972.

61. On the death of Aguilar García, see Cumsille Zapapa, *Recordando . . . Mi vida*, 105–109. See "120 mil comerciantes no abrirán en el día de hoy," *La Tercera de la Hora*, August 21, 1972; and "Gobierno decretó Zona de Emergencia," *La Tercera de la Hora,* August 22, 1972.

62. Cusmille Zapapa, *Recordando . . . Mi vida*, 83.

63. This shift reflects what food historian Sidney Mintz identifies as the tension between competing demands for regulation and individual choice. "[D]emocratic governments must struggle over food issues because, among other things, they are obliged to protect their citizens from harm, but can interfere only at some political risk with citizens' rights to buy as they wish," Mintz, "Food and Eating," 27–28.

64. Power, *Right-Wing Women*, 79–90. See also Baldez, *Why Women Protest*, 35–38. As Power notes, a similar campaign occurred against Allende in 1970, this one led not by the Christian Democrats but rather by Jorge Alessandri and the right-wing PN. See Power, *Right-Wing Women*, 126–137.

65. Power, *Right-Wing Women*, 83.

66. For participant accounts of these "mourning" marches, see María Correa, *La guerra de las mujeres* (Santiago: Editorial Universidad Técnica del Estado, 1974); and Teresa Donoso, *La epopeya de las ollas vacías* (Santiago: Editora Nacional Gabriela Mistral, 1974). For secondary accounts, see Baldez, *Why Women Protest*, 57–62; and Power, *Right-Wing Women*, 142.

67. Lisa Baldez notes that estimates of the crowd size vary greatly, but crowds most likely included around five thousand protestors. Baldez, *Why Women Protest*, 57–62

68. See "Women Lead the Opposition to Allende," 408.

69. For more participant accounts of the march, see Correa, *La guerra de las mujeres*. See also Donoso, *La epopeya de las ollas vacías*. For secondary accounts, see Baldez, *Why Women Protest*, 77–83; Power, *Right-Wing Women*, esp. 147–156; and Trumper, *Ephemeral Histories*, 43–64.

70. Power, *Right-Wing Women*, 165–166.

71. Carmen Puelma, "Las ollas vacías eran ... algo más," *Eva*, February 11–17, 1972, 36–41.

72. See Trumper, *Ephemeral Histories*, 46–47. As Trumper notes, organizers' calls to protest explicitly tried to "disassociate themselves from the posters, paintbrushes, and protests of the left" by encouraging women to bring empty pots or baskets to the demonstration instead of political placards. Organizers also noted that, unlike most marches, there would be no speeches to close the demonstration, just the sound of banging pots.

73. "Acordada formación del Frente Nacional de Actividad Privada," *La Tercera de la Hora*, December 5, 1971; and "Solidaridad del área privada," *La Tercera de la Hora*, December 6, 1971.

74. For examples of FRENAP's propaganda, see Santiago's *La Tercera de la Hora* in March and April 1972. For instance, see "El almacenero no tiene la culpa," *La Tercera de la Hora*, March 18, 1972; "El taxista no tiene la culpa," *La Tercera de la Hora*, March 19, 1972; "El farmacéutico no tiene la culpa," *La Tercera de la Hora*, March 21, 1972; and "El empleado no tiene la culpa," *La Tercera de la Hora*, April 8, 1972.

75. Power, *Right-Wing Women*, 173–174; and Baldez, *Why Women Protest*, 99–102.

76. Power, *Right-Wing Women*, 196–204; and Baldez, *Why Women Protest*, 102–104.

77. For example, "Productos del Mar," *Eva*, January 7–13, 1972, 80–83; "Cocina sin carne," *Eva*, January 7–13, 1972, 84–85; "Pollo . . . si es que encuentra," *Eva*, January 28–February 3, 80–83; and "Aun tenemos mariscos y frutas," *Eva*, February 4–10, 1972, 84–85.

78. "En Chile es pecado comer carne," *La Tercera de la Hora*, February 19, 1972.

79. Centro de Estudios Socioecónomicos-Facultad de Ciencias Económicas-Universidad de Chile, "Patrones socio-culturales de la población a la sustitución de alimentos—Informe preliminar," 1 (July 1966): 12. The cited figure includes those who said they would "easily accept" eating fresh merluza instead of fresh beef and those who said they would just simply "accept" said substitution.

80. "Pesca soviética en Chile"; "Hacia el consumo dirigido"; and "Escasez de merluza fresca." See also "La merluza tiene la palabra," *La Tercera de la Hora*, February 28, 1972; "Comerciantes acordaron no vender la merluza," *La Tercera de la Hora*, March 10, 1972; and Centro de Estudios Socioecónomicos, "Patrones socio-culturales," 10.

81. Centro de Estudios Socioecónomicos, "Patrones socio-culturales," 10. An additional problem with frozen fish was that its typical form of preparation, frying, required significant amounts of scarce, expensive cooking oil plus eggs, flour, and often beer. As such, it was perceived as uneconomical and wasteful.

82. The most prominent example was the Export-Import Bank's rejection of a relatively standard US$20 million loan request to finance the purchase of three new Boeing aircraft for Chile's state-owned airline, LAN. See "U.S. Aid: The Carrot and the Stick," in North American Congress on Latin America, *New Chile*, 45–46. See also Kornbluh, *Pinochet File*, 85.

83. Private lending fell most drastically after the government's November 1971 decision to suspend payments on its foreign debts. Up until that point, a few major banks had continued to lend to Allende's government. Robert J. Alexander, *The Tragedy of Chile* (Westport, CT: Greenwood Press, 1978), 223–224.

84. The World Bank, which had contributed US$275 million in loans to Chile from 1960 to 1970, also denied three loans to Allende during his presidency. See Kornbluh, *Pinochet File*, 84.

85. Kornbluh, *Pinochet File*, 83–87.

86. Select Committee to Study Governmental Operations with Respect to Intelligence Activities, *Covert Action in Chile, 1963–1973* (Washington, DC: US Government Printing Office, 1975), 2, 10, 30.

87. For an excellent recent account of the Bosses' Strike, see Trumper, *Ephemeral Histories*, 65–92.

88. "Cómo les falló todo recurren al sabotaje," *Puro Chile*, October 26, 1972.

89. "Comerciante quemó 200 kilos de carne," *Puro Chile*, October 26, 1972.

90. María de los Angeles Crummett, "El Poder Feminino: The Mobilization against Socialism in Chile," *Latin American Perspectives* 4, no. 4 (1977): 106.

91. Crummett, "El Poder Feminino," 106.

92. Carmen Puelma, "Plan de Acción Femenino," *Eva*, October 20–26, 1972, 47.

93. Frustration with the JAP is notable in the opposition's list of demands, known as the *pliego de Chile* (the demands of Chile), issued on October 21, 1972. The pliego demanded "immediate termination of the controlling actions of the JAPs," calling the organization "totalitarian" in nature. For excerpts of the demands, see Chilean Business and Professional Associations, "So That Chile Can Renew Its March Forward," in Hutchison et al., *Chile Reader*, 410–414.

94. During and after the October Strike, frustration with the ineffectiveness of the JAP and other state food agencies emerged for the first time in traditional strongholds of the organized left, like the working-class parish of San Miguel and the peripheral neighborhood of Población Caro. See "Persecución de la JAP denuncian comerciantes," *La Tercera de la Hora*, October 27, 1972. See also "Comerciantes repudiaron a la JAP en Población Caro," *La Tercera de la Hora*, November 6, 1972.

95. "Llaman a organizar la Resistencia contra racionamiento de alimentos," *La Tercera de la Hora*, January 12, 1973.

96. "Oposición llama a resistir las medidas del Gobierno," *La Tercera de la Hora*, January 13, 1973.

97. Carmen Puelma, "¿Sobrevivirán los supermercados?," *Eva*, October 20–26, 1972, 18–21, cited in Frens-String, "Communists, Commissars, and Consumers," 496. For analysis of modern supermarkets in Chile, see Bennett, *Government's Role in Retail Marketing*, 37–40.

98. For a good summary of Bardón's career and intellectual development, see Pablo Baroana, Hernán Felipe Errázuriz, and Cristián Larroulet, *Álvaro Bardón: Un libertario original* (Santiago: El Mercurio-Aguilar, 2008).

99. Álvaro Bardón, "Un nuevo récord chileno," *El Mercurio* (Santiago), May 29, 1971, reprinted in Álvaro Bardón Muñoz, *Una experiencia económica fallida: Crónicas sobre el Gobierno de la Unidad Popular* (Santiago: Universidad Finis Terrae, 1993), 2–9.

100. Bardón, "Un nuevo récord chileno," 3.

101. For an early assessment of competing analyses of inflation, see Baer, "Inflation Controversy in Latin America."

102. On the rise of monetarist explanations of inflation, see John H. Coatsworth, "Structures, Endowments, and Institutions in the Economic History of Latin America," *Latin American Research Review* 40, no. 3 (2005): 134. In Bardón's view, bias against the monetarist position "reached such an extreme point" during the early 1970s that some Allende sympathizers "began to propose a sort of cultural revolution, *a la chilena*," in the field of economics—a revolution that included discarding entirely the tenants of monetarist approaches. Álvaro Bardón, "El fracaso de una política económica," *El Mercurio* (Santiago), December 18, 1971, in *Una experiencia económica fallida*, 20.

103. Juan Gabriel Valdés, *Pinochet's Economists: The Chicago School in Chile* (Cambridge, UK: Cambridge University Press, 1995), 249.

104. Patricia Arancibia Clavel and Francisco Balart Páez, *Sergio de Castro: El arquitecto del modelo económico chileno* (Santiago: Editorial Biblioteca Americana, 2007), 149.

105. Arancibia Clavel and Balart Páez, *Sergio de Castro*, 152.

106. Álvaro Bardón, "Cómo superar la crisis económica," *El Mercurio* (Santiago), November 18, 1972, in *Una experiencia económica fallida*, 127.

107. For the conservative view of the UP, which maintained that the Allende government's economic policies represented the culmination of some fifty years of legal philosophy, see Brahm García, *Propiedad sin libertad*, esp. 225–259.

108. "Guerra a las JAP declaran los pobladores de la DC," *La Tercera de la Hora*, May 11, 1973.

109. "Protesta contra abastecimiento discriminado," *La Tercera de la Hora*, June 8, 1973; and "Concentración contra el hambre hicieron vecinos," *La Tercera de la Hora*, June 11, 1973.

110. "Cien mil campesinos iniciaron un paro," *La Tercera de la Hora*, June 20, 1973. On the state's attempt to create storehouses for wheat and potatoes in mid-1973, see "Estanco del Trigo es la única manera de asegurar abastecimiento nacional," *Poder Campesino* 2 (1973): n.p. See also "Editorial," *Poder Campesino* 6 (1973): 3.

111. Claudio Orrego Vicuña, "Ni pan, ni techo, ni abrigo," *La Tercera de la Hora*, May 23, 1973.

112. On the role of business leaders, economists, and military officials in the conspiracy to oust Allende, see Valdés, *Pinochet's Economists*, 247–252.

113. Arancibia Clavel and Balart Páez, *Sergio de Castro*, 154–157.

EPILOGUE

1. On Miguel Woodward's work in the JAP, see Edward Crouzet, *Sangre sobre La Esmeralda: Sacerdote Miguel Woodward, vida y martirio* (Santiago: Ediciones ChileAmérica, CESOC, 2005), 144–152. The Chinese government famously sent thousands of cans of canned pork to Chile to reduce meat shortages. The canned meat, similar to SPAM, was known in Chile as *chancho chino* (Chinese pork). See Alfredo Lamadrid Ojeda and Mario Gaete Jigins, dirs., *La dieta de la revolución* (Chile, 2009), available via Repositorio HISREDUC, http://repositorio .historiarecienteenlaeducacion.com/items/show/3212.

2. Crouzet, *Sangre sobre La Esmeralda*, 164–181.

3. "El paro y la escasez," *La Tercera de la Hora*, August 18, 1973; and "Van 35 días del paro camionero y aún no surge una solución," *La Tercera de la Hora*, August 30, 1973.

4. "El comercio paralizó por los incumplimientos del Gobierno," *La Tercera de la Hora*, August 10, 1973; "Paro de comerciantes detallistas: 48 horas," *La Tercera de la Hora*, August 21, 1973; and "Al comercio y la opinión pública," *La Tercera de la Hora*, August 28, 1973.

5. "El paro y la escasez."

6. "Con carne de caballo celebramos el '18,'" *La Tercera de la Hora*, August 29, 1973.

7. Salvador Allende Gossens, "Last Words to the Nation," trans. Yoshie Furuhashi, September 11, 1973,www.marxists.org/archive/allende/1973/september/11 .htm.

8. For more on the coup and the violence that followed, including US support, see Kornbluh, *Pinochet File*, esp. chs. 2–3.

9. One such case was that of Allende's agrarian reform guru, Jacques Chonchol. Chonchol was given temporary refuge in the Venezuelan embassy in Santiago three days after the coup. He remained there for nine months before leaving Chile for France in 1974. See Robles Ortiz, *Jacques Chonchol*, 282–293.

10. For Flores and Bitar's reflections on the Chilean economy while at Dawson Island, see Medina, *Cybernetic Revolutionaries*, 229.

11. This figure of fifteen hundred killed in the immediate wake of the coup comes from Peter Winn's excellent synthesis of the Pinochet dictatorship. See Winn, "The Pinochet Era," in Winn, *Victims of the Chilean Miracle*, 19.

12. On the case of Marta Ugarte, see Inter-American Commission on Human Rights, *Third Report on the Situation of Human Rights in Chile*, Chapter 2: The Right to Life, February 11, 1977, www.cidh.org/countryrep/Chile77eng/chap.2 .htm. For Patricio Palma's discussion of Ugarte and her death, see Patricio Palma, interview by Franck Gaudichaud, November 28, 2001, in Gaudichaud, *Poder popular y cordones industriales*, 410–411.

13. Arancibia Clavel and Balart Páez, *Sergio de Castro*, 162.

14. Patricia Arancibia Clavel, *Conversando con Roberto Kelly V.: Recuerdos de una vida* (Santiago: Editorial Biblioteca Americana, 2005), 142, 193.

15. As one of the first directors of the military government's economic planning office, Kelly helped implement market-oriented development policies in Chile during the Pinochet era. See Arancibia Clavel, *Conversando con Roberto Kelly V.*, 189–194, 263–268.

16. Cumsille Zapapa, *Recordando . . . Mi vida*, 138–139.

17. "Misión cumplida," *Revista Oficial del Comercio Detallista y de la Pequeña Industria de Chile* (October 1973): 3. For a complete list of the demands issued by Chile's small retailers' association, see "Acuerdo Confederación-Gobierno Militar," *Revista Oficial del Comercio Detallista y de la Pequeña Industria de Chile* (October 1973): 13, 15.

18. Cumsille Zapapa, *Recordando . . . Mi vida*, 140–142.

19. Cumsille Zapapa, *Recordando . . . Mi vida*, 141. Cumsille's words illustrate the common, military-promoted depiction of the Pinochet regime "saving" the distressed female consumers of Chile. As Heidi Tinsman has written, throughout the dictatorship's seventeen years in power, the regime consistently "invoked the specter of female outrage at consumer scarcity under Allende as justification for the coup." Tinsman, *Buying into the Regime*, 65.

20. Sáenz Terpelle, "Quichamahuida y Calatayud," 343. It is important to note the deeply classed nature of these memories. In contrast to the views of someone like

Carmen Sáenz, Alison J. Bruey has demonstrated how food insecurity became dire in poor shantytowns immediately after the coup. Describing the situation in the población of La Legua, Bruey writes that "the days fell into a pattern: wait for news, host visitors and refugees from outside the neighborhood, talk politics, and search for food." Bruey, *Bread, Justice, and Liberty*, 78.

21. Gloria Urgelles, "De las cacerolas a la reconstrucción," *Eva* (second half of October 1973): 13.

22. Sáenz Terpelle, , "Quichamahuida y Calatayud," 337–338.

23. "Entrevistas gremiales," *El Campesino* (September 1973): 11

24. Joseph Collins highlights the damning nature of the Pinochet dictatorship's Decree 208, in particular. He notes that the decree "disqualified from ever owning land all those who have *ever* participated in strikes, land seizures, and other conflicts with patrones." According to Collins, many large landowners collaborated with state intelligence agents to create lists of individuals who supported agrarian reform. See Collins, *Agrarian Reform and Counterreform in Chile* (San Francisco, CA: Institute for Food and Development Policy, 1979), 7.

25. See Thomas G. Sanders, "Counterreform in the Chilean Campo," American Universities Field Staff Reports, No. 32, 1980, 5, UWM, SML, LTCF, CH 7.5 S15. Sanders notes that Chile's sugar beet industry, which could not compete with cheap foreign sugar imports, was a major victim of the military government's new approach to trade and agriculture.

26. Sanders, "Counterreform in the Chilean Campo."

27. For a useful distinction between "food security" and "food sovereignty" that is drawn from the Mexican context, see Alyshia Gálvez, *Eating NAFTA: Trade, Food Policies, and the Destruction of Mexico* (Oakland: University of California Press, 2018), 81–82.

28. Gunder Frank, *Economic Genocide in Chile*, 62, cited in Naomi Klein, *The Shock Doctrine: The Rise of Disaster Capitalism* (New York: Metropolitan Books, 2007), 79. According to Gunder Frank, the inflation rate during the dictatorship's first year may have been closer to 500 percent overall, reaching as high as 1000 percent for certain essential goods, including many staple foods.

29. Cited in Orlando Letelier, "The Chicago Boys in Chile: Economic Freedom's Awful Toll," *Nation*, August 28, 1976.

30. While the Pinochet government froze automatic wage adjustments for blue collar workers almost immediately, on September 29, 1973, Pinochet's finance minister, Admiral Lorenzo Gotuzzo, announced a temporary, emergency initiative that subsidized essential popular consumer items for Chile's poorest citizens. This policy represented one point of difference between "moderate" opponents of the UP and their more economically conservative counterparts, who embraced orthodox monetarist prescriptions. See "Remuneraciones: Política de saneamiento y sacrificio," *Revista Oficial del Comercio Detallista y de la Pequeña Industria de Chile* (October 1973): 15.

31. Jorge González M., "Memorandum, Ref: Autoriza funcionamiento de vigilantes," December 18, 1973, ARNAD, CORFO-ECORFO, FSOCOAGRO, vol. 370;

Col. Jorge Domingo Vásquez Vásquez, "Memorandum, Ref. Establece niveles salarios mensuales a partir del 1 de octubre de 1973," October 12, 1973, ARNAD, CORFO-ECORFO, FSOCOAGRO, vol. 342; Jorge González, "Circular, Ref: Normas Transitorias Relativas a la Actividad Sindical," January 9, 1974, ARNAD, CORFO-ECORFO, FSOCOAGRO, vol. 342; Jorge González M., "Memorandum, Ref. Reformas al contrato de trabajo," February 25, 1974, 1–2, ARNAD, CORFO-ECORFO, FSOCOAGRO, vol. 37; and Miguel Ponce Vergara, "Memorandum, Ref: Utiles y materiales de Trabajo," March 20, 1974, ARNAD, CORFO-ECORFO, FSOCOAGRO, vol. 342.

32. Winn, *Weavers of Revolution*, 249. One area in which the military regime did make significant macroeconomic adjustments during its first few years in power was food imports. Between 1974 and 1975, the military cut Chile's national food import bill from US$561 million to US$361 million. While this diminished the country's trade deficit and eased its foreign exchange crisis, from a social perspective, the decision to reduce food imports had devastating consequences. Since it was not accompanied by any noticeable increases in domestic agrarian production, a reduction in imports of basic consumer goods led to the reemergence of hunger in many communities. Families living on the minimum wage were unable to consume more than one thousand calories and fifteen grams of protein per person per day in the mid-1970s, less than half the minimum satisfactory level of consumption established by the World Health Organization. Contrary to Cumsille's narration of the immediate post-Allende period, what many Chileans experienced after the coup was, to quote former Allende minister Orlando Letelier, "hunger and deprivation" on a scale "never before seen." Letelier, "Chicago Boys in Chile."

33. Mariana Schkolnik, *Sobrevivir en la población José M. Caro y en Lo Hermida* (Santiago: Programa de Economía del Trabajo, Academia de Humanismo Cristiano, 1986), 99–100, 103.

34. Schkolnik, *Sobrevivir en la población José M. Caro y en Lo Hermida*, 115.

35. See Tinsman, *Buying into the Regime*, 80–81. Sociologist Joel Stillerman's work has explicitly looked at the problems, contradictions, and social meanings produced through consumption during the Pinochet era. See, for example, "Gender, Class, and Generational Contexts for Consumption in Contemporary Chile," *Journal of Consumer Culture* 4, no. 51 (2004): 51–78.

36. Arancibia Clavel, *Conversando con Roberto Kelly V.*, 265.

37. Carola Fuentes and Rafael Valdeavellano, dir., *Chicago Boys* (Santiago: CNTV/CORFO/La Ventana Cine, 2015).

38. "Chile: Doce millones de consumidores," *Revista del Consumidor* 2, no. 7 (July 15, 1985): 2.

39. "Chile: Doce millones de consumidores," cited in Frens-String, "Communists, Commissars, and Consumers," 496.

40. "15 de marzo: Día Mundial del Consumidor," *Revista del Consumidor* 6, no. 54 (March 1988): 3.

41. Álvaro Bardón Muñoz, "El derecho humano a consumir," *El Mercurio* (Santiago), December 18, 1986, in *Chile bajo la pluma de Bardón: Política, economía,*

sociedad—Las mejores columnas de Álvaro Bardón publicadas en "El Mercurio" (Santiago: Ediciones Universidad Finis Terrae, 2008), 55–58.

42. Joana Ramiro (@joanaramiroUK), "Neoliberalism was born in Chile and will die in Chile (h/t: @saramsalem), Twitter, October 28, 2019, 6:10 a.m., https://twitter.com/JoanaRamiroUK/status/1188760016460890112. As I conclude writing this book, Chileans are again highlighting inequitable access to basic food staples as a defining failure of Chile's neoliberal order amid the COVID-19 pandemic. See, for example, "Coronavirus: Chile Protestors Clash with Police over Lockdowns," BBC News, May 19, 2020, www.bbc.com/news/world-latin-america-52717402?fbclid=IwAR08WfHqBtMFJm6eWFEiA1_1To8hBh_32IRvHto7269vY3lVYBau NEEMIvU.

BIBLIOGRAPHY

ARCHIVES CONSULTED

Chilean Archives

Archivo Histórico del Ministerio de Relaciones Exteriores—Santiago (ARREE)
    Fondo Hernán Santa Cruz (FHSC)
    Fondo Histórico (FH)
Archivo Nacional de la Administración—Santiago (ARNAD)
    Archivo de la Corporación de Fomento de la Producción—Empresas CORFO
        Fondo SOCOAGRO (FSOCOAGRO)
    Fondo Ministerio de Agricultura (FMA)
    Fondo Ministerio de Economía (MECO)
        Fondo Servicio Nacional del Consumidor (FSERNAC)
    Fondo Ministerio de Fomento (FMFO)
Archivo Nacional Histórico—Santiago (ANH)
    Fondo Gabriel González Videla (FGGV)
    Fondo Intendencia de Santiago (FIS)
    Fondo Salitre (FSAL)
Archivo Regional de Tarapacá—Iquique (ART)
    Fondo Intendencia de Tarapacá (FITAR)
Archivo Servicio Agrícola y Ganadero—Santiago
    Archivo de la ex-Corporación de Reforma Agraria
Biblioteca Nacional de Chile—Santiago (BNC)
    Colección José Arguedas (CJA)
    Sección Chilena (SC)
    Sección de Revistas (SR)

US Archives

National Archives and Record Administration II—College Park, Maryland (NARA)

Record Group (RG) 59

Record Group (RG) 229

University of Wisconsin, Steenbock Memorial Library—Madison, Wisconsin (UWM, SML)

Land Tenure Center Annual Reports (LTCAR)

Land Tenure Center Files (LTCF)

Other International Archives

International Institute of Social History—Amsterdam (IISH)

Marcelo Segall Rosenmann Collection (MSR)

Marco Rojas Turkowsky Collection (MRT)

NEWSPAPERS, MAGAZINES, AND JOURNALS

Boletín Oficial del Comisariato General de Subsistencias y Precios

Boletín del Ministerio de Higiene, Asistencia, Previsión y Trabajo

Boletín del Ministerio de Salubridad, Previsión y Asistencia Social

Boletín Municipal de la República

Chile Hoy

El Campesino

El Chileno

El Diario Ilustrado

El Ferrocarril

El Heraldo (Linares)

El Mercurio (Santiago)

El Mercurio (Valparaíso)

El Popular (Antofagasta)

El Rebelde

El Siglo

Eva

Federación de Obreros de Imprenta

Fiel

Frente Popular

Industria

La Mujer Nueva

La Opinión

La Tercera de la Hora

New York Times

Panorama Económico

Poder Campesino

Principios

Punto Final

Puro Chile

Quiubo Compadre

Revista Chilena de Higiene y Medicina Preventiva

Revista de Asistencia Social

Revista de la Alimentación Popular

Revista de la Sociedad Médica de Valparaíso

Revista de Medicina y Alimentación

Revista del Consumidor

Revista Médica de Chile

Revista Oficial del Comercio Detallista y de la Pequeña Industria de Chile

The Times (London)

Zig-Zag

DOCUMENT COLLECTIONS, MEMOIRS, REPORTS, SPEECHES, AND OTHER PUBLISHED PRIMARY SOURCES

Ahumada, Jorge. *En vez de la miseria.* Santiago: Editorial del Pacífico, S.A., 1958.

Aliaga Sánchez, Roberto. *Cultivo de remolacha azucarera en Chile: Aspectos generales y su desarrollo en el país.* Santiago: IANSA, 1973.

Allende Gossens, Salvador. "Discurso sobre la propiedad agraria." August 23, 1971. www.marxists.org/espanol/allende/1971/agosto23.htm.

———. *La contradicción de Chile: Régimen de izquierda, política económica de derecho.* Santiago: Talleres Gráficos, 1943.

———. *La realidad médico-social chilena.* Santiago: Editorial Cuarto Propio, 1999. First published 1939.

———. "Last Words to the Nation." Translated by Yoshie Furuhashi. September 11, 1973. www.marxists.org/archive/allende/1973/september/11.htm.

———. "Salitre: Historia trágica; Discurso en la Oficina Salitrera Pedro de Valdivia." February 6, 1971. www.marxists.org/espanol/allende/1971/febrero06.htm.

———. "Speech to the United Nations (Excerpts)." December 4, 1972. www.marxists .org/archive/allende/1972/december/04.htm.

———. "Trabajadores y participación: Discurso en ocasión de celebrarse el Día del Trabajador." May 1, 1972. www.marxists.org/espanol/allende/1972/may001.htm.

Alsworth Ross, Edward. *South of Panama.* New York: Century Company, 1917.

Arancibia Clavel, Patricia. *Conversando con Roberto Kelly V.: Recuerdos de una vida.* Santiago: Editorial Biblioteca Americana, 2005.

Arancibia Clavel, Patricia, and Francisco Balart Páez. *Sergio de Castro: El arquitecto del modelo económico chileno.* Santiago: Editorial Biblioteca Americana, 2007.

Arancibia Clavel, Patricia, and Andrea Novoa Mackenna. *Una mujer de la frontera: Carmen Sáenz Terpelle.* Santiago: Editoral Biblioteca Americana, 2006.

Banco Central de Chile. *Sexta memoria anual presentada a la superintendencia de bancos: Año 1931.* Santiago: Banco Central, 1932.

Barahona, Roberto, and Osvaldo Sotomayor. *El problema de la tuberculosis en Chile.* Santiago: Liga Social de Chile, 1935.

Bardón Muñoz, Álvaro. *Chile bajo la* pluma *de Bardón: Política, economía, sociedad— Las mejores columnas de Álvaro Bardón publicadas en "El Mercurio".* Santiago: Ediciones Universidad Finis Terrae, 2008.

———. *Una experiencia económica fallida: Crónicas sobre el Gobierno de la Unidad Popular.* Santiago: Universidad Finis Terrae, 1993.

Baroana, Pablo, Hernán Felipe Errázuriz, and Cristián Larroulet. *Álvaro Bardón: Un libertario original.* Santiago: El Mercurio-Aguilar, 2008.

Baroana Urzúa, Pablo, Martín Costabal Llona, and Álvaro Vial Gaete. *Mil días, mil por ciento: La economía chilena durante el gobierno de Allende.* Santiago: Universidad Finis Terrae, 1993.

Bennett, Peter D. *Government's Role in Retail Marketing of Food Products in Chile.* Austin: University of Texas Press, 1968.

Bitar, Sergio. *Chile, 1970–1973: Asumir la historia para construir el futuro.* Santiago: Pehuén, 1995.

Bitar, Sergio, and Eduardo Moyano. "Redistribución del consumo y transición al socialismo." *Cuadernos de la Realidad Nacional* 11 (January 1972): 25–44.

Braun, Juan, Matías Braun, Ignacio Briones, José Díaz, Rolf Lüders, and Gert Wagner. *Economía chilena, 1810–1995: Estadísticas históricas.* Documento de Trabajo No. 187. Santiago: Pontificia Universidad Católica de Chile—Instituto de Economía, 2000.

Bravo Elizondo, Pedro, ed. *Santa María de Iquique 1907: Documentos para su historia.* Santiago: Ediciones del Litoral, 1993.

Carrasco, Gamaliel, and Andrés Vergara. *Programa de fomento pecuario y desarrollo campesino de las colonias y asentamientos de la Corporación de la Reforma Agraria.* Santiago: CORA, 1970.

Casassus, Carlos. *El flagelo de la tuberculosis.* Santiago: Sección Bienestar de los Ferrocarriles del Estado, 1935.

Chacón, Juan. *El problema agrario y el Partido Comunista—Informe presentado ante el XI Congreso Nacional del Partido Comunista de Chile; Santiago, 19–25 December*

1939. Santiago: Ediciones del Comité Central del Partido Comunista de Chile, 1940.

Chile: Su futura alimentación. Ciclo de conferencias organizadas por la Dirección General de Bibliotecas, Archivos y Museos. Santiago: Editorial Nascimento, 1963.

Chonchol, Jacques. *El desarrollo de América Latina y la reforma agraria*. Santiago: Editorial del Pacífico, S.A., 1964.

Cobó, Julián. *Yo vi nacer y morir los pueblos salitreros*. Santiago: Editorial Quimantú, 1971.

Consejo Nacional para la Alimentación y Nutrición (CONPAN). *Chile: Estadísticas básicas en alimentación y nutrición; 1969–1978*. Santiago: Ministerio de Salud, 1980.

Corporación de Fomento de la Producción (CORFO). *Cinco años de labor, 1939–1943*. Santiago: CORFO, 1944.

———. *Geografía Económica de Chile*. Vol. 2. Santiago: Imprenta Universitaria, 1950.

Corporación de Fomento de la Producción (CORFO) and Ministerio de Agricultura. *Plan Agrario*. N.p., 1954.

Corporación de Reforma Agraria. *Qué sería del campesino sin su mujer?* Santiago: CORA, 1968.

Correa, María. *La guerra de las mujeres*. Santiago: Editorial Universidad Técnica del Estado, 1974.

Corvalán, Luis. *El gobierno de Salvador Allende*. Santiago: LOM Ediciones, 2003.

Cousiño Vicuña, Angélica, and María Angélica Ovalle Gana. *Reforma agraria chilena: Testimonios de sus protagonistas*. Santiago de Chile: Memoriter, 2013.

Crouzet, Edward. *Sangre sobre La Esmeralda: Sacerdote Miguel Woodward, vida y martirio*. Santiago: Ediciones ChileAmérica, CESOC, 2005.

Cruz-Coke, Eduardo. *Discursos: Política, economía, salubridad, habitación, relaciones exteriores agricultura*. Santiago: Editorial Nascimento, 1946.

———. *Plan de gobierno de Chile para mejorar la alimentación del pueblo*. Santiago: Consejo de Alimentación, 1937.

Cruz-Coke, Eduardo, and Marta Lagos Cruz-Coke. *Testimonios*. Santiago: Procultura Fundación, 2015.

Cumsille Zapapa, Rafael. *Recordando . . . Mi vida: De Don Arturo Alessandri Palma a Don Ricardo Lagos Escobar*. Santiago: Editorial Publival, 2005.

Donoso, Teresa. *La epopeya de las ollas vacías*. Santiago: Editora Nacional Gabriela Mistral, 1974.

Elgueta Guerin, Manuel. *Memorias de vida: 1902–1983*. Santiago: n.p., 1986.

Empresa de Comercio Agrícola. *Estudio de la comercialización de los productos alimenticios en la región geoeconómica del Bío-Bío: Antecedentes Generales de la Región del Bío-Bío*. Santiago: n.p., 1967.

Errázuriz Tagle, Jorge, and Guillermo Eyzaguirre Rouse. *Estudio social: Monografía de una familia obrera de Santiago*. Santiago: Barcelona, 1903.

Farías, Víctor, ed. *La izquierda chilena (1969–1973): Documentos para el estudio de su línea estratégica*. 5 vols. Santiago: Centro de Estudios Públicos, 2000.

Feinberg, Richard E. *The Triumph of Allende: Chile's Legal Revolution*. New York: New American Library, 1972.

Food and Agriculture Organization (FAO). *Evaluación preliminar de los asentamientos de Reforma Agraria de Chile: Aspectos socio-económicos*. Santiago: FAO, ICIRA, 1967.

Gaudichaud, Franck, ed. *Poder popular y cordones industriales: Testimonios sobre el movimiento popular urbano, 1970–1973*. Santiago: LOM Ediciones, 2004.

González Videla, Gabriel. *Memorias*. Vol. 1. Santiago: Editora Nacional Gabriela Mistral, 1974.

———. "Mensaje al Congreso—1947." Santiago: n.p., 1947.

Guzmán, Nicomedes. *La Sangre y la esperanza*. Santiago: Orbe, 1943.

Henfry, Colin, and Bernardo Sorj. *Chilean Voices: Activists Describe Their Experiences of the Popular Unity Period*. Hassocks, UK: Harvester Press, 1977.

Hobsbawm, Eric. *Viva la Revolucion: Revolución on Latin America*. London: Little, Brown 2016.

Hutchison, Elizabeth Quay, Thomas Miller Klubock, Nara B. Milanich, and Peter Winn, eds. *The Chile Reader: History, Culture, Politics*. Durham, NC: Duke University Press, 2014.

Instituto Nacional de Investigación Agrícola (INIA). *Cuarta memoria anual del Instituto de Investigaciones Agropecuarios, 1967–1968*. Santiago: Ministerio de Agricultura, 1968.

———. *Primera memoria anual del Instituto de Investigaciones Agropecuarios, 1964–1965*. Santiago: Ministerio de Agricultura, 1965.

Inter-American Commission on Human Rights. *Third Report on the Situation of Human Rights in Chile*, Chapter 2, "The Right to Life." February 11, 1977. www.cidh.org/countryrep/Chile77eng/chap.2.htm.

Interdepartmental Committee on Nutrition for National Defense. *Chile: Nutrition Survey, March–June 1960*. Washington, DC, April 1961.

Johnson, Dale L., ed. *The Chilean Road to Socialism*. New York: Anchor Books, 1973.

Keller, Carlos. *Cómo salir de la crisis*. Santiago: Editorial Nascimento, 1932.

Labarca, Santiago. "Memorias de Santiago Labarca—La Asamblea Obrera de Alimentación Nacional." *Claridad* 1, no. 9 (1920).

Lamadrid Ojeda, Alfredo, and Mario Gaete Jigins, dirs. *La dieta de la revolución*. Chile, 2009. Repositorio HISREDUC. http://repositorio.historiarecienteenla educacion.com/items/show/3212.

Landa Perroni, Francisco. *El problema de la leche en relación con la alimentación popular en Chile*. Santiago: Imprenta y Litografía Universo, S.A., 1939.

Larraín Bulnes, Lucía. *Manual de cocina: A beneficio de Lourdes*. Santiago: Imprenta Claret, 1913.

Lavín, Joaquín. *Chile, revolución silenciosa*. Santiago: Zig-Zag, 1987.

League of Nations. *The Problem of Nutrition: Interim Report of the Mixed Committee on the Problem of Nutrition*. Vol. 1. Geneva: League of Nations, 1936.

Letelier, Orlando. "The Chicago Boys in Chile: Economic Freedom's Awful Toll." *Nation*, August 28, 1976.

Mardones Restat, Jorge. *Aspecto médico de la aplicación de la Ley de Medicina Preventiva*. Santiago: Imprenta Universo, 1937.

———. *Efectos sociales de la Ley de Medicina Preventiva*. Santiago: Empresa Editora Zig-Zag, 1937.

Mardones Restat, Jorge, and Lidia Contreras. *Regímenes alimenticios para restaurantes económicos de adultos*. Santiago: Imprenta Leblanc, 1939.

Mardones Restat, Jorge, and Ricardo Cox. *La alimentación en Chile: Estudios del Consejo Nacional de Alimentación*. Santiago: Imprenta Universitaria, 1942.

Martell, Duquesa. *Cocina de Cuaresma*. 2nd ed. Santiago: Guillermo E. Miranda, 1904.

Martínez, Carlos Alberto. *Hacia la reforma agraria*. Santiago de Chile: Caja de Colonización Agrícola, 1939.

Martner, Gonzalo, ed. *El pensamiento económico del Gobierno de Allende*. Santiago: Editorial Universitaria, 1971.

McCaa, Robert, ed. *Chile: XI Censo de población (1940); Recopilación de cifras publicadas por la Dirección de Estadísticas y Censos*. Santiago: Centro Latinoamericano de Demografía, 1972.

Milos, Pedro, ed. *Chile 1971: El primer año del gobierno de la Unidad Popular*. Santiago: Ediciones Universidad Alberto Hurtado, 2013.

Morse Woodbury, Robert. *Food Consumption and Dietary Surveys in the Americas: Report Presented by the International Labour Office to the Eleventh Pan American Sanitary Conference, Rio de Janeiro, 7–18 September 1942*. Montreal: International Labour Office, 1942.

Muñoz, Heraldo. *The Dictator's Shadow: Life under Augusto Pinochet*. New York: Basic Books, 2008.

Murphy, Edward, ed. *Historias poblacionales: Hacia una memoria incluyente*. Santiago: CEDECO: World Vision, 2004.

Nehgme Rodríguez, Elías. *La economía nacional y el problema de las subsistencias en Chile*. Santiago: Imprenta Condor, 1943.

North American Congress on Latin America (NACLA), ed. *New Chile*. 2nd ed. New York: NACLA, 1973.

Palma, Arturo, and Juan Varas. *Efecto de la política de restricciones de carne de vacuno en el consumo y producción de sustitutos*. Santiago: Servicio Agrícola y Ganadero, 1968.

Palma, Patricio. Oral presentation at Seminario "Chile 1972". Universidad Alberto Hurtado, Santiago, December 6, 2012.

Poblete Troncoso, Moisés. *El subconsumo en América del Sur: Alimentos, vestuario y vivienda*. Santiago: Editorial Nascimento, 1946.

Prout, William. "On the Ultimate Composition of Simple Alimentary Substances." *Philosophical Transactions of the Royal Society of London* 117 (1827): 255–388.

Quilapayún. "A comer merluza" (single). Dicap, 1972.

Recabarren, Luis Emilio. *Ricos y pobres a través de un siglo de la vida repúblicana*. Santiago: LOM Ediciones, 2010. First published 1910.

Reid, William. *Nitrate Fields of Chile*. 4th ed. Baltimore, MD: Sun Book and Job Printing Office, 1935.

Reyes, Raquel. "Encuesta de nutrición a partir de censos agropecuarios y de población." Undergraduate thesis, Universidad de Chile, 1933.

Rios, Evaristo. *Socialismo y algunas fases de su doctrina*. Santiago: Imprenta el Progreso, 1919.

Robles Ortiz, Claudio. *Jacques Chonchol: Un Cristiano revolucionario en la política chilena del siglo XX*. Santiago: Ediciones Universidad Finis Terrae, 2016.

Romero, Alberto. *La viuda del conventillo*. Buenos Aires: Biblo Editorial, 1930.

Russell, William Howard. *A Visit to Chile and the Nitrate Fields of Tarapacá*. London: J. S. Virtue, 1890.

Salas Lavaqui, Manuel. *Trabajos y antecedentes presentados al Supremo Gobierno de Chile por la Comisión Consultiva del Norte*. Santiago: Imprenta Cervantes, 1908.

Santa Maria, Julio V. *La alimentación de nuestro pueblo*. Santiago: Talleres San Vicente, 1935.

Schatan, Jacobo. "El desabastecimiento: La conspiración de EE.UU. que derrotó a la UP." In *Salvador Allende: Presencia en la ausencia*, edited by Miguel Lawner, Hernán Soto, and Jacobo Schatan, 207–224. Santiago: LOM Ediciones, 2008.

Schkolnik. Mariana. *Sobrevivir en la población José M. Caro y en Lo Hermida*. Santiago: Programa de Economía del Trabajo, Academia de Humanismo Cristiano, 1986.

Select Committee to Study Governmental Operations with Respect to Intelligence Activities. *Covert Action in Chile, 1963–1973*. Washington, DC: US Government Printing Office, 1975.

Semper, E., and E. Michels. *La industria del salitre en Chile*. Santiago de Chile: Imprenta Barcelona, 1908.

Subercaseaux, Julio. *Reminiscencias*. Santiago: Editorial Nascimento, 1976.

Subercaseaux, Ramón. *Memorias de ochtena años*. Santiago: Editorial Nascimento, 1936.

Tagle, María Angélica. "La calidad y el valor proteico de la dieta del proletariado chileno." *Revista Médica de Chile* 98 (August 1970): 549–564.

Tapia Soko, Gonzálo, ed. *El derecho de todo ser: Testimonio biográfico del dirigente campesino Manuel Oliveros*. Santiago: Programa Interdisciplinario de Investigaciones en Educación, 1990.

Teitelboim, Volodia. *Un hombre de edad media (Antes del olvido II)*. Santiago: Editorial Sudamericana, 2000.

Torres Moncada, Inés. "Alimentación de las clases populares." Undergraduate thesis, Universidad de Chile, 1938.

Varas, José Miguel. *Chacón*. Santiago: Impresora Horizonte, 1968.

Wallace, Henry. *Century of the Common Man*. New York: Reynal & Hitchcock, 1943.

SECONDARY WORKS

Acevedo Arriaza, Nicolás. "La voz del campo: La política agraria del Partido Comunista de Chile durante el Frente Popular (1936–1940)." *Izquierdas* 13 (August 2012): 63–82.

Adair, Jennifer. *In Search of the Lost Decade: Everyday Rights in Post-Dictatorship Argentina*. Oakland: University of California Press, 2019.

Aguilar-Rodríguez, Sandra. "Cooking Modernity: Nutrition Policies, Class, and Gender in 1940s and 1950s Mexico City." *Americas* 64, no. 2 (October 2007): 177–205.

Alexander, Robert J. *The Tragedy of Chile*. Westport, CT: Greenwood, 1978.

Antezana-Pernet, Corinne. "Mobilizing Women in the Popular Front Era: Feminism, Class, and Politics in the *Movimiento Pro-Emancipación de la Mujer Chilena* (MEMCh), 1935–1950." PhD diss., University of California, Irvine, 1996.

Appadurai, Arjun. "How to Make a National Cuisine: Cookbooks in Contemporary India." *Comparative Studies in Society and History* 30, no. 1 (January 1988): 3–24.

Apple, Rima D. *Vitamania: Vitamins in American Culture*. New Brunswick, NJ: Rutgers University Press, 1996.

Astelerra, Judith. "Land Reform in Chile during Allende's Government." PhD diss, Cornell University, 1975.

Baer, Werner. "The Inflation Controversy in Latin America: A Survey." *Latin American Research Review* 2, no. 2 (Spring 1967): 3–25.

Baldez, Lisa. *Why Women Protest: Women's Movements in Chile*. Cambridge, UK: Cambridge University Press, 2002.

Barnard, Andrew. "Chile." In *Latin America Between the Second World War and the Cold War, 1944–1948*, edited by Leslie Bethell and Ian Roxborough, 66–91. Cambridge, UK: Cambridge University Press, 1992.

Barría Cerón, Jorge. "Chile: La cuestión política y social en 1920–1926," *Annales de la Universidad de Chile* 116 (1959): 56–73.

Bastías Saavedra, Manuel. "Intervención del estado y derechos sociales: Transformaciones en el pensamiento jurídico chileno en la era de la cuestión social, 1880–1925." *Historia* 48, no. 1 (2015): 11–42.

Bauer, Arnold J. *Chilean Rural Society from Spanish Conquest to 1930*. Cambridge, UK: Cambridge University Press, 1975.

———. *Goods, Power, History: Latin America's Material Culture*. Cambridge, UK: Cambridge University Press, 2001.

———. "Industry and the Missing Bourgeoisie: Consumption and Development in Chile, 1850–1950." *Hispanic American Historical Review* 70, no. 2 (May 1990): 227–253.

Bello, Walden. "The Roots and Dynamics of Revolution and Counterrevolution in Chile." PhD diss., Princeton University, 1975.

Bender, Daniel, and Jeffrey M. Pilcher. "Editors' Introduction: Radicalizing the History of Food." *Radical History Review* 110 (2001): 1–7.

Bengoa, José. *Historia rural de Chile central: Crisis y ruptura del poder hacendal*. Santiago: LOM Ediciones, 2015.

———. *Reforma agraria y revuelta campesina: Seguido de un homenaje a los campesinos desaparecidos*. Santiago, LOM Ediciones, 2016.

Bentley, Amy. *Eating for Victory: Food Rationing and the Politics of Domesticity*. Urbana: University of Illinois Press, 1998.

Bergquist, Charles W. "Exports, Labor, and the Left: An Essay on Twentieth-Century Chilean History." Wilson Center Latin America Program Working Papers 97, 1981.

Birchmeier Salgado, Cristián. "'Habrá carne para toda la población': El consumo de carnes como herramienta de igualación social en el proyecto de la Unidad Popular; Santiago, 1970–1973." Undergraduate thesis, Universidad Alberto Hurtado, 2012.

Bockman, Johanna. *Markets in the Name of Socialism: The Left-Wing Origins of Neoliberalism*. Palo Alto, CA: Stanford University Press, 2011.

Brahm Garcia, Enrique. *Propiedad sin libertad: Chile, 1925–1973; Aspectos relevantes en el avance de la legislación socializadora*. Santiago: Universidad de los Andes, 1999.

Bruey, Alison J. *Bread, Justice, and Liberty: Grassroots Activism and Human Rights in Pinochet's Chile*. Madison: University of Wisconsin Press, 2018.

Burger, Hilary. "An Intellectual History of ECLA Culture, 1948–1964." PhD diss., Harvard University, 1998.

Calvo Rebollar, Miguel. "Dinero no veían, solo fichas: El pago de salarios en las salitreras de Chile hasta 1925." *De Re Metallica* 2 (2009): 9–30.

Carmona C, Nicolás. "La Central de Leche 'Chile': Un caso de industrialización estatal fallido (1935–1960)." Undergraduate thesis, Universidad de Chile, 2008.

Casals, Marcelo. "The Insurrection of the Middle Class: Social Mobilization and Counterrevolution during the Popular Unity Government, Chile, 1970–1973." *Journal of Social History* shz110 (November 2019): 1–26. https://doi.org/10.1093/jsh/shz110.

Castillo Fernández, Simón. *El Río Mapocho y sus riberas: Espacio público e intervención urbana en Santiago de Chile (1885–1918)*. Santiago: Universidad Alberto Hurtado, 2014.

Castillo Soto, Sandra. *Cordones industriales: Nuevas formas de sociabilidad obrera y organización política popular (Chile 1970–1973)*. Santiago: Escaparate, 2009.

Cavarozzi, Marcelo. "The Government and the Industrial Bourgeoisie in Chile: 1938–1964." PhD diss., University of California–Berkeley, 1975.

Chase, Michelle. *Revolution within the Revolution: Women and Gender Politics in Cuba, 1952–1962*. Chapel Hill: University of North Carolina Press, 2015.

Coatsworth, John H. "Structures, Endowments, and Institutions in the Economic History of Latin America." *Latin American Research* Review 40, no. 3 (2005): 126–144.

Cofré, Boris. "Historia de los pobladores del campamento Nueva Habana durante la Unidad Popular (1970–1973)." Undergraduate thesis, Universidad ARCIS, 2007.

———. "La lucha por 'el pan' y la defensa del 'gobierno popular': las Juntas de Abastecimiento y Control de Precios en la vía chilena al socialismo." *Izquierdas* 41 (August 2018): 224–249.

Cohen, Lizabeth. "The Class Experience of Mass Consumption: Workers as Consumers in Interwar America." In *The Power of Culture: Critical Essays in American*

History, edited by Richard Wightman Fox and Jackson Lears, 135–160. Chicago: University of Chicago Press, 1993.

Collins, Joseph. *Agrarian Reform and Counterreform in Chile*. San Francisco, CA: Institute for Food and Development Policy, 1979.

Congreso Nacional de Chile. *Historia Política Legislativa del Congreso Nacional de Chile*. Biblioteca del Congreso Nacional de Chile, n.d. http://historiapolitica .bcn.cl/resenas_parlamentarias/wiki/Carlos_Alberto_Mart%C3%ADnez_Mart %C3%ADnez.

Craib, Raymond B. *The Cry of the Renegade: Politics and Poetry in Interwar Chile*. New York: Oxford University Press, 2016.

Cronon, William. *Nature's Metropolis: Chicago and the Great West*. New York: W. W. Norton, 1991.

Crummett, María de los Angeles. "El Poder Feminino: The Mobilization of Women against Socialism in Chile." *Latin American Perspectives* 4, no. 4 (1977): 103–113.

Cullather, Nick. "The Foreign Policy of the Calorie." *American Historical Review* 112, no. 2 (April 2007): 337–364.

———. *The Hungry World: America's Cold War Battle against Poverty in Asia*. Cambridge, MA: Harvard University Press, 2010.

de Ramón, Armando. *Santiago de Chile (1541–1991): Historia de una sociedad urbana*. Madrid: Editorial MAPFRE, 1992.

de Vylder, Stefan. *Allende's Chile: The Political Economy of the Rise and Fall of the Unidad Popular*. Cambridge, UK: Cambridge University Press, 1976.

DeShazo, Peter. *Urban Workers and Labor Unions in Chile, 1902–1927*. Madison: University of Wisconsin Press, 1983.

Drake, Paul W. *Socialism and Populism in Chile, 1932–52*. Urbana: University of Illinois Press, 1978.

Drinot, Paulo. "Food, Race, and Working-Class Identity: Restaurantes Populares in 1930s Peru." *Americas* 62, no. 2 (October 2005): 245–270.

Durán Bernales, Florencio. *Población, alimentos y reforma agraria*. Santiago: Editorial Universitaria, 1966.

Elena, Eduardo. *Dignifying Argentina: Peronism, Citizenship, and Mass Consumption*. Pittsburgh, PA: University of Pittsburgh Press, 2011.

Espinoza Muñoz, Francisca. "'La Batalla de la Merluza': Política y consumo alimenticio en el Chile de la Unidad Popular (1970–1973)." *Historia* 51, no. 1 (2018): 31–54.

Espinoza, Vicente. *Para una historia de los pobres de la ciudad*. Santiago: Ediciones Sur, 1988.

Etheridge, Elizabeth W. *The Butterfly Caste: A Social History of Pellagra*. Westport, CT: Greenwood, 1972.

Facusse Orellana, Fred Francisco. "La fijación de los precios en el comercio interno de Chile." Undergraduate thesis, Pontificia Universidad Católica de Chile, 1964.

Fermandois, Joaquín. *Abismo y cimiento: Gustavo Ross y las relaciones entre Chile y los Estados Unidos, 1932–1938*. Santiago: Ediciones Universidad Católica de Chile, 1997.

Fischer, Brodwyn. "The Red Menace Reconsidered: A Forgotten History of Communist Mobilization in Rio de Janeiro's Favelas, 1945–1964." *Hispanic American Historical Review* 94, no. 1 (2014): 1–33.

Frazier, Lessie Jo. *Salt in the Sand: Memory, Violence, and the Nation-State in Chile, 1890 to the Present*. Durham, NC: Duke University Press, 2007.

Frens-String, Joshua. "Communists, Commissars, and Consumers: The Politics of Food on the Chilean Road to Socialism." *Hispanic American Historical Review* 98, no. 3 (2018): 471–501.

———. "A 'Popular Option' for Development? Reconsidering the Rise and Fall of Chile's Political Economy of Socialism." *Radical Americas*. Forthcoming.

Fuentes, Carola, and Rafael Valdeavellano, dirs. *Chicago Boys*. Santiago: CNTV/CORFO/La Ventana Cine, 2015.

Gaffney, Adam. *To Heal Humankind: The Right to Health in History*. New York: Routledge, 2017.

Gálvez, Alyshia. *Eating NAFTA: Trade, Food Policies, and the Destruction of Mexico*. Oakland: University of California Press, 2018.

Garcés D., Mario. "Construyendo 'las poblaciones': El movimiento de pobladores durante la Unidad Popular." In *Cuando hicimos historia: La experiencia de la Unidad Popular*, edited by Julio Pinto Vallejos, 57–79. Santiago: LOM Ediciones: 2005.

Garrido Rojas, José, ed. *Historia de la reforma agraria chilena*. Santiago: Editorial Universitaria, 1988.

———. "Origen y alcances de la crisis alimenticia." In *Fuerzas armadas y seguridad nacional*, edited by Pablo Baroana et al., 160–233. Santiago: Ediciones Portada, 1973.

Gaudichaud, Franck. *Chile 1970–1973: Mil días que estremecieron el mundo*. Santiago: LOM Ediciones, 2016.

Giusti, Jorge. "Participación popular en Chile: Antecedentes para su estudio; Las JAP." *Revista Mexicana de Sociología* 37, no. 3 (1975): 767–788.

Glassner, Martin I. "Feeding a Desert City: Antofagasta, Chile." *Economic Geography* 45, no. 4 (October 1969): 339–348.

González Miranda, Sergio, ed. *A 90 años de los sucesos de la Escuela de Santa María de Iquique*. Santiago: LOM Ediciones, 1998.

———. *Matamunqui: El ciclo de expansión del nitrato de Chile: La sociedad pampina y su industria*. Santiago: RIL Editores, 2016.

———. *Ofrenda de una masacre: Claves e indicios históricos de la emancipación pampina de 1907*. Santiago: LOM Ediciones, 2007.

Grez Toso, Sergio. *Historia del comunismo en Chile: La era de Recabarren (1912–1924)*. Santiago: LOM Ediciones, 2011.

———. "La Asamblea Constituyente de Asalariados e Intelectuales, Chile, 1925: Entre el olvido y la mitificación." *Izquierdas* 29 (September 2016): 1–48.

Guard, Julie. "A Mighty Power against the Cost of Living: Canadian Housewives Organize in the 1930s." *International Labor and Working-Class History* 77 (2010): 27–47.

Gunder Frank, Andre. *Economic Genocide in Chile: Monetarist Theory versus Humanity*. Nottingham, UK: Spokesman Press, 1976.

Hagerman, Ann Louise. "Internal Migration in Chile to 1920: Its Relationship to the Labor Market, Agricultural Growth, and Urbanization." PhD diss., University of California–Davis, 1978.

Hakim, Peter, and Giorgio Solimano. *Development, Reform, and Malnutrition*. Cambridge, MA: MIT Press, 1978.

Henríquez Guaico, Renzo. *El poder del campo: Los campesinos de Maipú durante el gobierno de Allende*. Santiago: Londres 38 Espacio de Memorias, 2014.

———. "Industria Perlak: 'Dirigida y controlada por los trabajadores'; Desalieanción obrera en los tiempos de la Unidad Popular, 1970–1973." *Izquierdas* 20 (September 2014): 52–77.

Henríquez Vásquez, Rodrigo. *En "estado sólido": Políticas y politización en la construcción estatal, Chile 1920–1950*. Santiago: Ediciones UC, 2014.

Herrick, Bruce H. *Urban Migration and Economic Development in Chile*. Cambridge, MA: MIT Press, 1965.

Hirschman, Albert O. "Inflation in Chile." In *Journeys toward Progress: Studies of Economic Policy Making in Latin America*, 161–223. New York: Greenwood, 1968.

Hobsbawm, Eric. *Primitive Rebels: Studies in Archaic Forms of Social Movement in the 19th and 20th Centuries*. New York: W. W. Norton, 1965.

Huneeus, Carlos. *La guerra fría chilena: Gabriel González Videla y la ley maldita*. Santiago: Debate, 2009.

Huneeus, Carlos, and María Paz Lanas. "Ciencia política e historia: Eduardo Cruz-Coke y el estado de bienestar en Chile, 1937–1938." *Historia* 35 (2002): 151–186.

Hutchison, Elizabeth Quay. *Labors Appropriate to Their Sex: Gender, Labor, and Politics in Urban Chile*. Durham, NC: Duke University Press, 2000.

Illanes Oliva, María Angélica. "'El cuerpo nuestro de cada día': El pueblo como experiencia emancipatoria en tiempos de la Unidad Popular." In *Cuando hicimos historia: La experiencia de la Unidad Popular*, edited by Julio Pinto Vallejos, 127–145. Santiago: LOM Ediciones, 2005.

———. *En el nombre del pueblo, del estado y de la ciencia: Historia social de la salud pública, Chile 1880–1973 (Hacia una historia social del Siglo XX)*. Santiago: Ministerio de Salud, 2010.

Izquierdo Fernández, Gonzalo. "Octubre de 1905: Un episodio en la historia social chilena." *Historia* 13 (1976): 55–96.

Jacobs, Meg. "'How about Some Meat?' The Office of Price Administration, Consumption Politics, and State Building from the Bottom Up, 1941–1946." *Journal of American History* 84, no. 3 (December 1997): 910–941.

———. *Pocketbook Politics: Economic Citizenship in Twentieth-Century America*. Princeton, NJ: Princeton University Press, 2005.

———. "State of the Field: The Politics of Consumption." *Reviews in American History* 39 (2011): 561–573.

Jeffs Munizaga, José Gabriel. "Chile en el macrocircuito de la yerba mate: Auge y caída de un product típico del Cono Sur americano." *Revista Iberoamericana de Viticultura, Agroindustria y Ruralidad* 4, no. 11 (2017): 148–170.

Kaplan, Temma. "Female Consciousness and Collective Action: The Case of Barcelona, 1910–1918." *Signs* 7 (1982): 545–566.

Kaufman, Robert R. *The Politics of Land Reform in Chile, 1950–1970.* Cambridge, MA: Harvard University Press, 1972.

Klein, Naomi. *The Shock Doctrine: The Rise of Disaster Capitalism.* New York: Metropolitan Books, 2007.

Klubock, Thomas Miller. *Contested Communities: Class, Gender, and Politics in Chile's El Teniente Copper Mine, 1904–1951.* Durham, NC: Duke University Press, 1998.

———. *La Frontera: Forests and Ecological Conflict in Chile's Frontier Territory.* Durham, NC: Duke University Press, 2014.

———. "Ránquil: Violence and Peasant Politics on Chile's Southern Frontier." In *A Century of Violence: Insurgent and Counterinsurgent Violence during Latin America's Long Cold War,* edited by Greg Grandin and Gilbert M. Joseph, 121–159. Durham, NC: Duke University Press, 2010.

Kornbluh, Peter. *The Pinochet File: A Declassified Dossier of Atrocity and Accountability.* New York: New Press, 2013.

Laudan, Rachel. "A Plea for Culinary Modernism: Why We Should Love Fast, Modern, Processed Food (with a New Postscript)." In *Food Fights: How History Matters to Contemporary Food Debates,* edited by Charles C. Ludington and Matthew Morse Booker, 262–284. Chapel Hill: University of North Carolina Press, 2019.

Leonard Turner, Katherine. *How the Other Half Ate: A History of Working-Class Meals at the Turn of the Century.* Oakland: University of California Press, 2014.

Levenstein, Harvey. *Revolution at the Table: The Transformation of the American Diet.* New York: Oxford University Press, 1988.

Loveman, Brian. *Chile: The Legacy of Hispanic Capitalism.* New York: Oxford University Press, 2001.

———. *Struggle in the Countryside: Politics and Rural Labor in Chile, 1919–1973.* Bloomington: Indiana University Press, 1976.

———. "Unidad Popular in the Countryside: Ni Razón, Ni Fuerza." *Latin American Perspectives* 1, no. 2 (Summer 1974): 147–155.

Maestri de Diego, Patricio, Luis Peña Rojas, and Claudio Peralta Castillo. *La Asamblea Obrera de Alimentación Nacional: Un hito en la historia de Chile.* Santiago: Academia de Humanismo Cristiano, 2002.

Mallon, Florencia. *Courage Tastes of Blood: The Mapuche Community of Nicolás Ailío and the Chilean State, 1906–2001.* Durham, NC: Duke University Press, 2005.

Maureira, Hugo Alberto. "'Los culpables de la miseria': Poverty and Public Health during the Spanish Influenza Epidemic in Chile, 1918–1920." PhD diss., Georgetown University, 2011.

Medina, Eden. *Cybernetic Revolutionaries: Technology and Politics in Allende's Chile.* Cambridge, MA: MIT Press, 2011.

Melillo, Edward D. "The First Green Revolution: Debt Peonage and the Making of the Nitrogen Fertilizer Trade, 1840–1930." *American Historical Review* 117 (2012): 1028–1060.

———. *Strangers on Familiar Soil: Rediscovering the Chile-California Connection.* New Haven, CT: Yale University Press, 2015.

Meller, Patricio. *Un siglo de economía política chilena (1890–1990).* Santiago: Editorial Andrés Bello, 1996.

———. *The Unidad Popular and the Pinochet Dictatorship: A Political Economy Analysis.* London: Palgrave Macmillan, 2000.

Melo Contreras, Leonardo. "Las Juntas de Abastecimiento y Precios: Historia y memoria de una experiencia de participación popular; Chile, 1970–1973." Undergraduate thesis, Universidad Academia de Humanismo Cristiano, 2012.

Milanesio, Natalia. "Food Politics and Consumption in Peronist Argentina." *Hispanic American Historical Review* 90, no. 1 (2010): 84–85.

———. *Workers Go Shopping in Peronist Argentina: The Rise of Popular Consumer Culture.* Albuquerque: University of New Mexico Press, 2015.

Millas, Hernán. *Anatomía de un fracaso: La experiencia socialista chilena.* Santiago: Empresa Editora Zig-Zag, 1973.

Milos, Pedro. *Historia y memoria: 2 de abril de 1957.* Santiago: LOM Ediciones, 2007.

Mintz, Sidney W. "Food and Eating: Some Persisting Questions." In *Food Nations: Selling Taste in Consumer Societies,* edited by Warren Belasco and Philip Scranton, 24–33. New York: Routledge, 2002.

Mirow, M. C. "Origins of the Social Function of Property." *Fordham Law Review* 80, no. 3 (2011): 1183–1217.

Monteón, Michael. *Chile and the Great Depression: The Politics of Underdevelopment, 1927–1948.* Tempe: Center for Latin American Studies, Arizona State University, 1998.

———. "The *Enganche* in the Chilean Nitrate Sector, 1880–1930." *Latin American Perspectives* 6, no. 4 (1979): 66–79.

Moore, Jason W. *Capitalism in the Web of Life: Ecology and the Accumulation of Capital.* New York: Verso Books, 2015.

Moore, Jason W., and Raj Patel. *A History of the World in Seven Cheap Things: A Guide to Capitalism, Nature, and the Future of the Planet.* Oakland: University of California Press, 2017.

Moulian, Tomás. *El consumo me consume.* Santiago: LOM Ediciones, 1998.

———. *Fracturas: De Pedro Aguirre Cerda a Salvador Allende, 1938–1973.* Santiago: Ediciones LOM, 2006.

———. *La forja de ilusiones: el sistema de partidos (1932–1973).* Santiago: Universidad ARCIS-FLACSO, 1993.

Murphy, Edward. *For a Proper Home: Housing Rights in the Margins of Urban Chile, 1960–2010.* Pittsburgh, PA: University of Pittsburgh Press, 2015.

———. "In and Out of the Margins: Urban Land Seizures and Homeownership in Santiago, Chile." In *Cities from Scratch: Poverty and Informality in Urban Latin*

America, edited by Brodwyn Fischer, Bryan McCann, and Javier Auyero, 68–101. Durham, NC: Duke University Press, 2014.

Needham, Andrew. *Power Lines: Phoenix and the Making of the Modern Southwest*. Princeton, NJ: Princeton University Press, 2014

Ochoa, Enrique C. *Feeding Mexico: The Political Uses of Food since 1910*. Wilmington, DE: SR Books, 2000.

Offner, Amy. *Sorting Out the Mixed Economy: The Rise and Fall of Welfare and Developmental States in the Americas*. Princeton, NJ: Princeton University Press, 2019.

Orlove, Benjamin, ed. *The Allure of the Foreign: Imported Goods in Postcolonial Latin America*. Ann Arbor: University of Michigan Press, 1997.

———. "Meat and Strength: The Moral Economy of a Chilean Food Riot." *Cultural Anthropology* 12, no. 2 (May 1997): 234–268.

Orlove, Benjamin, and Arnold J. Bauer. "Chile in the Belle Epoque: Primitive Producers, Civilized Consumers." In *The Allure of the Foreign: Imported Goods in Postcolonial Latin America*, edited by Benjamin Orlove, 113–150. Ann Arbor: University of Michigan Press, 1997.

Ortega Martínez, Luis, Carmen Norambuena Carrasco, Julio Pinto Vallejos, and Guillermo Bravo Acevedo. *Corporación de Fomento de la Producción: 50 años de realizaciones, 1939–1989*. Santiago: Departamento de Historia, Facultad de Humanidades, Universidad de Santiago de Chile, 1989.

Oszlak, Oscar. *La trama oculta del poder: Reforma agraria y comportamiento político de los terratenientes chilenos, 1958–1973*. Santiago: LOM Ediciones, 2016.

Palma, Gabriel. "From an Export-Led to an Import-Substituting Economy, Chile 1914–1939." In *Latin America in the 1930s: The Role of the Periphery in World Crisis*, edited by Rosemary Thorp, 50–80. London: Palgrave Macmillan, 1984.

———. "Trying to 'Tax and Spend' Oneself Out of the 'Dutch Disease': The Chilean Economy from the War of the Pacific to the Great Depression." In *Economic History of Twentieth-Century Latin America*, vol. 1, *The Export Age*, edited by Enrique Cárdenas, José Antonio Ocampo, and Rosemary Thorp, 217–264. London: Palgrave Macmillan, 2000.

Palma Alvarado, Daniel. "De apetitos y de cañas: El consumo de alimentos y bebidas en Santiago a fines del siglo XIX." *Historia* 37, no. 2 (2004): 391–417.

Palmarola Sagredo, Hugo. "Productos y socialismo: Diseño Industrial Estatal en Chile." In *1973: La vida cotidiana de un año crucial*, edited by Claudio Rolle, 225–293. Santiago: Planeta, 2003.

Pastrana, Eduardo, and Monica Threlfall. *Pan, techo y poder: El movimiento de pobladores en Chile (1970–1973)*. Buenos Aires: Ediciones SIAP, 1974.

Pavilack, Jody. *Mining for the Nation: The Politics of Chile's Coal Communities from the Popular Front to the Cold War*. University Park: Pennsylvania State University Press, 2011.

Pérez, Louis A., Jr. *Rice in the Time of Sugar: The Political Economy of Food in Cuba*. Chapel Hill: University of North Carolina Press, 2019.

Pieper Mooney, Jagwida E. *The Politics of Motherhood: Maternity and Women's Rights in Twentieth-Century Chile*. Pittsburgh, PA: University of Pittsburgh Press, 2009.

Pike, Frederick B. *Chile and the United States, 1880–1962: The Emergence of Chile's Social Crisis and the Challenge to U.S. Diplomacy.* South Bend, IN: University of Notre Dame Press, 1963.

Pilcher, Jeffrey M. *Que Vivan los Tamales! Food and the Making of Mexican Identity.* Albuquerque: University of New Mexico Press, 1998.

———. *The Sausage Rebellion: Public Health, Private Enterprise, and Meat in Mexico City, 1890–1917.* Albuquerque: University of New Mexico Press, 2006.

Pinto Vallejos, Julio. *Desgarros y utopias en la pampa salitrera: La consolidación de la identidad obrera en tiempos de la cuestión social (1890–1923).* Santiago: LOM Ediciones, 2007.

———. "Socialismo y salitre: Recabarren, Tarapacá y la formación del Partido Obrero Socialista." *Historia* 32 (1999): 315–366.

Pite, Rebekah. *Creating a Common Table in Twentieth-Century Argentina: Doña Petrona, Women, and Food.* Chapel Hill: University of North Carolina Press, 2013.

Pohl-Valero, Stefan. "La Raza Entra Por La Boca: Energy, Diet, and Eugenics in Colombia, 1890–1940." *Hispanic American Historical Review* 94, no. 3 (2014): 455–486.

Pollan, Michael. *In Defense of Food: An Eater's Manifesto.* New York: Penguin Books, 2008.

Ponce, Miguel. *La industria de la carne en Chile, 1955–2005: Medio siglo de modernización.* Santiago: Editorial Puerto de Palos, 2005.

Povitz, Lana Dee. *Stirrings: How Activist New Yorkers Ignited a Food Justice Movement.* Chapel Hill: University of North Carolina Press, 2019.

Power, Margaret. *Right-Wing Women in Chile: Feminine Power and the Struggle against Allende, 1964–1973.* University Park: Pennsylvania State University Press, 2002.

Price, Catherine. *Vitamania: How Vitamins Revolutionized the Way We Think about Food.* New York: Penguin Press, 2015.

Reyes Navarro, Enrique. *Salitre chileno, mercado mundial y propaganda (1889–1916): Labor del Fiscal don Alejandro Bertrand.* Iquique: Centro de Investigación de la Realidad del Norte, 1986.

Robin, Corey. "Converting Hysterical Misery into Ordinary Unhappiness." *Jacobin*, December 10, 2013. www.jacobinmag.com/2013/12/socialism-converting-hysterical-misery-into-ordinary-unhappiness/.

Rodríguez Terrazas, Ignacio. "Protesta y soberanía popular: Las marchas del hambre en Santiago de Chile, 1918–1919." Undergraduate thesis, Pontificia Universidad Católica de Chile, 2001.

Rojas Flores, Jorge. "La lucha por la vivienda en tiempos de González Videla: Las experiencias de las poblaciones Los Nogales, Lo Zañartu y Luis Emilio Recabarren en Santiago de Chile, 1946–1947." *Izquierdas* 39 (April 2018): 1–33.

Rojas Sanford, Robinson. *The Murder of Allende and the End of the Chilean Way to Socialism.* Translated by Andree Conrad. New York: Harper & Row, 1975.

Rosemblatt, Karin Alejandra. *Gendered Compromises: Political Cultures and the State in Chile, 1920–1950.* Chapel Hill: University of North Carolina Press, 2000.

Rosenstein-Rodan, Paul N. "Why Allende Failed." *Challenge* (May–June 1974): 7–13.

Rudé, George. *The Crowd in the French Revolution*. London: Oxford University Press, 1959.

Salazar V., Gabriel. *Del poder constituyente de asalariados e intelectuales (Chile, siglos XX y XXI)*. Santiago: LOM Ediciones, 2012.

———. *Ferias libres: Espacio residual de soberanía ciudadana*. Santiago: Ediciones Sur, 2003.

San Martín, William. "Nitrogen Revolutions: Agricultural Expertise, Technology, and Policy in Cold War Chile." PhD diss., University of California–Davis, 2017.

Schlotterbeck, Marian. *Beyond the Vanguard: Everyday Revolutionaries in Allende's Chile*. Oakland: University of California Press, 2018.

Segall, Marcelo. "Biografía social de la ficha salario." *Mapocho* 2 (1964): 97–131.

Siegel, Benjamin. "Whither Agriculture? The 'Green Revolution' @50." Public Books, January 14, 2019. www.publicbooks.org/whither-agriculture-the-green-revolution-50/.

Silva, Patricio. "Modernization, Consumerism, and Politics in Chile." In *Neoliberalism with a Human Face? The Politics and Economics of the Chilean Model*, edited by David E. Hojman, 118–132. Liverpool, UK: Institute for Latin American Studies, University of Liverpool, 1995.

Silvert, Kalman H. "The Chilean Development Corporation." PhD diss, University of Pennsylvania, 1948.

Simmons, Dana. *Vital Minimum: Need, Science, and Politics in Modern France*. Chicago: University of Chicago Press, 2015.

Smil, Vaclav. *Enriching the Earth: Fritz Haber, Carl Bosch, and the Transformation of World Food Production*. Cambridge, MA: MIT Press, 2004.

Soto Cárdenas, Alejandro. *Influencia británica en el salitre: Origen, naturaleza y decadencia*. Santiago: Editorial Universidad de Santiago, 1998.

Stallings, Barbara, and Andy Zimbalist. "The Political Economy of the Unidad Popular." *Latin American Perspectives* 2, no. 1 (1975): 69–88.

Stickell, Lawrence A. "Migration and Mining: Labor in Northern Chile in the Nitrate Era." PhD diss., Indiana University, 1979.

Stillerman, Joel. "Gender, Class, and Generational Contexts for Consumption in Contemporary Chile." *Journal of Consumer Culture* 4, no. 51 (2004): 51–78.

Taffet, Jeffrey. *Foreign Aid as Foreign Policy: The Alliance for Progress in Latin America*. New York: Routledge, 2007.

Thompson, E. P. "The Moral Economy of the English Crowd in the Eighteenth Century." *Past and Present* 50 (1971): 76–136.

Tinsman, Heidi. *Buying into the Regime: Grapes and Consumption in Cold War Chile and the United States*. Durham, NC: Duke University Press, 2014.

———. *Partners in Conflict: The Politics of Gender, Sexuality, and Labor in the Chilean Agrarian Reform, 1950–1973*. Durham, NC: Duke University Press, 2002.

Torres Orrego, Guillermo. "El Comisariato General de Subsistencias y Precios de la República." Undergraduate thesis, Universidad de Chile, 1947.

Trumper, Camilo D. *Ephemeral Histories: Public Art, Politics, and the Struggle for the Streets in Chile*. Oakland: University of California Press, 2016.

Valdés, Juan Gabriel. *Pinochet's Economists: The Chicago School in Chile*. Cambridge, UK: Cambridge University Press, 1995.

Valdivia Ortiz de Zárate, Verónica. *Nacionales y gremialistas: El "parto" de la nueva derecha política chilena, 1964–1973*. Santiago: LOM Ediciones, 2008.

Valdivieso F., Patricio. *Dignidad humana y justicia: La historia de Chile, la política social y el cristianismo, 1880–1920*. Santiago: Ediciones Universidad Católica de Chile, 2006.

Vásquez V., David, and Felipe Rivera, eds. *Eduardo Cruz-Coke Lassabe: Política, ciencia y espíritu, 1899–1974*. Santiago: Biblioteca el Congreso Nacional, 2013.

Velasco, Alejandro. *Barrio Rising: Urban Popular Politics and the Making of Modern Venezuela*. Oakland: University of California Press, 2015.

Vergara, Ángela. "Chilean Workers and the Great Depression, 1930–1938." In *The Great Depression in Latin America*, edited by Paulo Drinot and Alan Knight, 51–80. Durham, NC: Duke University Press, 2014.

Vernon, James. *Hunger: A Modern History*. Cambridge, MA: Belknap Press of Harvard University Press, 2007.

Volk, Steven S. "Salvador Allende." In *Oxford Research Encyclopedia of Latin American History*, November 2015. https://oxfordre.com/latinamericanhistory/view/10.1093/acrefore/9780199366439.001.0001/acrefore-9780199366439-e-106.

Walter, Richard. *Politics and Urban Growth in Santiago, Chile, 1891–1941*. Palo Alto, CA: Stanford University Press, 2005.

Weinstein, Barbara. "Developing Inequality." *American Historical Review* 113, no. 1 (February 2008): 1–18.

Winn, Peter. "Furies of the Andes: Violence and Terror in the Chilean Revolution and Counterrevolution." In *A Century of Revolution: Insurgent and Counterinsurgent Violence during Latin America's Long Cold War*, edited by Greg Grandin and Gilbert M. Joseph, 239–275. Durham, NC: Duke University Press, 2010.

———. *La revolución chilena*. Santiago: LOM Ediciones, 2013.

———, ed. *Victims of the Chilean Miracle: Workers and Neoliberalism in the Pinochet Era, 1973–2002*. Durham, NC: Duke University Press, 2004.

———. *Weavers of Revolution: The Yarur Workers and Chile's Road to Socialism*. Oxford: Oxford University Press, 1986.

Winn, Peter, and Cristóbal Kay. "Agrarian Reform and Rural Revolution." *Journal of Latin American Studies* 6, no. 1 (1974): 135–159.

Wintersteen, Kristin. "Protein from the Sea: The Global Rise of Fishmeal and the Industrialization of Southeast Pacific Fisheries, 1918–1973." DesiguALdades.net Working Paper Series, No. 26. Berlin: Freie Universität, 2012.

Wright, Thomas C. *Landowners and Reform in Chile: The Sociedad Nacional de Agricultura, 1919–40*. Urbana: University of Illinois Press, 1982.

———. "Origins of the Politics of Inflation in Chile, 1888–1918." *Hispanic American Historical Review* 53, no. 2 (May 1973): 239–259.

Yáñez Andrade, Juan Carlos. "'Alimentación abundante, sana y barata': Los restaurantes populares en Santiago (1936–1942)." *Cuadernos de Historia* 45 (December 2016): 117–142.

———. "El problema de la alimentación: Un enfoque desde las encuestas de nutrición; Chile, 1928–1938." *América Latina en la Historia Económica: Revista de Investigación* 24, no. 1 (2017): 66–97.

———. *La intervención social en Chile, 1907–1932.* Santiago: RIL Editores, 2008.

———. "Los pobres están invitados a la mesa: Debates y proyectos transnacionales de alimentación popular en América del Sur, 1930–1950." *Historia Crítica* 71 (2019): 69–91.

Zárate, María Soledad. "Alimentación y previsión biológica: La política médico-asistencial de Eduardo Cruz-Coke." In *Medicina Preventiva y Medicina Dirigida/Eduardo Cruz-Coke L.*, edited by Rafael Sagredo Baeza, ix–lxv. Santiago: Cámara de la Construcción; Pontificia Universidad Católica de Chile, Dirección de Bibliotecas, Archivos y Museos, 2012.

Zeitlin, Maurice. *The Civil Wars in Chile (or the Bourgeois Revolutions That Never Were).* Princeton, NJ: Princeton University Press, 1984.

INDEX

cordón industrial, 157

corn, 111, 129*tab*

Corporación de Fomento (CORFO), 98, 99, 109

Corporation for Agricultural Construction. *See* Sociedad de Construcciones y Operaciones Agropecuarias (SOCOAGRO)

Costa Rica, 108

cost of living: committees, 141; increases after coup, 197; index, 45*tab*; persistently high, 17, 35–36, 56, 87; strikes about, 76, 79

counterfactuals, 67

courts, use by consumers, 199–200

Cox, Ricardo, 81, 82

Craib, Raymond, 29

credit, agricultural, 133, 168

credit, education about, 112

credit, international, 183

Crocco Ferrari, Juan, 88–89

crop production goals, 107

crop research, 98, 108–9

Cruz-Coke, Eduardo, Dr., 67–70, 69*fig*, 74, 79–80, 82–83, 88–89

Cuban Revolution, 138, 165

cultural history of food, 8

Cumsille, Rafael, 194–96, 199

currency, national, 26

currency devaluation, 156

Damned Law, 62

data, role of in reforms, 76–77, 79

Dawson Island, 192

debt, 112, 132

de Carpio, Enriqueta, 27

de Castro, Sergio, 187, 189, 199

Decree Law 520 (DL), 50, 125

defiance by rural workers, 95

delivery, product, 147, 159–60, 184

democracy, 68, 131, 142, 161, 185–86

Democratic Party (PD), 30

demographics, 19, 28, 39

deportation, 44

desaparecidos, 193

detention, state, 62, 193

Díaz, Eloisa, 5

diet quality, 72, 76, 78, 89

Dirección de Industria y Comercio (DIRINCO), 122, 143–44, 151–52, 156, 177–78, 194–95, 200

disease outbreaks, 24, 27–28

diseases of poverty, 42, 72

disillusionment with Popular Unity coalition, 150, 154

distribution, food. *See* food distribution

diversification, agricultural, 109

dockworkers, 56–57

domestic food production. *See* food production

Don Diego Crespo grocery store, 54

Dragoni, Carlo, 77, 78, 79, 80, 82

Drops of Milk, 72

earthquakes, 139

Economic Commission for Latin America (CEPAL), 92–93

economic depression, 46–47

economic development: conditions for, 68; experiments in, 123; interventionist approaches to, 92; Popular Unity efforts for, 124–25; wellbeing as purpose of, 43–44; working-class needs within, 38

economic planning: Allende's approach to, 124, 128, 132–33, 135; Chicago Boys' approach to, 187, 188–89, 199; Frei's approach to, 107; state-led, 99–100

economics: crisis of 1930s, 94; data, 128–29; declines, 91; democracy, 117; economic complementarity, 83; "economic crimes," 56; economic growth, 17–18, 127, 200–201; economic justice, 117, 124; economic liberalism, 33, 199; critique of, 46, 87; economic liberation, 128; economic rationalization, 104–5; economic reform, 1, 2, 140; international assistance, 183; marginalization, 18; national, 83, 91–92, 187, 201; prosperity, 18, 19; reports on, 126, 193–94; responses to depression, 47; substitution, 153

economy, substitution, 151

Editorial Lord Cochrane, 193

eggs, 78, 82, 129*tab*, 134, 176*tab*, 197

El Campesino bulletin, 170

El Despertar de los Trabajadores, 44

Elena, Eduardo, 7

meat, red: alternatives to, 1, 151; availability of, 102; consumption data on, 78; control of by JAPs, 150; hoarding of, 57; preparation of, 74; prices of, 31; reducing consumption of, 181; shortages of, 138–39; vitamin B in, 82
meat processing, 102
medical care, access to, 124
medical journals, 81
medical services, 24
Melillo, Edward, 27
mending clothes, 114
mercado popular, 162
merchants, small, 55, 146–47, 175, 178, 181, 186
merchants committees, 184
merluza, 1–2, 4, 5, 136–37, 151–53, 181. See also fish
merluza rusa, 182
Mery, Hernán, 169–70
middle class Chileans, 174, 196
migration, seasonal, 100
miguelitos, 184
Milanesio, Natalia, 7
military coup, 14; 1925, 46
military coup 1973, 190; description of, 191
military pursuit of Woodward, 190–91
military regime leaders, 194
military responses, 61–62
milk: access to before coup, 197; Allende program, 198*fig*; bars, 85; bottling technologies, 84*fig*; consumption, 78, 82, 129*tab*; distribution initiatives, 124; increasing access for children, 71–72, 130*fig*; and infant motality declines, 90; lost in transportation strike, 158; powdered, 129–30; powdered and condensed, 97; production of, 84–85, 127, 134, 171–72; state distribution of, 176*tab*; substitutes for infants, 49
Millas, Hernán, 171, 172
miners strike, 61, 68
minimum wage, 133
mining: coal, 56, 61, 62, 125; mineral exports, 20–21; miners, 24; nationalizing mineral deposits, 123–25
Minister of Agriculture, 132

Minister of Economy, 127, 143, 175
Minister of Health, 67, 75, 80, 82
Ministry of Agriculture, 92, 98, 116, 135
Ministry of Development, 135
Ministry of Hygiene, Social Assistance and Welfare, 72, 80
Ministry of Interior's Department of Municipalities, 81
Ministry of War of Chile, 32
Mintz, Sidney, 9
mobilizational capacity, 58
modernity-sacrifice paradox, 112–14
modernization, rural, 93
money supply, 186–87, 197
monopolies, of distribution, 147
moral economy, 55
Moreno Beiza, Tomás, 142–43
Mother-Child Law, 80
Mothers' Centers (CEMAs), 114
Moulian, Tomás, 128
Movement for the Emancipation of the Chilean Woman. See Movimiento Pro-Emancipación de la Mujer Chilena (MEMCh)
Movimiento de Acción Popular Unitario (MAPU), 190
Movimiento Pro-Emancipación de la Mujer Chilena (MEMCh), 49, 54, 58
Moyano, Eduardo, 125
murders, 169–70, 190–91, 193. See also violence
Mustakis, Gianoli, 57
Myers, William S., 22

narratives, 112–14, 121
National Agricultural Society (SNA), 30
National Committee of Pobladores of PDC, 187
National Distributor Company. See Compañía Distribuidora Nacional (CODINA)
national economy: democratic, 123; idea of, 10; need for interconnected, 131; purpose of, 43–44; relationship to food systems, 63; views on organization of, 164. See also economics
National Foundation on Infancy, 72

response to union demands, 143; revolution of, 1, 121–22, 123–25, 166; role in economic chaos, 182; slogans of revolution, 131; social programs and reforms of, 140; supporters of, 149–50, 159; supporters remembering, 199; support from small businesses, 175; viewed as totalitarianism, 184–85. *See also* Allende government

populism, 45–46

pork, 102–3, 103*fig*, 129*tab*, 134, 135

porotos, 29. *See also* Chilean food dishes

postwar Chile, 67, 88–89, 90, 96

potatoes, 47, 77, 78, 104, 108–9, 129*tab*, 196

potlucks, 149–50, 151–52, 152*fig*, 197

Power, Margaret, 154, 181

preservation methods of food, 102

presidential campaigns, 45–46, 69*fig*

Preventive Medicine Law, 67, 80, 89

price ceilings. *See* price controls

price controls, 50–51; citizen activists for, 159; dismantling after coup, 194; in early Popular Unity revolution, 122; end of, 197; enforcement of, 127; inspectors for, 59–60; policies for, 175; resistance to, 61; socialists supporting, 54; through JAPs, 141; violations of, 56, 57

price increases, 156

privatization of economy, 123, 196, 197

productionism, 96

progressive reformism, 86–87

"protective foods," 72–73, 82

proteins: alternatives to red meat, 102, 103*fig*, 113, 151; diets deficient in, 126; domestic production of, 110–11; fish as source of, 1, 137; as macronutrient, 72; shortages of, 89; state distribution of, 176*tab*; in tuberculosis recovery and prevention, 74. *See also* beef; fish; meat, red

protests and demonstrations: about cattle import tax, 31–32; about cost of living, 91, 101; about farmers' markets, 53; about food, 37, 40–42, 45; of DIRINCO death, 178; against fascism, 140–41; against food speculation, 57–58; government responses to, 44, 59, 61–62, 101; hunger marches, 48, 188;

Juan Chacón's reflections on, 17, 25; against the leftist coalition, 166; March of the Empty Pots and Pans, 179; by nitrate workers, 34; October Bosses' Strike, 183; against Popular Unity government, 139

Prout, William, Dr., 70

public education, 88, 112

public health: disease outbreaks, 27, 74; efforts of Chile as a model, 85–86; nutrition science and, 71; Popular Unity approaches to, 130; public education about, 88; regulations for, 130–31; research, 80–81; sanitation, 53; as success metric, 43–44; system, 68

Puelma, Carmen, 185

Puerto Rico, 92

pulpería, 25

Punta Arenas, 177–78

Punto FInal, MIR publication, 161

Puro Chile newspaper, 183

quality monitoring, 143

Qué Pasa newspaper, 189

Quilapayún (folk musicians), 152–53

Quinteros, Guillermo, 169

Quiubo Compadre, public bulletin, 107

rabbits, 113

Radical Party, 42, 59, 60, 63, 84, 128

railway construction, 23

rationing, 34–35, 116, 160–61, 162, 163

Recabarren, Luis Emilio, 11–12, 35–39, 46

redistribution, income, 128

red week, 33

reforestation, 99

refrigeration, 96, 102

regatones, 53

regional agrarian economy, 107

regulation, economic, 67–68, 173

Reid, William, 26–27

rent and eviction complaints, 52

rent controls, 124

repression, state supported, 32–33, 62, 67

research, agricultural, 107–9

research on nutrition habits, 88–89, 93

resistance by rural workers, 95

resource extraction. *See* mining

revolution, 163; support for ration cards, 160–61. *See also* Poder Femenino

Woodward, Miguel, 190–91, 194, 195

worker-led inspections, 57

worker mobilization, 57

worker productivity, 71

Workers' Assembly for National Nutrition (AOAN), 12

Workers' Federation of Chile. *See* Federación Obrera de Chile (FOCH)

Workers' Federation of Chile (FOCH), 38

working-class Chileans: economic challenge of after coup, 195; experiences of revolution, 121–22; exploitation of, 36–37; health outcomes of, 80; mobilization of, 57; nutrient deficiencies in, 76; nutritious lunches for, 83; in political campaigns,

45–46; political demands of, 50, 153; poltical power of, 63; socialism responding to, 164; struggle for enough food, 23

working conditions, 23–27, 34, 57, 71, 196–97

workplace health and safety, 24

workplace vigilance committees, 57

World Bank, 99, 183

World War II, 56–57

W. R. Grace Company, 57

xenophobia, 31

yeast fermentation, 97

Zapata, Emilio, 95

Zárate, María Soledad, 75

Founded in 1893,
UNIVERSITY OF CALIFORNIA PRESS
publishes bold, progressive books and journals
on topics in the arts, humanities, social sciences,
and natural sciences—with a focus on social
justice issues—that inspire thought and action
among readers worldwide.

The UC PRESS FOUNDATION
raises funds to uphold the press's vital role
as an independent, nonprofit publisher, and
receives philanthropic support from a wide
range of individuals and institutions—and from
committed readers like you. To learn more, visit
ucpress.edu/supportus.

Lightning Source UK Ltd.
Milton Keynes UK
UKHW012241270123
416084UK00004B/320